United Nations Conference on Trade and Development

INFORMATION ECONOMY REPORT 2005

Prepared by the UNCTAD secretariat

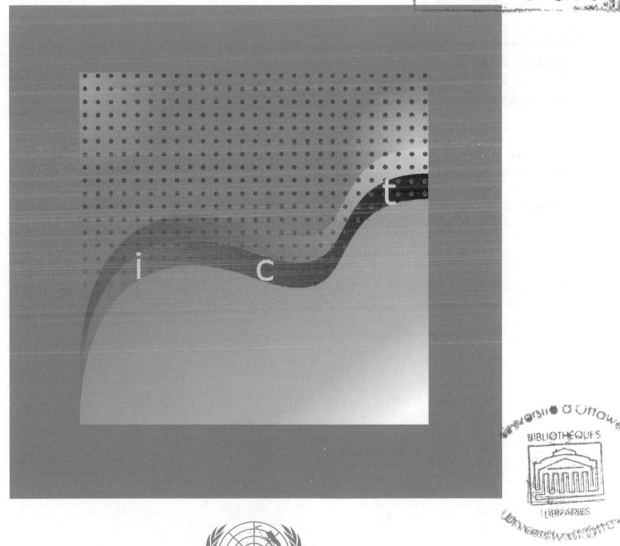

UNITED NATIONS
New York and Geneva, 2005

Note

Symbols of United Nations documents are composed of capital letters with figures. Mention of such a symbol indicates a reference to a United Nations document.

The designations employed and the presentation of the material in this publication do not imply the expression of any opinion whatsoever on the part of the Secretariat of the United Nations concerning the legal status of any country, territory, city or area, or of its authorities, or concerning the delimitation of its frontiers or boundaries.

Material in this publication may be freely quoted or reprinted, but full acknowledgement is requested, together with a reference to the document number. A copy of the publication containing the quotation or reprint should be sent to the UNCTAD secretariat at: Palais des Nations, CH-1211, Geneva 10, Switzerland.

The English version of the full report and the English, French and Spanish versions of its Overview section are currently available on the Internet at the address indicated below. Versions in other languages will be posted as they become available.

---

http://www.unctad.org/ecommerce/

UNCTAD/SDTE/ECB/2005/1

UNITED NATIONS PUBLICATION
Sales No. E.05.II.D.19
ISBN 92-1-112679-7

Foreword

Information and communication technologies (ICTs) have the potential to profoundly change global trade, finance and production. By making businesses more competitive and economies more productive, and most of all by empowering people with knowledge, ICTs can support faster economic growth and thus strengthen the material basis for development. Our challenge is to ensure that this potential is used to generate real gains in the global struggle against poverty, disease and ignorance – and their offspring, fear, intolerance and war.

This *Information Economy Report 2005* is being published by the United Nations Conference on Trade and Development to coincide with the second phase of the World Summit on the Information Society, at which the international community is expected to agree on further steps to realize the full potential of ICTs. The Report highlights the extent to which developing countries are striving to close the gap that separates the "information haves and have-nots". It also describes the enormous challenges the world still faces in key areas such as increasing access to the Internet and strengthening the security of the online environment. Most important, it shows that when there is awareness, political will and stakeholder involvement in national "e-strategies", progress in the use of ICTs for development is already an exciting reality.

New technologies and applications continue to emerge. Current technologies are maturing, and old ones are finding new uses. We must ensure that developing countries are not left further behind by all these dramatic changes, but can join in and benefit from them in their efforts to achieve the Millennium Development Goals. This Report is meant to contribute to that effort, and it is in that spirit that I commend its information, analysis and recommendations to participants in the Summit and to a wide global audience.

Kofi A. Annan
Secretary-General of the United Nations

Acknowledgments

The *Information Economy Report 2005* was prepared under the overall direction of Peter Fröhler, Officer-in-Charge of UNCTAD's Division for Services Infrastructure for Development and Trade Efficiency (SITE). It was written by a team led by Geneviève Féraud, Chief of the Electronic Commerce Branch, and consisting of the following UNCTAD staff members: Cécile Barayre, Dimo Calovski, Scarlett Fondeur Gil, Angel González Sanz, Muriel Guigue, Rouben Indjikian, Carlos Moreno, Marta Pérez Cusó and Susan Teltscher.

Pilar Borque Fernández and Marie Kamara provided administrative support.

Diego Oyarzun designed the cover and formatted the charts.

The UNCTAD team acknowledges the contribution of Ian Walden, consultant. The team also wishes to thank the following individuals for the information, comments and feedback they provided regarding various aspects of the Report: Jean-François Baylocq, Nelly Berthault, Gunter Fischer, Henri Laurencin, Nayana Mahajan, Lamon Rutten, Joachim Bartels, François Bédard, Noah Elkin, Vanessa Gray, John Hutchison, Karin Kosina, Esperanza Magpantay, Margaret Miller, Eduardo Moreno Lopez, Jean-François Outreville and Mondher Sahli.

Research assistance was provided by Wendy Hannan, Diana Korka and Arianna Rossi during their internship with UNCTAD.

Contents

List of Boxes

List of Charts

List of Tables

List of abbreviations

A

ADSL	asymmetric digital subscriber line
AES	advanced encryption standard
AfrISPA	African Internet Service Providers Association
AMU	Arab Maghreb Union
APCERT	Asia Pacific Computer Emergency Response Team
APEC	Asia-Pacific Economic Cooperation
ARPANET	Advance Research Projects Agency Network
AS	autonomous system
ASEAN	Association of South-East Asian Nations
ATI	Tunisian Internet Agency

B

B2B	business-to-business
B2C	business-to-consumer
Basel II	new capital adequacy framework endorsed by Basel Committee on Banking Supervision
BGP	Border Gateway Protocol
Bolero	Bill of Lading Electronic Registry Organisation
BQC	Bonjour Québec.com

C

CAD	Canadian dollars
CEE	Central and Eastern Europe
CERT	Computer Emergency Response Team
CIS	Commonwealth of Independent States
CISRT	Computer Security Incident Response Team
Coface	Compagnie Française d'Assurance pour le Commerce Extérieur
CRM	customer relationship management
CTO	Caribbean Tourism Organization

D

D&B	Dun and Bradstreet
DES	data encryption standard
DMO	destination management organization
DMS	destination management system
DNS	domain name system
DSA	digital signature algorithm
DSL	digital subscriber line

E

ebXML	Electronic business using Extensible Markup Language
ECA	Economic Commission for Africa
ECA	export credit agency
ECC	elliptic curve cryptography

ECD   *E-Commerce and Development Report*
ECLAC   Economic Commission for Latin America and the Caribbean
ECOSOC   Economic and Social Council
EDB   Economic Development Bank
EDI   electronic data interchange
ENISA   European Network and Information Security Agency
ESCAP   Economic and Social Commission for Asia and the Pacific
ESCWA   Economic and Social Commission for Western Asia
ETI   E-Tourism Initiative
ETP   E-Tourism Platform
EU   European Union
EU15   The 15 countries members of the European Union until May 2004
EU25   The current 25 member countries of the European Union
Eurostat   Statistical Office of the European Communities

F

FCI   Factors Chain International
FISMA   Federal Information Security Management Act
FOSS   free and open source software

G

GAISP   Generally Accepted Information Security Principles
GDP   gross domestic product
GDS   global distribution system
GNP   gross national product
GNU   Gnu is not Unix
GTC   Global Trade Corporation

I

ICANN   Internet Corporation for Assigned Names and Numbers
ICT   information and communication technology
IDEA   international data encryption algorithm
IEC   International Electrotechnical Commission
IFI   international financial institution
ISDN   Integrated Services Digital Network
ISO   International Organization for Standardization
ISP   Internet service provider
IT   information technology
ITES/BPO   information-technology-enabled services/business process outsourcing
ITU   International Telecommunication Union
IXP   Internet exchange point

K

Kbps   kilobits per second

L

LAN   local area network
LDC   least developed country

M

Mbps	megabits per second
MDG	Millennium Development Goal
MNC	multinational company

N

NAP	network access point
NEPAD	New Partnership for Africa's Development
NGO	non-governmental organization
NIST	National Institute of Standards and Technology
NSA	National Security Agency
NSFNet	National Science Foundation Network
NSO	National Statistical Office
NSP	network service provider
NTO	national tourism offices

O

OECD	Organisation for Economic Co-operation and Development
OS	operating systems
OTC	Online Travel Corporation Inc.

P

PC	personal computer
PCR	public credit registry
PGP	Pretty Good Privacy
PKI	public key infrastructure
PoP	point of presence

R

RCA	revealed comparative advantage
RSA	Rivest, Shamir and Adleman

S

SAS	statement on auditing standards
SDSL	symmetric digital subscriber line
SEE	South-East Europe
SHA	secure hash algorithm
SITA	Airline Telecommunications and Information Services
SME	small and medium-sized enterprise
SOX	Sarbanes-Oxley Act
SSL	secure sockets layer
SWIFT	Society for World Interbank Finance Telecommunication

T

TAT	Tourism Authority of Thailand
TCP/IP	Transmission Control Protocol/Internet Protocol
TLD	Top-Level Domains
TLS	transport layer security
TO	tour operators

U

UIS	UNESCO Institute for Statistics
UN/CEFACT	United Nations Centre for Trade Facilitation and Electronic Business
UNCTAD	United Nations Conference on Trade and Development
UNDESA	United Nations Department of Economic and Social Affairs
UneDocs	United Nations Electronic Trade Documents
USD	United States dollars

V

VPN	virtual private network
VSAT	very small aperture terminal

W

WAEMU	West African Economic and Monetary Union
WGIG	Working Group on Internet Governance
WMS	world market share
WPIIS	Working Party on Indicators for the Information Society
WSIS	World Summit on the Information Society
WTO	World Tourism Organization
WTSA	World Telecommunication Standardization Assembly
WTTC	World Travel and Tourism Council

X

XDSL	any type of digital subscriber line
XML	Extensible Markup Language

Explanatory Notes

The term "dollars" ($) refers to United States dollars unless otherwise stated. The term "billion" means 1,000 million.

Two dots (..) indicate that the data are not available or are not separately reported.

A hyphen (-) indicates that the amount is nil or negligible.

Because of rounding, details and percentages do not necessarily add up to totals.

Overview

1. The Information Economy

This Report illustrates the vigorous efforts being undertaken by many developing countries to catch up with their more developed partners in the dissemination and use of ICT. However, it also shows that the gaps are still far too wide and the catching-up far too uneven for the promise of a truly global information society, with its attendant benefits for sustainable social and economic development, to materialize without the sustained engagement of national Governments, the business sector and civil society, and the tangible solidarity of the international community.

Data show that the rate of growth in the number of Internet users worldwide slowed down to 15.1 per cent in 2003, from more than the 26 per cent in the previous two years. While some regions showed robust growth in the number of Internet users in 2003, such as Africa (56 per cent) and South-East Europe and the CIS (74 per cent), overall the gap between developed and developing countries remains wide: only 1.1 per cent of Africans had access to the Internet in 2003, compared with 55.7 per cent of North Americans. In order to benefit fully from the Internet, users need not just connections, but fast, good-quality ones. In particular, for some e-business applications broadband has become indispensable. If SMEs in developing countries do not have access to broadband, it will be difficult for them to implement ICT-enabled strategies to improve their productivity in areas such as customer acquisition and retention, logistics and inventory control. However, while some countries have shown a spectacular growth – for example, China, which went from close to zero to 23 million broadband subscribers in just three years – there are wide variations worldwide in broadband access. In many developing countries, however, data about broadband access are not even available.

It is essential to take action to address these developments. In order to take relevant decisions about priority areas for action and the allocation of resources, policymakers in developing countries require timely, accurate data and information about the situation of ICT in their countries. At a time when there is widespread realization of the importance of mainstreaming ICT in development strategies, the scarcity of data on ICT is a serious impediment to effective policymaking. Data about ICT diffusion and use also help SMEs to take informed business and investment decisions. At the national level, it is important to support, extend and replicate nascent initiatives to collect ICT data. At the regional and international levels, it is necessary to coordinate data collection in order to enhance global consistency and comparability. For these reasons, UNCTAD has been actively involved in the discussions that led to the establishment of a core list of internationally comparable ICT indicators, which is presented in chapter 1 of this Report and represents the beginning of a long-term international cooperative effort in the measurement of ICT for relevant policymaking.

Beyond the analysis of the disparities between countries in their access to ICTs, a more fundamental discussion concerns the economic and social impact of ICTs in the development process of individual countries and of developing countries as a group. The international debate has to focus on the impact of ICTs on the economic performance and trade competitiveness of developing countries. There is an urgent need to explore policies and best practices in order to enable enterprises, and particularly SMEs, to increase their productivity and their competitiveness through the use of ICTs. For example, Governments can help SMEs become integrated into national and international supply chains by using modern communication technologies, and examine the impact of such structural changes in enterprises on local, national and international labour markets. Therefore, it is important to support the debate between Governments, the representatives of workers and of employers and civil society that examines policies and practices that permit enterprises to employ ICTs as effective productivity-enhancing tools.

This debate will also help Governments and international organizations to identify strategies to ease the transition of developing countries to an information economy, a concept that for the purposes of UNCTAD's work refers to an economy in which the role of ICTs extends beyond e-commerce to embrace a broad range of social and economic consequences of the diffusion and use of ICTs, including the Internet and e-business. In such an economy, ICT policy frameworks shape economic growth, productivity, employment and business performance. The new name of this Report – Information Economy Report – previously called the *E-Commerce and Development Report*, is an acknowledgement of this evolution.

UNCTAD, in cooperation with the International Labour Organization, the International Trade Centre, and the Organisation for Economic Co-operation and Development, has been actively involved in supporting international dialogue on the economic and social implications of ICT through the WSIS Thematic Meeting on this subject.[1] This meeting acknowledged that the adoption of ICTs by enterprises plays a fundamental role in economic growth for developing countries. The growth - and productivity - enhancing effects of well-implemented investments in ICT can lead to increased trade and to more and better employment. But at the same time, a healthy business environment is fundamental for firms to thrive and benefit from ICTs; this includes an open and transparent competitive business framework, access to energy and communication facilities, and the availability of transaction facilities and trust mechanisms.[2] Such an environment will encourage the development of entrepreneurship, which is an indispensable component of any ICT implementation policy. For SMEs, particular efforts must be deployed to facilitate the promotion of business development services that may assist in the design of ICT-enabled business models, in the redefinition of production processes and in finding the most cost-effective means of implementing ICT solutions. At the same time, adopting trade policies that support local value-added and exports will encourage better integration of developing countries' SMEs into supply chains, and their improved access to customers through the greater reliability, low cost and security of connection services. In addition to that, an essential part of all national ICT policies is access to skills and capacity-building in ICT competencies. ICT training and retraining of the labour force might require a review of education and training systems so that the workforce will be able to adapt to increasingly frequent changes in work practices.

The potential of ICTs to facilitate and increase trade should be considered in national and multilateral trade policies and negotiations. International organizations and Governments have a major role to play in making the international debate more coherent, including through better coordination of policy development dialogues. Research organizations have a role to play in identifying the factors that may obstruct ICT adoption. Universities and research centres should be encouraged to research managerial practices, links between ICT investments and productivity growth, and the leveraging factors of firms' competitiveness in developing countries.

With the five-year review of progress towards the achievement of the development goals of the Millennium Declaration that took place at the UN General Assembly/Millennium Summit + 5 (MS+5) in New York in September 2005, and the second phase of the World Summit on the Information Society (WSIS) in Tunis in November 2005, there is a unique opportunity to maximize synergies between the work being done on ICT and the international endeavours in pursuit of the Millennium Development Goals (MDGs). In the follow-up process, international organizations and Governments are called on to support an intensification of the research and analytical work, increased cooperation between the different stakeholders, from civil society to business representatives, and a broad involvement of all stakeholders. Implementation efforts need to be integrated into national and international development plans and into poverty reduction strategy programmes. International organizations and Governments should also give priority to the integration of ICT into those sectors with the greatest potential impact for developing countries in priority policy areas such as trade, SME development and education.

There are indeed close links between the goals contained in the Millennium Declaration and the development potential of ICTs, which is explicitly related to Target 18 of Goal 8.[3] But ICT can also support the achievement of many, if not all, other MDGs. The eradication of extreme poverty (Goal 1), for example, will to a large extent depend on the achievement of sustained economic growth, which can be facilitated by the contribution of ICTs to economic growth and of ICT investments to development and job creation. ICTs can support the development of primary education (Goal 2) by broadening the availability of quality educational material and enhancing the effectiveness of educational administration and policy. ICTs can be used to improve health (Goals 4, 5 and 6) by providing efficient channels for the provision of health-care treatments and health-care services such as consultation, diagnosis and treatment.

The international community therefore needs to increase its commitment to mainstream ICT in all development efforts. As a contribution to this process, the various chapters of this Report highlight a number of current aspects of the information economy in which policy dialogue and concerted action can be of interest to developing countries. The subsequent sections of this Overview summarize their main elements and identify avenues for possible action.

2. ICT indicators for development: Trends and measurement issues

Analysing trends in the spread of the information economy in developing countries is a challenging task. Data are scarce, not always comparable and not yet at the level of detail necessary for measuring the impact of ICT on economic development and growth. The first chapter of the Report sets out to present an overview of basic developments in ICT access and use, in particular by enterprises in developing countries.

It finds that the number of Internet users continues to grow in all regions, in particular in Africa, whereas the market is almost mature in the United States. Despite high growth in many developing countries, Internet penetration rates are still very low; for example, China, the second largest Internet market in the world (after the United States), has a penetration rate of only 6.3 per 100 inhabitants. While the number of computers is increasing substantially in developing countries, particularly in some of the emerging markets, computer penetration remains very low, for example in China with 2.7 per cent, Brazil with 7.5 per cent and India with 0.7 per cent. Broadband, which plays a key role for enterprises to take full advantage of ICTs, is spreading quickly in developed countries and in a few Asian developing countries, whereas most other developing countries continue to have very low access rates.

Mobile phones, on the other hand, experienced a stunning growth in 2003 and developing countries have taken over from developed countries in respect of absolute numbers of cellular subscribers, mainly owing to Asian developing countries (e.g. China and India). This makes mobile phones the only ICT indicator with regard to which developing countries have

greater shares than developed countries, although penetration rates are still very low (whereas they have reached 100 per cent in some developed countries). This is an important development given that mobile telephony has been found to be a technology that has a significant impact on development, particularly in developing and least developed countries.

The Report reveals that enterprises' Internet use is high (up to 90 per cent) in developed countries and among medium-sized and large enterprises in developing countries; small and micro enterprises in developing countries are less connected, in particular those in rural areas. E-commerce continues to grow in all sectors. In the United States (the largest e-commerce market), it is most prominent in manufacturing and wholesale trade, although growth rates are highest in retail trade (B2C) and services. The Report also shows that the proportion of enterprises selling online decreases with size, but that online purchasing is more common than online selling. Most enterprises in developing countries use the Internet for e-mailing or basic information search, in particular those with slow modes of access; on the other hand, broadband access is spreading quickly among firms in developed countries and in Asian countries such as the Republic of Korea and Singapore, which use the Internet for more advanced e-business activities, banking and financial services, or filling out government forms.

As far as the ICT supply side is concerned, the chapter examines recent trends in international trade in ICT goods. It reveals that trade in ICT goods recovered strongly during 2003, after a sharp fall following the NASDAQ crash in 2000. In 2003, exports of ICT goods exceeded $1.1 trillion, accounting for 15 per cent of world merchandise exports and surpassing the combined value of international trade in agriculture, textiles and clothing. The growth of ICT trade was driven by developing economies (mainly from Asia), which accounted for almost 50 per cent of world exports of ICT goods; among these, China and Hong Kong (China) had the highest growth rates and gains in world market share.

As far as different ICT product groups are concerned, exports of electronic equipment fell sharply in 2001, and recovered strongly in 2003 to almost their level at the start of the millennium. Exports of telecommunications equipment, which also dropped in 2001, have not yet reached their 2000 levels. Exports of audio and video equipment fell less in 2001, and grew more than the other product groups during the same time period (by 25 per cent). While the Republic of Korea and China doubled their exports of telecommunication equipment between 2000 and 2003, those of the United States (the main exporter of telecommunication equipment in 2000) were halved. Developing countries have higher shares in the export of computer and related equipment, electronic components, and audio and video equipment. Trade in ICT goods among developing countries is increasing substantially, and trade in electronic components now represents over 50 per cent of all South–South ICT goods exports. On the other hand, audio and video equipment, as well as computer and related equipment, is largely exported from developing to developed countries.

As in any report that tries to quantitatively assess the information society in developing countries, the chapter is limited by the availability of comparable data and statistics. The second part of the chapter therefore examines the process of measuring the information economy in developing countries. It argues that improving the production of ICT statistics in those countries is critical not only to analysing trends and monitoring impact, but also to designing effective national ICT policies and strategies. It finds that a number of statistical offices in developing countries have started to compile ICT-related statistics, including on the use of ICTs by enterprises and e-business. A closer look at four developing countries shows that ICT statistics can play a critical role in national ICT policymaking through identifying areas where specific action is needed, monitoring ICT policies and international benchmarking.

However, most of the available data are not comparable across countries or even between surveys carried out in the same country. Hence, there is a great need for harmonization and standardization of ICT statistics. This is why several international and regional organizations have formed the global Partnership on Measuring ICT for Development, so as to coordinate their work on ICT statistics and to help developing countries in their development of comparable data. Under the umbrella of the Partnership, a core list of ICT indicators that could be collected by all countries was developed, as a first step towards a coherent and integrated approach to the development of internationally comparable ICT statistics. But much remains to be done in terms of assisting developing countries in this process, which will remain a major challenge in the years ahead.

3. International Internet backbone connectivity: Issues for developing countries

The commercial arrangements that currently determine the terms for interconnection between Internet service providers (ISPs) of developing countries and the major international Internet backbone providers have been criticized for reasons ranging from their alleged lack of equity to the negative effects that such arrangements might have on the cost of Internet access. There have been calls for regulatory intervention to remedy this situation.

The Report argues that the divergence between the model for financial settlements that was traditionally used among telephony networks and the arrangements in place for the Internet does not necessarily imply the existence of anti-competitive practices. It further argues that the cost of Internet access in developing countries is more heavily influenced by lack of competition in domestic Internet and telecommunications markets, and by small market sizes and lack of economies of scale, than by the terms for connectivity to global backbone providers or network service providers (NSPs).

In telephony networks the general principle applied to international interconnection was that operators shared the costs of calls terminated in each other's network. In the case of the Internet, most frequently the operator in the developing country has to pay the full cost of the connection between its network and that of the global NSP.

Internet traffic can be exchanged between networks on a peering (barter) or transit (purchase) basis. An analysis of the rationale for the decision to choose one or the other modality indicates that the choice of one or the other does not normally provide an indication of the intensity of competition among networks, but merely of the similarity or disparity between the cost structures of the various players. Networks of different sizes face different incentives to interconnect: they are much more significant for smaller networks, and a refusal to peer by the larger ones would not necessarily constitute anti-competitive behaviour.

In general, the international component of backbone connectivity represents only a small part of the total costs of ISPs, while costs determined at the domestic level are much more significant. The experience of several developing countries indicates that if restrictions on the provision of Internet backbone services are lifted, connectivity costs can be cut and infrastructure deployment accelerated. Restrictions on the provision of international connectivity (such as forcing ISPs to use the international gateway of the incumbent operator) have also been found to represent a heavy burden for ISPs.

Other restrictions in domestic Internet markets often make it difficult for developing countries' ISPs to lower their costs. For example, if ISPs in developing countries were allowed to create national or regional IXPs, they would be able to aggregate traffic, and this would make interconnection a more attractive proposition for global backbone networks. Transit arrangements could be negotiated on better terms and there would be more possibilities for peering. However, monopolies often oppose the creation of IXPs. In other cases, they impose high prices on leased lines, and these prices may represent up to 70 per cent of the total cost of ISPs.

Developing countries could facilitate Internet deployment by empowering their ISPs to make their own choices about the commercial modalities that are best suited to their connectivity needs. Some may prefer to buy transit services from regional or global networks. Others may decide to aggregate traffic with other operators and thus gain leverage in their dealings with global providers. Yet others may choose to build or buy their own end-to-end capacity.

Concerns remain, however, about those developing countries, particularly among the least developed countries, that have very limited access to international backbone networks. For reasons both of the small size of their markets and of geographical difficulties, it is unrealistic to expect that domestic liberalization will be enough to bring down the cost of Internet interconnection to levels that enable a significant improvement in Internet affordability. International cooperation has therefore an important role to play in accompanying and supporting the commercial development of Internet connectivity in these countries.

The creation of IXPs should be supported. Where they already exist, their operation at the national level should be facilitated and cooperation agreements at the regional level should be promoted.

It is important that Governments establish a competitive environment for ISPs. Particular attention should be paid to ISP domestic interconnection. New entrants should have guaranteed interconnection with other operators, particularly with the incumbent, quickly and at a reasonable cost. ISPs would benefit from more competitive conditions for the purchase of international leased circuit capacity. Another area of concern is ISP licensing, which in many developing countries is subject to very high fees that hamper the development of Internet markets. Finally, ISPs may benefit from capacity-building efforts to help them better understand the full range of international connectivity options open to them.

Very Small Aperture Terminal (VSAT) satellites may increase the availability of bandwidth and reduce its cost. However, in many developing countries regulatory restrictions are inhibiting their deployment. The development of policy consensus among developing countries at the regional level might facilitate their diffusion by creating economies of scale.

Finally, Internet policymaking and regulation is an area that requires levels of expertise and resources that are often scarce in developing countries. International support for capacity-building in this area might therefore be useful.

In conclusion, if abuses of dominant positions are prevented through enhanced transparency, commercial arrangements for global backbone access should offer Internet operators the right set of incentives to invest in infrastructure and increase connectivity in developing countries. Policies to promote Internet take-up by households, businesses and public entities by generating a critical mass of Internet users appear to be a more promising means of reducing Internet backbone interconnection costs than *ex-ante* regulatory intervention.

4. E-credit information, trade finance and e-finance: Overcoming information asymmetries

The Report notes that in most developing countries, financial service providers are not yet in a position to use modern credit risk management techniques to provide capital, and in particular trade finance, to local enterprises on competitive terms. One of the main reasons for this situation is the fragility and insufficient level of skills in the financial sector and in particular the lack of elaborate credit reporting systems. The inability of creditors to assess borrowers' risk owing to a lack of credit information, namely information on the financial state and payment record of the borrowers, is one of the main impediments to introducing a modern credit-based economy in those countries. Moreover, while enterprises in the formal sector face difficulties in accessing credit owing to their own weaknesses or to structural deficiencies of the economy, those in the informal economy lack a documented track record, and are therefore excluded from formal financial intermediation.

To improve on such major information asymmetries in creditor–borrower relations, those countries need to develop effective registration and bankruptcy laws, as well as public and court registers, acceptable standards for reporting and disclosure by private sector operators, international accounting standards and standards for auditors, and adequate public data dissemination and publishing requirements. Only in this way would institutions such as public credit registries, created mainly by banking regulators, and credit bureaux, put in place primarily by the private sector, be able to operate and to provide adequate and up-to-date electronic credit information. That in its turn would permit banks and other lenders to better assess enterprise risks on the basis of modern electronic credit risk assessment techniques and e-credit scoring or rating.

In point of fact, the emerging new international banking capital adequacy regulation, known as Basel II, makes the credit risks rating of potential borrowers a condition for their access to bank loans. Moreover, Basel II recommends a new, more differentiated and stricter regulatory capital criterion for various types of such ratings. Since the majority of more than 100 Central Banks that apply capital standards and other regulations based on the existing Basel I have announced their commitment to adopt Basel II, the development of e-credit information and related e-credit rating and scoring techniques should become a high priority for the financial sector in the developing and transition economies.

Lack of transparency and the existence of the informal sector are the major obstacles to introducing increasingly popular and innovative electronic credit information and risk management techniques. The persistence of these obstacles increases the risk of forgoing the opportunities that those techniques provide for considerable improvements in access to trade-related finance and e-finance. The recent and rapid introduction of the Internet and related innovative ICTs that make it possible to communicate, network and transact at much lower costs further underscore the importance of improving the quality of information flows in economies and hence making it possible to render more meaningful the use of modern ICTs. Moreover, actively using the Internet and ICTs, while building up from scratch modern credit information services, carries with it the promise of leapfrogging towards the latest and more efficient techniques and systems.

The recent migration of the credit information industry to the Internet has been followed by the migration of its main users and, the namely credit insurers, bankers, factors and other financial service providers. Moreover, as the experience of e-trade finance platforms of developing countries shows, many of them have the capacity to compete with major providers of similar services in terms of the use of sophisticated web-based technologies, which make it possible to develop e-credit information techniques, undertake e-trade finance operations and even reconcile the whole spectrum of online trade operations, which includes e-trade finance. The ability of many developing countries' operators to apply state-of the-art technologies might be constrained by their lack of access to the financial resources necessary for developing those systems. In some cases, operators might need to be supported by well-targeted technical assistance in the initial stages.

The Report argues that an important avenue for improving developing countries' access to trade-related finance and e-finance, and leading them towards the information economy, is the extensive use of opportunities provided by the Internet to overcome information asymmetry between creditors and borrowers. To substantiate that argument, the Report stresses the importance of strengthening credit infrastructure, meeting the regulatory challenge of Basel II and moving away from the informal economy by creating transparent conditions for collecting credit information on developing countries' enterprises, and by moving rapidly towards e-credit information infrastructures and e-credit scoring and e-rating techniques. In that respect, the Report also gives

examples of best practices, both in developed and in developing countries, of credit information and its migration towards Internet-based solutions. It analyses the recent trends in credit insurance, a financial service industry based on intensive use of credit and e-credit information. It also reviews the progress in e-banking and integrated e-trade finance platforms, other e-trade-finance-related techniques, and their applicability in the developing and transition countries. The Report stresses that while progressing towards paperless trade and e-trade finance, the industries, in addition to challenges related to e-credit information and e-trade finance business models, should treat adequately issues of a more general order such as IT security and interoperability.

Addressing the need to improve on the quality of credit information and simultaneously make it available at low cost by actively using opportunities provided by modern ICTs and the Internet is a task of great magnitude. Transacting economic agents are trying to overcome as much as possible information asymmetries. In that respect, modern ICTs are creating qualitatively a new environment permitting considerable advances in the right direction. That underscores the importance for developing countries of creating the necessary regulatory and institutional environment and making the establishment of credit information services a policy priority. Major international efforts, including public–private partnerships, technical assistance and other capacity-building, should not be spared to achieve that end.

5. Taking off: E-tourism opportunities for developing countries

One of the most important factors underlying the continuous evolution of the tourism industry is the Internet, which drives substantial changes in the market structure and consumer behaviour. Greater ICT access and availability, as well as comparison between the various tourism offers and price transparency, have seduced consumers, thus creating new expectations and accelerating the competition between online tourism providers. Consumers are increasingly mastering the online research and purchase processes. They expect to find high-quality and reliable information in order to be able to organize and

purchase the best product offering for each occasion and receive comprehensive feedback and confirmation. They are demanding flexible and customizable travel arrangements, including new travel experience based on cultural, natural, environmental and social resources. Understanding the opportunities offered by ICTs is a priority for public and private organizations, as well as tourism providers at national, regional and community levels in developing countries, including least developed countries (LDCs), where the tourism sector is of strategic importance and can meet consumers' demand.

Today's online tourism market is a very dynamic one, with highly competitive newcomers and powerful concentration mechanisms .Over the years, the number of online tourism providers, both generalists and niche players, has increased, and the market has experienced a gradual consolidation in the hands of the larger and better-funded companies. As was the case for the tourism industry before the Internet, information on tourism opportunities in developing countries is mainly generated and maintained by overseas service providers, who also conduct most of the sales transactions and take a large percentage of the profits. For a number of years, online giant travel agencies such as Expedia, Orbitz and Travelocity have dominated the online tourism business, but websites run by direct providers such as airlines, hotels and car rental services are attracting travellers seeking better prices by avoiding third-party distributors. In developed countries, large resources are being invested by tourism providers to design user-friendly destination management systems (DMSs) based on innovative ICT-based tools offering various functionalities (online reservation and booking systems) to meet their customers' expectations.

At the same time, ICTs are being deployed in developing countries at a slower pace. More and more destination management organizations (DMOs) in developing countries are using the Internet to market their tourism offerings. However, their websites are mainly an information window. Only a small number of DMOs have been able to gradually insert ICTs into the entire tourism value chain, developing effective DMSs capable of offering facilities for consumers to find what they are looking for, and for tourism producers to increase their competitiveness by networking globally with business partners. The chapter sets out to review the status of e-tourism initiatives undertaken by national DMOs in LDCs, on the basis of an informal survey of national tourism websites. It also presents some case studies on the e-tourism strategies developed both in developed and in developing destinations at a national or regional level. This will serve to shed light on similar challenges and the strategic options adopted to overcome them.

The Internet can help local tourism providers to benefit from global reach in international markets while promoting their tourism offer online. ICTs represent the most effective tools for destinations and tourism providers to help them remedy the existing imbalance and take charge of their destination promotion. The Internet is a complementary channel for distribution

of their tourism products, including niche tourism, through which they can offer a more complete set of tourism activities than the ones proposed by large online travel agencies and other distributors. The latter propose only tour vacations and a selection of international hotel chains. Small tourism producers have an opportunity to access international tourism markets on an equal footing, provided that they offer a well-conceived and effective e-tourism website that builds on technological and product innovations and enjoys consumers' confidence. For that purpose, effective e-tourism strategies should be adopted by policymakers and tourism enterprises in order to develop and maintain competitive advantages in the tourism global market.

ICT diffusion and use among tourism providers, and in particular within small and medium-sized tourism enterprises, are crucial for the effective development of e-tourism in developing countries. Governments and DMOs should create awareness of ICT benefits and emphasize local knowledge about tourism offerings as a competitive advantage to complement the actual promotion of their destinations by overseas tourism distributors. They should ensure that all local tourism providers at the national, regional and local levels are aware of the benefits of DMSs for promoting online their tourism products and services, and should encourage them to participate actively them in. The main priorities for destinations and tourism enterprises in developing countries are to foster the development of e-business in the local economy and to embrace new business models. In order to satisfy ever-demanding consumers, as well as ensuring sustainable development, they should develop and market innovative products and services such as eco-tourism for achieving a strong position in the global tourism market.

Building a dynamic, reliable and secure DMS with comprehensive packaging will be essential for DMOs in developing countries in order to meet consumers' information, purchasing, care and security needs. Public and private partnerships should be encouraged to gradually and successfully implement the DMS. Security issues, in particular those related to the transmission of credit card information, have to be addressed at the national level. In the end, the lack of confidence and security, and of user-friendly and high-quality frameworks, is influential in customers' decisions. This is an issue of particular relevance for the majority of developing countries, and particularly LDCs, which do not have transaction capabilities or

legal instruments to protect both businesses and consumers, or do not have the capacity to develop an
effective DMS and cannot rely only on uncertain
online revenue. For this reason, it is essential to propose different and complementary traditional distribution channels (travel agents, national tourism
offices, tourism producers, call centres, etc.). In addition, DMSs should work with certification authorities
to build consumers' confidence and allow e-tourism
to take off successfully.

6. Information technology and security
Risk management and policy implications

The mission of information security is to establish
trust in technologies that support or enable various
social and commercial activities. Information security
and the resulting trusted technological environment
are an essential component of digital development.
Trade, financial transactions, government administration and education are examples of activities that are
increasingly dependent on technology infrastructures
and therefore on information security.

In practice, information security is compromised on
a daily basis. Estimates of economic damage vary
but certainly reach into the tens, if not hundreds, of
billions of dollars per year. The threat of such losses
may, in turn, deter the application of information
technologies where they may bring about valuable
innovation, productivity gains and improved efficiency. In practice, electronic communication, network bandwidth and computing resources have
become critical infrastructures, and a default level of
security is expected. However, it has been argued
that a systematic underinvestment in security technologies may represent the current state of affairs,
and this, in consequence, validates and explains the
general and broad involvement of Governments in
developed and developing countries and at the highest level of international policy. Government
involvement in information security issues is rarely
disputed perhaps also because of strong historical
links with military and intelligence institutions.

A risk management approach can make significant
contributions to defining and implementing corporate strategy as well as government policy addressing
information security issues. Using risk management
means moving away from technology-centred treatment of information security towards a more holistic
approach. Instead of reacting to security attacks with
technical solutions, risk management requires consideration of the problem and its context; and this

includes analysing the balance of incentives and, in
particular from a government policy perspective, the
structure of the information security and technology
market. For any entity, the immediate and difficult
task is the evaluation of the information assets at risk.
This is followed by an assessment of the various
threats that affect these assets, their frequency and the
severity of the damage they may inflict. Risk mitigation activities and reducing the hazardous conditions
under which a threat can materialize are the next step.
This includes the application of security technologies,
security policies, regulations, standards and information security education and training. Having put in
place all feasible risk mitigation options, risk management moves towards finding ways to reduce the
severity of potential loss and damage and often
implies establishing safety and emergency response
teams, technologies and procedures. Inevitably, any
entity must accept that some damage will occur at
some point and must choose to transfer some risk
using insurance, thus securing a source of financial
compensation for part of the loss.

Governments are finding that the state of information
security technologies is unsatisfactory from a critical
infrastructure perspective. Their actions typically fall
into the risk mitigation or loss severity reduction
phases of the risk management process. In practice,
Governments often propose regulations mandating
general minimum standards or specific requirements
for certain industries or government suppliers. They
can also encourage self-regulation in response to consumer demands for quality certification. Government
can, and often does, support the establishment and
work of nations' computer emergency response teams.
Finally, Governments have engaged in international
policy processes for information security, initially
from the perspective of instituting a common understanding and platform on cybercrime issues, moving
thereafter to establish best practice guidelines often

imbued with the notion of the necessity of using risk management processes and techniques.

Given that Governments implement active policy, this can lead to several considerations for information security technology firms or firms that are heavy users of technology in the provision of their services, such as software and business process services exporters in developing countries. Increasingly stringent regulation aims to, among other issues, identify liabilities and fault in the event of security compromises. When judging its prospects, it may be insufficient to focus solely on the gauging of market demand: exporters will need to monitor international and national regulatory developments and adjust business expectations accordingly.

The position of developing countries is not conceptually different from that of developed countries. As electronic communication and interaction become part of everyday experience for many people, there may be an overall decrease in risk tolerance: early adopters of online technologies may have been less risk-averse or more technically capable of dealing with the security consequences. Thus, information security takes on strategic importance with growing digital penetration. Developing countries may, however, need to address several issues more specifically. The first is that the scope for human resource development may be greater, and government policy may reflect this by extending activities and support to all educational and training institutions. The second is

that disincentives for applying information security may be greater since there is less to protect, the most valuable information assets being owned or managed by entities in developed countries. This suggests that international technical and policy cooperation with developing countries should be encouraged and supported, in particular by the most technologically advanced countries, as there is only mutual benefit to be had. Since export and outsourcing opportunities increasingly depend on satisfying security regulations in the export destinations, undemanding domestic regulation does not facilitate technology or the outsourcing of export development.

The international community continues to address the issue of information security policy and practice and has recognized the threat posed by cybercrime for information economy development. International and national regulatory and standards bodies have also taken up this issue and are formulating and advising on minimum information security standards for international commercial partners. The substantive engagement of the international community in providing guidelines and addressing particular issues that may need policy consideration and action should offset the difficulties presented by increased regulatory requirements, provided that the latter are followed up with practical capacity-building and technical cooperation activities. The technologies that bring with them the inconvenience of increased security risks present stakeholders in the digital development process with many opportunities for the global sharing of security information and experience.

7. Protecting the information society: Addressing the phenomenon of cybercrime

As developing countries embrace, exploit and integrate computer and communications systems at an economic and social level, so concerns arise about the vulnerability of such systems to deliberate attack. An attack may target the data being processed by systems, or the integrity, confidentiality and availability of the systems themselves. Where such attacks are targeted at, or inadvertently impact on, a country's critical national infrastructure, such as power systems or transportation networks, their consequences may be disastrous.

Addressing the phenomenon of cybercrime is critically important in order to engender trust among Internet users. While the full economic cost of cybercrime is difficult to measure accurately, it is clear that the cost to individuals, businesses and Governments is substantial and increasing significantly. Since they have different levels of technological development, developing countries may experience patterns of threats and vulnerabilities different from those experienced by developed countries.

Protecting systems from attacks primarily relies on the implementation of appropriate technical, physical and operational security measures. Prevention being better than cure, it must therefore be the concern of policymakers that users, whether from the public or private sector, implement security measures to protect their data and systems. Greater awareness about the need for adequate data security must be promoted amongst users.

However, a reciprocal requirement for appropriate security is the establishment of a legal framework that deters such attacks by criminalizing the different forms of activities being carried out against systems and enabling law enforcement agencies to adequately investigate and prosecute such activities.

In general, law reform in respect of computer-related and content-related crime will involve adaptation designed to ensure that the criminal code is capable of being applied to acts involving the use of computers, rather than wholesale revision of the existing criminal code. In terms of substantive law, existing laws may need to be amended to reflect the involvement of computer and communication technologies. In addition, the penalties associated with certain crimes may need to be increased in order to address their greater prevalence in an Internet environment. Most countries also create new offences to cover criminal activities that specifically target computer and communication systems and the data they hold.

Reforming the criminal code is only one step towards the effective legal treatment of cybercrime. Public law enforcement agencies also require the necessary powers, training, expertise and resources to be able to tackle instances of cybercrime, often working in conjunction with the private sector. Countries will need to consider procedural law reforms, such as laws governing search and seizure and the interception of communications, to adequately equip their law enforcement agencies to investigate cybercrime. But Governments must also balance the need to tackle cybercrime with the protection of individual rights and liberties, such as freedom of expression and privacy.

Computer crime has an obvious international dimension and policymakers recognize the need to ensure that legal protection is harmonized among nations in order to prevent the emergence of cybercrime havens. Cybercrime is often international in nature, occurring across boundaries and impacting on users in different countries. Law enforcement, however, stops at the borders of nation States and must go through proper legal channels to receive assistance in cybercrime investigations.

While it is important for developing countries to have cybercrime laws in place, it is equally important that countries have the legal authority to assist foreign countries in an investigation, even if the country in question has not suffered any damage itself and is merely the location of the intruder or a pass-through site. Thus, inadequate regimes for international legal assistance and extradition might in effect shield criminals from law enforcement. Developing countries might be both the victim and source of cybercrime activities.

Attempts have been made in various international organizations and forums, such as the G8 member States and the United Nations, to achieve a harmonized approach to legislating against computer crime and thereby try to prevent the emergence of "computer crime havens". The most significant intergovernmental institution in the field has been the Council of Europe, which adopted on 23 November 2001 the Convention on Cybercrime, which is open for ratification by non-European countries. The Convention requires Parties to criminalize certain conduct that is committed through, against or in relation to computer systems, and provides for broad international cooperation in the form of extradition and mutual legal assistance. The Convention also requires Parties to have the ability to investigate computer-related crime effectively and to obtain electronic evidence in all types of investigations. The Convention entered into force on 18 March 2004.

The comprehensive nature of the Convention, as well as the geographical spread of its signatories, means that it is likely to remain the most significant international legal instrument in the field for the foreseeable future. However, concerns have been expressed about the Convention by both human rights groups and providers of communication services, and there have been calls for a treaty to be drafted under the auspices of the United Nations.

Notes

1. WSIS Thematic Meeting on the "Economic and Social Implications of ICT", 17–19 January 2005, Antigua, Guatemala. The meeting report can be downloaded at http://www.itu.int/wsis/docs2/thematic/ilo/final-report.pdf.

2. See chapter 5.

3. Goal 8 aims at developing a global partnership for development: "In cooperation with the private sector, make available the benefits of new technologies, especially information and communications."

Chapter 1

ICT INDICATORS FOR DEVELOPMENT: TRENDS AND MEASUREMENT ISSUES

A. INTRODUCTION

The present chapter is concerned with information society indicators, in terms of available statistics and of improving data and indicators in developing countries. This is based on recognition of the increasing need for reliable data and indicators regarding ICT readiness, use and impact. Such data are crucial for formulating policies and strategies concerning ICT-driven or ICT-enabled growth, for social inclusion and cohesion, and for monitoring and evaluating ICT-related economic and social developments. They help companies take the right investment and business decisions and allow developing countries to benchmark their information economies against those of other countries, both developed and developing. Finally, they contribute to documenting the impact of the information society on the implementation of internationally agreed development goals (e.g. the Millennium Development Goals) and measuring progress in the use of ICTs to achieve those goals.

The focus on the development of ICT statistical data stems from recent advances in measuring the information society at the international and regional levels, the increasing demand by policymakers and the international community for quantitative assessment of the impact of ICT on development and growth, and the attention the subject has attracted in international forums such as the World Summit on the Information Society (WSIS), the UN ICT Task Force and the UN Statistical Commission. It also reflects UNCTAD's ongoing work in this field, at both the analytical and the capacity-building levels.

The chapter is divided into two main parts. In the first part, it presents the latest developments in the spread and use of information and communication technology, particularly in e-business, as well as trade in ICT goods, on the basis of available statistical data (section B). In the second part, it draws the reader's attention to the need to improve the availability of comparable statistical data on ICT use and impact in developing countries, and describes progress made in this regard, including by the secretariat of UNCTAD (section C). The chapter ends with some suggestions about how the development of comparable statistics in developing countries could be enhanced, for the purpose of monitoring and assessing the information society.

B. Global and regional trends in ICT uptake

ICTs continue to spread in all parts of the world, particularly in the developing world. As illustrated below, more people have access to the Internet and at a higher speed, more have computers, and many more have mobile phones. More enterprises use the Internet for streamlining their business processes, for reaching out to potential clients, and in general, for increasing their competitive advantage. The continued spread of ICTs increases opportunities for users to benefit from the potential of ICTs for economic and social development.

At the same time, many of the poorest countries continue to have very low ICT penetration rates, in particular those with a large rural population and relatively high-priced basic ICT infrastructure. In these countries, the incorporation of ICT policies into the broader national social and economic development agenda will be crucial for the development of their information societies. They are also the countries that have the greatest need for assistance in this process.

This part of the chapter will first discuss the latest trends in basic ICT infrastructure and access, for example with regard to the Internet, broadband, computers and mobile phones, from a developing country point of view (section 1). These indicators, based on time series data compiled by the ITU, are essential to the development of an information economy. Then figures on the actual use of ICTs by enterprises will be presented, such as Internet and web use, and the types of activities that businesses carry out over the Internet, including e-commerce (section 2). The section will present data from selected developed and developing countries, drawing primarily from data provided by the Organisation for Economic Co-operation and Development (OECD), Eurostat and UNCTAD. Section 3 will focus on recent developments in the international trade of ICT goods, an important sector in the development of the information economy, and will use trade data from the UN Comtrade database. The classification of countries follows the *UNCTAD Handbook of Statistics* (2004) (see annex II).

1. Basic access to ICTs

Internet users

This section provides an overview of the number of Internet users in selected regions and countries, based on the latest available data. These data are based on estimates of all Internet users in a country, including those that use the Internet in public places, offices, Internet cafes, and so forth. In countries where no surveys on Internet users are carried out, estimates

are typically made on the basis of the number of subscribers. The indicator does not provide information on the intensity of Internet use, which would be better estimated by looking at the number of subscribers. In a developing country context, however, subscriber figures could be understated since many users share subscriptions or use public localities to access the Internet.

Between 2003 and 2004, the total number of Internet users continued to grow substantially (table 1.1 and annex I). At the end of 2004, most Internet users lived in Asia, followed by Europe. The United States still accounts for the largest Internet population, with 185 million users, about twice as many as China (in second place). On the basis of higher growth rates, Europe has now overtaken North America in terms of the number of Internet users. Developing countries continue to catch up (see chart 1.1), with the highest growth rates in Africa. There has been a considerable surge in the number of Internet users in South-East Europe and the CIS countries, with a growth rate of more than 70 per cent. The current take-up of ICTs in this region is also reflected in some of the other indicators presented below.

Table 1.1

Internet users by region and level of development, 2000-2004

	2000	% change 2000-2001	2001	% change 2001-2002	2002	% change 2002-2003	2003	% change 2003-2004	2004
Region									
Africa	4 314 700	36.2	5 876 800	57.5	9 255 620	41.5	13 096 650	66.6	21 813 872
Asia	110 958 867	37.2	152 262 521	39.0	211 582 599	20.8	255 668 777	28.6	328 887 039
Europe	107 999 345	27.6	137 834 925	23.9	170 817 495	17.9	201 324 310	20.7	242 951 272
Latin America and Caribbean	19 352 400	49.4	28 918 492	45.9	42 191 573	20.9	50 995 059	18.7	60 534 062
North America	136 971 000	14.5	156 823 000	11.1	174 200 000	2.9	179 232 400	14.4	205 000 000
Oceania	8 182 800	16.7	9 545 400	31.4	12 544 450	8.3	13 581 400	21.1	16 445 726
Level of development									
Developed countries	285 429 829	20.7	344 585 162	16.7	402 012 514	7.8	433 307 644	15.8	501 756 193
Developing countries	96 367 167	42.9	137 712 413	48.8	204 925 742	25.3	256 845 766	29.6	332 998 292
South-East Europe and CIS	5 982 116	49.8	8 963 563	52.3	13 653 481	73.9	23 745 186	72.2	40 877 486
Total	387 799 112	26.7	491 291 138	26.2	620 191 737	15.1	713 898 596	22.7	875 631 972

Source: UNCTAD calculations based on ITU World Telecommunication Indicators database, 2005.
Note: For those countries that had not reported data for 2004 at the time of publication, the 2004 values were derived by averaging the growth of the previous four years.

Chart 1.1

Internet users by level of development, 2000-2004

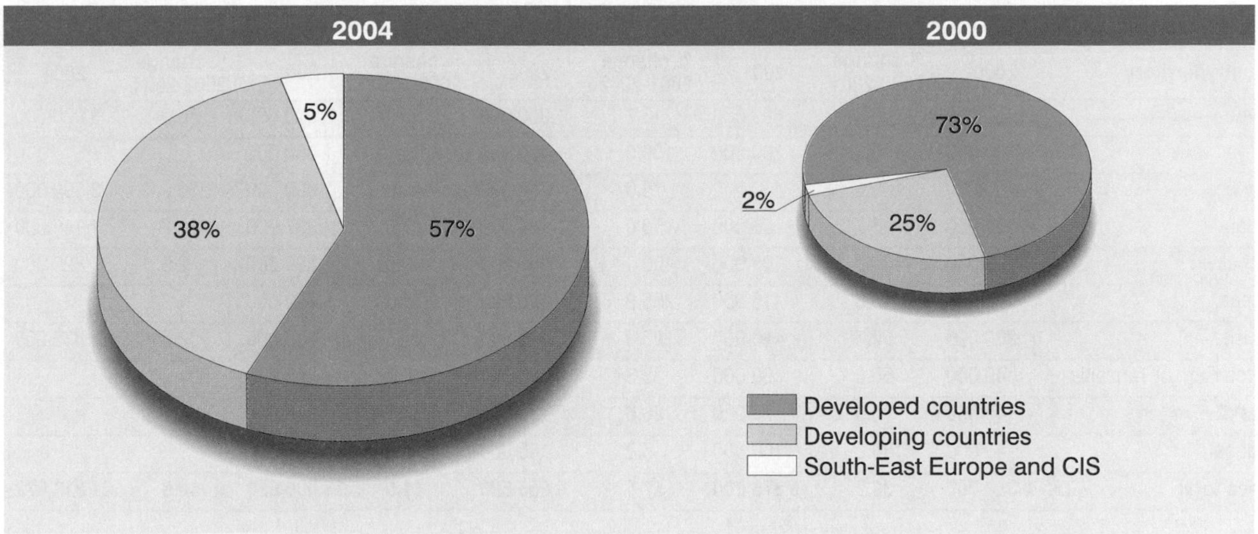

2004	2000
5% / 38% / 57%	73% / 2% / 25%

Developed countries
Developing countries
South-East Europe and CIS

Source: UNCTAD calculations based on the ITU World Telecommunication Indicators database, 2005.

At the regional level, Africa has very high growth rates (66 per cent), but many countries start from rather low levels (table 1.2). The highest growth in the number of Internet users has been in Eritrea, Sudan, Morocco, Congo, Libya, Lesotho and Nigeria. Egypt, with 3.9 million users, has caught up with South Africa (3.1 million users in 2002, no later data reported), and is now the country with the second largest number of Internet users in Africa.

In Asia, the top five countries together account for about 75 per cent of all Internet users in the region (China, Japan, India, Republic of Korea and Taiwan Province of China). China's growth has slowed down, from 35 per cent between 2002 and 2003 to 18 per cent between 2003 and 2004. The highest growth rates are in Myanmar, India, Turkey, Viet Nam and Pakistan. The almost doubling of the number of Internet users in India has contributed significantly to the increase in Asia during this period.

In Europe, more than 50 per cent of Internet users live in four countries (Germany, United Kingdom, Italy, and France). But the highest growth rates occur in Eastern European countries (such as Latvia, Ukraine and Bulgaria) and the Russian Federation. Western European countries usually have lower growth rates than the rest of Europe.

In the Americas, Brazil and Mexico, the two largest economies in the Latin American and Caribbean region, account for about 60 per cent of all Internet users there. But the highest growth rates are found in

Central America and the Caribbean, a region that is catching up with South America.

While the absolute number of Internet users provides important information about the dimensions and growth of national and regional Internet markets, figures on Internet penetration (i.e. users per 100 inhabitants) are crucial for assessing relative access to the Internet, in particular in population-rich countries (see annex I). Worldwide, 14.3 per cent of the population had access to Internet at the end of 2004. The Republic of Korea has overtaken the United States and now ranks number three worldwide (after New Zealand and Sweden), with a penetration rate of 65.7 per cent. In China, the second largest Internet market in 2004 as far as number of users is concerned, penetration is growing by 16.4 per cent. However, with 7.2 per cent penetration, still only a small proportion of the Chinese population use the Internet.

The gap between developed and developing countries continues to be impressive, as shown in table 1.3, although developing countries are slowly catching up, because of their high growth rates. Only 3.1 per cent of Africans had access to the Internet in 2004, compared with 62.6 per cent of North Americans. The relatively low figure for Europe (EU 25) is largely due to the low penetration rates in some of the Eastern European countries, whereas the EU15 country average is 50 per cent (the exception being Greece, which has both low penetration and low growth rates) (Eurostat, 2005). At the same time, many of the

Table 1.2

Internet users by region, 2000-2004 (top 10 countries/territories)

sorted by decreasing order of 2003 values

Country/territory	2000	% change 2000-2001	2001	% change 2001-2002	2002	% change 2002-2003	2003	% change 2003-2004	2004
Egypt	450 000	33.3	600 000	216.7	1 900 000	57.9	3 000 000	30.0	3 900 000
Kenya	100 000	100.0	200 000	100.0	400 000	150.0	1 000 000	..	..
Morocco	200 000	100.0	400 000	75.0	700 000	42.9	1 000 000	250.0	3 500 000
Sudan	30 000	86.7	56 000	50.0	84 000	1 015.5	937 000	21.7	1 140 000
Zimbabwe	50 000	100.0	100 000	400.0	500 000	60.0	800 000	2.5	820 000
Nigeria	80 000	43.8	115 000	265.2	420 000	78.6	750 000	..	..
Tunisia	260 000	57.7	410 000	23.3	505 500	24.6	630 000	32.5	835 000
United Rep. of Tanzania	40 000	50.0	60 000	33.3	80 000	212.5	250 000	..	..
Côte d'Ivoire	40 000	75.0	70 000	28.6	90 000	166.7	240 000	..	..
Senegal	40 000	150.0	100 000	5.0	105 000	114.3	225 000	..	..
Africa total	**4 314 700**	**36.2**	**5 876 800**	**57.5**	**9 255 620**	**41.5**	**13 096 650**	**66.6**	**21 813 872**
China	22 500 000	49.8	33 700 000	75.4	59 100 000	34.5	79 500 000	18.2	94 000 000
Japan	38 000 000	28.7	48 900 000	17.0	57 200 000	7.7	61 600 000	21.8	75 000 000
Rep. of Korea	19 040 000	28.0	24 380 000	7.8	26 270 000	11.2	29 220 000	8.1	31 580 000
India	5 500 000	27.3	7 000 000	136.9	16 580 000	11.5	18 481 044	89.4	35 000 000
Taiwan Province of China	6 260 000	24.9	7 820 000	37.1	10 720 000	9.5	11 740 000	4.0	12 210 000
Malaysia	4 977 000	27.5	6 346 650	23.5	7 840 640	10.5	8 661 000	14.1	9 878 214
Indonesia	1 900 000	121.1	4 200 000	7.1	4 500 000	79.6	8 080 000	..	..
Thailand	2 300 000	53.7	3 536 019	35.7	4 800 000	25.6	6 030 000	15.6	6 970 000
Turkey	2 000 000	75.0	3 500 000	22.9	4 300 000	39.5	6 000 000	70.3	10 220 000
Iran (Islamic Rep. of)	625 000	60.8	1 005 000	215.2	3 168 000	51.5	4 800 000	..	..
Asia total	**110 893 867**	**37.2**	**152 185 521**	**38.9**	**211 402 599**	**20.8**	**255 448 777**	**28.7**	**328 887 039**
United Kingdom	15 800 000	25.3	19 800 000	26.3	25 000 000	37.6	34 400 000	9.3	37 600 000
Germany	24 800 000	4.8	26 000 000	7.7	28 000 000	17.9	33 000 000	25.0	41 263 000
Italy	13 200 000	18.2	15 600 000	27.6	19 900 000	15.0	22 880 000	26.2	28 870 000
France	8 460 000	85.0	15 653 000	19.6	18 716 000	17.0	21 900 000	14.2	25 000 000
Russian Federation	2 900 000	48.3	4 300 000	39.5	6 000 000	66.7	10 000 000	60.0	16 000 000
Spain	5 486 000	34.7	7 388 000	6.3	7 856 000	24.6	9 789 000	32.8	13 000 000
Poland	2 800 000	35.7	3 800 000	133.7	8 880 000	1.0	8 970 000	0.3	9 000 000
Netherlands	7 000 000	12.9	7 900 000	3.8	8 200 000	3.7	8 500 000	17.6	10 000 000
Sweden	4 048 000	13.6	4 600 000	11.4	5 125 000	10.3	5 655 000	20.2	6 800 000
Belgium	3 000 000	6.7	3 200 000	6.3	3 400 000	17.6	4 000 000	5.0	4 200 000
Europe total	**107 999 345**	**27.6**	**137 834 925**	**23.9**	**170 817 495**	**15.3**	**196 944 310**	**23.4**	**242 951 272**
Brazil	5 000 000	60.0	8 000 000	78.8	14 300 000	25.9	18 000 000	22.2	22 000 000
Mexico	5 058 000	46.5	7 410 124	45.3	10 764 715	13.5	12 218 830	14.9	14 036 475
Argentina	2 600 000	40.4	3 650 000	12.3	4 100 000	10.5	4 530 000	13.0	5 120 000
Chile	2 537 308	22.3	3 102 200	15.2	3 575 000	11.9	4 000 000	7.5	4 300 000
Peru	800 000	150.0	2 000 000	20.0	2 400 000	18.8	2 850 000	13.0	3 220 000
Colombia	878 000	31.4	1 154 000	73.3	2 000 113	36.6	2 732 201	31.2	3 585 688
Venezuela	820 022	40.5	1 152 502	10.6	1 274 429	51.8	1 934 791	19.5	2 312 683
Costa Rica	228 000	68.4	384 000	108.3	800 000	12.5	900 000	11.1	1 000 000

Table 1.2 *(continued)*

Country/territory	2000	% change 2000-2001	2001	% change 2001-2002	2002	% change 2002-2003	2003	% change 2003-2004	2004
Dominican Rep.	327 118	21.5	397 333	25.8	500 000	30.0	650 000	23.1	800 000
Ecuador	180 000	85.0	333 000	61.5	537 881	5.9	569 727	9.6	624 579
Latin America and Caribbean total	**19 372 400**	**49.4**	**28 948 492**	**44.4**	**41 791 573**	**22.0**	**50 995 059**	**18.7**	**60 534 062**
United States	124 000 000	15.2	142 823 000	11.3	159 000 000	1.7	161 632 400	14.5	185 000 000
Canada	12 971 000	7.9	14 000 000	8.6	15 200 000	15.8	17 600 000	13.6	20 000 000
North America total	**136 971 000**	**14.5**	**156 823 000**	**11.1**	**174 200 000**	**2.9**	**179 232 400**	**14.4**	**205 000 000**
Australia	6 600 000	16.7	7 700 000	36.4	10 500 000	7.6	11 300 000	15.0	13 000 000
New Zealand	1 515 000	16.3	1 762 000	8.3	1 908 000	10.6	2 110 000	51.7	3 200 000
New Caledonia	30 000	33.3	40 000	25.0	50 000	20.0	60 000	16.7	70 000
Fiji	12 000	25.0	15 000	233.3	50 000	10.0	55 000	..	..
French Polynesia	15 000	0.0	15 000	33.3	20 000	75.0	35 000	..	..
Micronesia	4 000	25.0	5 000	20.0	6 000	66.7	10 000	20.0	12 000
Vanuatu	4 000	37.5	5 500	27.3	7 000	7.1	7 500	0.0	7 500
Solomon Islands	2 000	0.0	2 000	10.0	2 200	13.6	2 500	..	..
Marshall Islands	0 800	12.5	0 900	38.9	1 250	12.0	1 400	..	..
Oceania total	**8 182 800**	**16.7**	**9 545 400**	**31.4**	**12 544 450**	**8.3**	**13 581 400**	**20.6**	**16 383 400**

Source: UNCTAD calculations based on ITU World Telecommunication Indicators database, 2005.

Table 1.3

Internet penetration by region and level of development, 2000-2004

	2000	% change 2000-2001	2001	% change 2001-2002	2002	% change 2002-2003	2003	% change 2003-2004	2004
Region									
Africa	0.7	33.3	0.9	54.2	1.4	38.5	1.9	63.1	3.1
Asia	3.1	35.5	4.2	37.3	5.7	19.4	6.8	27.1	8.7
Europe	14.7	27.6	18.8	23.9	23.3	17.9	27.5	20.7	33.2
Latin America and Caribbean	3.9	47.3	5.7	43.8	8.2	19.2	9.7	17.1	11.4
North America	43.5	13.4	49.3	10.0	54.2	1.9	55.3	13.3	62.6
Oceania	32.8	15.3	37.9	29.9	49.2	7.0	52.6	19.7	63.0
Level of development									
Developed countries	30.7	20.1	36.9	16.0	42.8	7.2	45.9	15.2	52.9
Developing countries	2.1	40.8	3.0	46.7	4.4	23.6	5.4	27.9	6.9
South-East Europe and CIS	1.8	50.2	2.7	52.7	4.2	74.4	7.2	72.6	12.5
Total	**6.6**	**25.2**	**8.3**	**24.8**	**10.4**	**13.7**	**11.8**	**21.3**	**14.3**

Source: UNCTAD calculations based on ITU World Telecommunication Indicators database, 2005.
Note: For those countries that had not reported data for 2004 at the time of publication, the 2004 values were derived by averaging the growth of the previous four years.

Eastern European countries have on average very high growth rates, and it is thus expected that they will catch up quickly with the rest of Europe.

Broadband

Broadband access to the Internet has become a regular feature in developed countries' enterprises. By speeding up all Internet-related business activities, such as transferring web pages and data files, handling customer requests or automating supply chain management, broadband enables companies to work more efficiently and respond quickly to customers' needs. For certain e-business solutions, broadband has thus become indispensable.[1] Broadband access also allows companies to have multipurpose telecommunications lines, which can be particularly attractive to SMEs. It also supports the outsourcing of certain applications, distance learning and telecommuting. In some industries, such as media and entertainment, which involve the exchange of large data files, broadband is particularly important.

In a number of countries, mostly developed countries, policymakers have recognized the role of broadband in the spread and use of ICTs, including its ability to accelerate the contribution of ICTs to economic growth, and are taking action to foster the development and effective use of broadband at the national level (OECD, 2004; European Commission, 2005).

Available data for 2003 cover 98 countries (and for 2004, 83 countries), but data for many developing countries, especially in Latin America, are missing. Nevertheless, a few important observations can be made.

First of all, the top five broadband countries, measured by number of subscribers in 2004, were the United States, Japan, the Republic of Korea, China

Table 1.4

Top 25 countries/territories in terms of broadband subscribers, 2001-2004

sorted by decreasing order of 2004 values

Country/territory	2001	% change 2001-2002	2002	% change 2002-2003	2003	% change 2003-2004	2004
United States	12 792 812	55.4	19 881 549	26.3	25 110 000	50.9	37 890 646
Japan	3 835 000	145.0	9 397 426	58.7	14 917 165	25.1	18 660 000
China	339 510	1 480.8	5 367 000	96.0	10 519 000	61.0	16 935 000
Rep. Of Korea	7 806 000	33.3	10 405 486	7.4	11 178 000	4.7	11 700 000
Germany	2 100 000	52.6	3 205 000	42.3	4 560 000	51.4	6 905 159
France	601 500	179.8	1 682 992	112.1	3 569 381	89.2	6 754 035
United Kingdom	501 000	263.5	1 821 000	75.7	3 200 000	95.5	6 256 300
Canada	2 836 000	23.9	3 515 000	28.4	4 513 000	24.8	5 631 714
Italy	390 000	117.9	850 000	158.8	2 200 000	113.7	4 701 252
Taiwan, China	1 133 000	85.3	2 100 000	44.9	3 043 273	23.3	3 751 214
Spain	430 055	190.1	1 247 496	76.5	2 202 000	56.3	3 441 630
Netherlands	466 200	129.3	1 068 966	86.0	1 988 000	61.3	3 206 000
Brazil	331 000	120.8	731 000	64.0	1 199 000	88.2	2 256 000
Australia	122 800	110.2	258 100	132.6	600 400	157.9	1 548 300
Hong Kong, China	716 435	45.0	1 038 995	18.4	1 230 607	23.0	1 513 103
Sweden	356 500	100.9	716 085	35.1	967 464	34.7	1 302 861
Switzerland	140 000	225.2	455 220	72.2	783 874	53.3	1 202 000
Belgium	458 759	89.4	868 994	30.6	1 135 000	..	..
Israel	38 000	444.7	207 000	214.0	650 000	64.6	1 070 000
Denmark	223 276	97.3	440 492	63.0	718 000	41.2	1 013 500
Chile	59 975	214.2	188 454	257.8	674 305	35.4	913 172
Mexico	50 000	254.0	177 000	..	..	..	840 147
Austria	320 600	68.3	539 500	11.4	601 000	36.4	820 000
Finland	52 000	426.0	273 500	79.6	491 100	62.9	800 000
Portugal	96 324	169.4	259 491	93.9	503 119	31.6	661 948

Source: UNCTAD calculations based on ITU World Telecommunication Indicators database, 2005.

and Germany (see table 1.4). As far as penetration rates are concerned, the Republic of Korea is still the world leader (with 24.6 out of 100 inhabitants), followed by Hong Kong (China) and the Netherlands (see table 1.5). European countries have high penetration growth rates and are overtaking Canada, Japan and Taiwan Province of China. Eurostat data show wide variations in broadband uptake in households, led by Scandinavian countries (Iceland with 45 per cent, Denmark 36 per cent and Norway 30 per cent). At the other end of the range are countries such as Cyprus (2 per cent) and Ireland (3 per cent). This belies broadband uptake by EU enterprises (see section 2.a).

Table 1.5.

Broadband penetration, 2000-2004 (selected countries/territories)

Broadband subscribers per 100 inhabitants
sorted by decreasing order of 2004 values

Country/territory	2000	% change 2000-2001	2001	% change 2001-2002	2002	% change 2002-2003	2003	% change 2003-2004	2004
Republic of Korea	8.4	97.6	16.6	32.7	22.0	7.0	23.6	4.3	24.6
Hong Kong, China	6.7	59.1	10.7	43.3	15.3	17.1	17.9	21.6	21.7
Netherlands	1.6	82.3	2.9	128.1	6.7	85.0	12.3	60.5	19.8
Denmark	1.1	278.7	4.2	96.6	8.2	62.5	13.3	40.7	18.7
Iceland	0.8	358.8	3.7	130.6	8.5	65.0	14.0	32.2	18.5
Canada	4.6	98.9	9.2	22.7	11.2	27.1	14.3	23.5	17.6
Switzerland	0.6	224.5	1.9	224.3	6.3	71.8	10.8	53.0	16.6
Taiwan Province of China	1.0	407.1	5.1	84.3	9.3	44.3	13.5	22.8	16.6
Norway	0.5	291.1	2.0	130.6	4.5	92.3	8.7	88.1	16.3
Israel		..	0.6	400.0	3.0	207.8	10.0	61.5	16.2
Finland	0.4	150.5	1.0	424.5	5.3	79.0	9.4	62.4	15.3
Japan	0.7	330.4	3.0	144.6	7.4	58.5	11.7	24.9	14.6
Sweden	0.9	345.0	4.0	100.1	8.0	34.5	10.8	34.1	14.5
United States	2.5	78.3	4.5	53.9	6.9	25.1	8.6	49.5	12.8
Singapore	1.9	94.0	3.7	76.0	6.5	54.1	10.0	20.0	12.0
France	0.3	236.9	1.0	178.7	2.8	111.2	5.9	88.4	11.2
Belgium	1.2	270.0	4.4	89.0	8.4	30.3	10.9	..	..
United Kingdom	..	..	0.9	262.2	3.1	75.1	5.4	94.9	10.5
Austria	2.4	64.7	4.0	67.9	6.6	11.1	7.4	36.1	10.0
Macao, China	0.8	173.2	2.2	71.9	3.8	62.7	6.1	61.8	9.9
Luxembourg	..	..	0.3	362.6	1.3	165.9	3.4	183.9	9.6
Andorra	..	..	..	..	1.7	212.3	5.4	73.7	9.4
Estonia	..	..	1.3	166.4	3.4	75.1	5.9	41.0	8.4
Germany	0.3	749.2	2.5	52.5	3.9	42.1	5.5	51.3	8.4
Italy	0.2	237.4	0.7	117.6	1.5	158.5	3.8	113.4	8.1
Spain	0.2	423.0	1.0	186.6	3.0	74.3	5.2	54.5	8.1
Australia	0.4	59.1	0.6	107.8	1.3	130.1	3.0	155.1	7.8
Portugal	0.3	212.4	0.9	168.0	2.5	92.9	4.8	30.9	6.3
Chile	..	..	0.4	210.6	1.2	253.9	4.2	34.0	5.7
Malta	0.4	481.0	2.3	92.1	4.5	28.0	5.7	..	..
New Zealand	0.1	347.6	0.4	149.1	1.1	88.6	2.1	128.4	4.8
Dominica	..	..	0.2	82.5	0.4	727.2	3.4	22.4	4.1
Bahamas	..	..	..	..	6.3	- 44.8	3.5	15.4	4.0
Hungary	..	..	0.2	458.7	1.1	137.7	2.6	41.0	3.7
Ireland	..	..	..	..	0.3	287.1	1.0	216.8	3.3

Table 1.5. *(continued)*

Country/territory	2000	% change 2000-2001	2001	% change 2001-2002	2002	% change 2002-2003	2003	% change 2003-2004	2004
Slovenia	..	..	0.3	931.4	2.9	2.2	2.9	..	..
Lithuania	..	..	0.1	727.5	0.6	235.1	1.9	24.5	2.4
Latvia	..	..	0.1	211.0	0.4	96.4	0.8	152.9	2.1
Poland	..	..	0.0	914.6	0.3	59.3	0.5	319.3	2.1
Cyprus	..	..	0.3	132.2	0.7	68.6	1.2	31.7	1.6
El Salvador	..	..	..	..	..	..	0.3	380.1	1.4
Qatar	..	..	..	..	0.0	1 127.8	0.4	239.2	1.4
China	..	..	0.0	1 470.2	0.4	94.8	0.8	60.0	1.3
Argentina	..	..	0.2	34.0	0.3	102.1	0.6	110.0	1.3
Brazil	..	..	0.2	117.7	0.4	61.7	0.7	85.6	1.2
Belize	..	..	..	..	..	..	0.4	228.8	1.2
Malaysia	..	..	0.0	372.9	0.1	459.6	0.5	125.1	1.0
Slovak Republic	..	..	..	..	..	..	0.1	538.2	0.9
Kuwait	..	..	0.2	101.6	0.4	19.6	0.5	49.0	0.8
Czech Republic	..	..	0.1	147.0	0.1	126.9	0.3	118.3	0.7
Turkey	..	..	0.0	91.5	0.0	827.1	0.3	142.4	0.7
Costa Rica	..	..	..	..	0.0	3 920.7	0.4	84.3	0.7
Grenada	..	..	..	..	0.6	112.9	1.2	- 49.4	0.6
Panama	..	..	0.1	88.3	0.3	90.6	0.5	19.4	0.6
Peru	..	..	0.0	368.2	0.1	168.4	0.3	45.4	0.5
Greece	..	..	..	..	..	..	0.1	361.4	0.4
Romania	..	..	0.0	164.3	0.1	126.0	0.2	158.2	0.4
Trinidad & Tobago	..	..	..	..	0.0	476.6	0.1	347.5	0.4
Maldives	..	..	..	..	0.1	158.2	0.2	39.1	0.2
Mauritius	..	..	..	..	0.0	311.8	0.1	126.4	0.2
Morocco	..	..	..	..	0.0	33.0	0.0	2 259.9	0.2
Colombia	..	..	0.0	148.2	0.1	37.3	0.1	84.7	0.2
South Africa	..	..	..	..	0.0	655.3	0.0	193.6	0.1
Suriname	..	..	..	..	0.0	79.6	0.0	145.5	0.1
Nicaragua	..	..	0.0	41.7	0.0	86.1	0.1	11.3	0.1
Ecuador	..	..	..	..	..	..	0.1	65.6	0.1
Moldova	..	..	..	..	0.0	43.3	0.0	300.6	0.1
Gabon	..	..	..	..	..	..	0.0	1 051.9	0.0
Egypt	..	..	..	..	0.0	407.8	0.0	492.8	0.0
Armenia	..	..	..	..	0.0	25.5	0.0	9 936.7	0.0
Tunisia	..	..	..	..	..	..	0.0	8.4	0.0
India	..	..	0.0	62.2	0.0	67.7	0.0	64.9	0.0
Vanuatu	..	..	..	..	..	..	0.0	50.4	0.0
Sudan	..	..	..	..	..	..	0.0	37.4	0.0
Burkina Faso	..	..	..	..	0.0	180.8	0.0	2.9	0.0
Benin	..	..	..	..	..	..	0.0	195.1	0.0

Source: UNCTAD calculations based on ITU World Telecommunication Indicators database, 2005.

Second, China has experienced the most spectacular growth in the number of broadband subscribers: from close to zero (2001) to 17 million subscribers (2004) (see chart 1.2). This makes China the country with the second largest number of broadband subscribers, after the United States and Japan. Although broadband penetration in China has almost doubled compared with 2003, the country is still at the bottom of the list, with 1.3 subscribers per 100 inhabitants in 2004.

Third, with regard to developing country regions, only Asia has any significant broadband penetration. Even though subscriber growth rates in Africa and Latin America are very high, it will take years before they reach the subscriber levels of Asia, Europe or North America. Especially in Africa, the number of broadband subscribers in most countries is extremely small, and penetration rates are less than 1 per cent even in countries that are more advanced in ICT, such as South Africa, Mauritius, Egypt and Tunisia.

The digital divide in terms of broadband in many less developed countries could have serious implications for their enterprises as far as fully embracing ICTs is concerned. While previous research has demonstrated that dial-up access is sufficient for companies to start moving online, using e-mail and hosting a basic informational website, more advanced applications of ICTs, such as online ordering, customer acquisition and retention, finance and account management, product service and support, or logistics and inventory control, will benefit significantly from high-speed access (UNCTAD, 2004). These are also the areas where most ICT-related productivity gains

Chart 1.2

Broadband subscribers in China and the United States, 2001-2004

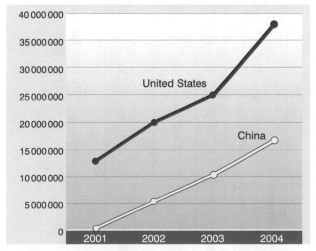

Source: Unctad calculations based on ITU World Telecommunications Indicators database, 2005

will be achieved. For many SMEs in developing countries, which do not currently have such access, the leap towards a more integrated adoption of ICTs in business processes will thus heavily depend on improved access to the Internet, in terms of both quality and speed.

Computers

Even though the Internet is increasingly being accessed through a variety of devices, computers are still by far the most important gateway to the Internet. Computers are indispensable for the development of the information economy and in particular for the application of ICT in e-business processes. An in-depth presentation of the presence of computers in developing countries is limited by the available data. Estimates about the number of PCs in countries are usually based on shipments (i.e. computers sold) or, if this information is not available, imports, coupled with a realistic replacement rate.[2] The latter obviously differs among countries, with many developing countries having significantly lower rates. The number of PCs by country is shown in annex I, while table 1.6 shows the penetration of PCs by region and level of country development.

The following observations can be made about the spread of computers:

- There is continued growth in the number of computers worldwide. In 2003, the highest growth was in developing countries/some emerging economies (such as China, Brazil, the Russian Federation, Mexico, India, the Islamic Republic of Iran and Malaysia). When it comes to computer penetration, however, these countries rank very low; for example, China at 3.7 per cent, Brazil at 8.9 per cent and India at 0.9 per cent – similar to most low-income countries.

- Switzerland leads in terms of penetration, with 74.2 computers per 100 inhabitants in 2003, followed by Singapore and Sweden.

- There are huge gaps among countries: for example, in 2003 the Republic of Korea had 26.7 million PCs, compared with only 11.5 million PCs in the whole of Africa. Some African countries have very few computers; for example, Malawi reported 15,800 computers for 2003. Similarly, computer penetration rates are lowest for Africa (1.4 per cent), compared with 66.8 per cent for North America.

Table 1.6

Personal computer penetration by region and level of development, 2000-2004

Region	2000 Number PCs	2000 Penetration	% Change 2000-2001	2001 Number PCs	2001 Penetration	% Change 2001-2002	2002 Number PCs	2002 Penetration	% Change 2002-2003	2003 Number PCs	2003 Penetration	% Change 2003-2004	2004 Number PCs	2004 Penetration
Africa	7'047'760	0.9	9.6	7'891'751	1.0	18.1	9'521'025	1.2	17.7	11'448'713	1.4	13.4	13'257'266	1.6
Asia	113'912'800	3.2	16.1	133'909'400	3.7	15.6	156'638'500	4.3	17.9	186'937'850	5.1	17.2	221'653'614	6.0
Europe	131'642'887	18.3	11.5	146'719'000	20.4	12.5	165'020'000	23.0	12.1	185'009'308	25.7	19.8	221'567'577	30.8
Latin America and the Caribbean	24'475'500	4.9	19.6	29'712'000	5.8	14.7	34'567'409	6.7	17.2	41'099'436	7.8	13.9	47'486'964	8.9
North America	173'900'000	55.2	9.4	192'200'000	60.4	5.8	205'300'000	63.9	4.5	216'663'536	66.8	10.8	242'390'000	74.0
Oceania	10'794'615	35.7	9.0	11'929'721	38.9	9.1	13'189'200	42.4	6.7	14'255'760	45.2	11.9	16'156'861	50.6
Level of development														
Developed countries	343'569'000	37.0	10.5	381'564'000	40.9	7.9	413'988'000	44.1	7.7	448'292'647	47.5	16.0	522'785'289	55.1
Developing countries	105'800'075	2.3	17.6	126'243'872	2.7	19.0	152'361'634	3.2	20.3	185'914'170	3.8	13.1	213'243'868	4.3
South-East Europe and CIS	12'404'487	4.6	17.9	14'554'000	5.4	23.5	17'886'500	6.7	19.1	21'207'786	7.9	25.5	26'483'125	10.0
Total	461'773'562	7.9	11.7	522'361'872	8.8	10.5	584'236'134	9.7	10.9	655'414'603	10.8	15.0	762'512'282	12.4

Source: UNCTAD calculations based on ITU World Telecommunication Indicators database, 2005.

Note: For those countries that had not reported data for 2004 at the time of publication, the 2004 values were derived by averaging the growth of the previous four years.

- On the basis of 2003 values, the United States and Canada combined had more computers than all of Europe or all of Asia.

Overall, the computer penetration rates are very similar to the Internet penetration rates presented earlier. However, it is important to bear in mind that these figures do not represent the number of computer *users*. Computers are often shared and the rate of sharing in developing countries is higher than in developed countries. This is particularly the case at the household and individual user level, but even small enterprises in rural areas often access computers in local village community centres and similar public places. In the absence of better data on the use of computers, the above figures suggest that the gap in computer use penetration rates between developed and developing countries is smaller than the gap in Internet user penetration rates. This leaves further room for increasing Internet user penetration in developing countries, based on computer access, given the same number of computers.

Mobile phones

One of the most significant developments in the spread of ICTs during the past few years is the stun-

ning growth of mobile phone access in all parts of the world, surpassing the number of fixed telephone lines in many countries. Given that an estimated 77 per cent of the world's population is able to access mobile networks, the number of cell phone subscribers worldwide continues to increase at a very rapid rate, with the most significant growth being in developing countries (see table 1.7) (World Bank, 2005) [3]. What is most significant, however, is that in 2003 developing countries overtook developed countries in terms of absolute numbers of cellular subscribers, mainly because of Asian developing countries (e.g. China and India). This makes mobile phones the only ICT indicator where developing countries have higher shares than developed countries (see chart 1.3).

In order to get a more realistic picture of the distribution of mobile phones among users, penetration rates, i.e. subscribers per 100 inhabitants, need to be taken into consideration. Although these are lower in the developing world, accounting for 17.8 per cent only when compared to the developed world with 77.5 per cent (table 1.8), the trend remains positive.

Table 1.7

Mobile phone subscribers by region and level of development, 2000-2004

	2000	% change 2000-2001	2001	% change 2001-2002	2002	% change 2002-2003	2003	% change 2003-2004	2004
Region									
Africa	15'633'872	63.6	25'583'344	45.3	37'170'404	38.0	51'313'043	56.1	80'103'000
Asia	256'460'391	40.6	360'685'744	39.1	501'832'608	19.3	598'435'765	24.7	745'993'223
Europe	275'415'270	23.5	340'171'811	13.1	384'594'128	15.9	445'853'766	23.0	548'367'260
Latin America and Caribbean	61'463'003	34.7	82'777'855	20.2	99'474'308	24.7	124'042'755	39.5	173'001'627
North America	118'358'031	17.6	139'177'512	9.8	152'763'842	12.6	171'949'981	14.0	196'089'531
Oceania	10'213'768	32.9	13'573'551	12.0	15'203'646	13.0	17'179'776	15.1	19'778'880
Level of development									
Developed countries	464'565'999	18.9	552'325'810	9.0	602'046'769	10.0	662'394'988	11.8	740'630'471
Developing countries	261'776'686	47.8	386'979'017	41.9	548'974'336	23.5	677'854'370	32.0	894'932'102
South-East Europe and CIS	11'201'650	102.3	22'664'990	76.6	40'017'831	71.2	68'525'728	86.5	127'770'948
Total	737'544'335	30.4	961'969'817	23.8	1'191'038'936	18.3	1'408'775'086	25.2	1'763'333'520

Source: UNCTAD calculations based on ITU World Telecommunication Indicators database, 2005.
Note: For those countries that had not reported data for 2004 at the time of publication, the 2004 values were derived by averaging the growth of the previous four years.

Chart 1.3

Mobile phone subscribers by level of development, 2000-2004

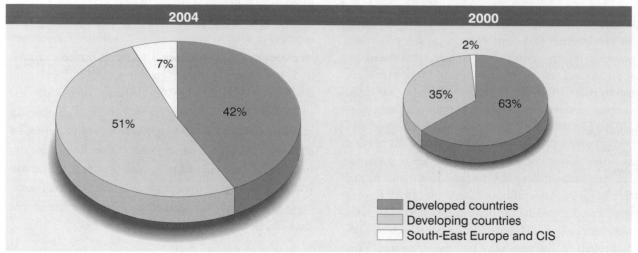

Source: Unctad calculations based on ITU World Telecommunications Indicators database, 2005

An important consideration here, however, is that in developing countries a single mobile phone is frequently shared by several people, particularly in poor, rural communities, and people at all income levels are able to access mobile services either through owning a phone or using someone else's. In India, for example, drivers pedal rickshaws equipped with mobile phones by a national mobile phone company throughout the state of Rajasthan offering mobile phone services for

a fee.[4] In other words, one subscriber could have many users, a fact which is not captured by the data provided here (see also box 1.1). That said, full penetration by mobile telephony is desired as much in developed as in developing countries.

Table 1.9 shows the mobile phone penetration rate in the top 10 countries in each region, next to the region average. Annex I contains the data on mobile phone

Table 1.8

Mobile phone penetration by region and level of development, 2000-2004

Mobile phone subscribers per 100 inhabitants (weighted averages)

	2000	% change 2000-2001	2001	% change 2001-2002	2002	% change 2002-2003	2003	% change 2003-2004	2004
Region									
Africa	2.0	60.1	3.2	42.1	4.5	35.1	6.1	52.9	9.4
Asia	7.0	38.9	9.8	37.4	13.4	17.8	15.8	23.2	19.5
Europe	37.5	23.5	46.4	13.1	52.4	15.9	60.8	23.0	74.7
Latin America and Caribbean	12.0	32.7	15.9	18.4	18.8	22.9	23.1	37.5	31.8
North America	37.6	16.4	43.8	8.7	47.6	11.5	53.0	13.0	59.9
Oceania	40.9	31.3	53.8	10.7	59.5	11.7	66.5	13.8	75.7
Level of development									
Developed countries	49.7	18.2	58.8	8.4	63.7	9.4	69.7	11.2	77.5
Developing countries	5.5	45.6	8.0	39.8	11.2	21.7	13.7	30.2	17.8
South-East Europe and CIS	3.3	102.8	6.8	77.0	12.0	71.7	20.5	86.9	38.4
Total	**12.3**	**28.8**	**15.8**	**22.3**	**19.3**	**16.9**	**22.6**	**23.7**	**27.9**

Source: UNCTAD calculations based on ITU World Telecommunication Indicators database, 2005.
Note: For those countries that had not reported data for 2004 at the time of publication, the 2004 values were derived by averaging the growth of the previous four years.

Table 1.9

Mobile phone penetration, regional country/territory performance, 2000-2004 (Top 10 countries)

sorted by decreasing order of 2003 values

Country/territory	2000	% change 2000-2001	2001	% change 2001-2002	2002	% change 2002-2003	2003	% change 2003-2004	2004
Réunion	39.5	45.8	57.6	14.4	65.9	13.4	74.7	..	..
Seychelles	32.0	41.2	45.2	18.3	53.4	11.3	59.5	2.2	60.8
South Africa	19.1	26.8	24.2	24.5	30.1	20.6	36.4	18.6	43.1
Botswana	12.2	54.4	18.8	34.5	25.3	17.5	29.7	5.7	31.4
Mauritius	15.1	50.5	22.7	26.7	28.8	-7.2	26.7	54.9	41.4
Morocco	8.2	100.5	16.4	27.8	20.9	16.8	24.4	23.0	30.1
Gabon	9.8	21.4	11.9	80.8	21.5	4.4	22.4	61.3	36.2
Mayotte	0.0	-	0.0	..	13.5	59.2	21.6	5.5	22.8
Tunisia	1.3	222.9	4.0	45.9	5.9	235.4	19.4	84.8	35.9
Mauritania	0.6	603.7	4.2	118.1	9.2	38.3	12.8	37.5	17.5
Africa total	**2.0**	**60.1**	**3.2**	**42.1**	**4.5**	**35.1**	**6.1**	**52.9**	**9.4**
Taiwan Province of China	80.2	21.2	97.2	114	108.3	5.4	114.0	12.3	100.0
Hong Kong (China)	81.7	5.1	85.9	9.7	94.3	14.5	108.0	6.0	114.5
Israel	70.2	29.2	90.7	5.3	95.5	0.7	96.0	9.1	104.7
Singapore	68.4	5.9	72.4	9.9	79.6	7.2	85.0	5.3	80.6
Macao (China)	32.1	38.9	44.5	40.4	62.6	20.8	81.0	14.3	92.6
United Arab Emirates	44.0	24.5	54.7	18.2	64.7	13.7	74.0	14.5	84.7
Rep. of Korea	58.3	5.2	61.4	10.7	67.9	3.2	70.0	8.7	76.1
Japan	52.6	11.7	58.8	8.3	63.7	6.7	68.0	5.3	71.6
Bahrain	32.4	42.7	46.2	25.2	57.9	10.3	64.0	37.4	87.9
Kuwait	21.7	77.5	38.6	34.5	51.9	10.1	57.0	35.2	77.1
Asia Total	**7.0**	**38.9**	**9.8**	**37.4**	**13.4**	**17.8**	**15.8**	**23.2**	**19.5**
Luxembourg	69.2	34.6	93.1	14.0	106.1	12.6	119.4	..	..
Italy	73.7	19.8	88.3	6.3	93.9	8.4	103.3	5.9	109.4
Sweden	71.8	12.3	80.6	10.3	88.9	10.3	98.1	5.3	103.2
Iceland	76.5	13.1	86.5	4.8	90.6	6.6	96.8	2.8	99.4
Czech Republic	42.3	60.6	68.0	24.9	84.9	13.7	96.5	9.2	105.3
Portugal	66.5	16.1	77.2	6.9	82.5	16.8	96.4	6.1	102.3
United Kingdom	72.7	6.0	77.0	9.1	84.1	8.4	91.2	12.8	102.8
Finland	72.0	11.6	80.4	7.9	86.7	4.9	91.0	5.1	95.6
Norway	74.8	11.1	83.1	1.5	84.4	7.7	90.9	..	..
Greece	56.2	33.8	75.2	12.5	84.5	6.7	90.2	11.5	100.6
Europe total	**37.5**	**23.5**	**46.4**	**13.1**	**52.4**	**15.9**	**60.8**	**23.0**	**74.7**
Jamaica	14.2	71.3	24.4	118.9	53.3	27.7	60.6	35.7	82.2
Saint Vincent	2.1	213.0	6.5	31.0	8.5	519.7	52.9	-11.0	47.1
Barbados	10.6	86.0	19.8	82.5	36.1	43.7	51.9	21.6	63.1
Chile	22.4	53.1	34.2	25.1	42.8	19.4	49.4	25.7	62.1

Table 1.9 (continued)

Country/territory	2000	% change 2000-2001	2001	% change 2001-2002	2002	% change 2002-2003	2003	% change 2003-2004	2004
Grenada	4.6	40.9	6.4	11.1	7.1	428.1	37.6	11.7	42.1
Trinidad & Tobago	12.5	57.5	19.7	41.2	27.8	43.5	37.3	32.9	49.6
Bahamas	10.3	90.8	19.7	97.8	39.0	-6.1	36.7	60.0	58.7
Suriname	9.5	109.1	19.8	13.9	22.5	42.2	32.0	51.4	48.5
Paraguay	14.9	36.6	20.4	41.3	28.8	3.5	29.9	- 50.3	14.9
Mexico	14.2	54.1	21.9	17.4	25.8	14.4	29.5	24.3	36.6
Latin America and Caribbean total	**12.0**	**32.7**	**15.9**	**18.4**	**18.8**	**22.9**	**23.1**	**37.5**	**31.8**
United States	38.9	15.7	45.0	8.6	48.9	11.7	54.6	11.7	61.0
Canada	28.8	20.4	34.7	10.0	38.2	9.7	41.7	13.3	47.2
North America total	**37.6**	**16.4**	**43.8**	**8.7**	**47.6**	**11.5**	**53.0**	**13.0**	**59.9**
Australia	44.7	28.5	57.4	11.4	64.0	12.8	72.2	14.5	82.6
New Zealand	40.0	47.5	59.0	5.4	62.2	4.3	64.8	19.6	77.5
New Caledonia	23.3	33.1	31.0	15.3	35.7	18.7	42.4	18.4	50.2
Fiji	6.8	46.5	9.9	10.2	11.0	21.3	13.3	..	..
Samoa	1.4	-1.0	1.4	6.9	1.5	285.0	5.8	..	..
Micronesia	..	..	..	..	0.1	5752.7	5.4	111.8	11.5
Vanuatu	0.2	-6.6	0.2	1263.3	2.4	55.0	3.8	28.9	4.8
Marshall Islands	0.9	7.8	0.9	11.2	1.0	6.7	1.1	..	..
Kiribati	0.4	29.5	0.5	23.3	0.6	4.5	0.6	..	..
Solomon Islands	0.3	-18.3	0.2	0.5	0.2	38.8	0.3	..	..
Oceania total	**40.9**	**31.3**	**53.8**	**10.7**	**59.5**	**11.7**	**66.5**	**13.8**	**75.7**
World total	**12.3**	**28.8**	**15.8**	**22.3**	**19.3**	**16.9**	**22.6**	**23.7**	**27.9**

Source: UNCTAD calculations based on ITU World Telecommunication Indicators database, 2005.

subscribers and penetration for all countries. With regard to regional differences, Africa is catching up in general terms, but one fourth of subscribers are in South Africa. The top four countries (South Africa, Morocco, Nigeria and Egypt) account for 57 per cent of all subscribers in the region. Very high subscriber growth rates can be observed in many countries, such as Algeria, Nigeria, Ghana and Sudan, to name the larger ones. The small countries start from very low levels. However, if we look at penetration rates, even the highest rate, which is in South Africa (at 43 per cent, followed by Mauritius, Gabon, Tunisia and Botswana), is still low compared with some European countries, which have approximately one mobile phone per inhabitant (e.g. Italy, the Czech Republic, Sweden, the United Kingdom and Portugal). Tunisia has experienced a surge in mobile phone penetration,

from only 6 per cent (2002) to 36 per cent (2004), mainly owing to the deregulation of the market and the subsequent fall in prices.[5] Other countries that have both high penetration growth and penetration rates above 10 per cent, are Algeria, Mauritania and Namibia.

In Asia, China is clearly the outstanding case in terms of absolute numbers, with about 45 per cent of all subscribers in the region. It is followed by Japan, India, the Republic of Korea, Turkey, the Philippines, Indonesia and Thailand. While Taiwan Province of China and Hong Kong (China) are the two economies with the highest penetration rates in the region, with more than one subscriber per inhabitant (reflecting double subscriptions), mainland China has a penetration rate of 25 per cent. Meanwhile, India and Pakistan, with a penetration rate of 4.4 per cent and

3.2 per cent respectively, are at the bottom level of penetration. Countries/territories with high mobile phone penetration growth between 2003 and 2004 include Kazakhstan, Palestine, Syria, Azerbaijan and Sri Lanka.

Brazil and Mexico account for about 60 per cent of all cellular subscribers in the Latin American and the Caribbean region, but their penetration rates, at 36.3 per cent and 36.6 per cent respectively, are not among the highest but are just about average for the region. The small States of the Caribbean have the highest penetration rates, together with Chile. Similarly, as with the number of Internet users, the countries in the Caribbean and Central America have the highest growth rates in the region as far as mobile phone penetration is concerned, in addition to their overall already higher penetration levels. Exceptions here are Cuba and Haiti, which are at the bottom of the list with almost 0 per cent (Cuba) and 4 per cent (Haiti).

With regard to other regions, it is worthwhile pointing out the dynamics of the countries of South-East Europe and the Commonwealth of Independent States, which have on average the highest growth rate for mobile subscribers. Mobile subscribers in the United States and Canada are growing in numbers but are still only at half the penetration rate of many European countries.

The substantial growth of mobile telephony in developing countries is largely explained by the fact that mobile phones are more widely accessible to users compared with fixed line telephony, for which waiting periods can be up to two years (ITU, 2003). Furthermore, mobile telephony has contributed to reducing the costs of telecommunications and facilitating the connection of rural areas. This continued growth can have significant implications for economic development in these countries. Apart from plenty of anecdotal evidence about how mobile phones have created business opportunities for the poor, there is an emerging literature examining the link between the use of mobile phones and economic growth in developing countries (Torero et al., 2002; Sridhar and Sridhar, 2004). According to a recent study by researchers at the London School of Economics, an increase of 10 mobile phones per 100 people in African developing countries would increase GDP growth by 0.6 per cent (Waverman et al., 2005).

It is argued that mobile telephony is the information and communication technology that has the most significant impact on development, particularly in developing and least developed countries. In these countries, mobile phones are used for more than simple communication, often as a business tool by means of which producers and buyers can shop around for prices and vendors can be paid.[6] The importance accorded to these economic benefits is reflected in the larger share of income that developing country users spend on telecommunications as compared with users in developed countries. African countries, and particularly sub-Saharan ones, are a good example of this (see box 1.1). The number of mobile phone subscribers in Africa increased from 15 million in 2000 to over 80 million in 2004, an increase of 433 per cent (table 1.7).

Box 1.1

Use of mobile phones by African businesses

A recent study surveyed the use of mobile phones among small businesses (under 50 employees) in rural and urban communities in Egypt and South Africa (Waverman et al., 2005). In those countries, tradesmen such as bricklayers and painters advertise themselves by giving a mobile phone number, taxi drivers are contacted by phone, and retailers avoid unnecessary travel by pre-shopping over the phone for supplies. The study found that the large majority of small businesses used mobiles (85 per cent in Egypt and 89 per cent in South Africa) and had overtaken fixed-line phones and other communication tools, despite the relatively higher price for mobile telephone calls. Nonetheless, it is significant that many of the businesses had no form of telephone access before the acquisition of a mobile phone, and in the South African sample, 85 per cent of the businesses depended solely on mobiles. Nearly a third of the businesses also indicated that their start-up was partly influenced by the availability of mobile phones, particularly in the service sector, and that higher spending was not detrimental to profitability. In fact, this spending was compensated for by greater efficiency, and a larger number of customers and turnover, all of which were indicated by the majority of the businesses surveyed.

2.   ICT access and use in enterprises

In its *E-Commerce and Development Report 2004*, UNCTAD noted that the focus on measuring e-commerce transactions might divert attention from measuring other uses of ICTs in businesses and therefore provide only limited information on the adoption of ICTs by enterprises. Therefore, increasing attention is being paid to the measurement of e-business – or more broadly the use of ICTs in enterprises for a variety of business activities that go beyond e-commerce. Many of the efficiency gains related to the adoption of ICTs result from changes in business processes, such as logistics and inventory control, order fulfilment and tracking, and customer acquisition and retention. Also, the growing adoption of ICTs by businesses in developing countries can be analysed for its impact on development, and better data on ICT readiness, use and impact are needed in order to design, implement and evaluate ICT development policies.

In that context, the UNCTAD secretariat launched an annual data collection exercise, starting with the E-Commerce and Development Report 2004, to compile e-business statistics from developing countries. On the basis of the list of core ICT indicators agreed upon at the WSIS Thematic Meeting on "Measuring the Information Society" (see section C), an extended group of selected developing countries were surveyed in 2005 regarding their e-business statistics.[7] While the data are still very limited, they give an initial indication on the adoption of ICTs by enterprises in developing countries. OECD and Eurostat provide complementary data on developed countries. A table summarizing the information available from selected economies can be found in annex I, table 6.

Internet access and use

In developed countries, a very high proportion of enterprises are connected to the Internet. Eighty-nine per cent of enterprises in EU countries are connected. There are however significant differences between European countries; for example, Denmark and Finland report that 97 per cent of enterprises are connected to the Internet while Romania (a EU candidate country) reports 52 per cent. Some differences also persist between SMEs and large enterprises (see chart 1.4). As a group, OECD countries also show high proportions of Internet access by enterprises. Among non-European members, for example, Australia reported 88.6 per cent, New Zealand reported 84 per cent and Canada reported 82 per cent (2004).

It is harder to obtain comparable information on Internet access by enterprises in developing countries. The diversity of surveys conducted in developing countries affects the comparability between countries and prevents from drawing conclusions at the regional level, or for developing countries as a whole. Several developing countries report high percentages of Internet access by enterprises, on a par with developed countries, such as the Republic of Korea (94 per cent), Trinidad and Tobago (77 per cent) and Singapore (76 per cent). Others report very low proportions, such as Mauritius (5 per cent) and Thailand (9 per cent). The reference years for the data reported vary from 2001 to 2004, and the samples vary from economy-wide to focused on specific sectors, such as manufacturing. In some cases, samples are made up predominantly of small enterprises. There is virtually no information on Internet access by enterprises disaggregated by urban or rural areas, although it is likely that results for some countries have a strong bias towards urban areas, which tend to concentrate overall ICT infrastructure and commercial activities (data for Morocco's survey, for example, was disaggregated by major cities and towns).

Nonetheless, in the cases in which data are disaggregated according to the size of enterprises, it appears that also in developing countries access to Internet is more prevalent among larger businesses. Since small and medium-sized enterprises represent a significant share of developing economies, it is important to look at the weight they have in the overall picture of ICT

Chart 1.4

Proportion of EU 15 enterprises with access to the Internet by size, 2002-2004

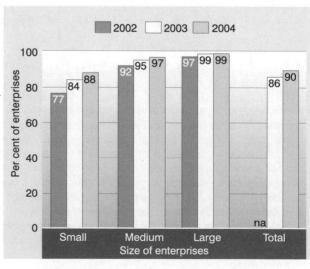

Source: Eurostat database, 2005.

Table 1.10

Proportion of businesses using the Internet in Thailand, 2003

	Number of Employees					
	1-15	**16-25**	**26-30**	**31-50**	**51-200**	**200+**
Number of enterprises in the survey	800'425	12'096	2'793	5'879	6'556	2'119
Proportion of businesses using the Internet (%)	7.2	45.6	52.6	59.4	73.3	90.1

Source: UNCTAD e-business database 2005.

uptake in these countries. In Thailand, for example, although the overall proportion of business access to Internet is merely 9 per cent in a survey with an overwhelming share of microenterprises, the proportion increases tenfold among large enterprises to 90 per cent, as shown in table 1.10.

Regarding modes of access to the Internet in enterprises, these are not always equally defined and there are significant differences among countries, depending on the availability of certain technologies. For example, in Europe the broadband roll-out is gathering speed and is overtaking ISDN.[8] Eurostat data show that the percentage of enterprises with Internet in the EU 15 that had broadband access grew from 46 per cent in 2003 to 61 per cent in 2004. For the EU 25, the percentage was of 58 per cent in 2004. Although the proportion of enterprises with broadband access increases with the size of the enterprise, recent growth in adoption has been stronger among SMEs (see chart 1.5).

The data received from developing countries indicate that many businesses connect to the Internet through an analogue modem (87.8 per cent in Colombia and 74.5 per cent in Moldova) or with fixed line connections under 2 Mbps (76.7 per cent in Morocco). Notable exceptions are some Asian countries/territories: Hong Kong SAR reports that 31.9 per cent of businesses have fixed line connections over 3 Mbps rather than 2 Mbps; Macao SAR reports that 75 per cent of businesses connect through ADSL; and the Republic of Korea reports that 98 per cent of businesses connect through fixed line connections of 2 Mbps or more, including XDSL, dedicated lines and cable modem. Classifications for modes of access that were provided by countries, although not requested by the UNCTAD survey, include dedicated and leased lines, cable modem and wireless connections, including mobiles.

Regarding the proportion of businesses with a website (or a web presence over which the business has control with regard to content), 58 per cent of businesses in the European Union have them. Including EU candidate countries, the same differences that can be found with respect to Internet access can also be found in terms of websites; the largest proportion is found in Denmark, with 81 per cent, and the lowest is found in Romania, with 19 per cent (35 per cent of businesses that have Internet). Also, as in the case of Internet access, the prevalence of websites is higher the larger the enterprise: 53 per cent of small companies, 76 per cent of medium sized companies and 89 per cent of large companies.

Among developing countries reporting data, proportions of businesses with Internet that have a website are generally lower, the lowest being Colombia with

Chart 1.5

Proportion of EU 15 entreprises with access to the Internet having broadband access, by size, 2003-2004

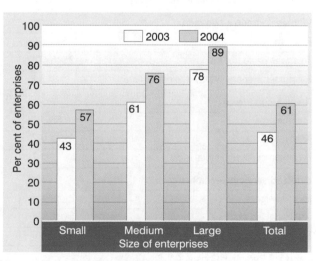

Source: Eurostat database, 2005.

12 per cent and the highest Trinidad and Tobago, with 57.6 per cent. Where disaggregated data are available, aside from the presence of websites according to size of companies, which follows a trend similar to that for more developed countries, the presence of websites can vary significantly among industrial classifications and can affect the weighted total. For example, Chile reported an overall proportion of 8.6 per cent, although approximately 73 per cent of utility companies (electricity, gas and water supply) had websites. In the Philippines, with a proportion of 10 per cent overall, it is the financial intermediation sector that reported the highest proportion of websites, with 26.4 per cent. Other sectors that reported higher or lower proportions of businesses with websites, ranging from 25 to 70 per cent, were real estate, renting and business activities (Chile, Colombia, Hong Kong SAR, Thailand), education (Russian Federation), heavy industry (Republic of Korea), and post and telecommunications (Romania).

E-commerce

E-commerce, understood as placing and receiving orders over the Internet and other networks,[9] continues to grow in most countries, although exact data on the value of e-commerce sales and purchases are not very common, in particular on a time-series basis.

In the United States, the largest global e-commerce market, e-commerce sales (including both Internet and other networks) continued to grow during 2003 (see table 1.11). E-commerce is most prominent in manufacturing shipments, followed by wholesale trade (accounting for 21.1 per cent and 13.1 per cent of total sales respectively). Online sales are less common in retail trade (B2C) or in services industries, with 1.7 per cent and 1 per cent of total sales respectively. However, with a growth rate significantly higher than for total retail trade, the share of e-commerce in total retail trade is also growing. The latest available figures (2005) indicate that its share has more than doubled since 2000.[10]

In Canada, Internet sales continued to increase substantially reaching $22.9 million (C$ 28.3 billion) in 2004, primarily on the basis of private sector sales (see table 1.12). Seventy-five per cent of Internet sales is B2B, up from 68 per cent in 2003, mainly between large firms, whereas small firms tend to sell more to households. As far as industries are concerned, one quarter of all Internet sales took place in the whole-

Table 1.11

E-commerce sales in the United States, 2000-2003 (million USD)

	2003	% change 2002-2003	2002	% change 2001-2002	2001	% change 2000-2001	2000
Manufacturing e-commerce							
E-commerce	842'666	12.1	751'985	3.7	725'149	-4.1	755'807
Total manufacturing	3'979'917	1.5	3'920'632	-1.3	3'970'500	-5.7	4'208'582
E-commerce share in total manufacturing	21.2	10.4	19.2	5.0	18.3	1.7	18.0
Wholesale trade e-commerce							
E-commerce	386'922	12.7	343'327	26.1	272'183	12.9	241'109
Total wholesale trade	2'946'473	4.3	2'824'417	4.3	2'708'666	-1.2	2'742'593
E-commerce share in total wholesale trade	13.1	8.0	12.2	21.0	10.0	14.3	8.8
Retail e-commerce							
E-commerce	55'731	24.7	44'706	30.5	34'263	21.7	28'152
Total retail	3'275'407	4.3	3'141'468	-0.5	3'156'754	3.2	3'059'173
E-commerce share in total retail	1.7	19.6	1.4	31.1	1.1	17.9	0.9
Selected services e-commerce							
E-commerce	49'945	21.3	41'185	10.5	37'261	-0.1	37'312
Total selected services	5'076'846	4.3	4'868'907	2.3	4'759'796	2.4	4'647'156
E-commerce share in total selected services	1.0	16.3	0.8	8.1	0.8	-2.5	0.8

Source: US Bureau of Census, 2005.

Table 1.12

Internet sales in Canada, 2000-2004 (million USD)

	2000	% change 2000-2001	2001	% change 2001-2002	2002	% change 2002-2003	2003	% change 2003-2004	2004
Private sector	4'496	14.2	5'134	70.7	8'762	68.0	14'716	45.5	21'419
Public sector	90	62.1	146	46.2	214	187.0	613	148.7	1'524
Total	4'586	15.1	5'280	70.0	8'976	70.8	15'329	49.7	22'944

Source: Statistics Canada, 2005.
FX rate: 1.00 C$ = 0.810174 US$, live mid-market rate as at 23.06.2005, XE.com.

sale trade sector, followed by transportation and warehousing (17 per cent).[11]

Other than for North America, available information on the value of e-commerce is fragmentary, although there appears to be clear growth. Eurostat data indicate that e-commerce sales over the Internet increased from 0.9 per cent in 2002 to 2.2 per cent in 2004.[12] The highest shares were reported by enterprises in Ireland (12.9 per cent), which has an important software sector, and Denmark (4.4 per cent). When online sales using other networks (in particular EDI) are added, the value increases from 6.2 per cent to 7.7 per cent over the same period (United Kingdom 12.5 per cent, Denmark 8.5 per cent and Ireland 8.3 per cent). Partial data also indicate that the percentage of enterprises' total turnover from e-commerce increased from 5.9 per cent in 2003 to 9.4 per cent in 2004. Compilations by the OECD suggest that online sales represent a small but growing share of total sales in most member countries, and that there is solid growth in B2C e-commerce (OECD, 2004). Because of the current difficulties in determining, collecting and comparing data on the value of e-commerce even in developed countries, these data are not currently included in the core list of indicators (see box 1.3) nor are they requested of countries in the UNCTAD survey.

In the case of developing countries, information on the value of e-commerce is virtually non-existent, as well as measures of the share of e-commerce in the turnover of enterprises. Only some developing countries covered by the UNCTAD survey were able to provide information on businesses receiving orders over the Internet (see annex I, table 6). However, as a general observation, countries reported fewer orders being received than placed, the main country receiving orders being Singapore (33.7 per cent), followed by Trinidad and Tobago (21.9 per cent) and Colombia (15.3 per cent).[13]

There is, however, more information from developed countries. In 2004, 15 per cent of enterprises in the EU 15 received orders over the Internet, as compared with 10 per cent in 2003. However, in 2004 the proportion for the 25 EU countries was 15 per cent. The proportion of enterprises selling online increases with the size of the company, since 29 per cent of large enterprises placed orders as compared with medium-sized enterprises (19 per cent) and small enterprises (12 per cent). Among non-European OECD countries, Japan reported in 2002 the largest percentage of businesses receiving orders over the Internet (18 per cent), although this refers only to enterprises with 100 or more employees, while Australia reported 13 per cent in the same year. Chart 1.6 illustrates the proportion of enterprises placing and receiving orders over the Internet in selected countries.

Regarding online purchases, 27 per cent of EU 25 enterprises reported having placed orders over the Internet in 2004, almost double that of online sales. The proportion was greater for large enterprises, 45 per cent of which reported online purchases. This is confirmed by data from selected OECD countries, which report a much larger proportion of businesses purchasing products and placing orders online than there were selling or receiving orders. The developing countries that reported the largest proportions of online purchases, of businesses with Internet were Singapore (45.5 per cent), Trinidad and Tobago (42.0 per cent) and the Republic of Korea (25.5 per cent).

Other e-business

As regards other e-business, there is limited but growing information on the use of ICT by enterprises for internal business processes, and on the use of the Internet by type of activity. As may be expected, developed countries collect more advanced e-business data and more frequently, since they are also

Chart 1.6

Enterprises placing and receiving orders over the Internet, 2004 or latest available year (selected countries)

of enterprises using the Internet

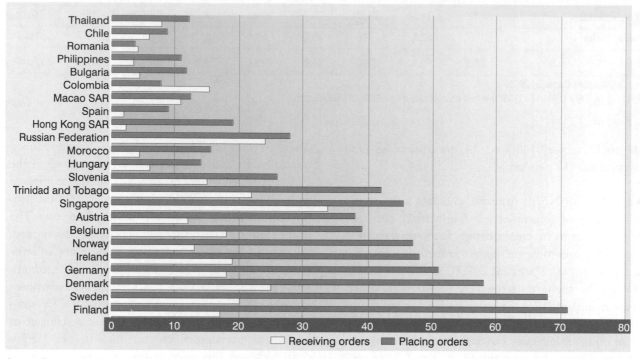

Source: Eurostat database, 2005; UNCTAD e-business database, 2005.

more advanced users of ICTs. For example, business operations might be linked to online orders (see chart 1.7), or ICTs can be used as tools for management (see chart 1.8).

As far as the use of the Internet by enterprises is concerned, it is difficult to obtain comparable data from developing countries in this regard. Many countries do not collect data specifically on the use of the Internet, but among those that do, unsurprisingly, e-mail is the most common type of Internet activity, followed by information search (about goods and services, the market, government and public authorities) and other research (see table 6 in annex I). Also, response categories can vary from country to country. As can be seen in table 1.13, Thailand requests different information from enterprises as regards their use of the Internet, and more of the larger enterprises use the Internet for different types of activity.

The Internet is also used by enterprises for e-banking and other financial services. In the EU 25, 68 per cent of enterprises used the Internet for financial services in 2004. In the OECD countries, a selected number of countries had a very high proportion of firms that use the Internet for banking and financial services,

from 45 per cent in Cyprus to 87 per cent in Slovenia. Bulgaria and Romania, reported 26 per cent and 23 per cent respectively. Almost none of the developing economies covered by the UNCTAD survey reported the use of the Internet for these purposes, with the exceptions of Hong Kong SAR (34.1 per cent) and Thailand (5.6 per cent).

Even in the EU, which has a strong e-government agenda, transacting with public authorities over the Internet is still not widespread, although enterprises do so more than individuals and the level of interactivity is growing slowly. In 2004, only 18 per cent of enterprises in the EU 25 with Internet access used it for full electronic case handling[14] with Governments. However, 51 per cent of enterprises with Internet access used the Internet to obtain information from public authorities, 46 per cent for obtaining forms and 32 per cent for returning filled-in forms. The countries covered by the UNCTAD survey have not provided much information on businesses using the Internet to transact with Government or public authorities, despite the increase in e-government initiatives. Notable, but not surprising exceptions are Bulgaria and Romania, which are EU candidate countries, and Andorra, which is not in the EU but is in

Chart 1.7

Proportion of enterprises carrying out e-business activities in selected European countries, 2003

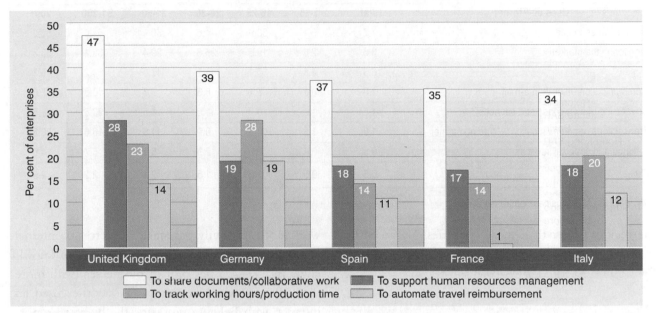

Source: OECD, 2004.

Chart 1.8

Business processes linked to online orders in selected OECD countries, 2003

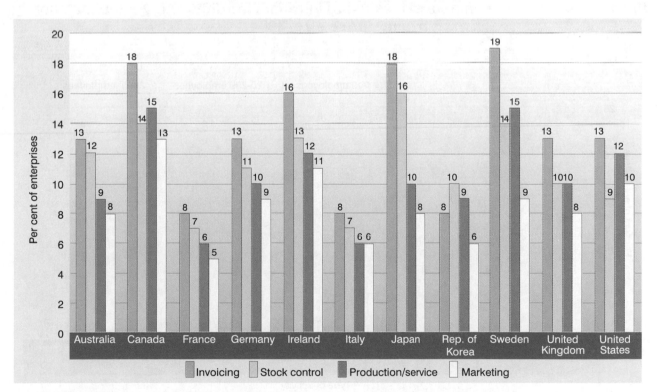

Source: OECD, 2004.

Table 1.13

Different uses of Internet by enterprises in Thailand by number of employees, 2003 *(percentages)*

Uses of Internet	total	1-15	16-25	26-30	31-50	51-200	200+
Information searches	7.7	6.1	38.9	44.6	50.9	64.0	82.2
Monitoring the market	3.6	2.6	19.5	25.6	29.4	38.1	53.8
E-mail	6.3	4.8	35.4	41.9	47.0	61.2	78.3
Communication other than e-mail	1.0	0.8	5.1	5.8	7.7	10.3	17.6
Advertising of own goods and services	1.5	1.0	10.2	11.5	14.5	23.6	38.8
Transactions or communication w/ trading partner	1.6	1.3	8.1	9.9	11.5	16.6	26.2
Banking and financial services	0.5	0.4	2.5	2.9	5.1	6.7	14.9
Other	0.5	0.5	1.0	1.5	2.1	2.2	2.5

Source: UNCTAD e-business database 2005.

the region. Other than these countries, Macao SAR reported that 9.4 per cent of enterprises use the Internet to transact with public authorities.

Other ICT use indicators

The proportion of businesses with an intranet is also a core indicator owing to the importance of such networks in e-business.[15] Intranets help an organization

work more efficiently, particularly in terms of internal communication, coordination and sharing of knowledge. In 2004, 33 per cent of businesses (with more than 10 employees) in European countries used an intranet, with Belgium reporting the highest proportion (45 per cent). Bulgaria reported that 27.2 per cent of enterprises have an intranet, and Romania reported 16 per cent. Although many countries still do not collect information on the use of intranets by enter-

Chart 1.9

Proportion of Moroccan enterprises using intranets for different types of activity, by enterprise size, 2004

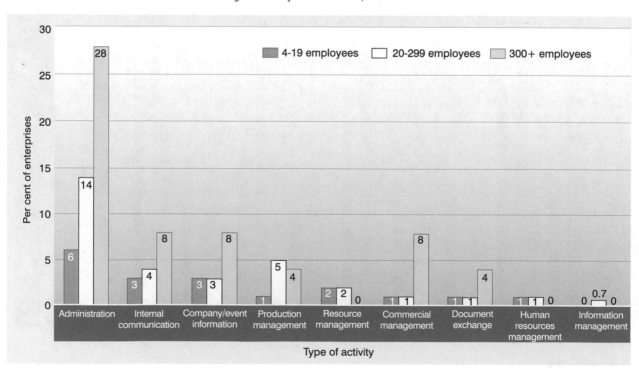

Source: UNCTAD e-business database 2005.

Table 1.14

Proportion of businesses with extranet and intranet, 2003 or latest available year (selected countries)

of businesses with Internet

Country	Businesses with an intranet	Businesses with an extranet
Singapore	84.7	36.1
Madagascar	57.0	..
Republic of Korea	37.4	..
Argentina	50.2	15.6
Morocco	33.3	
Bulgaria	44.0	5.5
Philippines	33.1	7.8
Trinidad & Tobago	24.2	..
Romania	31.0	9.5
Chile	22.7	7.2
Colombia	0.8	0.4

Source: UNCTAD e-business database 2005.

prises, among those covered by the UNCTAD survey the use of intranets is not far from European numbers and even surpasses them. The outperformer is Singapore, reporting that 64.3 per cent of enterprises use an intranet, followed by Madagascar with 38.2 per cent and the Republic of Korea with 35.2 per cent. At the lower end is Chile with 4.6 per cent, a result which is weighted downwards by retail trade enterprises (63 per cent of the sample), which have a low prevalence of intranets; as can be expected, enterprises in computer and related activities (less than 1 per cent of the sample), report 40 per cent of intranet prevalence. In Morocco, the national regulatory authority also collects data on the types of activities for which intranets are used by enterprises (see chart 1.9).

It should be noted that size also matters here. In the EU 25, 76 per cent of large enterprises have an intranet, as opposed to 27 per cent of small enterprises and 54 per cent of medium-sized enterprises. This may be due to several factors: for example, SMEs have fewer resources available for development and maintenance of an intranet, their size might not justify the use of an intranet, or there is less management awareness of the potential benefits of such a network. A certain basic infrastructure, such as a LAN, is also required. In this sense, there is a definite correspondence between the proportion of businesses with a LAN and those with an intranet, in

which the former is always equal to or greater than the latter (see table 6 in annex I).

The use of an extranet is less common, perhaps a combination of security concerns related to allowing external users into parts of an enterprise's system, and the technical challenge of expanding the functionalities of the system to allow for external interaction.[16] Extranets also entail changes in business processes and structures, since resources are required for maintaining and following up on this additional avenue for interaction with clients, suppliers and the general public. Such an indicator provides information on the level of e-business sophistication and interactivity in countries. In particular, more in-depth analysis of this indicator could also help assess the relative importance of B2B extranets for enterprise productivity.

In 2004, only 12 per cent of businesses in European countries had extranets, with Belgium also reporting the highest proportion (23 per cent). Bulgaria and Romania reported 3.4 per cent and 4.9 per cent respectively. Among developing countries, this indicator is collected less frequently than that on intranets, and in those cases where data are available the proportion of businesses with extranets is also lower than the proportion of businesses with intranets. Singapore, which is more advanced in ICT uptake than most developing countries, reported the highest proportion with 27.4 per cent.

3.   International trade in ICT goods

Another set of core indicators related to measuring the information economy concerns the ICT-producing sector and international trade in ICT goods and services (see section C.2). Currently, very little internationally comparable data are available on the ICT sector in developing countries. Similarly, comparable data on international trade in ICT services suffer from a lack of an internationally agreed upon definition of ICT trade in services.[17] By contrast, data on international trade in goods are collected at national borders by most countries and compiled in the UN Comtrade database. This section will thus provide an overview of trends in the international trade of ICT goods from a developing country perspective.

The data presented in this section are based on the classification of ICT goods developed by the OECD Working Party on Indicators for the Information Society (WPIIS) and are currently under consideration by the UN Statistical Commission for final

Chart 1.10

Evolution of ICT goods and total merchandise exports, 1996-2003 (1996 = 100)

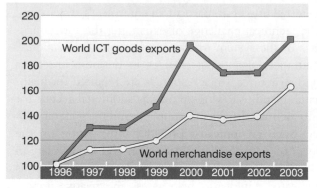

Source: UN COMTRADE database.

approval. A detailed list (at the six-digit level of the Harmonized System) of all the items covered under this classification is provided in annex III.

Global trends in international trade of ICT goods

Since 1996, exports of ICT goods have doubled and have grown at a faster pace than merchandise exports. Between 1996 and 2003 merchandise exports

increased by 60 per cent, while ICT goods exports increased by 100 per cent (see chart 1.10). In 2003, exports of ICT goods exceeded $ 1.1 trillion, accounting for 15 per cent of world merchandise exports. The value of international trade in ICT goods thus exceeded the combined value of international trade in agriculture, textiles and clothing.[18]

This growth has taken place despite a general stagnation in international merchandise trade at the turn of the millennium and following the crash of the NAS-DAQ stock market, which particularly impacted on trade in ICT goods. In 2001, trade in ICT goods plummeted by 11 per cent, a fall far greater than the decline in merchandise trade. ICT goods exports started to recover in 2002, and grew strongly again in 2003, as well as merchandise trade in general, with an average annual growth rate of 15 per cent.[19]

Trade in ICT goods continues to be highly concentrated: the top ten exporters account for 72 per cent of global ICT exports, and the top ten importers for slightly less (66 per cent of global ICT imports). Concentration is even higher in developing countries: the top ten developing country exporters amount for over 98 per cent of all developing countries' exports in ICT goods (the top ten importers amount for

Table 1.15

ICT goods exports by region and level of development, 2000-2003 (million USD)

	2000	2001	2002	2003	% change 2000-2001	% change 2001-2002	% change 2002-2003	% of world exports in ICT goods 2003
Level of development								
Developed countries	635'468	560'468	528'510	569'916	-12	-6	8	50.7
South-East Europe and CIS	1'790	2'223	2'391	2'360	24	8	-1	0.2
Developing countries	461'529	410'961	442'853	551'690	-11	8	25	49.1
Region								
Africa	797	800	1'386	1'661	0	73	20	0.1
North America	204'886	167'161	144'631	148'645	-18	-13	3	13.2
Latin America and Caribbean	42'944	42'066	40'139	40'253	-2	-5	0	3.6
Asia	549'203	469'306	501'451	621'265	-15	7	24	55.3
Europe	298'969	292'365	284'151	309'938	-2	-3	9	27.6
Oceania	1'988	1'954	1'996	2'204	-2	2	10	0.2
World ICT goods exports	1'098'787	973'651	973'754	1'123'967	-11.4	0.0	15.4	100.0
World merchandise exports	5'970'375	5'826'804	5'951'043	6'962'775	-2.5	2.1	14.5	–

Source: UNCTAD calculations based on UN COMTRADE database.

Chart 1.11

Share of ICT goods in total merchandise exports, 1996-2003

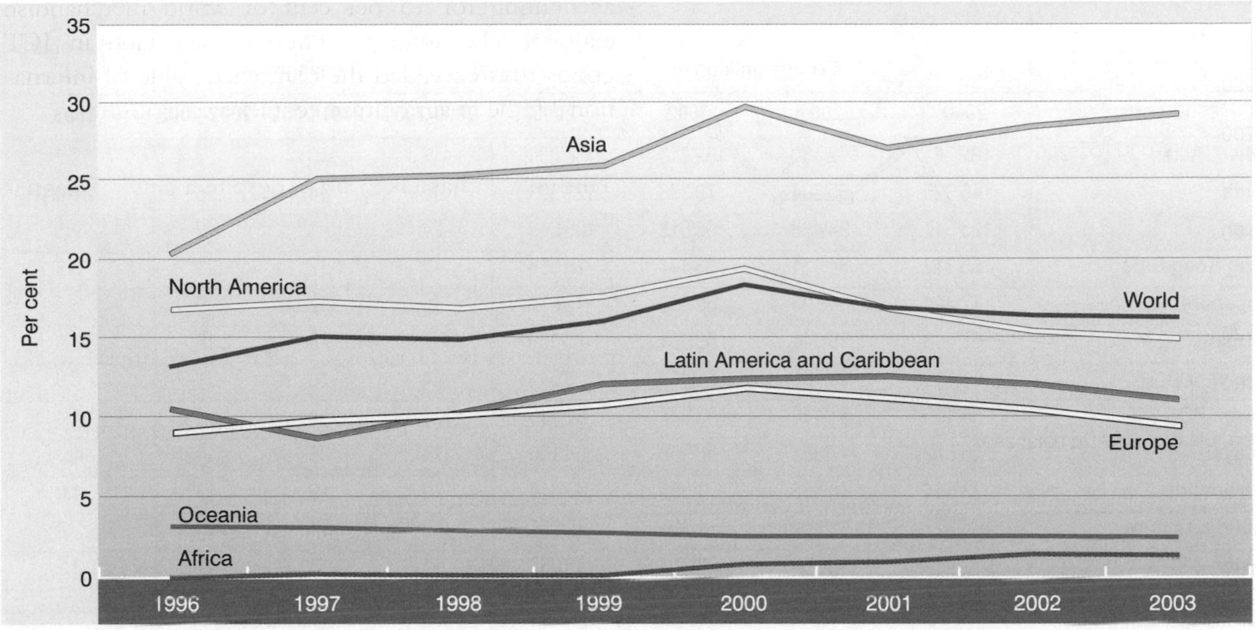

Source: UN COMTRADE database.

90 per cent of the developing countries' ICT goods imports). China alone takes 22 per cent of all developing countries' trade in ICT goods.

Major exporters

As table 1.15 shows, the growth in global ICT goods exports was particularly driven by increased exports from developing countries, which grew by 25 per cent in 2003. Developing countries now amount for almost 50 per cent of world exports in ICT goods.

Regionally, Africa and Asia experienced stronger growth rates, although Africa started from very low levels. Characterized by impressive growth and high initial levels of exports, the Asian region dominates the international market with a 55 per cent world market share, followed by Europe (27 per cent) and North America (13 per cent). Latin America and the Caribbean represent under 4 per cent of the world market, while neither Oceania nor Africa accounts for 1 per cent of world exports of ICT goods.

Asian exporters continue to be highly specialized in ICT trade (30 per cent of total merchandise trade) whereas since 2001 North America's relative exports in ICT goods have decreased, from 20 per cent to 15 per cent of total merchandise trade. For Europe and Latin America, ICT goods continue to represent about 10 per cent of their total merchandise exports. Finally, for Oceania and Africa, exports of ICT goods

represent less than 5 per cent of total merchandise exports (see chart 1.11).

The recent growth in market share of developing countries has been driven by a small number of economies, namely China, Hong Kong SAR and the Republic of Korea. In three years, China has more than doubled its market share and, in 2003, became the second major exporter after the United States. The market share of Hong Kong SAR increased by 40 per cent during the same period, and in 2003 it became the fourth largest exporter of ICT goods (see table 1.16 and chart 1.12).

This growth in developing countries' market shares was also due to the fact that some of the largest developed country exporters (such as the United States, Japan, the United Kingdom, France, Ireland, Italy and Canada) had decreased their exports (in absolute values) since 2000.

Furthermore, lower production costs, economies of scale, an increased interest in investing in certain developing countries and perhaps a move towards ICT services rather than goods by developed countries prompted the reallocation of ICT goods production to developing countries. This development, coupled with a surge in local ICT productive sectors in some developing countries contributed to the increase in ICT goods exports from developing countries. Except for Germany, the ten major developed

Table 1.16

Major exporters of ICT goods, 2000-2003

Exports	Exports (million $)				% change			World market share (%)
	2000	2001	2002	2003	2000-2001	2001-2002	2002-2003	2003
United States	182'261	152'150	132'613	136'630	-17	-13	3	12.2
China	46'996	55'304	79'376	123'303	18	44	55	11.0
Japan	123'547	94'498	95'013	106'649	-24	1	12	9.5
Hong Kong SAR	55'312	54'431	63'494	78'056	-2	17	23	6.9
Singapore	77'344	64'693	65'863	72'670	-16	2	10	6.5
Germany	57'608	59'041	59'064	70'336	2	0	19	6.3
Rep. of Korea	61'516	46'786	55'018	66'541	-24	18	21	5.9
Taiwan PC	64'406	51'140	52'977	61'085	-21	4	15	5.4
Malaysia	55'572	47'981	50'966	53'126	-14	6	4	4.7
Netherlands	33'644	34'533	31'580	45'110	3	-9	43	4.0
United Kingdom	54'927	53'394	51'394	43'051	-3	-4	-16	3.8
Mexico	38'262	38'054	36'313	36'062	-1	-5	-1	3.2
France	35'149	29'920	27'240	28'152	-15	-9	3	2.5
Philippines	26'421	21'394	24'080	24'157	-19	13	0	2.1
Ireland	25'607	28'999	26'489	22'453	13	-9	-15	2.0
Thailand	20'360	17'428	-	20'844	-14	0	0	1.9
Italy	12'830	12'801	11'406	12'524	0	-11	10	1.1
Belgium	11'432	11'813	10'218	12'125	3	-14	19	1.1
Canada	22'625	15'011	12'018	12'015	-34	-20	0	1.1
Hungary	7'776	7'510	8'938	11'967	-3	19	34	1.1
Finland	11'555	9'413	9'789	11'085	-19	4	13	1.0
Sweden	14'705	9'352	10'250	10'754	-36	10	5	1.0
Spain	6'135	6'158	5'896	7'615	0	-4	29	0.7
Indonesia	7'843	6'500	6'680	6'274	-17	3	-6	0.6
Austria	4'883	5'189	5'721	6'080	6	10	6	0.5
Rest of the world	40'072	40'158	41'358	45'302	0	3	10	4.0
World exports	1'098'787	973'651	973'754	1'123'967	-11	0	15	100.0

Source: UN COMTRADE database.

country exporters saw their market share in exports of ICT goods eroded during the period 2000–2003.

However, some of the previously leading developing countries also lost market share in exports of ICT goods. Malaysia and Singapore both lost 8 per cent and 6.5 per cent respectively of their market share in these three years.[20] This may be explained by a reallocation of ICT manufacturing businesses to lower-wage countries such as China. Other developing countries among the top 25 exporters – Mexico, the Philippines, Thailand and Indonesia – also experienced negative and/or sluggish growth rates and a

loss in market share in global ICT goods exports (see table 1.16).

African and Latin American regions are scarcely represented in the list of 25 major exporters. The three major African exporters are Morocco, South Africa and Tunisia. Together they account for 94 per cent of Africa's ICT goods exports. Nevertheless, these figures need to be considered with caution as few African countries report data on trade in ICT goods, and export data from important African exporters such as Egypt are lacking. Mexico is by far the largest exporter of ICT goods in Latin America and the Caribbean, accounting for 90 per cent of all the Latin

Chart 1.12

Major exporters of ICT goods, 2003

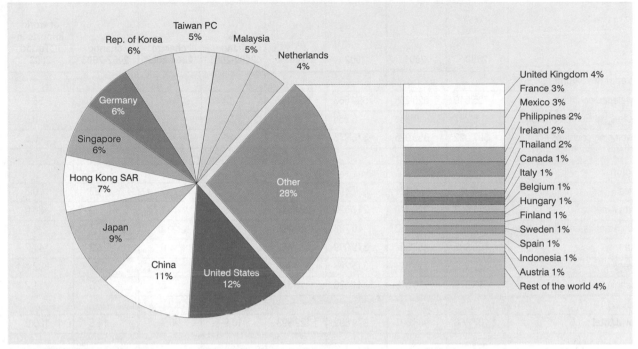

Source: UN COMTRADE database

Tables 1.17a and 1.17b

WMS and RCA by country/territory, 2000-2003

Countries/territories with 2003 RCA >1

	RCA	RCA growth (%)
	2003	2000-2003
Philippines	4.13	10
Malaysia	3.14	2
Singapore	3.13	3
Taiwan PC	2.54	7
Rep. of Korea	2.13	10
Hong Kong SAR	2.12	42
Hungary	1.75	16
China	1.74	70
Costa Rica	1.65	-5
Thailand	1.61	0
Ireland	1.51	-19
Japan	1.40	0
Mexico	1.35	8
Finland	1.35	-5
Netherlands	1.25	15
United States	1.17	-8

Source: UNCTAD calculations based on UN COMTRADE database

Countries/territories with WMS>1, 2003 RCA >1 and positive growth rates

	Three year Av. WMS Index	WMS growth (%)	RCA	RCA growth (%)
	2001-2003	2000-2003	2003	2000-2003
China	1.37	156	1.74	70
Hong Kong SAR	1.11	38	2.12	42
Hungary	1.15	50	1.75	16
Netherlands	1.10	31	1.25	15
Rep. of Korea	1.03	6	2.13	10

American ICT goods exports, followed by Brazil (5.8 per cent) and Costa Rica (3.8 per cent).

A useful measure to assess the export performance in ICT goods of individual countries is the revealed comparative advantage (RCA) index, combined with world market share (WMS) data.[21] The following will thus take a closer look at the countries that have gained comparative advantage and world market share in ICT goods exports.

According to table 1.17a, only a few economies have a revealed comparative advantage in ICT goods

Table 1.18

ICT goods imports by region and level of development, 2000-2003 (million USD)

	2000	2001	2002	2003	% change 2000-2001	% change 2001-2002	% change 2002-2003	% of world imports in ICTgood 2003
Level of development								
Developed countries	705'549	620'235	594'663	657'457	-12	-4	11	58.5
South-East Europe and CIS	5'297	7'341	8'256	9'600	39	12	16	0.9
Developing countries	397'022	359'026	376'973	455'937	-10	5	21	40.6
Region								
Africa	6'041	6'124	7'142	8'766	1	17	23	0.8
North America	271'963	220'110	217'526	224'546	-19	-1	3	20.0
Latin America and Caribbean	58'484	58'132	49'705	50'139	-1	-14	1	4.5
Asia	405'825	357'807	379'099	462'462	-12	6	22	41.2
Europe	352'177	333'812	315'293	363'705	-5	-6	15	32.4
Oceania	13'379	10'616	11'126	13'376	-21	5	20	1.2
World total	1'107'868	986'601	979'892	1'122'993	-10.9	-0.7	14.6	100.0
World merchandise imports	6'220'711	6'012'925	6'110'719	7'222'408	-3.5	1.6	15.4	

Source: UNCTAD calculations based on UN COMTRADE database.

exports, demonstrated by an RCA index of > 1. They are mostly Asian developing economies (China, Hong Kong SAR, Malaysia, Philippines, Republic of Korea, Singapore, Taiwan Province of China and Thailand), some developed countries (Finland, Hungary, Ireland, Japan, Netherlands and the United States) and two Latin American countries (Costa Rica and Mexico). Most of them (except Costa Rica, Ireland, Finland and the United States) have increased their revealed comparative advantage in the last three years.

Table 1.17b highlights countries with high export performance in terms of both gaining world market shares and increasing their specialization in ICT trade (i.e. growing RCA indices). The five best performers (with WMS and RCA indices above one and positive growth rates) during the period 2000–2003 were China, Hong Kong SAR, Hungary, the Netherlands and the Republic of Korea.

Major importers

In 2003, developed countries imported nearly 50 per cent more ICT goods than developing countries (table 1.18). However, if we look at the trend during the last three years, developed countries' imports have

fallen since 2000 and developing countries have higher import growth rates.

The three major importers are the United States, China and Hong Kong SAR. Despite a very low average growth in the last five years, the United States remains the major importer of ICT goods (accounting for 17 per cent of total reported imports) (see table 1.19 and chart 1.13). China and Hong Kong SAR experienced high import growth rates, although somewhat lower than their export growth rates. For instance, China had a 40 per cent growth in ICT goods imports in just one year (2002–2003), while its exports increased by 55 per cent in the same period. It has to be mentioned that 98 per cent of the goods imported by Hong Kong SAR are re-exported, and half of those go to China.

In 2001 and 2002, as in the case of exports, the value of ICT imports decreased in most countries. The only two countries, among the 25 major exporters, that have consistently increased their ICT goods imports since 2000 are China and Hungary. Overall, imports picked up strongly again in 2003. Among the major importers, Ireland is an exceptional case: since 2001 its imports have declined (in terms of total value), and in 2003 they dropped by 20 per cent, largely owing to

Table 1.19

Major importers of ICT goods, 2000-2003

Exports	Imports (million $)				% change			World market share (%)
	2000	2001	2002	2003	2000-2001	2001-2002	2002-2003	2003
United States	237'942	193'797	193'873	199'852	-19	0	3	17.8
China	47'479	53'192	68'724	96'536	12	29	40	8.6
HongKongSAR	64'403	61'552	69'082	82'686	-4	12	20	7.4
Germany	65'432	67'831	63'255	73'779	4	-7	17	6.6
Japan	66'871	58'207	55'092	61'220	-13	-5	11	5.5
UnitedKingdom	66'934	55'388	49'353	54'465	-17	-11	10	4.9
Singapore	59'769	47'950	48'144	53'153	-20	0	10	4.7
Netherlands	36'535	34'767	29'816	43'020	-5	-14	44	3.8
Rep.of Korea	39'085	30'334	32'288	37'543	-22	6	16	3.3
Malaysia	36'390	30'821	35'057	37'399	-15	14	7	3.3
Taiwan PC	43'410	31'353	33'756	34'698	-28	8	3	3.1
France	38'760	33'391	30'893	34'670	-14	-7	12	3.1
Mexico	36'308	36'568	34'394	33'980	1	-6	-1	3.0
Canada	34'021	26'313	23'653	24'694	-23	-10	4	2.2
Italy	23'511	21'508	20'879	24'018	-9	-3	15	2.1
Philippines	12'621	12'020	17'300	18'288	-5	44	6	1.6
Spain	14'238	13'276	13'080	16'045	-7	-1	25	1.5
Thailand	15'276	14'329	-	16'214	-6	0	0	1.4
Belgium	13'096	13'344	12'560	14'280	2	-6	14	1.3
Ireland	16'680	18'492	17'525	13'925	11	-5	-21	1.2
Australia	11'551	8'995	9'372	11'194	-22	4	19	1.0
Hungary	7'612	8'050	8'668	10'425	8	8	20	0.9
Sweden	10'982	9'073	8'632	10'093	-17	5	17	0.9
Switzerland	9'225	8'180	7'504	8'269	-11	-8	10	0.7
Austria	7'057	6'906	6'945	8'043	-2	1	16	0.7
Rest of the world	92'680	90'964	90'047	104'204	-2	-1	16	9.3
World imports	1'107'868	986'601	979'892	1'122'993	-11	-1	15	100.0

Source: UNCTAD calculations based on UN COMTRADE database.

a 50 per cent drop in the exports of electronic components.

As far as developing regions are concerned, the three major African importers of ICT goods are South Africa (45 per cent of all African imports), Algeria (12 per cent) and Morocco (11 per cent). They are followed by Nigeria (9 per cent) and Tunisia (8 per cent), all of which experienced positive growth in 2003. As in the case of global imports, Africa's imports of ICT goods are less concentrated than its exports.

In Latin America, Mexico, Brazil and Costa Rica are the largest importers. Mexico's share in imports is more modest (68 per cent of all ICT goods imported by Latin American countries) compared with its exports (90 per cent).

A final look at the role of LDCs in international trade of ICT goods reveals that it is extremely small, accounting for only $13 million (2003) or 0.001 per cent of world ICT goods exports.[22] This ratio is much smaller than LDCs' share in overall world merchandise exports (0.22 per cent). On the other hand, imports of ICT goods are 100 times greater than their exports and, with a value of $1,277 million represent 0.1 per cent of world ICT goods imports.[23] This shows that, unlike major exporters in this field, most LDCs do not import ICT goods as inputs into other goods to be exported; rather, the final destination of such goods is

Chart 1.13

Major importers of ICT goods, 2003

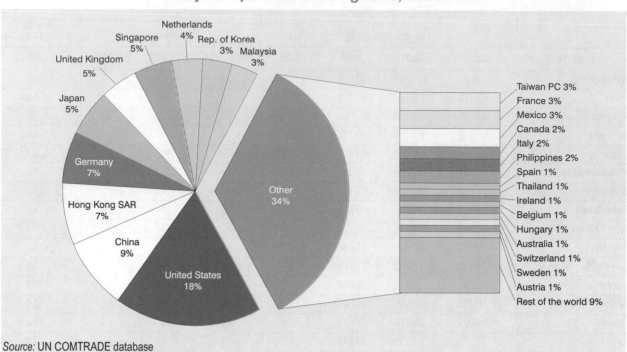

Source: UN COMTRADE database

local use. However, LDCs share in ICT goods imports (0.1 per cent) is much smaller than LDCs' share in total merchandise imports (0.36 per cent).

Seven out of the 10 LDCs that reported export data in 2000 and 2003 have experienced a negative compound annual growth rate. The only exceptions were Cambodia, Togo and Senegal (60 per cent, 48 per cent and 27 per cent compound annual growth rate). On the other hand, of the 13 LDCs that reported import data for 2000 and 2003, all have increased their imports (except for Cambodia). On average, LDCs' imports of ICT goods have grown at a 19 per cent compound annual growth rate. Given the lack of data on trade in ICT goods from LDCs, a note of caution should be exercised regarding any interpretation of the data provided above.

Trade patterns by category of ICT product

The above trends refer to a large number of ICT products. Therefore, this section disaggregates trade trends by category of ICT good. Following the OECD classification, ICT goods fall into five groups:[24]

- Telecommunications equipment;
- Computer and related equipment;
- Electronic components;
- Audio and video equipment;
- Other ICT goods.

Charts 1.14 and 1.15 show that two thirds of trade in ICT goods is in electronic components (34 per cent) and computer and related equipment (32 per cent). Trade in telecommunications equipment represents only about 15 per cent and decreased in the last few years. Audio and video equipment now represents 12 per cent of world ICT goods trade, with a slight increase from three years ago. Furthermore, the general category of "Other ICT goods" represents 8 per cent of global exports.

However, the share of the five product groups differs in some regions. Regarding exports, African countries export mainly electronic components (52 per cent) but few computers (8 per cent); and Latin American countries export mainly computers (37 per cent) but relatively few electronic components (13 per cent). In terms of imports, African countries import mainly telecommunications equipment (37 per cent) and Latin American countries mainly electronic components (40 per cent) (tables 1.20 and 1.21).

Since 2000, and following the NASDAQ stock market crash, each of the five ICT goods categories has been performing very differently (chart 1.16). Exports in electronic equipment fell sharply in 2001 and recovered strongly in 2003, to almost their level at the start of the millennium. However, exports of telecommunications equipment, which dropped in 2001 and 2002, have not yet reached their 2000 levels.

Table 1.20   Exports of ICT goods by category of good, 2000-2003 (million USD)

	Telecommunications				Computer				Electronic components				Audio & video				Other ICT goods				All ICT goods			
	2000	2001	2002	2003	2000	2001	2002	2003	2000	2001	2002	2003	2000	2001	2002	2003	2000	2001	2002	2003	2000	2001	2002	2003
Level of development																								
Developed countries	124'872	109'964	96'774	93'618	188'660	172'046	154'178	164'425	205'500	166'133	162'550	178'093	49'432	46'869	48'480	56'333	67'003	65'456	66'557	76'447	635'468	560'468	528'510	569'916
SEE&CIS	342	537	501	585	211	171	153	177	621	527	847	611	125	167	194	334	491	820	697	654	1'790	2'223	2'391	2'360
Developing countries	43'525	47'364	49'086	59'455	160'452	145'723	153'787	191'476	186'422	147'599	161'511	206'824	60'201	58'810	65'540	79'255	10'929	11'465	12'930	14'680	461'529	410'961	442'853	551'690
Region																								
Africa	287	277	277	286	141	134	118	139	158	192	712	857	35	80	90	141	126	116	189	239	797	800	1'386	1'661
North America	34'440	25'596	20'190	18'670	59'985	50'353	40'697	41'951	79'341	61'209	56'165	59'582	7'902	7'375	6'733	6'759	23'218	22'124	20'846	21'683	204'886	167'161	144'631	148'645
LatinAmerican and the Caribbean	10'226	10'564	8'901	7'556	13'434	13'931	13'022	14'810	7'125	5'113	4'943	5'426	9'939	9'936	10'564	9'816	2'220	2'522	2'704	2'645	42'944	42'066	40'139	40'253
Asia	47'355	47'731	47'457	59'409	175'026	154'314	164'146	198'751	236'123	182'564	197'370	243'851	69'848	65'245	73'107	90'266	20'852	19'152	19'370	22'987	549'203	469'306	501'451	621'265
Europe	75'984	73'277	69'177	67'360	99'962	97'863	89'248	99'543	69'473	64'615	65'408	70'458	21'907	23'132	23'644	28'836	31'643	33'478	36'674	43'741	298'969	292'365	284'151	309'938
Oceania	448	421	359	378	775	840	886	884	324	266	276	352	77	73	76	104	364	349	400	486	1'988	1'954	1'996	2'204
World	168'740	157'865	146'361	153'659	349'323	317'940	308'118	356'078	392'543	314'259	324'878	386'528	109'758	105'846	114'214	135'921	78'423	77'741	80'184	91'781	1'098'787	973'651	973'754	1'123'967

Source: UNCTAD calculations based on UN COMTRADE database.

Table 1.21   Imports of ICT goods by category of good, 2000-2003 (million USD)

	Telecommunications				Computer				Electronic components				Audio & Video				Other ICT goods				All ICT goods			
	2000	2001	2002	2003	2000	2001	2002	2003	2000	2001	2002	2003	2000	2001	2002	2003	2000	2001	2002	2003	2000	2001	2002	2003
Level of development																								
Developed countries	117'058	104'694	92'101	100'965	271'467	240'057	231'324	254'335	181'985	140'980	128'643	140'171	81'423	79'712	87'605	100'076	53'616	54'793	54'990	61'909	705'549	620'235	594'663	657'457
SEE&CIS	1'892	2'569	2'735	2'992	1'047	1'552	1'796	2'065	823	970	1'375	1'705	395	723	908	1'068	1'141	1'546	1'442	1'770	5'297	7'341	8'256	9'600
Developing countries	45'866	45'906	38'381	43'898	84'192	80'864	83'425	93'282	213'718	182'825	202'774	251'453	28'347	26'881	29'854	34'707	24'900	22'549	22'539	27'597	397'022	359'026	376'973	455'937
Region																								
Africa	2'337	2'211	2'509	3'261	1'553	1'707	1'874	2'398	794	593	851	1'074	652	754	886	995	706	754	922	1'037	6'041	6'124	7'142	8'766
North America	43'577	36'316	34'322	37'769	99'932	82'760	83'369	84'844	72'037	45'566	39'994	38'301	36'192	34'040	38'724	41'356	20'224	20'428	20'617	22'277	271'963	220'110	217'526	224'546
LatinAmerican and the Caribbean	11'520	10'743	6'540	6'644	10'686	12'528	12'353	13'811	26'404	23'945	21'031	20'191	5'299	5'830	5'433	5'128	4'574	4'786	4'348	4'364	58'484	58'132	49'705	50'139
Asia	39'071	38'741	33'784	38'387	100'178	90'755	91'543	106'547	211'844	178'887	201'031	253'815	29'914	28'095	30'636	36'200	24'818	22'029	22'104	27'512	405'825	357'807	379'099	462'462
Europe	64'562	62'470	53'149	58'966	139'117	130'360	122'792	141'790	83'984	73'655	68'862	73'706	36'333	37'046	40'697	49'579	28'180	29'781	29'793	34'664	352'177	333'812	315'293	363'705
Oceania	3'748	2'688	2'312	2'828	5'240	4'243	4'614	5'293	1'462	1'022	1'023	1'243	1'774	1'551	1'991	2'592	1'154	1'111	1'186	1'421	13'379	10'616	11'126	13'376
World	164'815	153'169	133'216	147'855	356'706	322'453	316'546	354'682	396'325	324'775	332'791	353'329	110'165	107'316	118'367	135'851	79'657	78'888	78'971	91'276	1'107'868	986'601	979'892	1'122'993

Source: UNCTAD calculations based on UN COMTRADE database.

Chart 1.14

Exports of ICT goods by category of good, 2003

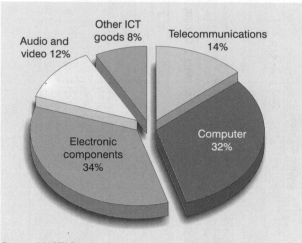

Source: UNCTAD calculations based on UN COMTRADE database.

Chart 1.15

Imports of ICT goods by category of good, 2003

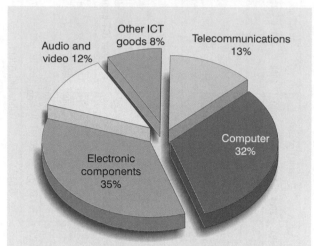

Source: UNCTAD calculations based on UN COMTRADE database.

Exports of audio and video equipment fell less in 2001, and have since grown by 25 per cent.

As far as the origin of exports is concerned, telecommunications equipment is mainly exported from developed countries, and particularly Europe, although their share of global telecommunications exports decreased from 74 per cent in 2000 to just over 60 per cent in 2003. In 2000, the United States was the main exporter of telecommunications equip-

ment, with 14 per cent of the global share. However, between 2000 and 2003 it halved its exports of telecommunications equipment, while the Republic of Korea and China doubled them. Thus, by 2003, the largest exporters of telecommunications equipment were the Republic of Korea, the United States and China, accounting for about 10 per cent of the market each. They are followed closely by Germany and the United Kingdom (see table 1.22 and charts 1.17a to 1.17d).

Chart 1.16

Evolution of ICT goods exports by category, 2000-2003 (2000 =100)

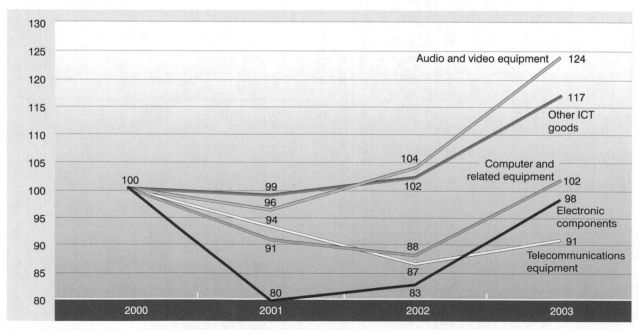

Source: UNCTAD calculations based on UN COMTRADE database.

Table 1.22

Major exporters by category of ICT goods, 2003 (million USD)

Telecommunications

	Value	%
Rep. of Korea	15'169	10
United States	14'871	10
China	14'558	9
Germany	13'407	9
United Kingdom	11'806	8
Finland	8'359	5
France	6'684	4
Hong Kong SAR	6'664	4
Mexico	6'133	4
Sweden	5'793	4
Rest of the world	50'216	33
Total telecom	**153'659**	**100**

Computers

	Value	%
China	59'245	17
United States	39'196	11
Netherlands	25'205	7
Singapore	24'883	7
Japan	21'838	6
Hong Kong SAR	21'816	6
Taiwan, PC	19'220	5
Germany	17'807	5
Rep. of Korea	17'638	5
Malaysia	15'662	5
Rest of the world	92'567	26
Total computers	**356'078**	**100**

Electronic components

	Value	%
United States	56'625	15
Japan	47'734	12
Singapore	38'645	10
Hong Kong SAR	31'808	8
Taiwan, PC	29'253	8
Rep. of Korea	25'660	7
Malaysia	25'288	7
China	22'879	6
Germany	18'477	5
Philippines	16'564	4
Rest of the world	73'596	19
Total electronic components	**336'528**	**100**

Audio & Video

	Value	%
China	24'289	18
Japan	20'709	15
Hong Kong SAR	15'391	11
Mexico	9'518	7
Rep. of Korea	7'251	5
Malaysia	6'595	5
United States	6'328	5
Germany	5'589	4
Taiwan, PC	4'364	3
Singapore	3'710	3
Rest of the world	32'177	24
Total audio & video	**135'921**	**100**

Other ICT goods

	Value	%
United States	19'610	21
Germany	15'055	16
Japan	10'682	12
United Kingdom	6'201	7
France	4'453	5
Netherlands	4'192	5
Taiwan, PC	3'164	3
Hong Kong SAR	2'376	3
Mexico	2'359	3
China	2'332	3
Rest of the world	21'356	23
Total other ITC goods	**91'781**	**100**

Source: UNCTAD calculations based on UN COMTRADE database

Chart 1.17 a, b, c, d
Major exporters by category of ICT goods, 2003 (million USD)

17a. Telecommunications equipment

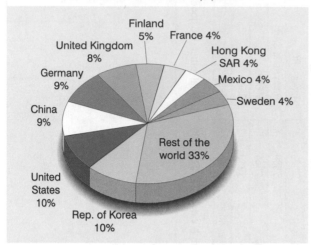

17b. Computers and related equipment

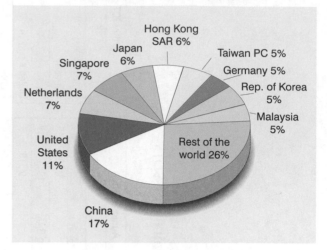

17c. Electronic components

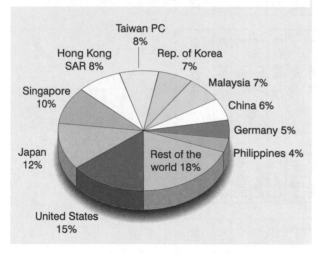

17d. Audio and video equipment

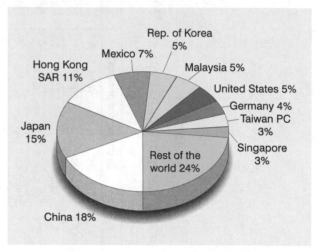

Source: UNCTAD calculations based on UN COMTRADE database.

Developing countries have exported slightly more computers and related equipment than developed countries. At the country level, China dominates the computer export market. In only three years, China's share in the global market tripled to reach 17 per cent of world exports in computers by 2003. During the same period, the United States' exports of computers decreased by 30 per cent, and this resulted in a drop to second place (with 11 per cent of the market).

Developing countries also have higher shares than developed ones in exports of electronic components (54 per cent in 2003). Furthermore, while the United States and Japan have seen their exports of electronic components drop by 25 per cent and 13 per cent

respectively, they continued to be the major exporters in 2003.

In 2003, almost 60 per cent of exports of audio and video equipment originated from developing countries. Between 2000 and 2003 China doubled its exports of audio and video equipment, and by 2003 had the largest share of the market (18 per cent). During the same period, exports from Japan stagnated and in 2003 Japan moved from the leading position to second place with 15 per cent of the market.

Table 1.23 and charts 1.18a to 1.18d show the major importers by category of ICT good in 2003. Developed countries account for about 70 per cent of

Table 1.23

Major importers by category of ICT goods, 2003 (million USD)3

Telecommunications

	Value	%
United States	34'046	23
United Kingdom	10'392	7
Germany	8'900	6
Hong Kong SAR	7'785	5
China	7'320	5
France	5'018	3
Italy	4'937	3
Singapore	4'382	3
Netherlands	4'164	3
Spain	3'748	3
Rest of the world	57'164	39
World	147'855	100

Computers

	Value	%
United States	76'149	21
Germany	28'495	8
Netherlands	24'379	7
Japan	23'194	7
United Kingdom	22'254	6
Hong Kong SAR	21'498	6
China	17'203	5
Singapore	13'247	4
France	12'674	4
Mexico	9'947	3
Rest of the world	105'642	30
World	354'682	100

Electronic components

	Value	%
China	62'138	16
Hong Kong SAR	37'227	9
United States	33'955	9
Singapore	31'628	8
Malaysia	27'763	7
Rep. of Korea	24'699	6
Japan	22'601	6
Taiwan, PC	22'310	6
Germany	18'975	5
Mexico	15'218	4
Rest of the world	97'817	25
World	395'329	100

Audio & Video

	Value	%
United States	37'551	28
Hong Kong SAR	13'923	10
Germany	10'138	7
United Kingdom	7'508	6
Japan	7'306	5
France	5'291	4
Netherlands	4'377	3
Italy	3'832	3
Canada	3'805	3
Singapore	3'487	3
Rest of the world	38'633	28
World	135'851	100

Other ICT goods

	Value	%
United States	18'151	20
Germany	7'271	8
China	6'844	7
United Kingdom	5'320	6
Japan	4'684	5
France	4'175	5
Canada	4'125	5
Rep. of Korea	3'646	4
Taiwan, PC	3'359	4
Italy	3'028	3
Rest of the world	30'672	34
World	91'276	100

Source: UNCTAD calculations based on UN COMTRADE database.

Chart 1.18 a, b, c, d

Major importers by category of ICT goods, 2003 (million USD)

18a. Telecommunications equipment

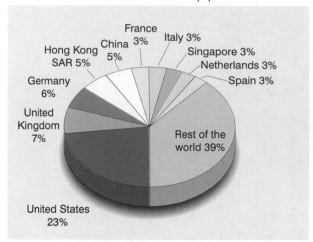

18b. Computers and related equipment

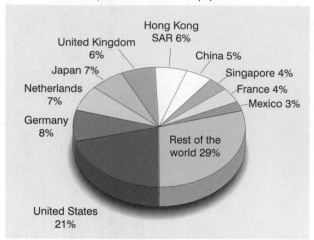

18c. Electronic components

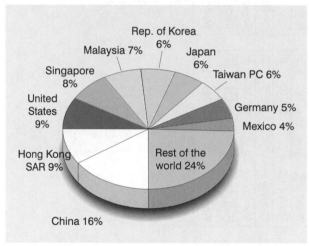

18d. Audio and video equipment

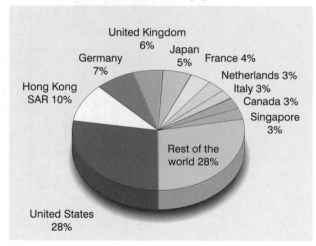

Source: UNCTAD calculations based on UN COMTRADE database.

imports of telecommunications equipment and computer and related equipment. The United States alone imports one fifth of all telecommunications equipment and computers. The percentage of imports among developing regions and major importers did not undergo a significant change in the period 2000–2003. On the other hand, the subsector of electronic components has seen some changes, and developing countries now account for 64 per cent of imports (up from previous 54 per cent). This is largely due to China, which has more than doubled its imports of electronic components in these three years, and in 2003 imported 16 per cent of all electronic components. It is worth noting that China, together with Hong Kong SAR and Singapore, amount for half of the developing countries' imports of electronic components.

Directions of trade and South–South trade

When one looks at the direction of trade flows (exports) by development blocs (see table 1.24), the increasing significance of trade among, and between, southern (developing) and transition economies is striking. They experienced positive growth rates in the last three years in all ICT goods categories.

The most important trade flows in telecommunications equipment, computers and related equipment (35 per cent of all North–North trade), and other ICT goods are between developed countries, while trade in electronic components is largely between developing countries. Audio and video equipment is mostly exported to developed countries from developing countries.

Table 1.24

Direction of exports of ICT goods, 2003

Trade flow	Value of exports (million USD), 2003					CAGR (%) 2000-2003					
	Tele-commu-nications equipment	Computers and related equipment	Electronic components	Audio & video equipment	Other ICT goods	Tele-commu-nications equipment	Computers and related equipment	Electronic components	Audio & video equipment	Other ICT goods	Total ICT
North-North	64'720	127'701	76'084	45'808	52'872	-11	-5	-8	5	5	-5%
North-SEE & CIS	4'591	3'245	1'277	779	1'581	30	20	14	27	21	23%
North-South	24'306	33'476	101'731	9'744	21'992	-8	-4	-2	0	2	-2%
SEE & CIS-North	273	98	407	232	178	5	-18	-6	55	-10	0%
SEE & CIS-SEE & CIS	99	49	45	92	157	13	26	6	17	7	12%
SEE & CIS-South	213	30	159	9	319	81	41	19	29	37	40%
South-North	36'479	116'273	65'867	52'502	8'800	7	2	-7	8	9	1%
South-SEE & CIS	592	688	407	658	92	58	41	66	27	25	42%
South-South	22'384	74'516	140'550	26'095	5'787	19	15	11	12	13	13%

Source: UNCTAD calculations based on UN COMTRADE database.

South–South trade is particularly substantial in electronic components, which represent over 50 per cent of all South-South ICT goods exports. But trade in the other sectors is growing at a slightly higher rate, particularly in telecommunications equipment (with a 9 per cent annual average growth rate for 2000–2003). Trade among SEE and CIS economies is most significant in the "other ICT goods" categories, while trade of computer and related components has experienced the highest compound annual growth rate during this period (25 per cent).

C. Measuring ICT in developing countries

The previous part of this chapter clearly reflects the limited availability of internationally comparable data on ICTs, in particular on the use and impact of ICTs in developing countries. This severely restricts an empirical analysis of the trends and impact of ICTs in the context of the information economy. At the same time, as ICTs become key elements of national development strategies, policymakers have an increasing need for reliable data and indicators on the information society (UNCTAD, 2003a). Such data help formulate strategies for ICT-driven growth and monitor and evaluate economic and social developments related to ICTs; they also help companies take informed business and investment decisions. Being

able to measure the information society is thus a precondition for:

- Fine-tuning and assessing ICT policies and strategies;

- Monitoring the digital divide;

- Evaluating and benchmarking information society developments; and

- Documenting the impact of the information society on the implementation of internationally agreed development goals and measuring progress in the use of ICTs to achieve those goals.

The lack of comparable data not only hampers the ability of policymakers and business people to take strategic decisions, but also makes it difficult to carry out meaningful macroeconomic analyses of the impact of ICTs on economic growth, trade, investment and employment. Current research is limited to the use of data on basic ICT infrastructure, such as the number of telephone lines, PCs or Internet hosts available in countries. However, cross-sectoral studies on the economic impact of ICTs would require statistical data such as firm-level data on investments in, and use of, ICTs; the enabling resources that have led to the effective use of ICTs; the performance of these enterprises; the cost of ICTs; productivity growth in the ICT-producing sector; changes in the patterns of occupations and skill requirements demanded of the labour force; and general data on the shifts of employment patterns related to changes in production processes.

This section sheds further light on the process of improving data on the information society and particularly on the adoption of ICTs by enterprises. It first presents work currently undertaken at the global level and its link to the WSIS process. It then provides an overview of the status of the collection of official ICT business statistics in developing countries based on the results of a metadata survey carried out with all developing countries in the second half of 2004. A few country examples follow, demonstrating how ICT statistics have been successfully linked to national ICT policymaking.

1. Global e-measurement initiatives

The striking absence of comparable data on ICTs in developing countries, and the resulting difficulties in carrying out meaningful assessments of the information society and its impact on development, have prompted a number of stakeholders at national, regional and international levels to take action in this regard. At the national level, an increasing number of offices responsible for producing statistical data have started to incorporate basic questions on ICTs into their national data collections or have carried out new ICT-specific surveys. An assessment of the current availability of ICT data in developing countries will be provided below (section C.3).

At the regional and international levels, several organizations involved in ICT-related research and policymaking, including e-measurement, started to cooperate, recognizing that coordination of their work was indispensable for reaching global harmonization of ICT indicators. Today, the global "Partnership on Measuring ICT for Development" is widely recognized as playing a leading role in this process. Current partners include Eurostat, the ITU, OECD, UNCTAD, UNESCO Institute for Statistics, four UN Regional Commissions (ECA, ECLAC, ESCAP, ESCWA), the UN ICT Task Force and the World Bank. The Partnership provides an open framework for coordinating ongoing and future activities in the area of information society measurements, and for developing a coherent and structured approach to advancing the development of ICT indicators globally, and in particular in the developing countries. National statistics offices from statistically advanced countries are invited to contribute to the Partnership's

activities and provide expertise and advice to NSOs from developing countries, as well as to transfer knowledge in areas such as methodologies and survey programmes.

The Partnership, which was officially launched on the occasion of UNCTAD XI, held in Brazil in June 2004, has three main objectives:

- To achieve a common set of core ICT indicators, to be harmonized and agreed upon internationally, which will constitute the basis for a database on ICT statistics;

- To enhance the capacities of NSOs in developing countries to develop their compilation of statistics on the information society on the basis of internationally agreed upon indicators;

- To develop a global database on ICT indicators and to make it available on the Internet.

Since its launch, the following activities have been carried out under the umbrella of the Partnership:

(a) A global stocktaking exercise to examine the current and future availability of official information society statistics and indicators in all countries (see section C.3).

(b) A series of regional workshops to identify priorities for action in the area of ICT indicators and agree on a common set of core indicators at the regional level. Workshops have taken place in Western Asia (Beirut, October 2004 and June 2005), Africa (Gaborone, October 2004, and Addis Ababa, June 2005), and Latin America and the Caribbean (Santiago de Chile, November 2004 and Santo Domingo, October 2005).

(c) The development of a core list of ICT indicators that could be collected by all countries (see section C.2.). The list covers four broad areas of measurement: basic ICT infrastructure and access, ICT access and use by households, ICT use by businesses and the ICT sector and trade in ICT goods. The list was adopted by delegates attending the WSIS Thematic Meeting in Geneva (see next item).

(d) A WSIS Thematic Meeting on "Measuring the Information Society", held in Geneva from 7 to 9 February 2005. The meeting agreed on a list of core ICT indicators that could be collected by all countries; made suggestions on how the production of ICT statistics in developing countries could be enhanced through effective capacity-building measures; and stressed the need to formalize the link

Box 1.2

Measuring the Information Society and the WSIS

The WSIS Plan of Action (para. 28), which was adopted by delegates at the Geneva Summit in December 2003, calls for action to develop comparable ICT indicators:

"A realistic international performance evaluation and benchmarking (both qualitative and quantitative), through comparable statistical indicators and research results, should be developed to follow up the implementation of the objectives, goals and targets in the Plan of Action, taking into account different national circumstances.

... All countries and regions should develop tools so as to provide statistical information on the Information Society, with basic indicators and analysis of its key dimensions. Priority should be given to setting up coherent and internationally comparable indicator systems, taking into account different levels of development."

During the Tunis phase of the Summit, further progress was made at both the political and the substantive level:

- The WSIS Thematic Meeting on Measuring the Information Society (Geneva, 7–9 February 2005) adopted a core set of ICT indicators that could be collected by all countries. The outcome of the meeting was reported to the WSIS PrepCom2 as a concrete input into the Tunis Phase of the Summit.

- Several regional WSIS conferences addressed the subject of ICT indicators: the WSIS Africa Regional Preparatory Conference (Accra, 31 January – 1 February 2005); the Pan-Arab regional conference WSIS-Phase II (Cairo, 8–10 May 2005); and the Regional Preparatory Ministerial Conference of Latin America and the Caribbean for WSIS II (Rio de Janeiro, 8–10 June 2005), together with its regional action plan, eLAC 2007

The subject of ICT indicators thus became an accepted element of the WSIS process and its follow-up. At the time of finalizing this report, the draft text of the final Tunis document makes reference to the subject of indicators calling for a continuation of the work of the Partnership.

---

[1] The document, WSIS-II/PC-2/DOC/3-E, is available at http://www.itu.int/wsis/docs2/pc2/

---

between ICT and the development agenda, notably regarding measurement of the achievement of the internationally agreed development goals, including those contained in the Millennium Declaration.

In addition, a WSIS parallel event on measuring the information society will be held in Tunis on 15 November 2005. The event will bring together ICT policymakers, statistical offices and telecom regulators to discuss the need for internationally comparable data on ICT access, use and impact, share best practices in ICT measurement and examine some of the policy issues impeding effective measurement of the information society. Thematic sessions will be held on related policy issues such as measuring the impact of ICT on progress towards the achievement of international development goals.

As a result of the initiatives taken by the different stakeholders, discussions in international forums such as the WSIS started to pay increasing attention to the measurement of the information society (box 1.2). This was reinforced by pressure from the international development community for empirical evidence about the impact of ICTs on development, in particular on pro-poor growth, and the contribution of ICTs to the progress made towards the achievement of the MDGs.

2.   Towards a core list of ICT indicators

As indicated in the previous section, comparable statistical indicators should contribute to the follow-up and implementation of the WSIS Geneva Plan of Action and to monitoring progress in bridging the digital divide. But most importantly, a list of core ICT indicators should help countries to carry out their collection of ICT data so that results are internationally comparable, to understand their development path into the information society, and to design ICT for development policies. Within the framework of the Partnership on Measuring ICT for Development,

Box 1.3

Core ICT business indicators

The core list of ICT indicators contains 12 business indicators:

Basic core

- Proportion of businesses using computers;

- Proportion of employees using computers;

- Proportion of businesses using the Internet;

- Proportion of employees using the Internet;

- Proportion of businesses with a website (or web presence where the business has control over the content)

- Proportion of businesses with an intranet;

- Proportion of businesses receiving orders over the Internet;

- Proportion of businesses placing orders over the Internet.

Extended core

- Proportion of businesses accessing the Internet by modes of access (response categories);

- Proportion of businesses with a local area network (LAN);

- Proportion of businesses with an extranet;

- Proportion of businesses using the Internet by type of activity (response categories).

These indicators cover basic, policy-relevant information on the use of ICTs in enterprises. They are well defined, reflecting an international consensus on measuring ICT in enterprises; they have been tested for several years and are easy to collect; and there are model questions available that can be used in national surveys. Most importantly, however, from a policy perspective, the core list contains basic use indicators, such as the kind of activities enterprises carry out over the Internet. Most developing countries that have collected ICT business indicators thus far have mainly asked questions about whether a company has computers, Internet access or a website. Little information has been collected about what companies actually do on the Internet. The core list provides useful guidance on the type of information that could be collected in this regard, and in a way that makes the results be comparable internationally.

much progress has been made during the past year in establishing such a core list; indeed, this has been one of the three key objectives of the Partnership.

Following a broad consultation process involving the Partners and NSOs, a proposal for a core list of indicators was prepared as an input to the WSIS Thematic Meeting on Measuring the Information Society, held in Geneva from 7 to 9 February 2005.[25] It contained four sets of indicators: basic ICT infrastructure indicators, ICT access and use by households and individuals, ICT use by enterprises, and the ICT sector (see table 1.25 and box 1.3). The list of core indicators was accepted as an agreed outcome of the meeting and is contained in annex IV of this chapter.

Table 1.25

Number of core indicators by classification

Set of indicators	Basic core	Extended core	Reference	Total
ICT infrastructure and access	10	2		12
ICT access and use by households and individuals	10	3	1	14
ICT use by businesses	8	4		12
ICT sector	4			4
Total	32	9	1	42

Source: Partnership on Measuring ICT for Development (2005a).

The selection of indicators reflects the key actors in the information society (individuals, households and enterprises). Most importantly, however, it reflects an emerging consensus on definitions, guidelines and methodologies regarding individual, household and business ICT indicators, based on the outcome of various national, regional and international initiatives. For example, most of the basic core ICT access indicators are compiled by the ITU; OECD and Eurostat have developed model household and business surveys.[26] Less progress has been made on other ICT-related indicators, such as government or health. The latter will thus be dealt with at a later stage.

Future work on the list of core ICT indicators can address issues such as characteristics of Internet users (gender, language, disability, indigenous status, resident status and geographical location), content language, community access, trade in ICT services, or ICT investment and information security data. Methodological issues regarding definitions of the Internet, intranets, extranets, LANs and websites, and the distinction between fixed and mobile broadband, are currently being added to the list.

The list of core indicators provides useful guidance for countries wishing to start collecting ICT indicators, and constitutes the basis for developing internationally comparable statistics on the information society. There is plenty of scope for further developing the core list, which can be amended or expanded with new policy-relevant statistical indicators as experience is gained. This work has continued throughout 2005 and will be presented at the WSIS Tunis parallel event organized by the Partnership.

Not all countries are at the same level of development or have well-developed statistical systems. Countries with little or no ICT infrastructure may not see the need to collect ICT indicators. Countries with growing investment in ICT may want to monitor this growth by starting to measure ICT; these countries may want only to collect the most basic information, while others, with higher levels of ICT investment, may want to go further. To give further guidance to the different collection efforts by countries, a distinction was made between "basic core" indicators (for countries in the initial stages of ICT data collection, and covering mainly basic access indicators), and "extended core" indicators (for countries with more advanced ICT data collection, with some basic use indicators added).

In addition, developing countries will always have to respond to national policy needs, which may be only partially covered by the core list, and might choose to supplement this core list with additional indicators. In particular, the discussions held in 2004 and 2005 in various forums point to a marked interest in developing ICT indicators related to education, government, health or agriculture. Unlike in the case of the indicators that are already in the core list, which have been well defined and repeatedly tested and for which there is a critical mass level of consensus, the development of ICT indicators in the areas mentioned before is an ongoing process that still requires further widespread consultation and consideration. The indicators have to be adequately defined so that they can be truly measurable and useful. ICT indicators in these additional areas will become readily available only at a later stage, most likely in the medium term.

3. Status of ICT business indicators in developing countries

This chapter is primarily concerned with the use of ICTs by enterprises in developing countries. Therefore, efforts to enhance the availability of relevant data need to start with an assessment of current data collection concerning ICT business indicators. This section presents a summary of the results of a survey on the status of ICT indicators in developing countries, focusing on ICT business indicators.[27] They highlight differences among regions in the developing world and underline the best performers and the regions that are most active in the planning of future data collection, as well as the gaps in the availability of ICT-related statistics.[28] The questionnaire was sent to 179 countries in Africa, Asia-Pacific, Central Asia and Central and Eastern Europe, Latin America and the Caribbean, and Western Asia. Of those countries, 85 returned the questionnaire, a response rate of 47 per cent.

NSOs were asked to indicate, on the basis of their institution's perspective, the level of demand for collecting ICT business indicators (see chart 1.19). Excluding the countries that did not respond to this question, the median value of all replies is "high" demand, with 37 per cent (31 countries) answering either "very high" or "high". The NSOs in the 26 countries that did not respond to this question were probably unable to answer because the issue has not been addressed or discussed at the policy level.

Chart 1.19

Global level of demand of ICT business indicators

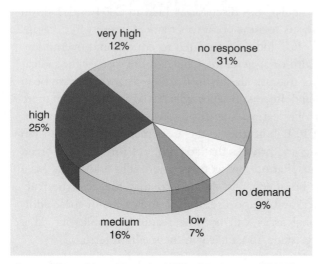

Source: Partnership on Measuring ICT for Development (2005 b).

access). This area of statistics is frequently surveyed through specific ICT business surveys.

Indicators referring to the type of Internet activities and e-commerce are collected by a small portion of NSOs across all regions (excluding Western Asia) (average of 12 countries). The least collected indicators are those on customer groups or destination of Internet sales (8 per cent), barriers to e-commerce (9 per cent) and geographical location of sales (6 per cent). These types of indicators are produced through more specific surveys aimed at collecting information about ICTs in particular. Therefore, it is mainly the countries that have specific "ICT in business" surveys that can provide information on these indicators. However, it was also noted that "ICT in business" surveys tend not to be carried out on a regular basis, unlike the other types of surveys. Indicators on barriers to ICTs are rarely collected through surveys that are not explicitly aimed at investigating ICT use in enterprises.

The key part of the questionnaire was a list of 20 indicators concerning access to and use of ICTs in enterprises. Respondents were asked whether the individual indicators are currently available from official statistical sources, whether they intend to produce them in the next year or three years, or whether they are not planning to do so.

Table 1.26 shows the number of countries that collect each indicator across regions. OECD member countries are added as a comparison.[29] Table 1.27 shows the number of countries that already collect, plan to collect or do not plan to collect ICT business indicators (65 out of 179 respondents replied to this question), for both developing countries/CEE and OECD countries.

The results show that, overall, data and official statistics on ICT in enterprises are still limited in most developing countries. However, 65 countries (59 per cent of respondents) do collect some type of ICT business indicator. Most of these are indicators related to basic access to ICTs (such as presence of telephones, computers and the Internet). The information is frequently collected through manufacturing and services establishment surveys, which most NSOs already have in place. All regions, except Western Asia, also collect a limited number of more advanced ICT access and use indicators (such as presence of website, local network and modes of Internet

In the OECD countries, ICT data collection is considerably more advanced and the planning process largely completed (see low figures in "planning" column, table 1.27). Most countries have been collecting a large number of ICT-in-enterprise statistics for the past few years. This is largely the result of the work of the OECD Working Party on Indicators for the Information Society (WPIIS), a group that has met since 1997 and is composed of representatives from NSOs of OECD member countries.

Observations can also be made concerning the regional distribution of the responses. In Africa, Asia-Pacific and Central Asia, and CEE, each indicator is collected, although not by all countries. Asia-Pacific and Central Asia, and CEE, are the regions that have the highest number of countries collecting ICT business indicators. In these regions the level of demand for ICT-related business statistics is on average high, and NSOs respond effectively to this demand. In Latin America and the Caribbean, each indicator except "geographical location of sales" is collected, although not by all countries. In Western Asia, six indicators out of 20 ("basic access to ICT" indicators and indicator 12 on "services the Internet is used for") are collected; nevertheless, this is also the region where the highest percentage of countries plans to collect business indicators within one or three years.

Table 1.26

Number of countries collecting each indicator by region

Indicator	Africa (12/53)	Asia-Pacific (11/53)	Central Asia and CEE (17/24)	Latin America and the Caribbean (18/36)	Western Asia (9/13)	Total developing/ CEE (65/179)	OECD (28/30)
Fixed telephone	9	9	10	8	4	40	1
Mobile devices	5	9	11	8	1	34	3
Computer	6	7	6	7	2	28	25
Number of computer	6	6	6	3	1	22	1
Internet	6	9	11	11	1	38	25
Type of Internet access	5	5	6	4	0	20	24
Local network	4	5	5	5	0	19	23
Website	7	5	5	9	0	26	25
ICT Investment	5	5	6	2	0	18	5
Share of PC	3	4	7	2	0	16	22
Share of Internet	1	3	5	2	0	11	22
Services the Internet is used for	2	5	4	4	1	16	22
Value of purchases	4	1	3	3	0	11	17
Value of sales	4	1	3	5	0	13	24
Customer group	2	1	2	2	0	7	20
ICT training	4	1	1	4	0	10	18
Barriers to PC	4	4	2	1	0	11	0
Barriers to Internet	3	4	3	1	0	11	1
Barriers to e-commerce	2	2	2	2	0	8	21
Geographical location	1	1	3	0	0	5	17

Source: Partnership on Measuring ICT for Development (2005 b).

In Africa, where 13 countries out of the 19 respondents are LDCs, few NSOs collect ICT indicators and many have no defined plans to collect most of them in the near future. However, since the indicated demand for this region is on average high, it can be assumed that the collection of ICT business statistics is on the agenda but will be implemented over a period longer than three years. These countries are likely to be in particular need of capacity building and training at the national level. In particular, NSOs in developing countries that have limited or no experience in data collection would benefit from technical assistance in the establishment of such collection (or in the inclusion of ICT statistics in existing mechanisms), as well as in collecting information society statistics more broadly. This will be further addressed in section D.

4.   ICT policymaking and ICT measurement

This section will give examples of developing countries that are actively collecting data and statistics and have used such data for ICT policy design, evaluation, monitoring and benchmarking. Observations will then be made on what these examples show about the relationship between ICT data collection and policymaking, making the case for enhanced ICT statistics, particularly for business. The selection of countries was made based on the results of the global ICT

Table 1.27

Number of countries planning to collect each indicator

Indicator	Collecting		Planning to collect		No plan to collect	
	Non-OECD	OECD	Non-OECD	OECD	Non-OECD	OECD
Fixed telephone	40	1	9	0	16	27
Mobile devices	34	3	11	1	18	24
Computer	28	25	11	2	20	1
Number of computer	22	1	14	1	25	26
Internet	38	25	10	2	16	0
Type of Internet access	20	24	12	3	28	0
Local network	19	23	15	1	28	3
Website	26	25	13	2	25	0
ICT Investment	18	5	14	0	29	23
Share of PC	16	22	18	2	27	4
Share of Internet	11	22	21	2	29	4
Services the Internet is used for	16	22	19	3	27	2
Value of purchases	11	17	15	8	35	2
Value of sales	13	24	15	4	33	0
Customer group	7	20	15	5	37	3
ICT training	10	18	18	5	32	5
Barriers to PC	11	0	18	0	31	28
Barriers to Internet	11	1	19	1	31	26
Barriers to e-commerce	8	21	19	2	32	5
Geographical location	5	17	16	7	38	4

Source: Partnership on Measuring ICT for Development (2005 b).

statistics stocktaking and the availability of complementary background material.

The case of Trinidad and Tobago

The national ICT agenda of Trinidad and Tobago aims to make the country into a knowledge-based society by 2008 and is part of the country's overall development agenda to transform the country into a developed nation by the year 2020.[31] The national ICT plan is led by the Ministry of Public Administration and Information and seeks to "spur the next wave of social and economic development" through national ICT planning, of which one programme is focused on e-commerce/e-business development. Phase 2 of the plan (Research and Mapping Current Capabilities) explicitly contemplated the production of national statistics to support ICT planning, which was done with the 2003 National Survey of E-Commerce Usage and Awareness among Businesses.

The results of the above-mentioned survey served to provide a baseline snapshot of the situation of ICTs in the country at the start of the implementation of its ICT agenda.[32] The survey was conducted on the basis of a register of businesses listed by the Central Statistical Office.[33] Although several business sectors were represented, approximately half of the respondents were under the national classification of "Distribution, restaurants and bars".[34] At least half of the respondents were also microenterprises (under 10 employees). The results showed that although most businesses have computers and Internet access through the telephone (87 per cent), only the major industries have had the wherewithal to invest in the switch to broadband, dedicated data lines and business automation. B2C is underdeveloped and websites lack functionality for online sales, since only a very small percentage of potential clients are currently using the Internet (only 9 per cent of regular Internet users). B2B and other applications of e-business are almost non-existent, most companies using the Internet for e-mail and basic web presence.[35] Employee use of ICTs in enterprises is also limited, since computers are shared and there are few work e-mail addresses.

In addition, it is interesting to note that Trinidad and Tobago has also used ICT indicators to conduct some benchmarking of its own, including with two of the countries highlighted in this section: Mauritius and Singapore (Ministry of Public Administration and Information of Trinidad and Tobago, 2003a). They were chosen among others because they were small island nations with a similar population, albeit with different income levels. The benchmarking was comprehensive and covered several aspects of the information society, from basic infrastructure to e-government. On e-business (referred to as economy and finance in the study), the benchmarking indicated that although national enterprises have been slow to adopt websites, for example, this seemed to be consistent with the other developing countries in the study (Costa Rica, Jamaica and Mauritius). Trinidad and Tobago also recognized low levels of B2B or B2C e-commerce applications, on a par with Mauritius. This was despite the apparent pervasiveness of e-payment systems (in this context, the study compared its survey results with the rankings of the Global Information Technology Report).

ICT data collection and the benchmarking study allowed Trinidad and Tobago to identify the building blocks for its ICT development (high GNP per capita for a country in this geographical region, strong use of fixed line and cellular telephone service, high quality of public schools, high availability of venture capital, adequate overall infrastructure quality) and the weaknesses on which work is needed (low general Internet use, mirrored by low availability of business and government online services; no definitive bandwidth policy; telecommunications sector characterized by poor access, bandwidth and affordability; a high incidence of IT brain drain). As Trinidad and Tobago's national ICT plan unfolds, the Ministry of Public Administration and Information Communications has recognized that ongoing measures to track development progress must be implemented, and regularly updated. This will require coordination between the competent ministry and the Central Statistical Office to conduct regular surveys, using the initial e-readiness study as reference. Certainly, a follow-up survey should be conducted in 2008, the target date for the Fast Forward Agenda.

The case of Singapore

The Infocomm Development Authority of Singapore (IDA) has been the competent authority for the development of Singapore's information economy since 1999, operating under the Ministry of Information, Communications and The Arts (MICA) for the implementation of the national ICT plan, "Connected Singapore". IDA has a comprehensive mandate to oversee everything from the development of Singapore's ICT industry to its e-government. Since 1996, the Government of Singapore has had a very clear policy thrust for the development of e-commerce.[36] In terms of e-business, IDA aims to create an environment conducive to its development, focused on the legal and policy framework, infrastructure and building businesses' capabilities.

The Singapore Department of Statistics (DOS) and IDA are the main government agencies responsible for the compilation of ICT related statistics in Singapore.[37] The DOS compiles and publishes ICT-related data from existing nationwide and economy-wide business and household surveys, while data on e-commerce and ICT use in businesses are periodically collected as part of IDA's mandate.

The combined results of the multiple surveys thus far clearly show that Singapore is well advanced in the information economy. The last survey on ICT use by businesses showed that access to basic ICT infrastructure could be reaching saturation point at about 83 per cent penetration, but that there is dynamism in the adoption of new technologies (narrowband to broadband, wireless) and applications (web-based services), in particular those aimed at increasing productivity and business relationships (IDA, 2002a and 2003b). Regarding the use of ICT by employees, another survey indicated that about 13 per cent of working Singapore residents were telecommuters, and that the more frequently used broadband Internet applications used by these telecommuters for business purposes were e-mail (99 per cent), access to their enterprises' Virtual Private Networks (21 per cent), videoconferencing (16 per cent) and telephony (13 per cent) (IDA, 2002a).

It should be noted that Singapore has consistently used its ICT data collection exercises as opportunities to obtain inputs from individual and corporate stakeholders to guide future policy actions, including on barriers to e-commerce (cost of systems implementation, lack of awareness, security concerns), perceived benefits of ICT (enhanced productivity, flexibility, reduced costs) and opportunities for government-led action (skills development, financial grants for ICT implementation). For example, the 2002 survey on broadband and wireless use asked about the perceived benefits of telecommuting through broadband Internet, namely increased flexibility, reduction of travel time and cost, increased productivity with less distraction, better balance between "work and play", and extended employment opportunities for people with disabilities. Such perceptions play a determining role in the ongoing adoption of such practices by enterprises and the implementation of policy actions to encourage it.

In terms of benchmarking, Singapore's policy measures and data clearly show the country to be the leader in ICT uptake and use by most stakeholders, both in the Asian region and worldwide. Singapore is repeatedly at the top of the various ICT indices and rankings, which are used as leverage for the development of its ICT industry through foreign investments and public–private partnerships. In the case of Singapore there is a virtuous circle between positive benchmarking and advancing ICT policy objectives and actions, the Government feeling compelled to preserve its leading position (IDA, 2003c). In this sense, Singapore is proactively involved in regional efforts to develop the information economy, both to develop the regional market for ICT goods and services (see section C.3) and to become a regional hub for e-business. Benchmarking has highlighted Singapore's example for other developing countries that are developing their information economies, in particular with regard to policy formulation and follow-up, of which statistical data are an integral part for diagnosis, monitoring and evaluation.

Singapore's increasingly significant investments in developing its information economy will require continued and expanded ICT business data collection. For example, in the case of a large project to develop ICT-enabled integrated supply chains for high-tech manufacturing,[38] future collection of data on use of e-business applications will show progress in the adoption of such supply chains. ICT sector indicators should also be used to evaluate the impact of such a project, in particular regarding value added. Periodical

data on Internet modes of access should indicate progress in the adoption of wireless, broadband and other technologies that have an impact on enterprise productivity, particularly in developing B2B e-commerce.

The building of stakeholder confidence and trust in e-commerce and e-business was a main goal of Singapore's policy to develop the adoption of e-commerce (IDA, 2001).[39] Indicators on ICT uptake and use, in particular Internet use by households, individuals and businesses, can serve to show the progress in adoption of, and thus of confidence in, e-commerce and e-business. Business ICT data should also serve to evaluate the effectiveness of extensive efforts by IDA in developing capabilities for e-businesses. Current data collected by Singapore reflect workforce proficiency in ICT, but not the frequency or intensity of such use, or the proportion of employees in an enterprise that will use ICTs on a regular basis.[40]

The case of Mauritius

Mauritius has had a strong national IT strategic plan in place since 1998, modelled on Singapore's ICT policy. The National Computer Board (NCB) and the Ministry of Information Technology and Telecommunications are the competent authorities in charge of its implementation, which includes the liberalization of telecommunications, the diffusion of ICT in the workforce and e-government. To support its mandate, the NCB has an ongoing project for data collection and analysis, mostly focused on the ICT sector. Chapter 5 of the *E-Commerce and Development Report 2003*, which dealt with business process outsourcing services for development, examined Mauritius' plan to become a "cyber island" and a regional ICT hub, including through the Ebene Cyber City project.[41]

A reduced survey in 2001 (300 businesses with more than 10 employees) indicated that 83 per cent of businesses had at least one computer and 75 per cent had Internet access (National Computer Board of Mauritius, 2001). However, this result is affected by the fact that it excluded microenterprises, nearly half of the sample was made up of services industries and more than half had a turnover of almost $700,000, which is not insignificant in Mauritius' economy. The Census of Economic Activities in 2002 (excluding agricultural enterprises) indicated a nationwide proportion of businesses' Internet access of only 4.9 per cent. Nonetheless, it is precisely on the high-use enterprise sector that Mauritius is concentrating its ICT policies (including manufacturing, wholesale and retail trade, hotels and restaurants, transport, storage and communication, and banking and finance).

Owing to the size of the country, Mauritius' internal ICT market is very small and businesses must look to external markets for significant growth and economies of scale that would justify ICT investments. In May 2005 there were 78 ICT companies in Mauritius, employing approximately 3,500 people, with several projected new arrivals. This does not mean that attention is not being paid to the overall diffusion of ICTs in Mauritius, since broader diffusion of ICTs, including through e-government, would reduce the cost of connectivity.[42] Local diffusion is particularly important for the development of a local ICT workforce to benefit from ICT sector growth and to use ICTs to develop other service-based industries, such as tourism (see chapter 4 on e-tourism).

Since the IT household surveys (1998, 2000 and 2002) have enabled Mauritius to track progress in household access to and use of ICTs, it would seem obvious that the country should ensure that periodic ICT surveys are also carried out in the business sector. Mauritius has already taken a step in the right direction, the NCB having issued in 2004-2005 an invitation to tender for conducting an assessment of ICT indicators aimed at evaluating the use of ICTs in key economic sectors in Mauritius and serving as an input for the elaboration of specific ICT policies. The projected assessment includes an ICT use survey in businesses that will update the 2001 information and will measure (by sector) the computerization level, ICT use, investment and spending, infrastructure, human resource profile and the extent of e-commerce adoption. The assessment should also include a benchmarking exercise based on ITU's Digital Access Index, which is partly based on the core indicators discussed in this chapter (National Computer Board of Mauritius, 2002).[43]

The case of Colombia

Colombia's Connectivity Agenda is led by the Ministry of Communications and aims at the diffusion of ICTs as a catalyst for economic and social development. The Agenda is geared towards citizens, enterprises and public administration. In the case of enterprises, ICTs are to be encouraged to support growth and competitiveness, improve market access for the productive sector and promote job creation. For these purposes, ICT policy includes the development of electronic commerce, the promotion of the ICT sector and the use of e-business by SMEs (62 per cent of GDP and 31 per cent of exports).[44]

In 2001, Colombia's NSO conducted a survey-cum-model for the measurement of ICTs that was the result of an agreement with the Ministry of Communications; it aimed to provide a diagnosis of the status of the information society in Colombia that would be the basis for future work on ICT (including information gathering) (Departamento Administrativo Nacional de Estadística, 2003). Regarding the productive sector, the survey focused on manufacturing, trade, services and microenterprises. It yielded some interesting findings, such as that in terms of e-business, manufacturing makes extensive use of management software (83.1 per cent), but not of production software (19.6 per cent). In terms of e-commerce, in the trade sector there was extensive use of websites for marketing products (81.1 per cent), but not for order processing (10.3 per cent), online payments (11 per cent) or secure transactions (3.2 per cent). Also, there were low percentages of ICT-trained personnel in all sectors (from 2.1 per cent in microenterprises to 11 per cent in manufacturing).

In 2005, Colombia conducted a benchmarking exercise that took into consideration several international indices and rankings, and compared the country's performance with that of developed countries and countries in the region.[45] Despite the recognition that the indices were not comparable the one with the other or from one year to the other, the benchmarking served to identify desirable goals with respect to certain indicators, such as increasing broadband and Internet user rates, and to the policies that influence them, such as liberalization of the telecommunications sector. The benchmarking also identified positive developments, such as the increase in local websites and e-government services, which triggered an increase in Colombia's ranking in the e-government readiness index of the UN Department of Economic and Social Affairs (UNDESA).

Although Colombia's survey on ICT use was released at the end of 2003, the reference year is 2001 and the information is thus somewhat dated. In view of the Government's programme to promote ICTs among SMEs, expected developments in the spread of broadband and the elaboration of a strategy to develop a software industry,[46] the Connectivity Agenda will be well served by an updated survey on ICT use by businesses in the short to medium term.

At the same time, the survey should provide a more in-depth analysis of the reasons for any progress or deterioration in the indicators and assist the competent authority for the Connectivity Agenda in formulating the actions to address those findings.

Observations

Some observations can be made taking into account the experience of the above-mentioned countries, as well as others surveyed for this report.

- Since ICT data collection in developing countries, particularly data on business, is nascent, the data are being used mainly for diagnosis of the status of the information society/information economy of a country.

- There is an increased interest on the part of several developing countries in international benchmarking. Benchmarking can highlight exceptional cases such as Singapore, which incidentally takes advantage of benchmarking to attract ICT investments. Developing countries that are less digitally advanced can also draw lessons from such exceptions, particularly on the thoroughness of ICT policy planning and implementation, and on the use of updated data for regular assessment of progress in ICT uptake.

- As data from initial or one-time surveys age there is a growing interest in updating collections. There appears to be increased awareness of the need for periodic data collection for the monitoring and evaluation of policies, and cross-verification of international rankings. The WSIS and the MDGs have increased awareness and the political will of countries to develop their information society policies, including data collection to support those policies.

- Data collection still remains largely focused on infrastructure and household and individual access. The availability of business ICT indicators from developing countries could and should be increased, in a manner that can be comparable internationally. Just as household and individual indicators serve as measures of a country's progress in the information society, so business indicators will indicate a country's progress in the information economy.

- It is worthwhile further exploring the extent to which the collection, or lack thereof, of certain ICT business statistics is related to the level of demand in countries, and to what extent it is related to the level of resources available to NSOs. The type of data collected officially by countries may also respond to the real or perceived usefulness of such data to policymakers. For example, countries with explicit ICT-related development policies or with active ICT sectors would need more specific indicators for policy evaluation or benchmarking. Of course, the comparability of such indicators should also be considered in order to make them relevant to a benchmarking exercise.

- Coordination between national statistical offices and ICT-related competent national authorities (ministries of communication, education, finance, science and technology, trade, etc.) is essential to the ability to collect, disseminate, and meaningfully use ICT statistical data. This should include awareness creation and a transparent arrangement for information sharing, coordinated work for the inclusion of ICT questions in censuses, identification of samples, statistical capacity building and sharing of logistical resources. To this end, several countries have established high-level task forces or coordination bodies that monitor the implementation of ICT policies, for which indicators are needed. Coordination will also involve the private sector, which is determinant in ICT investments, business adoption of ICTs and the development of the ICT sector.

- Although a coordinating body with a strong mandate and sufficient resources can perform effective data collection, such as IDA in Singapore, it is important that NSOs and relevant sector ministries as the main source of official statistics in a country be the main players in both data collection and analysis. This ensures that data are mainstreamed as a policymaking tool.

D. The road ahead

Analysing trends in the spread of the information economy in developing countries is a challenging task. Data are scarce, not always comparable, and not yet at the level of detail necessary for measuring the impact of ICTs on economic development and growth. The overview of basic developments in ICT access and use presented in the first part of this chapter showed that while rates of growth of basic access to ICTs are high in most developing countries, more advanced use of ICTs for business activities such as enhanced customer services or supply chain management is nascent. At the same time, the impressive growth in the numbers of cellular subscribers in many developing countries could generate additional business opportunities in some of the poorest countries.

While there are clear deficits of comparable ICT-related data, in particular data on the adoption of ICT by enterprises, there are also clear signs that an increasing number of developing countries pay attention to the development of ICT statistics, recognizing the need to monitor their information societies and take informed decisions concerning ICT policies for development. The country examples in the previous section demonstrated how ICT measurement can contribute effectively to improving the national ICT policy agenda.

In order to make further progress in this work the following suggestions for policy action are provided.

1. Policy commitment and coordination

The development of comparable data, and the creation of the necessary statistical tools, constitute a long-term process. Therefore, even countries with relatively less advanced information societies should start the process early in order to have some initial data in the medium term.

In many countries, there is still an important need for awareness building both at the political and technical level. In some cases, ICT-driven ministries are keen on having the data, while statistical offices are slow to react. In other cases, statistical offices are aware of ICT measurement issues but lack the resources and related political mandates to further develop the necessary programmes. Hence, there is a need to link the national policy agenda with the e-measurement agenda, and this requires effective cooperation between policymakers and national statistical systems.

As at the national level, it is essential to establish the link between ICT policymaking and ICT measurement in international forums dealing with the information society. Follow-up to and review of the WSIS process will require the continuous monitoring of the

progress of information society developments, in particular in developing countries. This will require all countries to develop comparable statistical indicators, which will become a critical element of the implementation and evaluation of the Geneva Plan of Action.

2. Data collection and capacity-building

Coordination among different entities of national statistical systems involved in the collection and dissemination of statistical data is essential, owing to the cross-cutting nature of ICTs. The "statistical system" is stressed, as not all countries have a centralized statistical office, and statistics may be the responsibility of sector ministries, regulators or special agencies outside the NSO.

The list of core ICT indicators presented in section C.2 provides a basis for starting to collect a small number of ICT statistics, such as statistics on Internet use by businesses or web presence. Countries that lack resources to implement special ICT surveys should follow a pragmatic approach, for example by incorporating a few basic questions into existing surveys.

Building capacity in statistical offices of developing countries will be essential to improving the production of official information society statistics. National Governments, with the support of the international community, are called on to provide the necessary support to relevant statistical offices in designing and implementing ICT statistical compilation programmes. The Partnership on Measuring ICT for Development can play an important role in this regard. During the first phase of the Partnership, much emphasis has been put on establishing a list of core ICT indicators as a starting point for the collection of internationally comparable data on ICT. In the next phase, partners need to put more emphasis on the building of capacity in developing countries' statistical systems, which will include seeking the funds necessary for carrying out such activities.

Capacity-building for ICT statistics should be integrated with existing activities into statistical capacity-building and focus on sustainable systems. Capacity-building and technical assistance programmes should cover areas such as methodologies and definitions, survey implementation and data collection, data verification, database development and analysis.

More specifically, capacity-building activities should aim at:

- Developing specialized training courses on ICT statistics for practitioners from statistical offices in developing countries, including the preparation of guidebooks on core indicators, comprising best practices, model question-naires and suggestions about methodologies and data collection measures for developing countries;

- Conducting training workshops for local staff involved in the collection of ICT indicators; and for policy-makers and regulators to raise awareness about the importance of indicators for monitoring ICT policies and carrying out impact analysis;

- Assisting NSOs in developing ICT data collection (e.g. defining frameworks, methodologies or survey measures), database development and dissemination;

- Building regional statistical networks for ICT indicators (including the establishment of technical working groups on ICT indicators at the regional level and conducting of technical workshops) to advance the development of information society indicators, to continue discussions on indicators, model questions and survey implementation at the regional level, and to ensure the harmonization of ICT data and statistics across countries in the region;

- Developing common approaches to the collection of ICT data and statistics and the harmonization of the work on ICT indicators at the global level, so as to increase comparability between countries and to develop a global database on ICT indicators.

Annex I

Statistical annex

Table 1. Internet users by country/territory, 2000–2004

Country/territory	2000	% change 2000-2001	2001	% change 2001-2002	2002	% change 2002-2003	2003	% change 2003-2004	2004
Afghanistan	..	..	..	..	1 000	1 900.0	20 000	25.0	25 000
Albania	3 500	185.7	10 000	20.0	12 000	150.0	30 000	..	..
Algeria	150 000	33.3	200 000	150.0	500 000	..	..	..	..
Andorra	7 000	..	..	..	..	..	10 049	..	..
Angola	15 000	33.3	20 000	105.0	41 000	..	..	..	..
Antigua & Barbuda	5 000	40.0	7 000	42.9	10 000	..	..	..	..
Argentina	2 600 000	40.4	3 650 000	12.3	4 100 000	10.5	4 530 000	13.0	5 120 000
Armenia	40 000	25.0	50 000	20.0	60 000	133.3	140 000	7.1	150 000
Aruba	14 000	71.4	24 000	..	..	..	..	..	..
Australia	6 600 000	16.7	7 700 000	36.4	10 500 000	7.6	11 300 000	15.0	13 000 000
Austria	2 700 000	16.7	3 150 000	6.0	3 340 000	11.7	3 730 000	4.6	3 900 000
Azerbaijan	12 000	108.3	25 000	1 100.0	300 000	16.7	350 000	..	..
Bahamas	13 130	28.9	16 923	254.5	60 000	40.0	84 000	10.7	93 000
Bahrain	40 000	150.0	100 000	22.8	122 794	22.2	150 000	1.8	152 721
Bangladesh	100 000	86.0	186 000	9.7	204 000	19.1	243 000	23.5	300 000
Barbados	10 000	50.0	15 000	100.0	30 000	233.3	100 000	..	..
Belarus	187 036	130.0	430 263	87.9	808 481	72.2	1 391 903	..	..
Belgium	3 000 000	6.7	3 200 000	6.3	3 400 000	17.6	4 000 000	5.0	4 200 000
Belize	15 000	20.0	18 000	66.7	30 000	..	..	..	..
Benin	15 000	66.7	25 000	100.0	50 000	40.0	70 000	42.9	100 000
Bermuda	27 000	11.1	30 000	..	..	..	..	..	..
Bhutan	2 250	122.2	5 000	100.0	10 000	50.0	15 000	33.3	20 000
Bolivia	120 000	50.0	180 000	50.0	270 000	14.8	310 000	12.9	350 000
Bosnia and Herzegovina	40 000	12.5	45 000	122.2	100 000	50.0	150 000	..	..
Botswana	25 000	100.0	50 000	20.0	60 000	0.0	60 000	0.0	60 000
Brazil	5 000 000	60.0	8 000 000	78.8	14 300 000	25.9	18 000 000	22.2	22 000 000
Brunei Darussalam	30 000	16.7	35 000	..	..	..	..	..	..
Bulgaria	430 000	40.7	605 000	4.1	630 000	145.3	1 545 143	..	..
Burkina Faso	9 000	111.1	19 000	31.6	25 000	92.0	48 000	10.8	53 200
Burundi	5 000	40.0	7 000	14.3	8 000	75.0	14 000	..	..
Cambodia	6 000	66.7	10 000	200.0	30 000	16.7	35 000	..	..
Cameroon	40 000	12.5	45 000	33.3	60 000	66.7	100 000	..	..
Canada	12 971 000	7.9	14 000 000	8.6	15 200 000	15.8	17 600 000	13.6	20 000 000
Cape Verde	8 000	50.0	12 000	33.3	16 000	25.0	20 000	25.0	25 000
Central African Rep.	2 000	50.0	3 000	66.7	5 000	20.0	6 000	50.0	9 000
Chad	3 000	33.3	4 000	275.0	15 000	100.0	30 000	..	..
Chile	2 537 308	22.3	3 102 200	15.2	3 575 000	11.9	4 000 000	7.5	4 300 000
China	22 500 000	49.8	33 700 000	75.4	59 100 000	34.5	79 500 000	18.2	94 000 000
Colombia	878 000	31.4	1 154 000	73.3	2 000 113	36.6	2 732 201	31.2	3 585 688
Comoros	1 500	66.7	2 500	28.0	3 200	56.3	5 000	..	..

Table 1 (continued)

Country/territory	2000	% change 2000-2001	2001	% change 2001-2002	2002	% change 2002-2003	2003	% change 2003-2004	2004
Congo	0 800	25.0	1 000	400.0	5 000	200.0	15 000	..	..
Costa Rica	228 000	68.4	384 000	108.3	800 000	12.5	900 000	11.1	1 000 000
Côte d'Ivoire	40 000	75.0	70 000	28.6	90 000	166.7	240 000	..	..
Croatia	299 380	73.0	518 000	52.3	789 000	28.5	1 014 000	..	..
Cuba	60 000	100.0	120 000	33.3	160 000	- 38.8	98 000	53.1	150 000
Cyprus	120 000	25.0	150 000	40.0	210 000	19.0	250 000	..	..
Czech Republic	1 000 000	50.0	1 500 000	73.3	2 600 000	19.2	3 100 000	54.8	4 800 000
DR Congo	3 000	100.0	6 000	733.3	50 000	..	..	..	..
Denmark	2 090 000	10.0	2 300 000	19.8	2 756 000	10.1	3 034 000	..	..
Djibouti	1 400	135.7	3 300	36.4	4 500	44.4	6 500	..	..
Dominica	6 000	50.0	9 000	38.9	12 500	..	..	..	..
Dominican Rep.	327 118	21.5	397 333	25.8	500 000	30.0	650 000	23.1	800 000
Ecuador	180 000	85.0	333 000	61.5	537 881	5.9	569 727	9.6	624 579
Egypt	450 000	33.3	600 000	216.7	1 900 000	57.9	3 000 000	30.0	3 900 000
El Salvador	70 000	114.3	150 000	100.0	300 000	83.3	550 000	6.8	587 475
Equatorial Guinea	0 700	28.6	0 900	100.0	1 800	..	..	..	..
Eritrea	5 000	20.0	6 000	50.0	9 000	5.6	9 500	426.3	50 000
Estonia	391 600	9.7	429 656	3.3	444 000	35.1	600 000	11.7	670 000
Ethiopia	10 000	150.0	25 000	100.0	50 000	50.0	75 000	..	..
Faeroe Islands	15 000	33.3	20 000	25.0	25 000	..	..	..	..
Fiji	12 000	25.0	15 000	233.3	50 000	10.0	55 000	..	..
Finland	1 927 000	16.0	2 235 320	18.7	2 654 000	- 3.5	2 560 000	2.3	2 620 000
France	8 460 000	85.0	15 653 000	19.6	18 716 000	17.0	21 900 000	14.2	25 000 000
French Guiana	16 000	25.0	20 000	25.0	25 000	..	..	..	..
French Polynesia	15 000	0.0	15 000	33.3	20 000	75.0	35 000	..	..
Gabon	15 000	13.3	17 000	47.1	25 000	40.0	35 000	14.3	40 000
Gambia	12 000	50.0	18 000	38.9	25 000	..	..	..	..
Georgia	23 000	102.2	46 500	58.1	73 500	59.2	117 020	50.1	175 600
Germany	24 800 000	4.8	26 000 000	7.7	28 000 000	17.9	33 000 000	25.0	41 263 000
Ghana	30 000	33.3	40 000	325.0	170 000	..	..	..	..
Greece	1 000 000	-8.5	915 347	62.3	1 485 281	15.7	1 718 435	13.8	1 955 000
Greenland	17 841	12.1	20 000	25.0	25 000	..	..	..	..
Grenada	4 113	26.4	5 200	188.5	15 000	26.7	19 000	- 57.9	8 000
Guadeloupe	25 000	60.0	40 000	25.0	50 000	..	..	..	..
Guam	25 007	60.0	40 000	25.0	50 000	..	..	..	..
Guatemala	80 000	150.0	200 000	100.0	400 000	..	..	..	..
Guernsey	20 000	25.0	25 000	20.0	30 000	10.0	33 000	..	..
Guinea	8 000	87.5	15 000	133.3	35 000	14.3	40 000	..	..
Guinea-Bissau	3 000	33.3	4 000	250.0	14 000	35.7	19 000	..	..
Guyana	50 000	100.0	100 000	25.0	125 000	12.0	140 000	3.6	145 000
Haiti	20 000	50.0	30 000	166.7	80 000	87.5	150 000	233.3	500 000
Honduras	55 000	63.6	90 000	87.3	168 560	10.1	185 510	19.8	222 273
Hong Kong (China)	1 855 200	40.2	2 601 300	12.2	2 918 800	10.1	3 212 800	8.3	3 479 700
Hungary	715 000	107.0	1 480 000	8.1	1 600 000	50.0	2 400 000	12.5	2 700 000
Iceland	168 000	2.4	172 000	8.5	186 600	4.5	195 000	..	..
India	5 500 000	27.3	7 000 000	136.9	16 580 000	11.5	18 481 044	89.4	35 000 000

Table 1 (continued)

Country/territory	2000	% change 2000-2001	2001	% change 2001-2002	2002	% change 2002-2003	2003	% change 2003-2004	2004
Indonesia	1 900 000	121.1	4 200 000	7.1	4 500 000	79.6	8 080 000	..	..
Iran (Islamic Rep. of)	625 000	60.8	1 005 000	215.2	3 168 000	51.5	4 800 000	..	..
Iraq	..	..	12 500	100.0	25 000	20.0	30 000	..	
Ireland	679 000	31.8	895 000	23.1	1 102 000	14.3	1 260 000	- 20.1	1 006 400
Israel	1 270 000	41.7	1 800 000	11.1	2 000 000	..	..	..	3 200 000
Italy	13 200 000	18.2	15 600 000	27.6	19 900 000	15.0	22 880 000	26.2	28 870 000
Jamaica	80 000	25.0	100 000	500.0	600 000	..	..	..	..
Japan	38 000 000	28.7	48 900 000	17.0	57 200 000	7.7	61 600 000	21.8	75 000 000
Jersey	8 000	..	..	..	..	..	..	..	..
Jordan	127 317	83.8	234 000	31.4	307 469	44.4	444 000	35.1	600 000
Kazakhstan	100 000	50.0	150 000	66.7	250 000	20.0	300 000	33.3	400 000
Kenya	100 000	100.0	200 000	100.0	400 000	150.0	1 000 000	..	..
Kiribati	1 500	33.3	2 000	0.0	2 000	..	..	..	..
Kuwait	150 000	33.3	200 000	25.0	250 000	126.8	567 000	5.8	600 000
Kyrgyzstan	51 600	191.9	150 600	0.9	152 000	31.6	200 000	..	..
Lao PDR	6 000	66.7	10 000	50.0	15 000	26.7	19 000	10.0	20 900
Latvia	150 000	13.3	170 000	82.4	310 000	201.9	936 000	- 13.5	810 000
Lebanon	300 000	-13.3	260 000	53.8	400 000	25.0	500 000	20.0	600 000
Lesotho	4 000	25.0	5 000	320.0	21 000	42.9	30 000	..	..
Liberia	0 500	100.0	1 000	..	..	..	..	..	
Libyan AJ	10 000	100.0	20 000	525.0	125 000	28.0	160 000	..	..
Lithuania	225 000	11.1	250 000	100.0	500 000	39.1	695 700	..	..
Luxembourg	100 000	60.0	160 000	3.1	165 000	3.0	170 000	..	..
Macao (China)	60 000	68.3	101 000	13.9	115 000	4.3	120 000	25.0	150 000
Madagascar	30 000	16.7	35 000	57.1	55 000	28.2	70 500	..	..
Malawi	15 000	33.3	20 000	35.0	27 000	33.3	36 000	20.2	46 140
Malaysia	4 977 000	27.5	6 346 650	23.5	7 840 640	10.5	8 661 000	14.1	9 878 214
Maldives	6 000	66.7	10 000	50.0	15 000	..	..	..	..
Mali	15 000	33.3	20 000	25.0	25 000	40.0	35 000	42.9	50 000
Malta	51 000	94.1	99 000	21.2	120 000	58.3	190 000	..	..
Marshall Islands	0 800	12.5	0 900	38.9	1 250	12.0	1 400	..	..
Martinique	30 000	33.3	40 000	50.0	60 000	33.3	80 000	..	..
Mauritania	5 000	40.0	7 000	42.9	10 000	20.0	12 000	..	..
Mauritius	87 000	21.8	106 000	17.9	125 000	20.0	150 000	..	..
Mayotte	1 800	..	..	..	..	..	..	..	..
Mexico	5 058 000	46.5	7 410 124	45.3	10 764 715	13.5	12 218 830	14.9	14 036 475
Micronesia	4 000	25.0	5 000	20.0	6 000	66.7	10 000	20.0	12 000
Mongolia	30 000	33.3	40 000	25.0	50 000	185.6	142 800	..	..
Morocco	200 000	100.0	400 000	75.0	700 000	42.9	1 000 000	250.0	3 500 000
Mozambique	20 000	50.0	30 000	66.7	50 000	..	..	..	..
Myanmar	7 000	42.9	10 000	150.0	25 000	12.0	28 002	127.4	63 688
Namibia	30 000	50.0	45 000	11.1	50 000	30.0	65 000	15.4	75 000
Nepal	50 000	20.0	60 000	33.3	80 000	25.0	100 000	75.0	175 000
Netherlands	7 000 000	12.9	7 900 000	3.8	8 200 000	3.7	8 500 000	17.6	10 000 000
New Caledonia	30 000	33.3	40 000	25.0	50 000	20.0	60 000	16.7	70 000
New Zealand	1 515 000	16.3	1 762 000	8.3	1 908 000	10.6	2 110 000	51.7	3 200 000

Table 1 *(continued)*

Country/territory	2000	% change 2000-2001	2001	% change 2001-2002	2002	% change 2002-2003	2003	% change 2003-2004	2004
Nicaragua	50 000	50.0	75 000	20.0	90 000	11.1	100 000	25.0	125 000
Niger	4 000	200.0	12 000	25.0	15 000	..	..	..	..
Nigeria	80 000	43.8	115 000	265.2	420 000	78.6	750 000	..	..
Norway	1 950 000	-32.3	1 319 400	6.0	1 398 600	13.2	1 583 300	..	..
Oman	90 000	33.3	120 000	50.0	180 000	..	..	..	..
Pakistan	300 000	66.7	500 000	100.0	1 000 000	20.0	1 200 000	66.7	2 000 000
Palestine	35 000	71.4	60 000	75.0	105 000	38.1	145 000	10.3	160 000
Panama	90 000	87.4	168 690	10.2	185 875	39.9	260 000	15.4	300 000
Papua New Guinea	45 000	11.1	50 000	50.0	75 000	..	..	..	..
Paraguay	40 000	50.0	60 000	66.7	100 000	20.0	120 000	25.0	150 000
Peru	800 000	150.0	2 000 000	20.0	2 400 000	18.8	2 850 000	13.0	3 220 000
Philippines	1 540 000	29.9	2 000 000	75.0	3 500 000	..	..	..	..
Poland	2 800 000	35.7	3 800 000	133.7	8 880 000	1.0	8 970 000	0.3	9 000 000
Portugal	1 680 200	10.7	1 860 400	21.9	2 267 200	17.9	2 674 000	10.4	2 951 000
Puerto Rico	400 000	50.0	600 000	12.8	677 000	..	..	..	..
Qatar	30 000	33.3	40 000	75.0	70 000	101.1	140 760	17.2	165 000
Rep. of Korea	19 040 000	28.0	24 380 000	7.8	26 270 000	11.2	29 220 000	8.1	31 580 000
Rep. of Moldova	52 600	14.1	60 000	150.0	150 000	92.0	288 000	41.0	406 000
Réunion	100 000	20.0	120 000	25.0	150 000	20.0	180 000	..	..
Romania	800 000	25.0	1 000 000	120.0	2 200 000	81.8	4 000 000	..	..
Russian Fed.	2 900 000	48.3	4 300 000	39.5	6 000 000	66.7	10 000 000	60.0	16 000 000
Rwanda	5 000	300.0	20 000	25.0	25 000	..	..	..	..
S. Tome & Principe	6 500	38.5	9 000	22.2	11 000	36.4	15 000	..	..
Samoa	1 000	200.0	3 000	33.3	4 000	..	..	..	..
Saudi Arabia	460 000	120.9	1 016 208	39.6	1 418 880	5.7	1 500 000	..	..
Senegal	40 000	150.0	100 000	5.0	105 000	114.3	225 000	..	..
Serbia and Montenegro	400 000	50.0	600 000	6.7	640 000	32.3	847 000	41.7	1 200 000
Seychelles	6 000	50.0	9 000	30.4	11 736	..	..	..	..
Sierra Leone	5 000	40.0	7 000	14.3	8 000	..	..	..	..
Singapore	1 300 000	30.8	1 700 000	23.5	2 100 000	1.7	2 135 034	13.4	2 421 782
Slovakia	507 029	32.9	674 039	28.0	862 833	59.5	1 375 809	65.4	2 276 000
Slovenia	300 000	100.0	600 000	25.0	750 000	6.7	800 000	18.8	950 000
Solomon Islands	2 000	0.0	2 000	10.0	2 200	13.6	2 500	..	..
Somalia	0 500	100.0	1 000	1 400.0	15 000	500.0	90 000	122.2	200 000
South Africa	2 400 000	20.4	2 890 000	7.3	3 100 000	..	..	..	..
Spain	5 486 000	34.7	7 388 000	6.3	7 856 000	24.6	9 789 000	32.8	13 000 000
Sri Lanka	121 500	23.5	150 000	33.3	200 000	25.0	250 000	12.0	280 000
Saint Kitts and Nevis	2 700	33.3	3 600	177.8	10 000	..	..	..	..
Saint Lucia	8 000	62.5	13 000	..	..	..	..	..	..
Saint Vincent	3 500	57.1	5 500	27.3	7 000	0.0	7 000	14.3	8 000
Sudan	30 000	86.7	56 000	50.0	84 000	1 015.5	937 000	21.7	1 140 000
Suriname	11 709	24.0	14 520	37.7	20 000	15.0	23 000	30.4	30 000
Swaziland	10 000	40.0	14 000	42.9	20 000	35.0	27 000	..	..
Sweden	4 048 000	13.6	4 600 000	11.4	5 125 000	10.3	5 655 000	20.2	6 800 000
Switzerland	2 096 000	6.1	2 224 000	14.9	2 556 000	14.1	2 916 000	61.2	4 700 000
Syrian Arab Rep.	30 000	100.0	60 000	508.3	365 000	67.1	610 000	31.1	800 000
Taiwan PC	6 260 000	24.9	7 820 000	37.1	10 720 000	9.5	11 740 000	4.0	12 210 000

Table 1 (continued)

Country/territory	2000	% change 2000-2001	2001	% change 2001-2002	2002	% change 2002-2003	2003	% change 2003-2004	2004
Tajikistan	3 000	6.7	3 200	9.4	3 500	17.7	4 120	..	..
TFYR Macedonia	50 000	40.0	70 000	42.9	100 000	26.0	126 000	..	..
Thailand	2 300 000	53.7	3 536 019	35.7	4 800 000	25.6	6 030 000	15.6	6 970 000
Togo	100 000	50.0	150 000	33.3	200 000	5.0	210 000	..	..
Tonga	2 400	16.7	2 800	3.6	2 900	..	..	..	..
Trinidad & Tobago	100 000	20.0	120 000	15.0	138 000	..	..	..	..
Tunisia	260 000	57.7	410 000	23.3	505 500	24.6	630 000	32.5	835 000
Turkey	2 000 000	75.0	3 500 000	22.9	4 300 000	39.5	6 000 000	70.3	10 220 000
Turkmenistan	6 000	33.3	8 000	..	..	..	20 000	..	..
Uganda	40 000	50.0	60 000	66.7	100 000	25.0	125 000	60.0	200 000
Ukraine	350 000	71.4	600 000	50.0	900 000	177.8	2 500 000	..	..
United Arab Emirates	765 000	27.6	976 000	20.4	1 175 516	16.8	1 373 217	0.8	1 384 837
United Kingdom	15 800 000	25.3	19 800 000	26.3	25 000 000	37.6	34 400 000	9.3	37 600 000
United States	124 000 000	15.2	142 823 000	11.3	159 000 000	1.7	161 632 400	14.5	185 000 000
UR of Tanzania	40 000	50.0	60 000	33.3	80 000	212.5	250 000	..	..
Uruguay	370 000	8.1	400 000	..	,,		530 000	28.3	080 000
US Virgin Islands	15 000	33.3	20 000	50.0	30 000	..	..	..	..
Uzbekistan	120 000	25.0	150 000	83.3	275 000	70.9	492 000	..	..
Vanuatu	4 000	37.5	5 500	27.3	7 000	7.1	7 500	0.0	7 500
Venezuela	820 022	40.5	1 152 502	10.6	1 274 429	51.8	1 934 791	19.5	2 312 683
Viet Nam	200 000	404.8	1 009 544	48.6	1 500 000	133.3	3 500 000	67.7	5 870 000
Yemen	15 000	13.3	17 000	488.2	100 000	20.0	120 000	50.0	180 000
Zambia	20 000	25.0	25 000	109.7	52 420	30.0	68 150	..	..
Zimbabwe	50 000	100.0	100 000	400.0	500 000	60.0	800 000	2.5	820 000

Source: UNCTAD calculations based on ITU World Telecommunication Indicators Database, 2005.

Table 2.   Internet penetration, by country/territory, 2000–2004

Internet users per 100 inhabitants
sorted by decreasing order of 2003 values

Country/territory	2000	% change 2000-2001	2001	% change 2001-2002	2002	% change 2002-2003	2003	% change 2003-2004	2004
Iceland	59.8	0.2	59.9	8.2	64.8	4.1	67.5	..	..
Sweden	45.6	13.2	51.6	11.0	57.3	9.9	63.0	19.8	75.5
Rep. of Korea	41.4	24.4	51.5	7.0	55.1	10.8	61.1	7.5	65.7
United Kingdom	26.4	25.0	33.0	28.2	42.3	39.9	59.2	6.9	63.3
Guernsey	31.9	39.5	44.5	20.4	53.6	10.3	59.1	..	..
Australia	34.5	15.1	39.7	34.5	53.4	6.4	56.8	14.8	65.3
Denmark	39.2	9.4	42.9	19.6	51.3	9.6	56.2	..	..
United States	44.1	13.6	50.1	10.2	55.2	0.7	55.6	12.1	62.3
Canada	42.1	6.9	45.0	7.6	48.4	14.5	55.4	13.7	63.0
New Zealand	39.3	15.5	45.4	6.6	48.4	8.7	52.6	55.7	82.0
Netherlands	43.8	12.1	49.1	3.1	50.6	3.1	52.2	18.1	61.6
Taiwan Province of China	28.1	24.2	34.9	36.4	47.6	9.1	51.9	3.3	53.6
Singapore	32.4	27.2	41.2	22.3	50.4	1.0	50.9	10.3	56.1
Finland	37.2	15.6	43.0	18.6	51.0	- 3.8	49.1	2.4	50.2
Japan	29.9	28.4	38.4	16.9	44.9	7.5	48.3	21.6	58.7
Malta	13.1	93.1	25.3	19.8	30.3	56.8	47.5	..	..
Hong Kong (China)	27.8	39.2	38.7	11.1	43.0	9.7	47.2	3.7	48.9
Austria	33.7	16.3	39.2	5.9	41.5	11.3	46.2	4.0	48.0
Estonia	27.2	10.3	30.0	9.3	32.8	35.4	44.4	15.3	51.2
Italy	23.0	17.0	26.9	30.5	35.1	18.6	41.6	20.9	50.3
Latvia	6.2	16.1	7.2	84.7	13.3	203.5	40.4	- 12.2	35.4
Slovenia	15.1	99.3	30.1	24.9	37.6	6.5	40.1	19.7	48.0
Germany	30.1	4.7	31.5	7.6	33.9	17.9	40.0	6.1	42.4
Switzerland	29.1	5.5	30.7	14.3	35.1	13.5	39.9	64.6	65.6
Belgium	29.2	6.2	31.0	5.8	32.8	17.6	38.6	5.3	40.6
Israel*	20.3	36.5	27.7	9.0	30.1	27.4	38.4	21.4	46.6
Luxembourg	22.8	59.6	36.4	1.6	37.0	1.8	37.7	..	..
Barbados	3.7	51.4	5.6	100.0	11.2	231.1	37.1	..	..
France	14.4	83.3	26.4	18.9	31.4	16.4	36.6	13.2	41.4
Norway	43.3	- 32.6	29.2	5.1	30.7	12.6	34.6	..	..
Malaysia	21.4	24.3	26.6	20.3	32.0	7.5	34.4	15.4	39.7
United Arab Emirates	23.6	18.6	28.0	11.8	31.3	8.6	34.0	- 6.3	31.9
Cyprus	17.7	23.2	21.8	34.9	29.4	14.7	33.7	..	..
Ireland	17.9	30.2	23.3	20.2	28.0	13.1	31.7	- 20.5	25.2
Czech Republic	9.7	51.5	14.7	74.1	25.6	20.3	30.8	52.4	46.9
Macao (China)	13.6	69.9	23.1	12.6	26.0	2.9	26.8	20.0	32.1
Bahamas	4.3	27.9	5.5	249.1	19.2	38.0	26.5	10.8	29.3
Chile	16.7	20.4	20.1	18.4	23.8	10.3	26.3	6.2	27.9
New Caledonia	14.0	30.0	18.2	22.5	22.3	17.5	26.2	15.2	30.2
Portugal	16.8	7.1	18.0	21.7	21.9	17.3	25.7	14.1	29.3
Réunion	14.3	14.7	16.4	23.2	20.2	17.9	23.8	..	..
Hungary	7.1	108.5	14.8	6.8	15.8	50.1	23.7	15.8	27.5
Poland	7.2	36.1	9.8	134.7	23.0	1.0	23.2	0.5	23.4

Table 2 *(continued)*

Country/territory	2000	% change 2000-2001	2001	% change 2001-2002	2002	% change 2002-2003	2003	% change 2003-2004	2004
Croatia	6.7	76.1	11.8	52.5	18.0	28.8	23.2	..	..
Spain	13.7	33.6	18.3	5.5	19.3	18.8	22.9	37.9	31.6
Kuwait	6.9	27.5	8.8	20.5	10.6	115.3	22.8	1.3	23.1
Bahrain	6.3	144.4	15.4	18.8	18.3	18.0	21.6	- 4.3	20.7
Costa Rica	5.7	63.2	9.3	111.8	19.7	9.5	21.6	9.1	23.5
Slovakia	9.4	33.0	12.5	28.0	16.0	34.8	21.6	95.2	42.1
Martinique	7.8	32.1	10.3	49.5	15.4	32.5	20.4	..	..
Lithuania	6.1	11.5	6.8	111.8	14.4	39.9	20.1	..	..
Qatar	4.9	28.6	6.3	65.1	10.4	91.6	19.9	33.8	26.7
Bulgaria	5.3	41.5	7.5	8.0	8.1	144.6	19.8	..	..
Romania	3.6	25.0	4.5	124.4	10.1	82.7	18.5	..	..
Grenada	4.4	18.2	5.2	173.1	14.2	19.0	16.9	- 54.0	7.8
Uruguay	10.9	5.5	11.5	2.6	11.8	39.0	16.4	27.9	21.0
Greece	9.5	- 9.5	8.6	57.0	13.5	11.1	15.0	18.7	17.8
Lebanon	9.1	- 14.3	7.8	50.0	11.7	22.1	14.3	18.3	16.9
Belarus	1.9	126.3	4.3	90.7	8.2	72.0	14.1	..	..
French Polynesia	6.3	- 1.6	6.2	30.6	8.1	72.8	14.0	..	..
Mauritius	7.3	20.5	8.8	17.0	10.3	19.3	12.3	..	..
Argentina	7.3	38.9	10.1	11.2	11.2	6.8	12.0	10.1	13.2
Mexico	5.1	47.1	7.5	42.7	10.7	11.8	12.0	11.9	13.4
Andorra	9.0	..	..	..	..	..	11.9	..	..
Peru	3.1	148.4	7.7	16.9	9.0	15.4	10.4	12.4	11.7
Brazil	2.9	62.1	4.7	74.5	8.2	24.4	10.2	19.4	12.2
S. Tome & Principe	4.4	36.4	6.0	21.7	7.3	35.2	9.9	..	..
Thailand	3.8	52.6	5.8	34.5	7.8	22.6	9.6	14.9	11.0
Micronesia	3.7	27.0	4.7	19.1	5.6	65.5	9.3	16.6	10.8
Turkey	3.1	64.5	5.1	21.6	6.2	36.9	8.5	66.4	14.1
Panama	3.2	81.3	5.8	25.9	7.3	14.2	8.3	13.4	9.5
El Salvador	1.1	109.1	2.3	100.0	4.6	80.2	8.3	7.1	8.9
Jordan	2.5	80.0	4.5	28.9	5.8	39.8	8.1	31.8	10.7
Rep. of Moldova	1.4	21.4	1.7	141.2	4.1	94.6	8.0	19.3	9.5
Serbia and Montenegro	3.8	47.4	5.6	7.1	6.0	31.2	7.9	45.0	11.4
Venezuela	3.4	38.2	4.7	8.5	5.1	47.6	7.5	17.4	8.8
Dominican Rep.	3.8	21.1	4.6	32.6	6.1	22.8	7.5	21.5	9.1
Iran (Islamic Rep. of)	1.0	60.0	1.6	200.0	4.8	50.8	7.2	..	..
Russian Fed.	2.0	45.0	2.9	41.4	4.1	66.6	6.8	62.5	11.1
Zimbabwe	0.4	125.0	0.9	377.8	4.3	58.1	6.8	- 6.8	6.3
Fiji	1.5	20.0	1.8	238.9	6.1	9.2	6.7	..	..
Saudi Arabia	2.2	113.6	4.7	38.3	6.5	2.5	6.7	..	..
Tunisia	2.7	55.6	4.2	23.8	5.2	22.7	6.4	31.7	8.4
Colombia	2.1	28.6	2.7	70.4	4.6	35.7	6.2	27.9	8.0
China	1.7	52.9	2.6	76.9	4.6	33.7	6.2	16.4	7.2
TFYR Macedonia	2.5	36.0	3.4	41.2	4.8	26.0	6.1	..	..
Mongolia	1.3	30.8	1.7	23.5	2.1	176.7	5.8	..	..
Ukraine	0.7	71.4	1.2	58.3	1.9	176.3	5.3	..	..
Egypt	0.7	28.6	0.9	211.1	2.8	56.1	4.4	27.5	5.6

Table 2 (continued)

Country/territory	2000	% change 2000-2001	2001	% change 2001-2002	2002	% change 2002-2003	2003	% change 2003-2004	2004
Suriname	2.7	22.2	3.3	27.3	4.2	4.0	4.4	56.3	6.8
Cape Verde	1.8	50.0	2.7	33.3	3.6	21.1	4.4	21.6	5.3
Ecuador	1.4	85.7	2.6	65.4	4.3	1.2	4.4	8.7	4.7
Philippines	2.0	27.0	2.6	72.2	4.4	- 2.0	4.3	35.0	5.8
Viet Nam	0.3	300.0	1.2	50.0	1.8	138.9	4.3	65.6	7.1
Azerbaijan	0.2	50.0	0.3	1 133.3	3.7	14.3	4.2	..	..
Togo	2.2	45.5	3.2	28.1	4.1	2.4	4.2	..	..
Palestine	1.1	63.6	1.8	66.7	3.0	33.7	4.0	8.2	4.3
Kyrgyzstan	1.1	172.7	3.0	0.0	3.0	32.3	4.0	..	..
Bosnia	1.1	9.1	1.2	116.7	2.6	50.4	3.9	..	..
Indonesia	0.9	122.2	2.0	5.0	2.1	79.0	3.8	..	..
Bolivia	1.5	46.7	2.2	45.5	3.2	15.3	3.7	5.7	3.9
Armenia	1.1	18.2	1.3	23.1	1.6	130.0	3.7	33.4	4.9
Vanuatu	2.1	33.3	2.8	25.0	3.5	3.1	3.6	- 4.2	3.5
Syrian Arab Rep.	0.2	100.0	0.4	425.0	2.1	65.7	3.5	26.1	4.4
Botswana	1.5	100.0	3.0	16.7	3.5	- 2.6	3.4	- 2.1	3.3
Namibia	1.7	47.1	2.5	8.0	2.7	25.2	3.4	10.4	3.7
Morocco	0.7	100.0	1.4	71.4	2.4	38.3	3.3	239.5	11.3
Kenya	0.3	93.9	0.6	98.4	1.3	148.0	3.2	..	..
Libyan AJ	0.2	100.0	0.4	475.0	2.3	25.7	2.9	..	..
Sudan	0.1	100.0	0.2	50.0	0.3	836.7	2.8	17.4	3.3
Honduras	0.9	55.6	1.4	78.6	2.5	9.2	2.7	16.5	3.2
Gabon	1.2	8.3	1.3	46.2	1.9	37.9	2.6	13.0	3.0
Marshall Islands	1.6	6.2	1.7	41.2	2.4	7.9	2.6	..	..
Swaziland	1.0	40.0	1.4	35.7	1.9	36.3	2.6	..	..
Georgia	0.5	80.0	0.9	66.7	1.5	59.3	2.4	44.8	3.5
Senegal	0.4	150.0	1.0	0.0	1.0	117.0	2.2	..	..
Bhutan	0.3	133.3	0.7	100.0	1.4	45.7	2.0	- 57.8	0.9
Paraguay	0.7	57.1	1.1	54.5	1.7	18.8	2.0	23.3	2.5
Uzbekistan	0.5	20.0	0.6	83.3	1.1	74.5	1.9	..	..
Kazakhstan	0.6	50.0	0.9	77.8	1.6	18.1	1.9	37.6	2.6
Nicaragua	1.0	45.5	1.4	20.1	1.7	5.2	1.8	22.5	2.2
Haiti	0.2	100.0	0.4	150.0	1.0	80.0	1.8	229.4	5.9
India	0.5	40.0	0.7	128.6	1.6	9.4	1.8	85.1	3.2
Guinea-Bissau	0.2	50.0	0.3	266.7	1.1	34.5	1.5	..	..
Côte d'Ivoire	0.3	33.3	0.4	25.0	0.5	188.0	1.4	..	..
Lesotho	0.2	0.0	0.2	400.0	1.0	38.0	1.4	..	..
Sri Lanka	0.7	14.3	0.8	37.5	1.1	18.2	1.3	11.5	1.5
Benin	0.2	100.0	0.4	75.0	0.7	42.9	1.0	45.0	1.5
Albania	0.1	200.0	0.3	33.3	0.4	145.0	1.0	..	..
Djibouti	0.2	150.0	0.5	40.0	0.7	38.6	1.0	..	..
Cuba	0.5	120.0	1.1	27.3	1.4	- 37.9	0.9	51.7	1.3
Pakistan	0.2	100.0	0.4	75.0	0.7	14.3	0.8	58.8	1.3
Somalia	0.0	..	0.0	..	0.2	275.0	0.8	122.7	1.7
UR of Tanzania	0.1	100.0	0.2	0.0	0.2	255.0	0.7	..	..
Comoros	0.2	50.0	0.3	33.3	0.4	57.5	0.6	..	..

Table 2 *(continued)*

Country/territory	2000	% change 2000-2001	2001	% change 2001-2002	2002	% change 2002-2003	2003	% change 2003-2004	2004
Cameroon	0.3	7.4	0.3	31.0	0.4	63.2	0.6	..	..
Nigeria	0.1	0.0	0.1	200.0	0.3	103.3	0.6	..	..
Zambia	0.2	0.0	0.2	150.0	0.5	20.0	0.6	..	..
Guinea	0.1	100.0	0.2	150.0	0.5	4.0	0.5	..	..
Solomon Islands	0.5	0.0	0.5	0.0	0.5	4.0	0.5	..	..
Uganda	0.2	50.0	0.3	33.3	0.4	22.5	0.5	53.1	0.8
Mauritania	0.2	50.0	0.3	33.3	0.4	10.0	0.4	..	..
Congo	0.0	..	0.0	..	0.2	115.0	0.4	..	..
Madagascar	0.2	0.0	0.2	50.0	0.3	43.3	0.4	..	..
Turkmenistan	0.1	100.0	0.2	..	..	..	0.4	..	..
Burkina Faso	0.1	100.0	0.2	0.0	0.2	95.0	0.4	2.6	0.4
Chad	0.0	25.0	0.1	280.0	0.2	94.7	0.4	..	..
Malawi	0.1	100.0	0.2	50.0	0.3	13.3	0.3	8.8	0.4
Lao PDR	0.1	100.0	0.2	50.0	0.3	10.0	0.3	9.1	0.4
Mali	0.1	100.0	0.2	0.0	0.2	60.0	0.3	40.6	0.5
Cambodia	0.0	..	0.1	100.0	0.2	25.0	0.3	..	..
Eritrea	0.1	100.0	0.2	0.0	0.2	15.0	0.2	404.3	1.2
Burundi	0.1	0.0	0.1	0.0	0.1	100.0	0.2	..	..
Bangladesh	0.1	0.0	0.1	100.0	0.2	- 10.0	0.2	11.1	0.2
Central African Rep.	0.1	0.0	0.1	0.0	0.1	40.0	0.1	64.3	0.2
Ethiopia	0.0	..	0.0	..	0.1	10.0	0.1	..	..
Afghanistan	0.0	..	..	..	0.0	..	0.1	0.0	0.1
Tajikistan	0.0	..	0.1	0.0	0.1	0.0	0.1	..	..
Myanmar	0.0	..	0.0	..	0.1	0.0	0.1	140.0	0.1

* UNCTAD estimate for 2003
Source: UNCTAD calculations based on ITU World Telecommunication Indicators Database, 2005.

Table 3.   Number of personal computers, by country/territory, 2000–2004

sorted by decreasing order of 2002 values

Country/territory	2000	% change 2000-2001	2001	% change 2001-2002	2002	% change 2002-2003	2003	% change 2003-2004	2004
United States	161 000 000	10.6	178 000 000	6.7	190 000 000	5.3	200 000 000	10.0	220 000 000
Japan	40 000 000	14.0	45 600 000	6.8	48 700 000	..	..	..	69 200 000
Germany	27 640 000	13.3	31 317 000	13.7	35 600 000	12.4	40 000 000	15.8	46 300 000
China	20 600 000	21.4	25 000 000	42.0	35 500 000	..	..	..	52 990 000
United Kingdom	20 190 000	9.0	22 000 000	9.0	23 972 000	..	..	..	35 890 000
Rep. of Korea	18 615 000	20.8	22 495 000	4.5	23 502 000	3.2	24 248 000	8.1	26 201 000
France	17 920 000	8.8	19 500 000	6.2	20 700 000	20.8	25 000 000	17.6	29 410 000
Canada	12 900 000	10.1	14 200 000	7.7	15 300 000	..	..	..	22 390 000
Italy	10 300 000	9.7	11 300 000	15.3	13 025 000	..	15 480 000	..	18 150 000
Brazil	8 500 000	27.1	10 800 000	20.4	13 000 000	..	..	..	19 350 000
Russian Fed.	9 300 000	18.3	11 000 000	18.2	13 000 000	..	..	..	19 010 000
Australia	9 000 000	11.1	10 000 000	11.0	11 100 000	8.1	12 000 000	14.3	13 720 000
Taiwan PC	7 063 200	15.5	8 160 900	16.7	9 521 000	11.9	10 655 000	..	..
Mexico	5 700 000	21.1	6 900 000	21.1	8 353 000	19.7	10 000 000	12.1	11 210 000
Spain	5 800 000	17.2	6 800 000	17.2	7 972 000	..	..	..	..
Netherlands	6 300 000	9.5	6 900 000	9.5	7 557 000	..	..	..	11 110 000
India	4 600 000	30.4	6 000 000	25.0	7 500 000	..	..	..	13 030 000
Sweden	4 500 000	11.1	5 000 000	11.1	5 556 000	..	..	..	..
Switzerland	4 700 000	5.1	4 940 000	4.5	5 160 000	5.2	5 430 000	12.4	6 105 000
Iran (Islamic Rep. of)	4 000 000	12.5	4 500 000	8.9	4 900 000	22.4	6 000 000	..	..
Poland	2 670 000	23.6	3 300 000	23.6	4 079 000	34.3	5 480 000	..	..
Malaysia	2 200 000	36.4	3 000 000	20.0	3 600 000	16.7	4 200 000	..	..
South Africa	2 900 000	6.9	3 100 000	6.5	3 300 000	..	..	..	..
Hong Kong (China)	2 360 000	10.2	2 600 000	25.9	3 273 000	15.4	3 777 000	10.9	4 187 000
Denmark	2 700 000	7.4	2 900 000	6.9	3 100 000	..	..	..	..
Austria	2 261 000	20.6	2 727 000	10.5	3 013 000	6.2	3 200 000	6.9	3 419 600
Saudi Arabia	1 300 000	37.5	1 787 500	68.0	3 003 000	..	..	..	..
Argentina	2 560 000	13.3	2 900 000	3.4	3 000 000	..	..	..	..
Turkey	2 500 000	8.0	2 700 000	11.1	3 000 000	..	..	..	..
Belgium	2 300 000	4.3	2 400 000	16.7	2 800 000	17.9	3 300 000	9.9	3 627 000
Singapore	1 941 000	8.2	2 100 000	23.3	2 590 000	..	..	..	..
Indonesia	2 100 000	9.5	2 300 000	9.5	2 519 000	..	..	..	..
Thailand	1 714 000	16.9	2 003 000	22.9	2 461 000	..	..	..	..
Norway	2 200 000	4.5	2 300 000	4.6	2 405 000	..	..	..	..
Finland	2 050 000	7.3	2 200 000	4.5	2 300 000	..	..	..	..
Philippines	1 480 000	14.9	1 700 000	29.4	2 200 000	..	..	..	..
Colombia	1 500 000	20.0	1 800 000	18.5	2 133 000	..	..	..	..
Czech Republic	1 250 000	20.0	1 500 000	20.0	1 800 000	..	..	..	..
Romania	713 000	12.2	800 000	125.0	1 800 000	16.7	2 100 000	..	..
Chile	1 420 000	15.5	1 640 000	9.5	1 795 814	11.4	2 000 000	6.9	2 137 934
Ireland	1 360 000	10.3	1 500 000	10.3	1 654 000	..	..	..	..
New Zealand	1 380 000	8.7	1 500 000	8.7	1 630 000	..	..	..	..
Israel	1 590 000	0.6	1 600 000	0.6	1 610 000	..	..	..	5 037 000
Venezuela	1 100 000	18.2	1 300 000	18.2	1 536 000	..	..	..	..
Portugal	1 050 000	15.2	1 210 000	15.2	1 394 000	0.3	1 398 240	..	..
Peru	1 050 000	19.0	1 250 000	- 8.1	1 149 300	53.0	1 758 000	..	..

Table 3 *(continued)*

Country/territory	2000	% change 2000-2001	2001	% change 2001-2002	2002	% change 2002-2003	2003	% change 2003-2004	2004
Egypt	800 000	25.0	1 000 000	12.0	1 120 000	78.6	2 000 000	15.0	2 300 000
Hungary	870 000	9.2	950 000	15.8	1 100 000	..	..	..	..
Slovakia	740 000	8.1	800 000	26.3	1 010 000	25.7	1 270 000	25.4	1 593 000
Ukraine	890 000	3.4	920 000	3.4	951 000	18.1	1 123 220	..	..
Greece	750 000	14.7	860 000	4.7	900 000	..	..	..	..
Nigeria	750 000	6.7	800 000	6.6	853 000	0.8	860 000	..	..
Costa Rica	600 000	16.7	700 000	16.7	817 000	11.4	910 000	..	..
Viet Nam	600 000	16.7	700 000	14.3	800 000	..	..	..	..
Croatia	498 987	24.3	620 000	22.6	760 000	..	..	..	..
Slovenia	548 000	0.4	550 000	9.1	600 000	8.3	650 000	..	..
Zimbabwe	195 000	2.6	200 000	200.0	600 000	3.3	620 000	61.3	1 000 000
Morocco	350 000	14.3	400 000	25.0	500 000	20.0	600 000	3.3	620 000
Bangladesh	200 000	25.0	250 000	80.0	450 000	133.3	1 050 000	57.1	1 650 000
United Arab Emirates	400 000	5.0	420 000	7.1	450 000	..	..	..	..
Bulgaria	361 400	5.1	380 000	6.6	405 000	..	..	..	..
Ecuador	275 000	9.1	300 000	34.2	402 652	..	..	..	..
Latvia	340 000	5.9	360 000	11.1	400 000	9.0	436 000	14.9	501 000
Lithuania	240 000	8.3	260 000	46.2	380 000	..	..	..	..
Tunisia	219 100	16.5	255 245	31.4	335 325	19.4	400 372	17.9	472 132
Syrian Arab Rep.	250 000	8.0	270 000	22.2	330 000	51.5	500 000	20.0	600 000
Papua New Guinea	280 000	7.1	300 000	7.0	321 000	..	..	..	..
Lebanon	175 000	42.9	250 000	20.0	300 000	16.7	350 000	14.3	400 000
Serbia and Montenegro	240 000	4.2	250 000	16.0	290 000	..	..	..	..
Estonia	220 000	13.6	250 000	14.0	285 000	108.8	595 000	..	..
Kuwait	250 000	8.8	272 000	4.8	285 000	40.4	400 000	12.5	450 000
Luxembourg	200 000	15.0	230 000	15.2	265 000	5.7	280 000	..	..
Cuba	135 000	63.0	220 000	13.6	250 000	8.0	270 000	11.1	300 000
Myanmar	100 000	50.0	150 000	66.7	250 000	20.0	300 000	8.3	325 000
Sri Lanka	135 000	29.6	175 000	42.9	250 000	30.0	325 000	63.0	529 650
Algeria	200 000	10.0	220 000	10.0	242 000	9.5	265 000	..	..
Kenya	150 000	16.7	175 000	16.6	204 000	47.1	300 000	..	..
Iraq	..	..	..	..	200 000	..	..	..	..
Jordan	150 000	13.3	170 000	17.6	200 000	22.5	245 000	..	..
Paraguay	70 000	114.3	150 000	33.3	200 000	..	..	..	..
Senegal	160 000	12.5	180 000	11.1	200 000	10.0	220 000	..	..
Sudan	100 000	15.0	115 000	73.9	200 000	..	..	..	..
Cyprus	150 000	13.3	170 000	13.5	193 000	..	..	..	..
Bolivia	140 000	21.4	170 000	11.8	190 000	..	..	..	..
Mauritius	120 000	8.3	130 000	38.5	180 000	..	..	..	..
Guatemala	130 000	15.4	150 000	15.3	173 000	..	..	..	..
El Salvador	120 000	16.7	140 000	16.4	163 000	35.0	220 000	..	..
Georgia	112 000	27.7	143 000	9.1	156 000	10.3	172 000	11.6	192 000
Côte d'Ivoire	90 000	30.8	117 700	30.8	154 000	..	..	..	..
Nicaragua	120 000	8.3	130 000	15.4	150 000	..	..	..	..
Togo	100 000	20.0	120 000	25.0	150 000	6.7	160 000	..	..
Yemen	35 000	5.7	37 000	291.9	145 000	37.9	200 000	50.0	300 000
UR of Tanzania	100 000	20.0	120 000	20.0	144 000	38.9	200 000	..	..
Jamaica	120 000	8.3	130 000	8.5	141 000	..	..	..	..

Table 3 *(continued)*

Country/territory	2000	% change 2000-2001	2001	% change 2001-2002	2002	% change 2002-2003	2003	% change 2003-2004	2004
Namibia	75 000	37.1	102 806	29.4	133 000	43.7	191 100	15.1	220 000
Iceland	110 000	9.1	120 000	8.3	130 000	3.1	134 000	..	..
Libyan AJ	..	..	..	..	130 000	..	..	..	..
Palestine	..	..	..	..	125 000	14.4	143 000	18.2	169 000
Panama	105 000	4.8	110 000	4.5	115 000	4.3	120 000	8.3	130 000
Guadeloupe	90 000	11.1	100 000	11.0	111 000	..	..	..	..
Qatar	90 000	11.1	100 000	10.0	110 000	..	..	..	..
Bahrain	95 000	5.3	100 000	7.0	107 000	..	..	..	..
Trinidad & Tobago	80 000	12.5	90 000	15.0	103 500	..	..	..	..
Malta	80 000	12.5	90 000	12.2	101 000	..	..	..	..
Ethiopia	60 000	25.0	75 000	33.3	100 000	50.0	150 000	..	..
Oman	80 000	6.3	85 000	11.8	95 000	..	..	..	..
TFYR Macedonia	..	..	72 000	30.6	94 000	25.5	118 000	18.6	140 000
Macao (China)	70 000	14.3	80 000	15.0	92 000	27.2	117 000	11.1	130 000
Honduras	70 000	14.3	80 000	13.8	91 000	9.9	100 000	..	..
Cameroon	50 000	20.0	60 000	50.0	90 000	33.3	120 000	..	..
Nepal	70 000	14.3	80 000	6.3	85 000	17.8	100 172	..	..
Ghana	60 000	16.7	70 000	17.1	82 000	..	..	..	..
Mozambique	60 000	16.7	70 000	17.1	82 000	..	..	..	..
Uganda	60 000	16.7	70 000	17.1	82 000	25.0	102 500	17.6	120 500
Zambia	70 000	7.1	75 000	6.7	80 000	18.8	95 000	..	..
Martinique	65 000	10.8	72 000	8.3	78 000	2.6	80 000	..	..
Rep. of Moldova	63 500	10.2	70 000	10.0	77 000	..	..	..	112 200
Botswana	60 000	8.3	65 000	7.7	70 000	..	..	..	..
French Polynesia	75 115	- 11.8	66 221	5.7	70 000	..	..	..	..
Madagascar	35 000	14.3	40 000	75.0	70 000	14.3	80 000	..	..
Mongolia	32 000	31.3	42 000	64.3	69 000	175.4	190 000	..	..
Kyrgyzstan	25 600	150.0	64 000	0.8	64 500	16.3	75 000	..	..
Armenia	25 000	40.0	35 000	71.4	60 000	..	..	..	200 000
Réunion	35 000	22.9	43 000	23.3	53 000	..	..	..	..
Guinea	29 000	10.3	32 000	31.3	42 000	2.4	43 000	..	..
Fiji	36 000	5.6	38 000	5.3	40 000	5.0	42 000	..	..
Albania	25 000	20.0	30 000	20.0	36 000	..	..	..	..
Belize	30 000	10.0	33 000	6.1	35 000	..	..	..	..
Cape Verde	25 000	20.0	30 000	16.7	35 000	..	..	..	..
Bermuda	30 000	6.7	32 000	6.3	34 000	..	..	..	..
French Guiana	25 000	8.0	27 000	7.4	29 000	..	..	..	..
Mauritania	25 000	8.0	27 000	7.4	29 000	20.7	35 000	..	..
Barbados	22 000	13.6	25 000	12.0	28 000	..	..	..	..
Angola	15 000	13.3	17 000	58.8	27 000	..	..	..	..
Brunei Darussalam	23 000	8.7	25 000	8.0	27 000	..	..	..	..
Cambodia	15 000	33.3	20 000	35.0	27 000	18.5	32 000	..	..
Gabon	12 000	66.7	20 000	25.0	25 000	20.0	30 000	66.7	50 000
Swaziland	12 000	33.3	16 000	56.3	25 000	20.0	30 000	..	..
Guyana	22 000	4.5	23 000	4.3	24 000	8.3	26 000	3.8	27 000
Saint Lucia	22 000	4.5	23 000	4.3	24 000	..	..	..	..
Maldives	10 000	50.0	15 000	33.3	20 000	..	..	..	..
Burkina Faso	15 000	13.3	17 000	11.8	19 000	36.8	26 000	10.0	28 600

Table 3 *(continued)*

Country/territory	2000	% change 2000-2001	2001	% change 2001-2002	2002	% change 2002-2003	2003	% change 2003-2004	2004
Gambia	15 000	13.3	17 000	11.8	19 000	..	..	..	..
Lao PDR	14 000	14.3	16 000	12.5	18 000	11.1	20 000	10.0	22 000
Solomon Islands	16 000	6.3	17 000	5.9	18 000	..	..	..	..
Benin	10 000	10.0	11 000	36.4	15 000	72.2	25 825	16.2	30 000
Mali	13 000	7.7	14 000	7.1	15 000	66.7	25 000	..	..
Somalia	..	..	..	..	15 000	66.7	25 000	100.0	50 000
Grenada	12 000	8.3	13 000	7.7	14 000	..	..	..	..
Malawi	12 000	8.3	13 000	7.7	14 000	12.9	15 800	24.7	19 710
Saint Vincent	12 000	8.3	13 000	7.7	14 000	..	..	..	..
Chad	11 000	9.1	12 000	8.3	13 000	..	..	..	..
Congo	11 000	9.1	12 000	8.3	13 000	15.4	15 000	..	..
Seychelles	11 000	9.1	12 000	8.3	13 000	..	..	..	..
Bhutan	5 000	40.0	7 000	42.9	10 000	0.0	10 000	10.0	11 000
Djibouti	6 500	7.7	7 000	42.9	10 000	45.0	14 500	..	..
Eritrea	6 160	13.6	7 000	42.9	10 000	20.0	12 000	25.0	15 000
Saint Kitts and Nevis	7 000	14.3	8 000	12.5	9 000	..	..	..	..
Central African Rep.	6 000	16.7	7 000	14.3	8 000	25.0	10 000	10.0	11 000
Dominica	5 500	9.1	6 000	16.7	7 000	..	..	..	..
Niger	5 000	20.0	6 000	16.7	7 000	..	..	..	..
Burundi	4 000	12.5	4 500	11.1	5 000	160.0	13 000	..	..
Comoros	3 000	33.3	4 000	5.0	4 200	9.5	4 600	..	..
Equatorial Guinea	2 000	25.0	2 500	40.0	3 500	..	..	..	..
Marshall Islands	2 000	25.0	2 500	20.0	3 000	..	..	..	..
Vanuatu	2 400	8.3	2 600	15.4	3 000	0.0	3 000	0.0	3 000
Tonga	1 300	7.7	1 400	42.9	2 000	..	..	..	..
Samoa	1 000	10.0	1 100	9.1	1 200	..	..	..	..
Kiribati	0 800	12.5	0 900	11.1	1 000	..	..	..	..
Uruguay	350 000	5.7	370 000	..	..	..	410 000	4.9	430 000

Source: UNCTAD calculations based on ITU World Telecommunication Indicators Database, 2005.

Table 4.   Mobile phone subscribers by country/territory, 2000–2004

(alphabetical order)

Country/territory	2000	% change 2000-2001	2001	% change 2001-2002	2002	% change 2002-2003	2003	% change 2003-2004	2004
Afghanistan	..	..	..	..	25 000	700.0	200 000	200.0	600 000
Albania	29 791	1 218.0	392 650	116.7	851 000	29.3	1 100 000	..	..
Algeria	86 000	16.3	100 000	300.0	400 000	260.4	1 441 400	224.9	4 682 690
Andorra	23 543	25.0	29 429	11.4	32 790	58.3	51 893	..	..
Argentina	6 049 963	15.3	6 974 939	- 5.9	6 566 740	19.4	7 842 233	72.3	13 512 383
Armenia	17 486	45.9	25 504	182.1	71 949	59.0	114 379	77.8	203 309
Australia	8 562 000	30.0	11 132 000	13.0	12 575 000	14.1	14 347 000	14.7	16 449 000
Austria	6 117 000	6.9	6 541 000	3.0	6 736 000	5.3	7 094 502	12.6	7 989 955
Azerbaijan	420 400	73.6	730 000	19.2	870 000	21.5	1 057 000	68.7	1 782 900
Bahamas	31 524	92.1	60 555	101.1	121 759	- 4.5	116 267	60.0	186 007
Bahrain	205 727	46.2	300 829	29.3	388 990	13.9	443 109	46.6	649 764
Bangladesh	279 000	86.4	520 000	106.7	1 075 000	27.0	1 365 000	217.0	4 327 516
Barbados	28 467	86.6	53 111	83.0	97 193	44.0	140 000	22.1	171 000
Belarus	49 353	180.3	138 329	234.4	462 630	141.7	1 118 000	..	..
Belgium	5 629 000	36.7	7 697 000	5.7	8 135 512	5.8	8 605 834	6.1	9 131 705
Belize	16 812	132.9	39 155	32.1	51 729	16.8	60 403	61.8	97 755
Benin	55 476	125.3	125 000	75.0	218 770	8.0	236 175	..	..
Bhutan	..	..	..	..	..	..	7 998	122.6	17 800
Bolivia	582 620	33.9	779 917	31.5	1 025 451	24.7	1 278 844	40.8	1 800 789
Bosnia	93 386	376.2	444 711	68.4	748 780	40.2	1 050 000	..	..
Botswana	200 000	58.0	316 000	37.7	435 000	20.2	522 840	7.8	563 782
Brazil	23 188 171	24.0	28 745 769	21.3	34 880 964	32.9	46 373 266	41.5	65 605 000
Bulgaria	738 000	110.0	1 550 000	67.6	2 597 548	34.8	3 500 869	35.1	4 729 731
Burkina Faso	25 245	201.0	76 000	48.7	113 000	100.9	227 000	75.3	398 000
Burundi	16 320	88.0	30 687	69.5	52 000	23.1	64 000	..	..
Cambodia	130 547	71.2	223 458	70.1	380 000	31.2	498 388	..	..
Cameroon	103 279	304.0	417 295	68.1	701 507	53.5	1 077 000	42.7	1 536 594
Canada	8 880 000	21.7	10 803 000	11.1	11 997 000	10.3	13 228 000	13.3	14 984 396
Cape Verde	19 729	59.7	31 507	36.3	42 949	24.2	53 342	23.3	65 780
Central African Rep.	4 967	121.5	11 000	14.5	12 600	217.5	40 000	50.0	60 000
Chad	5 500	300.0	22 000	55.5	34 200	90.1	65 000	..	..
Chile	3 401 525	55.0	5 271 565	22.3	6 445 698	16.7	7 520 280	27.2	9 566 581
China	85 260 000	69.9	144 820 000	42.2	206 005 000	31.0	269 953 000	24.0	334 824 000
Colombia	2 256 801	44.7	3 265 261	40.8	4 596 594	34.6	6 186 206	68.1	10 400 578
Comoros	..	..	..	..	..	..	2 000	..	..
Congo	70 000	114.3	150 000	47.9	221 800	48.8	330 000	34.0	442 200
Costa Rica	205 275	51.7	311 329	47.7	459 757	64.5	756 235	20.5	911 539
Côte d'Ivoire	472 952	54.0	728 545	41.0	1 027 058	24.7	1 280 696	19.6	1 531 846
Croatia	1 033 000	69.9	1 755 000	33.3	2 340 000	9.1	2 553 000	..	..
Cuba	6 536	31.3	8 579	108.1	17 851	98.1	35 356	114.4	75 797
Cyprus	218 324	44.0	314 355	32.9	417 933	32.0	551 752	16.1	640 515
Czech Republic	4 346 009	59.9	6 947 151	23.9	8 610 177	12.8	9 708 683	10.9	10 771 270
DR Congo	15 000	900.0	150 000	273.3	560 000	78.6	1 000 000	..	..
Denmark	3 363 552	17.7	3 960 165	13.1	4 477 752	6.5	4 767 277	8.4	5 165 546

Table 4 *(continued)*

Country/territory	2000	% change 2000-2001	2001	% change 2001-2002	2002	% change 2002-2003	2003	% change 2003-2004	2004
Djibouti	0 230	1 204.3	3 000	400.0	15 000	53.3	23 000	..	..
Dominican Rep.	705 431	80.0	1 270 082	33.9	1 700 609	24.8	2 122 543	19.4	2 534 063
Ecuador	482 213	78.2	859 152	81.7	1 560 861	53.6	2 398 161	89.5	4 544 174
Egypt	1 359 900	105.4	2 793 800	60.9	4 494 700	29.0	5 797 530	31.8	7 643 060
El Salvador	743 628	15.4	857 782	3.6	888 818	29.4	1 149 790	59.4	1 832 579
Equatorial Guinea	5 000	200.0	15 000	113.3	32 000	29.7	41 500	33.7	55 500
Estonia	557 000	16.9	651 200	35.3	881 000	19.2	1 050 241	19.6	1 255 731
Ethiopia	17 757	54.9	27 500	83.2	50 369	94.2	97 827	82.0	178 000
Faeroe Islands	16 971	44.3	24 487	25.4	30 709	25.8	38 640	..	..
Fiji	55 057	47.0	80 933	11.1	89 900	22.2	109 882	..	..
Finland	3 728 625	12.0	4 175 587	8.2	4 516 772	5.1	4 747 126	5.1	4 988 000
France	29 052 360	27.3	36 997 400	4.3	38 585 300	8.0	41 683 100	6.9	44 551 800
Gabon	120 000	25.0	150 000	86.2	279 289	7.4	300 000	63.1	489 367
Georgia	194 741	54.7	301 327	67.1	503 619	41.2	711 224	18.2	840 600
Germany	48 202 000	16.4	56 126 000	5.3	59 128 000	9.6	64 800 000	10.1	71 316 000
Ghana	130 045	49.0	193 773	131.9	449 435	78.0	799 873	111.9	1 695 000
Greece	5 932 403	34.2	7 963 742	17.0	9 314 260	11.0	10 337 000	6.8	11 044 232
Grenada	4 300	49.2	6 414	17.8	7 553	459.9	42 293	2.4	43 313
Guatemala	856 831	33.8	1 146 441	37.6	1 577 085	29.0	2 034 776	55.7	3 168 256
Guernsey	21 885	44.1	31 539	16.0	36 580	13.5	41 530	5.5	43 824
Guinea	42 112	32.2	55 670	63.1	90 772	22.8	111 500	..	..
Guinea-Bissau	..	..	..	..	..	..	1 275	..	..
Haiti	55 000	66.4	91 500	53.0	140 000	128.6	320 000	25.0	400 000
Honduras	155 271	53.0	237 629	37.4	326 508	16.2	379 362	86.4	707 201
Hong Kong (China)	5 447 346	6.0	5 776 360	10.7	6 395 725	14.9	7 349 202	10.9	8 148 685
Hungary	3 076 279	61.5	4 967 430	38.2	6 862 766	15.8	7 944 586	9.9	8 727 188
Iceland	214 896	15.5	248 131	5.2	260 938	7.2	279 670	4.2	291 372
India	3 577 095	79.8	6 431 520	97.3	12 687 637	106.1	26 154 405	80.8	47 300 000
Indonesia	3 669 327	77.7	6 520 947	79.4	11 700 000	60.7	18 800 000	59.6	30 000 000
Iran (Islamic Rep. of)	962 595	116.8	2 087 353	4.8	2 186 958	54.4	3 376 526	27.3	4 300 000
Iraq	..	..	..	..	20 000	300.0	80 000	617.5	574 000
Ireland	2 461 000	20.7	2 970 000	1.0	3 000 000	16.7	3 500 000	8.0	3 780 000
Israel	4 400 000	34.1	5 900 000	7.4	6 334 000	2.6	6 500 000	10.6	7 187 500
Italy	42 246 000	21.3	51 246 000	3.4	53 003 000	7.1	56 770 000	10.5	62 750 000
Jamaica	366 952	73.0	635 000	120.5	1 400 000	14.3	1 600 000	37.5	2 200 000
Japan	66 784 374	12.0	74 819 158	8.4	81 118 324	6.8	86 654 962	5.6	91 473 940
Jordan	388 949	122.7	866 000	40.8	1 219 597	8.7	1 325 313	20.3	1 594 513
Kazakhstan	197 300	195.0	582 000	76.5	1 027 000	29.6	1 330 730	107.3	2 758 940
Kenya	127 404	370.9	600 000	97.9	1 187 122	34.0	1 590 785	60.1	2 546 157
Kiribati	0 300	31.7	0 395	25.3	0 495	6.3	0 526	..	..
Kuwait	476 000	84.4	877 920	39.8	1 227 000	15.7	1 420 000	40.8	2 000 000
Kyrgyzstan	9 000	200.0	27 000	96.6	53 084	160.5	138 279	117.0	300 000
Lao PDR	12 681	133.0	29 545	86.7	55 160	103.5	112 275	81.9	204 191
Latvia	401 272	63.7	656 835	39.6	917 196	33.0	1 219 550	26.0	1 536 712
Lebanon	743 000	3.2	766 754	1.1	775 104	5.8	820 000	8.3	888 000
Lesotho	21 600	163.9	57 000	69.9	96 843	4.8	101 474	56.7	159 000

Table 4 *(continued)*

Country/territory	2000	% change 2000-2001	2001	% change 2001-2002	2002	% change 2002-2003	2003	% change 2003-2004	2004
Libyan AJ	40 000	25.0	50 000	40.0	70 000	81.4	127 000	..	..
Lithuania	524 000	94.3	1 017 999	61.6	1 645 568	31.9	2 169 866	57.7	3 421 538
Luxembourg	303 274	34.9	409 064	15.6	473 000	14.0	539 000	..	..
Macao (China)	141 052	37.9	194 475	42.0	276 138	31.8	364 031	18.8	432 450
Madagascar	63 094	133.8	147 500	10.5	163 010	74.0	283 666	17.7	333 888
Malawi	49 000	13.7	55 730	54.4	86 047	57.0	135 114	64.4	222 135
Malaysia	5 121 748	44.2	7 385 240	25.3	9 253 387	20.2	11 124 112	31.4	14 611 902
Mali	10 398	336.0	45 340	16.1	52 639	365.3	244 930	63.3	400 000
Malta	114 444	109.2	239 416	15.6	276 859	4.7	289 992	..	..
Marshall Islands	0 447	9.4	0 489	12.9	0 552	8.3	0 598	..	..
Mauritania	15 300	622.0	110 463	123.8	247 238	41.9	350 870	48.9	522 400
Mauritius	180 000	51.3	272 416	27.8	348 137	- 6.3	326 033	56.4	510 000
Mayotte	..	..	..	..	21 700	65.9	36 000	5.6	38 000
Mexico	14 077 880	54.6	21 757 559	19.2	25 928 266	16.1	30 097 700	27.8	38 451 135
Micronesia	..	..	..	..	0 100	5 769.0	5 869	117.8	12 782
Mongolia	154 600	26.1	195 000	10.8	216 000	47.7	319 000	..	..
Morocco	2 342 000	103.7	4 771 739	29.9	6 198 670	18.7	7 359 870	26.9	9 336 878
Mozambique	51 065	198.9	152 652	66.9	254 759	71.0	435 757	62.5	708 000
Myanmar	13 397	69.2	22 671	111.6	47 982	38.6	66 517	38.3	92 007
Namibia	82 000	30.0	106 600	40.7	150 000	49.1	223 671	27.9	286 095
Nepal	10 226	69.0	17 286	26.6	21 881	130.2	50 367	255.6	179 126
Netherlands	10 755 000	14.8	12 352 000	- 2.4	12 060 000	3.6	12 500 000	18.6	14 821 000
New Caledonia	49 948	36.0	67 917	17.8	80 000	21.4	97 113	19.9	116 443
New Zealand	1 542 000	48.4	2 288 000	7.0	2 449 000	6.1	2 599 000	16.5	3 027 000
Nicaragua	90 294	82.2	164 509	44.2	237 248	96.7	466 706	58.3	738 624
Niger	2 056	3.4	2 126	683.1	16 648	360.0	76 580	93.6	148 276
Nigeria	30 000	1 233.3	400 000	302.0	1 607 931	95.9	3 149 473	190.4	9 147 209
Norway	3 367 763	11.8	3 766 431	3.8	3 911 136	6.4	4 163 381	..	..
Oman	164 348	97.5	324 540	43.2	464 896	27.7	593 450	35.6	805 000
Pakistan	349 460	132.4	812 000	52.5	1 238 602	111.9	2 624 799	91.3	5 020 000
Palestine	175 941	70.5	300 000	6.7	320 000	50.0	480 000	103.0	974 345
Panama	410 401	15.8	475 141	10.7	525 845	31.7	692 406	23.6	855 852
Paraguay	820 810	40.1	1 150 000	45.0	1 667 018	6.2	1 770 345	- 0.1	1 767 824
Peru	1 273 857	40.8	1 793 284	28.6	2 306 944	27.0	2 930 343	39.7	4 092 558
Philippines	6 454 359	88.4	12 159 163	25.0	15 201 000	48.1	22 509 560	46.3	32 935 875
Poland	6 747 000	48.3	10 004 661	38.9	13 898 471	25.2	17 401 222	32.7	23 096 065
Portugal	6 664 951	19.7	7 977 537	6.9	8 528 900	17.6	10 030 000	2.7	10 300 000
Qatar	120 856	47.2	177 929	49.9	266 703	41.2	376 535	30.2	490 333
Rep. of Korea	26 816 398	8.3	29 045 596	11.4	32 342 493	3.9	33 591 758	8.9	36 586 052
Rep. of Moldova	139 000	61.9	225 000	50.3	338 225	40.7	475 942	65.4	787 000
Réunion	276 100	52.5	421 100	16.3	489 800	15.4	565 000	..	..
Romania	2 499 000	53.9	3 845 116	32.9	5 110 591	37.8	7 039 898	45.1	10 215 388
Russia	3 263 200	137.5	7 750 499	127.2	17 608 756	107.3	36 500 000	103.9	74 420 000
Rwanda	39 000	66.7	65 000	70.4	110 762	21.0	134 000	11.9	150 000
S. Tome & Principe	..	..	..	..	1 980	143.4	4 819	..	..
Samoa	2 500	0.0	2 500	8.0	2 700	288.9	10 500	..	..

Table 4 *(continued)*

Country/territory	2000	% change 2000-2001	2001	% change 2001-2002	2002	% change 2002-2003	2003	% change 2003-2004	2004
Saudi Arabia	1 375 881	83.8	2 528 640	98.0	5 007 965	44.5	7 238 224	26.8	9 175 764
Senegal	250 251	20.6	301 811	51.0	455 645	26.4	575 917	78.5	1 028 061
Serbia and Montenegro	1 303 609	53.3	1 997 809	37.7	2 750 397	32.1	3 634 613	30.1	4 729 629
Seychelles	25 961	41.3	36 683	21.9	44 731	10.1	49 229	0.0	49 230
Singapore	2 747 400	8.9	2 991 600	11.8	3 344 800	4.0	3 477 100	11.0	3 860 600
Slovakia	1 109 888	93.5	2 147 331	36.1	2 923 383	25.8	3 678 774	16.2	4 275 164
Slovenia	1 215 601	20.9	1 470 085	13.4	1 667 234	4.3	1 739 146	..	..
Solomon Islands	1 151	- 16.0	0 967	3.3	0 999	48.9	1 488	..	..
South Africa	8 339 000	29.4	10 787 000	27.0	13 702 000	23.0	16 860 000	15.7	19 500 000
Spain	24 265 059	22.2	29 655 729	13.1	33 530 997	11.0	37 219 839	..	..
Sri Lanka	430 202	55.2	667 662	39.5	931 580	49.6	1 393 403	58.7	2 211 158
St. Vincent	2 361	217.3	7 492	33.2	9 982	530.2	62 911	- 9.5	56 950
Sudan	23 000	351.5	103 846	83.7	190 778	176.4	527 233	98.9	1 048 558
Suriname	41 048	111.9	87 000	24.6	108 363	55.5	168 522	26.3	212 819
Swaziland	33 000	66.7	55 000	23.6	68 000	25.0	85 000	32.9	113 000
Sweden	6 372 300	12.6	7 177 000	10.8	7 949 000	10.7	8 801 000	5.7	9 302 000
Switzerland	4 638 519	13.7	5 275 791	8.7	5 736 303	7.9	6 189 000	1.4	6 275 000
Syrian Arab Rep.	30 000	566.7	200 000	100.0	400 000	196.3	1 185 000	97.9	2 345 000
Taiwan PC	17 873 829	21.9	21 786 384	12.0	24 390 520	5.8	25 799 839	- 11.8	22 760 144
Tajikistan	1 160	40.5	1 630	700.8	13 200	260.7	47 617	..	..
TFYR Macedonia	115 748	92.9	223 275	63.6	365 346	112.4	776 000	..	..
Thailand	3 056 000	147.1	7 550 000	113.5	16 117 000	54.3	24 864 019	12.6	28 000 000
Togo	50 000	90.0	95 000	78.9	170 000	29.4	220 000	..	..
Trinidad & Tobago	161 860	58.2	256 106	41.3	361 911	34.3	485 871	33.3	647 870
Tunisia	119 165	226.6	389 208	47.6	574 334	233.9	1 917 530	85.8	3 562 970
Turkey	16 133 405	21.3	19 572 897	19.2	23 323 118	19.6	27 887 535	24.5	34 707 549
Turkmenistan	7 500	9.0	8 173	0.0	8 173	12.4	9 187	..	..
Uganda	126 913	123.4	283 520	38.7	393 310	97.3	776 169	50.1	1 165 035
Ukraine	818 524	171.8	2 224 600	66.0	3 692 700	76.0	6 498 423	111.4	13 735 000
United Arab Emirates	1 428 115	33.7	1 909 303	27.2	2 428 071	22.4	2 972 331	23.9	3 683 117
United Kingdom	43 452 000	6.5	46 283 000	7.3	49 677 000	6.7	52 984 000	15.3	61 100 000
United States	109 478 031	17.3	128 374 512	9.7	140 766 842	12.8	158 721 981	14.1	181 105 135
UR of Tanzania	180 200	136.9	426 964	78.0	760 000	36.9	1 040 640	57.6	1 640 000
Uzbekistan	53 128	141.0	128 012	46.0	186 900	71.7	320 815	69.6	544 100
Vanuatu	0 365	- 4.1	0 350	1 300.0	4 900	59.2	7 800	34.7	10 504
Venezuela	5 447 172	18.8	6 472 584	- 0.1	6 463 561	8.5	7 015 735	20.0	8 420 980
Viet Nam	788 559	58.7	1 251 195	52.0	1 902 388	44.1	2 742 000	80.9	4 960 000
Yemen	32 000	375.0	152 000	170.4	411 083	70.3	700 000	53.1	1 072 000
Zambia	98 853	22.6	121 200	14.8	139 092	73.3	241 000	24.5	300 000
Zimbabwe	309 000	6.4	328 669	3.1	338 779	7.3	363 365	9.4	397 500

Source: UNCTAD calculations based on ITU World Telecommunication Indicators Database, 2005.

Table 5.   Mobile phone penetration, by country/territory 2000–2004

Mobile phone subscribers per 100 inhabitants
(alphabetical order)

Country/territory	2000	% change 2000-2001	2001	% change 2001-2002	2002	% change 2002-2003	2003	% change 2003-2004	2004
Afghanistan	..	..	..	..	0.1	829.2	1.0	141.7	2.4
Albania	1.0	1 220.9	12.7	117.2	27.6	29.6	35.8	..	..
Algeria	0.3	14.6	0.3	294.2	1.3	255.1	4.5	219.0	14.5
Andorra	30.2	22.1	36.9	8.5	40.0	54.1	61.6	..	..
Argentina	16.9	14.1	19.3	- 7.8	17.8	16.6	20.7	67.8	34.8
Armenia	0.5	45.9	0.7	182.2	1.9	59.0	3.0	..	..
Australia	44.7	28.5	57.4	11.4	64.0	12.8	72.2	14.5	82.6
Austria	76.4	6.7	81.4	2.7	83.6	5.1	87.9	12.0	98.4
Azerbaijan	5.4	70.4	9.1	17.0	10.7	19.7	12.8	65.1	21.1
Bahamas	10.3	90.8	19.7	97.8	39.0	- 6.0	36.7	60.0	58.7
Bahrain	32.4	42.7	46.2	25.2	57.9	10.3	63.8	37.7	87.9
Bangladesh	0.2	83.6	0.4	103.7	0.8	25.1	1.0	186.1	2.9
Barbados	10.6	86.0	19.8	82.5	36.1	43.7	51.9	21.6	63.1
Belarus	0.5	181.4	1.4	235.8	4.7	142.5	11.3	..	..
Belgium	54.8	36.1	74.7	5.2	78.6	5.6	83.0	6.4	88.3
Belize	7.0	117.4	15.2	23.3	18.8	9.0	20.5	83.0	37.5
Benin	0.9	118.1	1.9	69.4	3.2	4.5	3.4	..	..
Bhutan	..	..	..	..	..	..	1.1	- 29.4	0.8
Bolivia	7.1	32.8	9.4	30.4	12.3	23.7	15.2	36.1	20.7
Bosnia	2.5	374.1	11.7	67.6	19.6	39.6	27.4	..	..
Botswana	12.2	54.4	18.8	34.5	25.3	17.5	29.7	5.7	31.4
Brazil	13.7	22.5	16.7	19.9	20.1	31.1	26.3	38.2	36.3
Bulgaria	9.1	111.1	19.1	74.2	33.3	34.8	44.9	34.6	60.4
Burkina Faso	0.2	193.7	0.7	45.1	0.9	95.8	1.9	60.5	3.0
Burundi	0.2	84.3	0.4	66.4	0.7	20.8	0.9	..	..
Cambodia	1.0	66.9	1.7	65.8	2.8	27.7	3.5	..	..
Cameroon	0.7	295.4	2.7	63.7	4.4	49.4	6.6	42.4	9.4
Canada	28.8	20.4	34.7	10.0	38.2	9.1	41.7	13.3	47.2
Cape Verde	4.5	56.9	7.1	33.9	9.5	22.0	11.6	19.9	13.9
Central African Rep.	0.1	111.7	0.3	9.5	0.3	204.6	1.0	57.7	1.5
Chad	0.1	289.5	0.3	51.4	0.4	85.1	0.8	..	..
Chile	22.4	53.1	34.2	25.1	42.8	15.3	49.4	25.7	62.1
China	6.6	67.6	11.0	45.4	16.0	30.3	20.9	22.0	25.5
Colombia	5.3	43.1	7.6	39.2	10.6	33.1	14.1	63.9	23.2
Comoros	..	..	..	..	..	..	0.3	..	..
Congo	2.4	102.7	4.8	39.4	6.7	40.3	9.4	22.8	11.6
Costa Rica	5.1	48.3	7.6	46.6	11.1	63.3	18.1	18.4	21.5
Côte d'Ivoire	3.2	39.3	4.5	39.8	6.2	23.6	7.7	17.8	9.1
Croatia	23.1	73.7	40.1	33.3	53.5	9.1	58.4	..	..
Cuba	0.1	30.8	0.1	107.4	0.2	95.8	0.3	116.1	0.7
Cyprus	32.2	41.8	45.6	28.2	58.4	27.3	74.4	6.7	79.4
Czech Republic	42.3	60.6	67.9	24.9	84.9	13.6	96.5	9.2	105.3
DR Congo	0.0	883.5	0.3	272.5	1.1	78.2	1.9	..	..

Table 5 (continued)

Country/territory	2000	% change 2000-2001	2001	% change 2001-2002	2002	% change 2002-2003	2003	% change 2003-2004	2004
Denmark	63.1	17.2	74.0	12.7	83.3	6.0	88.3	8.8	96.1
Djibouti	0.0	1 180.0	0.5	390.9	2.3	50.6	3.4	..	..
Dominican Rep.	8.2	77.6	14.6	41.0	20.7	18.4	24.5	17.8	28.8
Ecuador	3.8	74.9	6.7	88.5	12.6	45.6	18.3	88.1	34.4
Egypt	2.1	102.0	4.3	54.3	6.7	26.5	8.4	29.3	10.9
El Salvador	11.8	13.1	13.4	2.7	13.8	25.8	17.3	60.0	27.7
Equatorial Guinea	1.1	189.1	3.2	98.5	6.3	20.6	7.6	43.3	11.0
Eritrea	..	..	..	..	..	..	..	..	0.5
Estonia	38.7	17.7	45.5	42.8	65.0	19.6	77.7	23.5	96.0
Ethiopia	0.0	50.4	0.0	77.8	0.1	88.6	0.1	77.3	0.3
Faeroe Islands	37.7	44.1	54.3	18.4	64.4	18.9	76.5	..	..
Fiji	6.8	46.5	9.9	10.2	11.0	21.3	13.3	..	..
Finland	72.0	11.6	80.4	7.9	86.7	4.9	91.0	5.1	95.6
France	49.3	26.4	62.3	3.8	64.7	7.6	69.6	5.9	73.7
Gabon	9.8	21.4	11.9	80.8	21.5	4.4	22.4	61.3	36.2
Georgia	3.9	56.0	6.1	68.5	10.2	42.4	14.5	14.0	16.6
Germany	58.6	16.2	68.1	5.2	71.6	9.6	78.5	10.1	86.4
Ghana	0.6	43.9	0.9	124.0	2.1	71.9	3.6	122.5	7.0
Greece	56.2	33.8	75.2	12.5	84.5	6.7	90.2	11.5	100.6
Grenada	4.8	40.9	6.4	11.1	7.1	420.1	37.0	11.8	42.1
Guatemala	7.5	30.3	9.8	34.0	13.1	25.7	16.5	51.4	25.0
Guinea	0.6	30.7	0.7	61.2	1.2	21.5	1.4	..	..
Guinea-Bissau	..	..	..	..	..	..	0.1	..	..
Haiti	0.7	63.8	1.1	52.5	1.7	127.8	3.8	23.3	4.7
Honduras	2.5	46.9	3.6	34.1	4.9	14.5	5.6	81.0	10.1
Hong Kong (China)	81.7	5.1	85.9	9.7	94.2	14.5	107.9	6.1	114.5
Hungary	30.7	62.0	49.8	35.7	67.6	16.2	78.5	13.0	88.8
Iceland	76.5	13.1	86.5	4.8	90.6	6.8	96.8	2.8	99.4
India	0.4	77.2	0.6	94.5	1.2	103.2	2.5	76.6	4.4
Indonesia	1.8	75.2	3.1	76.9	5.5	58.5	8.7	54.2	13.5
Iran (Islamic Rep. of)	1.5	113.7	3.2	3.5	3.3	52.2	5.1	21.0	6.2
Iraq	..	..	..	..	0.1	289.2	0.3	591.5	2.2
Ireland	65.0	19.0	77.4	- 1.4	76.3	15.3	88.0	7.5	94.5
Israel	70.2	29.2	90.7	5.3	95.5	0.6	96.1	9.0	104.7
Italy	73.7	19.8	88.3	6.3	93.9	10.1	103.3	5.9	109.4
Jamaica	14.2	71.3	24.4	118.9	53.3	13.6	60.6	35.7	82.2
Japan	52.6	11.7	58.8	8.3	63.7	6.7	67.9	5.4	71.6
Jordan	7.7	116.5	16.7	36.9	22.9	5.7	24.2	17.4	28.4
Kazakhstan	1.2	197.3	3.6	77.9	6.4	30.6	8.4	113.2	17.9
Kenya	0.4	361.5	1.9	96.6	3.8	33.1	5.0	56.5	7.9
Kiribati	0.4	29.5	0.5	23.3	0.6	4.5	0.6	..	..
Kuwait	21.7	77.5	38.6	34.5	51.9	10.1	57.2	34.8	77.1
Kyrgyzstan	0.2	193.6	0.5	92.4	1.0	163.9	2.8	109.5	5.8
Lao PDR	0.2	127.1	0.5	81.9	1.0	98.6	2.0	78.3	3.5
Latvia	16.6	68.8	27.9	41.0	39.4	33.5	52.6	27.8	67.2
Lebanon	22.6	1.2	22.9	- 0.8	22.7	3.2	23.4	6.8	25.0

Table 5 (continued)

Country/territory	2000	% change 2000-2001	2001	% change 2001-2002	2002	% change 2002-2003	2003	% change 2003-2004	2004
Lesotho	1.0	163.0	2.6	69.4	4.5	4.4	4.7	89.2	8.8
Libya AJ	0.7	25.6	0.9	40.6	1.3	82.2	2.3	..	..
Lithuania	14.2	94.9	27.7	71.8	47.5	32.2	62.8	58.1	99.3
Luxembourg	69.2	34.6	93.1	14.0	106.1	12.6	119.4	..	..
Macao (China)	32.1	38.9	44.5	40.4	62.5	29.8	81.2	14.1	92.6
Madagascar	0.4	127.6	1.0	7.6	1.0	69.4	1.7	7.7	1.9
Malawi	0.5	13.2	0.5	53.6	0.8	56.3	1.3	39.7	1.8
Malaysia	22.0	40.4	30.9	22.1	37.7	17.1	44.2	32.9	58.7
Mali	0.1	328.8	0.4	13.6	0.5	355.3	2.3	59.7	3.6
Malta	29.3	108.1	61.1	14.5	69.9	3.7	72.5	..	..
Marshall Islands	0.9	7.8	0.9	11.2	1.0	6.7	1.1	..	..
Mauritania	0.6	603.7	4.2	118.1	9.2	38.3	12.7	37.5	17.5
Mauritius	15.1	50.5	22.7	26.7	28.8	- 7.2	26.7	54.9	41.4
Mayotte	..	..	..	..	13.5	59.2	21.6	5.5	22.8
Mexico	14.2	54.1	21.9	17.4	25.8	14.4	29.5	24.3	36.6
Micronesia	..	..	..	..	0.1	5 752.7	5.4	111.8	11.5
Mongolia	6.5	24.7	8.1	9.5	8.9	46.0	13.0	..	..
Morocco	8.2	100.5	16.4	27.8	20.9	16.8	24.4	23.0	30.1
Mozambique	0.3	189.5	0.9	63.0	1.4	61.7	2.3	63.8	3.7
Myanmar	0.0	67.1	0.0	109.0	0.1	27.6	0.1	36.0	0.2
Namibia	4.6	26.7	5.8	37.1	8.0	45.3	11.6	22.4	14.2
Nepal	0.0	65.6	0.1	24.0	0.1	125.6	0.2	229.1	0.7
Netherlands	67.3	14.0	76.7	- 2.9	74.5	3.1	76.8	19.0	91.3
New Caledonia	23.3	33.1	31.0	15.3	35.7	18.7	42.4	18.4	50.2
New Zealand	40.0	47.5	59.0	5.4	62.2	4.3	64.8	19.6	77.5
Nicaragua	1.8	77.6	3.2	44.2	4.6	86.8	8.5	55.1	13.2
Niger	0.0	- 1.2	0.0	648.4	0.1	339.6	0.6	91.0	1.2
Nigeria	0.0	1 198.4	0.3	291.4	1.3	90.7	2.6	181.9	7.2
Norway	74.8	11.1	83.1	1.5	84.4	7.7	90.9	..	..
Oman	6.8	91.4	13.1	39.9	18.3	24.6	22.8	20.2	27.4
Pakistan	0.3	126.7	0.6	48.8	0.8	106.8	1.8	81.8	3.2
Palestine	5.6	62.8	9.1	1.8	9.3	43.2	13.3	99.3	26.4
Panama	14.5	13.4	16.4	6.7	17.5	27.0	22.2	21.4	27.0
Paraguay	14.9	36.6	20.4	41.3	28.8	3.5	29.9	- 1.6	29.4
Peru	5.0	38.5	6.9	25.5	8.6	24.0	10.7	38.9	14.9
Philippines	8.4	84.2	15.5	23.0	19.1	45.2	27.8	43.5	39.9
Poland	17.5	48.3	25.9	39.0	36.0	25.3	45.1	32.9	59.9
Portugal	66.5	16.1	77.2	6.9	82.5	16.8	96.4	6.1	102.3
Qatar	19.9	40.0	27.9	42.5	39.7	34.2	53.3	48.6	79.2
Rep. of Korea	58.3	5.2	61.4	10.7	67.9	3.4	70.2	8.4	76.1
Réunion	39.5	45.8	57.6	14.4	65.9	13.4	74.7	..	..
Rep. of Moldova	3.8	62.3	6.2	50.8	9.3	41.2	13.2	39.9	18.5
Romania	11.1	54.1	17.2	36.6	23.5	38.5	32.5	41.2	45.9
Russian Fed.	2.2	137.8	5.3	127.5	12.0	107.5	24.9	107.0	51.6
Rwanda	0.5	62.1	0.8	65.8	1.4	17.7	1.6	10.9	1.8
S. Tome & Principe	..	..	..	..	1.3	141.8	3.2	..	..

Table 5 (continued)

Country/territory	2000	% change 2000-2001	2001	% change 2001-2002	2002	% change 2002-2003	2003	% change 2003-2004	2004
Samoa	1.4	- 1.0	1.4	6.9	1.5	285.0	5.8	..	..
Saudi Arabia	6.6	79.1	11.8	93.0	22.8	40.8	32.1	14.7	36.8
Senegal	2.6	17.2	3.1	46.9	4.5	23.0	5.6	78.8	9.9
Serbia and Montenegro	12.3	52.7	18.7	37.2	25.7	31.7	33.8	33.1	45.0
Seychelles	32.0	41.2	45.2	18.3	53.4	11.3	59.5	2.2	60.8
Singapore	68.4	5.9	72.4	9.9	79.6	4.1	82.9	8.0	89.5
Slovakia	20.5	94.3	39.9	36.2	54.4	6.1	57.7	37.1	79.1
Slovenia	61.1	20.6	73.7	13.4	83.5	4.3	87.1	..	..
Solomon Islands	0.3	- 18.3	0.2	0.5	0.2	38.8	0.3	..	..
South Africa	19.1	26.8	24.2	24.5	30.1	20.6	36.4	18.6	43.1
Spain	60.5	21.3	73.4	12.4	82.4	5.8	87.2	..	..
Sri Lanka	2.3	53.0	3.6	37.9	4.9	47.9	7.3	57.8	11.5
Saint Vincent	2.1	213.0	6.5	31.0	8.5	519.7	52.9	- 11.0	47.1
Sudan	0.1	339.1	0.3	78.7	0.6	172.1	1.6	92.4	3.0
Suriname	9.5	109.1	19.8	13.9	22.5	42.2	32.0	51.3	48.5
Swaziland	3.3	64.7	5.4	22.2	6.6	23.6	0.1	28.1	10.4
Sweden	71.8	12.3	80.5	10.3	88.9	10.3	98.0	5.3	103.2
Switzerland	64.3	13.2	72.8	8.2	78.8	7.4	84.6	3.6	87.6
Syrian Arab Rep.	0.2	545.5	1.2	95.2	2.3	189.2	6.8	90.6	12.9
Taiwan PC	80.2	21.2	97.2	11.4	108.3	5.4	114.1	12.4	100.0
Tajikistan	0.0	38.6	0.0	689.2	0.2	251.5	0.7	..	..
TFYR Macedonia	5.7	91.0	10.9	62.0	17.7	110.3	37.2	..	..
Thailand	5.0	144.5	12.3	111.3	26.0	51.4	39.4	11.9	44.1
Togo	1.1	85.2	2.0	74.4	3.5	26.1	4.4	..	..
Trinidad & Tobago	12.5	57.5	19.7	41.2	27.8	34.1	37.3	32.9	49.6
Tunisia	1.2	222.9	4.0	45.9	5.9	230.6	19.4	84.8	35.9
Turkey	24.7	15.6	28.6	17.5	33.6	17.5	39.4	21.7	48.0
Turkmenistan	0.2	0.5	0.2	- 0.3	0.2	12.0	0.2	..	..
Uganda	0.6	115.6	1.2	33.9	1.6	90.4	3.0	43.8	4.4
Ukraine	1.6	184.5	4.6	66.7	7.7	77.4	13.7	108.9	28.5
United Arab Emirates	44.0	24.5	54.7	18.2	64.7	13.7	73.6	15.1	84.7
United Kingdom	72.7	6.0	77.0	9.1	84.1	8.4	91.2	12.8	102.8
United States	38.9	15.7	45.0	8.6	48.9	11.7	54.6	11.7	61.0
UR of Tanzania	0.6	130.3	1.3	73.6	2.2	33.7	3.0	47.5	4.4
Uruguay	12.3	25.7	15.5	24.5	19.3	- 20.0	15.4	20.2	18.5
Uzbekistan	0.2	137.9	0.5	44.2	0.7	69.5	1.3	63.7	2.1
Vanuatu	0.2	- 6.6	0.2	1 263.3	2.4	55.0	3.8	28.9	4.8
Venezuela	22.5	16.2	26.2	- 2.1	25.6	6.5	27.3	17.8	32.2
Viet Nam	1.0	56.1	1.5	51.8	2.3	43.9	3.4	78.4	6.0
Yemen	0.2	362.1	0.8	161.7	2.1	64.8	3.5	48.8	5.2
Zambia	1.0	19.2	1.1	11.6	1.3	68.2	2.2	27.9	2.8
Zimbabwe	2.7	5.2	2.9	6.2	3.0	2.2	3.1	0.0	3.1

Source: UNCTAD calculations based on ITU World Telecommunication Indicators Database, 2005.

Table 6. E-business statistics of selected countries/territories, 2004 or latest available year

Percentage of businesses

Country/Territory	Andorra	Argentina[8]	Bulgaria	Chile	Colombia	Hong Kong (China)	Kazakhstan	Macao (China)	Madagascar	Mauritius[9]	Morocco	Philippines	Republic of Korea	Rep. of Moldova	Romania	Russian Federation	Singapore	Thailand	Trinidad & Tobago	Ukraine
Reference year	2004	2003	2003	2003	2001	2004	2004	2003	2004	2002	2004	2002	2003	2003	2003	2003	2003	2004	2003	2003
Businesses using computers	73.1	..	83.5	24.7	16.8	58.4	64.4	33.0	80.2	7.4	100.0	84.8	95.6	10.6	84.2	84.6	83.1	20.6	86.2	100.0
Employees using computers	..	..	16.0	..	30.6	..	..	..	..	7.9	36.0	..	..	9.2	14.3	30.5	..	19.3	..	..
Businesses using the Internet	63.0	68.0	61.8	20.3	8.9	50.4	37.3	64.0	67.0	4.9	90.0	58.6	94.0	51.6	51.4	43.4	75.9	9.0	77.3	28.0
Employees using the Internet	..	..	8.8	..	9.0	..	..	..	..	..	19.0	..	..	..	7.2	7.8	..	8.2	..	..
Businesses with Internet that have a website[1]	76.2	67.7	40.3	42.6	12.0	29.4	16.9	12.5	50.1	24.5	42.2	17.1	41.4	..	35.3	31.0	..	32.2	57.6	..
Businesses with an intranet[2]	..	50.2	44.0	22.7	0.8	..	..	..	57.0	..	33.3	33.1	37.4	..	31.0	..	84.7	..	24.2	..
Businesses receiving orders over the Internet[3]	42.9	..	4.4	5.9	15.3	2.4	30.0	10.9	..	..	4.4	3.4	7.2	..	4.1	24.1	33.7	7.8	21.9	..
Businesses placing orders over the Internet[4]	31.7	..	11.8	8.7	7.7	19.0	29.5	12.5	..	..	15.6	10.8	25.5	..	3.6	27.9	45.5	12.2	42.0	..
Businesses accessing the Internet by modes of access:[5]	..	..		..	..	..	..	..	..	..	..	..	..	..	..	..	..	..	..	..
Analogue modem	27.0	..	56.5	28.9	87.8	16.1	..	19.0	..	..	21.1	..	..	74.5	75.6	68.9	47.0	87.8	71.0	..
ISDN	..	..	11.0	10.2	17.9	..	..	..	..	..	2.9	..	..	..	9.3	..	17.7	4.4	..	..
Fixed line connection under 2 Mbps	71.4	..	4.9	42.4	..	31.9	..	6.0	..	..	76.7	..	..	4.2	4.1	..	..	14.4	..	..
Fixed line connection of 2 Mbps or more	..	..	1.8	76.4		52.4	..	..	..	..	2.2	..	98.0	..	1.7	..	5.8	..	..	..
Other	..	..	See notes	..	See notes	7.5	55.2	75.0	..	..	5.6	..	1.9	..	8.0	31.1	..	3.3	See notes	..
Businesses with a local area network (LAN)	64.6	..	46.3	22.7	..	..	..	..	..	..	76.7	88.4	64.6	18.4	54.9	45.8	84.7	..	..	36.1
Businesses with an extranet[6]	..	15.6	5.5	7.2	0.4	..	..	..	..	..	..	7.8	..	3.7	9.5	15.4	36.1	..	..	..
Businesses using the Internet by type of activity:[7]	..	..		..	..	..	..	..	..	..	..	..	..	..	..	..	..	..	..	..
Internet e-mail	90.0	72.1	..	91.1	79.9	96.2	87.9	65.6	99.6	..	..	..	..	..	..	93.8	..	70.0	97.7	..
Getting information about goods or services	70.0	68.2	..	..	..	93.8	61.7	54.7	..	..	..	..	..	..	61.8	56.6	..	..	..	..

Table 6 (continued)

Country/Territory	Andorra	Argentina[8]	Bulgaria	Chile	Colombia	Hong Kong (China)	Kazakhstan	Macao (China)	Madagascar	Mauritius[9]	Morocco	Philippines	Republic of Korea	Rep. of Moldova	Romania	Russian Federation	Singapore	Thailand	Trinidad & Tobago	Ukraine
Reference year	2004	2003	2003	2003	2001	2004	2004	2003	2004	2002	2004	2002	2003	2003	2003	2003	2003	2004	2003	2003
Getting information from government organizations/public authorities	..	..	59.1	..	..	58.5	..	..	..	..	.	..	..	..	56.1	..	..	..	..	..
Other information searches and research	..	..	..	..	..	..	86.1	..	64.2	..	..	..	..	..	..	..	..	85.6	83.7	..
Internet banking or accessing other financial services	62.0	..	41.7	..	..	34.1	..	..	..	..	..	..	..	..	43.4	..	..	5.6	..	..
Transacting with government organizations/public authorities	25.0	..	61.0	..	..	..	..	9.4	..	..	..	..	..	..	12.6	..	..	..	..	..
Providing customer services	34.0	21.0	..	..	..	17.3	45.0	23.4	..	..	..	..	..	..	..	5.1	..	..	36.2	..
Delivering products online	22.0	..	..	..	..	21.8	92.0	..	..	..	..	..	..	..	..	5.7	..	..	..	..
Other	20.0	..	..	..	..	46.8	..	3.1	16.4	..	..	..	..	..	..	..	..	See notes	See notes	..

Notes:

1 Or web presence where the business has control over the content.

2 Morocco: Intranet is used for administration 12.4 per cent; internal messaging 4.4 per cent; events information 3.3 per cent; production management 3.6 per cent; resource management 2 per cent; sales management 2 per cent; document exchange 2 per cent; human resource management 0.5 per cent; and information management 0.4 per cent.

3 Philippines: Receiving orders is based on proportion of enterprises with on line sales/revenue.

4 Philippines: Placing orders is based on proportion of enterprises with online purchases.

5 Russian Federation: Placing orders over all global information networks, including the Internet.
Bulgaria: Other broadband connection, e.g. cable etc. 25.6 per cent; wireless, e.g. satellite, mobiles, 8.9 per cent.
Hong Kong (China): Fixed line connection is measured at 3Mbps or under and over 3Mbps; other mode of access refers to mobile network.
Macao (China): Fixed line connection was reported indistinctly of speed; other modes of access refers to XDSL.
Republic of Moldova: Fixed line connection was reported irrespective of speed.
Morocco: Other modes of access refer to mobile phone.
Republic of Korea: Fixed line connection of 2Mbps or more includes xDSL, dedicated line and cable modem; no explanation given for other modes of access.
Russian Federation: Other modes of access refer to dedicated communication lines.
Trinidad and Tobago: Other modes of access include leased lines 4.7 per cent; both dial-up and leased lines 4.7 per cent; and wireless 4.7 per cent.

6 Hong Kong (China): Getting information on goods and services other than the Internet.

7 Hong Kong (China): Getting information on goods and services refers to getting information in general; providing customer services includes purchases and sales.
Macao (China): Getting information on goods and services refers to getting information n general; providing customer services refers to after-sales services.
Russian Federation: E-mail refers not only to Internet e-mail; providing customer services refers to after-sales services.
Thailand: Also reported monitoring the market 40 per cent; communication other than e-mail 11.1 per cent; advertising of own goods and services 16.7 per cent; transactions or communications with trading partners 17.8 per cent; other 5.6 per cent.

8 Argentina survey on manufacturing sector only.

9 Mauritius census/survey conducted only in microenterprises (1–9 employees).

Source: UNCTAD e-business database (2005).

Annex II

Distribution of countries

The distribution of countries by regional groups and type of development is based on UNCTAD's distribution of countries as set out in the *UNCTAD Handbook of Statistics, 2004*.

Level of Development / Region	Developed economies	Developing economies	South-East Europe and Commonwealth of Independent States
North America	Canada, USA (includes Puerto Rico and Guam)		
Latin America and the Caribbean, other America		Anguilla, Antigua and Barbuda, Argentina, Aruba, Bahamas, Barbados, Belize, Bolivia, Br. Virgin Isds, Brazil, Cayman Isds, Chile, Colombia, Costa Rica, Cuba, Dominica, Dominican Rep., Ecuador, El Salvador, Falkland Isds (Malvinas), French Guiana, Grenada, Guadeloupe, Guatemala, Guyana, Haiti, Honduras, Jamaica, Martinique, Mexico, Montserrat, Neth. Antilles, Nicaragua, Panama, Paraguay, Peru, Saint Kitts and Nevis, Saint Lucia, Saint Vincent and the Grenadines, Suriname, Trinidad and Tobago, Turks and Caicos Isds, Uruguay, US Virgin Isds, Venezuela	
Africa		Algeria, Angola, Benin, Botswana, Burkina Faso, Burundi, Cameroon, Cape Verde, Central African Rep., Chad, Comoros, Congo, Côte d'Ivoire, Dem. Rep. of the Congo, Djibouti, Egypt, Equatorial Guinea, Eritrea, Ethiopia, Gabon, Gambia, Ghana, Guinea, Guinea-Bissau, Kenya, Lesotho, Liberia, Libyan Arab Jamahiriya, Madagascar, Malawi, Mali, Mauritania, Mauritius, Mayotte, Morocco, Mozambique, Namibia, Niger, Nigeria, Réunion, Rwanda, Saint Helena, Sao Tome and Principe, Senegal, Seychelles, Sierra Leone, Somalia, South Africa, Sudan, Swaziland, Togo, Tunisia, Uganda, United Rep. of Tanzania, Zambia, Zimbabwe	
Asia	Israel, Japan	Afghanistan, Bahrain, Bangladesh, Bhutan, Brunei Darussalam, Cambodia, China, Dem. People's Rep. of Korea, Hong Kong SAR, India, Indonesia, Islamic Rep. of Iran, Iraq, Jordan, Kuwait, Lao People's Dem. Rep., Lebanon, Macao SAR, Malaysia, Maldives, Mongolia, Myanmar, Nepal, Palestinian Territory, Oman, Pakistan, Philippines, Qatar, Rep. of Korea, Saudi Arabia, Singapore, Sri Lanka, Syrian Arab Rep., Thailand, Timor-Leste, Turkey, United Arab Emirates, Viet Nam, Yemen	Armenia, Azerbaijan, Georgia, Kazakhstan, Kyrgyzstan, Tajikistan, Turkmenistan, Uzbekistan
Europe	Andorra, Austria, Belgium, Belgium-Luxembourg, Cyprus, Czech Rep., Denmark, Estonia, Faeroe Isds, Finland, France, Germany, Gibraltar, Greece, Hungary, Iceland, Ireland, Italy, Latvia, Lithuania, Luxembourg, Malta, Netherlands, Norway, Poland, Portugal, Slovakia, Slovenia, Spain, Sweden, Switzerland, United Kingdom		Albania, Belarus, Bosnia and Herzegovina, Bulgaria, Croatia, Rep. of Moldova, Romania, Russian Federation, Serbia and Montenegro, TFYR of Macedonia, Ukraine
Oceania	Australia, New Zealand	Cook Isds, Fiji, French Polynesia, FS Micronesia, Kiribati, Marshall Isds, N. Mariana Isds, Nauru, New Caledonia, Niue, Palau, Papua New Guinea, Samoa, Solomon Isds, Tokelau, Tonga, Tuvalu, Vanuatu, Wallis and Futuna Isds	

Source: UNCTAD Handbook of Statistics, 2004

Annex III

Classification of ICT goods

ICT goods classification, based on HS 1996, proposed by OECD

Telecommunications equipment

851711	Line telephone sets with cordless handsets
851719	Other telephone sets, video phones
851721	Facsimile machines
851722	Teleprinters
851730	Telephonic or telegraphic switching apparatus
851750	Other apparatus, for carrier-current line systems or for digital line systems
851780	Other electrical apparatus for line telephony or line telegraphy
851790	Parts for other electrical apparatus for line telephony or line telegraphy
852020	Telephone answering machines
852510	Transmission apparatus for radiotelephony, radiotelegraphy, radiobroadcasting or television not incorporating reception apparatus
852520	Transmission apparatus for radiotelephony, radiotelegraphy, radiobroadcasting or television incorporating reception apparatus
852530	Television cameras
852610	Radar apparatus
852790	Reception apparatus for radiotelephony, radiotelegraphy or radiobroadcasting, whether or not combined, in the same housing, with sound recording or reproducing apparatus or a clock, n.e.s
852910	Aerials and aerial reflectors of all kinds; parts suitable for use therewith
853110	Burglar or fire alarms and similar apparatus (2)
854420	Co-axial cable and other co-axial electric conductors
854470	Optical fibre cables

Computer and related equipment

847110	Analogue or hybrid automatic data processing machines
847130	Portable digital automatic data processing machines, weighing not more than 10 kg, consisting of at least a central processing unit, a keyboard and a display
847141	Digital automatic data processing machines comprising in the same housing at least a central processing unit and an input and output unit, whether or not combined
847149	Other digital automatic data processing machines, presented in the form of systems
847150	Digital processing units other than those of subheadings 8471.41 and 8471.49, whether or not containing in the same housing one or two of the following types of unit: storage units, input units, output units
847160	Automatic data processing machines, input or output units, whether or not containing storage units in the same housing
847170	Automatic data processing machines, storage units
847180	Other units of automatic data processing machines
847190	Magnetic or optical readers, machines for transcribing data onto data media in coded form and machines for processing such data, not elsewhere specified or included
847330	Parts and accessories of the machines of heading No. 84.71

Electronic components

850431	Electrical transformers having a power handling capacity not exceeding 1 kVA (2)
850450	Inductors (2)
850490	Parts of: electrical transformers, static converters (for example, rectifiers) and inductors (2)
852330	Cards incorporating a magnetic stripe, unrecorded (2)
852460	Cards incorporating a magnetic stripe, recorded (2)
852990	Parts suitable for use solely or principally with the apparatus of headings Nos. 85.25 to 85.28 except aerials and aerials reflectors
853221	Capacitors, fixed, tantalum having a reactive power handling capacity of less than 0.5 kvar
853224	Capacitors, fixed, ceramic dielectric, multilayer having a reactive power handling capacity of less than 0.5 kvar
853230	Variable or adjustable (pre-set) capacitors
853310	Fixed carbon resistors, composition or film types
853321	Electrical resistors, fixed, (including rheostats and potentiometers), other than heating resistors, for a power handling capacity <= 20 W
853329	Electrical resistors, fixed, (including rheostats and potentiometers), other than heating resistors, n.e.s..
853331	Wirewound variable resistors, for a power handling capacity <= 20 W
853339	Wirewound variable resistors, for a power handling capacity <= 20 W
853340	Other variable resistors, including rheostats and potentiometers
853390	Parts for electrical resistors (including rheostats and potentiometers), other than heating resistors
853400	Printed circuits
854011	Cathode-ray television picture tubes, including video monitor tubes, colour
854012	Cathode-ray television picture tubes, including video monitor tubes, black and white or other monochrome
854020	Television camera tubes; image converters and intensifiers; other photo-cathode tubes
854040	Data/graphic display tubes, colour, with a phosphor dot screen pitch smaller than 0.4 mm
854050	Data/graphic display tubes, black and white or other monochrome
854060	Other cathode-ray tubes
854071	Microwave tubes, magnetrons, excluding grid-controlled tubes
854072	Microwave tubes klystrons, excluding grid-controlled tubes
854079	Microwave tubes, other, excluding grid-controlled tubes
854081	Receiver or amplifier valves and tubes
854089	Valve and tubes, n.e.s.
854091	Parts of cathode-ray tubes
854099	Parts of thermionic or photo-cathode, valve and tubes, other than cathode-ray tubes
854110	Diodes, other than photosensitive or light emitting diodes
854121	Transistors, other than photosensitive, dissipation rate < 1 W
854129	Transistors, other than photosensitive transistors, n.e.s.
854130	Thyristors, diacs and triacs, other than photosensitive devices
854140	Photosensitive semiconductor devices, including photovoltaic cells whether or not assembled in modules or made up into panels; light emitting diodes
854150	Other semiconductor devices
854160	Mounted piezo-electric crystals
854190	Parts for semiconductor devices
854212	Cards incorporating electronic integrated circuits ("smart" cards)
854213	Metal oxide semiconductors (MOS technology)
854214	Circuits obtained by bipolar technology
854219	Integrated circuits monolitihic non-digital
854230	Other monolithic integrated circuits
854240	Hybrid integrated circuits
854250	Electronic microassemblies
854290	Parts for electronic integrated circuits and microassemblies

Audio and video equipment

851810	Microphones and stands therefor
851821	Single loudspeakers, mounted in their enclosures
851822	Multiple loudspeakers, mounted in the same enclosure
851829	Other loudspeakers, n.e.s
851830	Headphones and earphones, whether or not combined with a microphone, and sets consisting of a microphone and one or more loudspeakers
851840	Audio-frequency electric amplifiers
851850	Electric sound amplifier sets
851890	Parts of microphones, loudspeakers, headphones, earphones, combined microphone/loudspeaker sets, audio-frequency electric amplifiers and electric sound amplifier sets
851910	Coin- or disc-operated record-players
851921	Record-players, without loudspeaker
851929	Record-players, n.e.s.
851931	Turntables with automatic record changing mechanism
851939	Turntables, n.e.s.
851940	Transcribing machines
851992	Pocket-size cassette-players
851993	Other sound reproducing apparatus, cassette-type
851999	Sound reproducing apparatus, not incorporating a sound recording device, n.e.s.
852010	Dictating machines not capable of operating without an external source of power
852032	Other magnetic tape recorders incorporating sound reproducing apparatus, digital audio type
852033	Other magnetic tape recorders incorporating sound reproducing apparatus, cassette-type
852039	Other magnetic tape recorders incorporating sound reproducing apparatus
852090	Magnetic tape recorders and other sound recording apparatus, whether or not incorporating a sound reproducing device, n.e.s.
852110	Video recording or reproducing apparatus, whether or not incorporating a video tuner magnetic tape type
852190	Video recording or reproducing apparatus, whether or not incorporating a video tuner other type
852210	Parts and accessories suitable for use solely or principally with the apparatus of headings Nos. 85.19 to 85.21 pick-up cartridges
852290	Parts and accessories suitable for use solely or principally with the apparatus of headings Nos. 85.19 to 85.21 other
852311	Magnetic tapes, unrecorded, width <= 4 mm (1/6 in.) (2)
852312	Magnetic tapes, unrecorded, width > 4 mm (1/6 in.) but <= 6.5 mm (1/4 in.) (2)
852313	Magnetic tapes, unrecorded, width > 6.5 mm (1/4 in.) (2)
852320	Magnetic discs, unrecorded (2)
852390	Other prepared unrecorded media for sound recording or similar recording of other phenomena, other than products of Chapter 37
852540	Still image video cameras and other video camera recorders, digital cameras
852712	Pocket-size radio cassette-players capable of operating without an external source of power
852713	Radio-broadcast receivers, capable of operating without an external source of power, combined with sound recording or reproducing apparatus
852719	Other radio-broadcast receivers, capable of operating without an external source of power, not combined with sound recording or reproducing apparatus
852721	Radio-broadcast receivers with sound recording or reproducing apparatus, for motor vehicles, requiring external source of power
852729	Other radio-broadcast receivers for motor vehicles, not combined with sound recording or reproducing apparatus
852731	Other radio-broadcast receivers, including apparatus capable of receiving also radio-telephony or radiotelegraphy, combined with sound recording or reproducing apparatus
852732	Other radio-broadcast receivers, including apparatus capable of receiving also radio-telephony or radiotelegraphy, not combined with sound recording or reproducing apparatus but combined with a clock
852739	Other radio-broadcast receivers, including apparatus capable of receiving radio-telephony or radiotelegraphy, n.e.s.
852812	Reception apparatus for television, whether or not incorporating radio-broadcast receivers or sound or video recording or reproducing apparatus, colour

852813	Reception apparatus for television, whether or not incorporating radio-broadcast receivers or sound or video recording or reproducing apparatus, black and white or other monochrome
852821	Video monitors, colour
852822	Video monitors, black and white or other monochrome
852830	Video projectors

Other ICT goods

846911	Word-processing machines
847010	Electronic calculators capable of operation without an external source of electric power and pocket-size data recording, reproducing and displaying machines with calculating functions
847021	Other electronic calculating machines incorporating a printing device
847029	Other electronic calculating machines
847040	Accounting machines
847050	Cash registers
847310	Parts and accessories (other than covers, carrying cases and the like) suitable for use solely or principally with machines of heading No. 84.69
847321	Parts and accessories of the electronic calculating machines of subheading No. 8470.10, 8470.21 or 8470.29
847350	Parts and accessories equally suitable for use with machines of two or more of the headings Nos. 84.69 to 84.72
852691	Radio navigational aid apparatus
852692	Radio remote control apparatus
901041	Apparatus for the projection or drawing of circuit patterns on sensitised semiconductor materials – direct write-on-wafer apparatus
901042	Apparatus for the projection or drawing of circuit patterns on sensitised semiconductor materials – step and repeat aligners
901049	Apparatus for the projection or drawing of circuit patterns on sensitised semiconductor materials other
901410	Direction finding compasses
901420	Instruments and appliances for aeronautical or space navigation (other than compasses)
901480	Other navigational instruments and appliances
901490	Parts and accessories of direction finding compasses, other navigational instruments and appliances
901540	Photogrammetrical surveying instruments and appliances
901580	Other surveying instruments and appliances
901811	Electro-cardiographs
901812	Ultrasonic scanning apparatus
901813	Magnetic resonance imaging apparatus
901814	Scintigraphic apparatus
901819	Other electro-diagnostic apparatus (including apparatus for functional exploratory examination or for checking physiological parameters)
902212	Computed tomography apparatus
902213	Other apparatus based on the use of X-rays, for dental uses
902214	Other apparatus based on the use of X-rays, for medical, surgical or veterinary uses
902219	Other apparatus based on the use of X-rays, for other uses
902410	Machines and appliances for testing the hardness, strength, compressibility, elasticity or other mechanical properties of materials, metals
902480	Other machines and appliances for testing the hardness, strength, compressibility, elasticity or other mechanical properties of materials
902490	Parts and accessories for machines and appliances for testing the hardness, strength, compressibility, elasticity or other mechanical properties of materials
902620	Instruments and apparatus for measuring or checking the pressure of liquids or gases, excluding instruments and apparatus of heading Nos. 9014, 9015, 9028 or 9032
902710	Instruments and apparatus for physical or chemical analysis, gas or smoke analysis apparatus
902730	Spectrometers, spectrophotometers and spectrographs using optical radiations (UV, visible, IR)
902740	Instruments and apparatus for measuring or checking quantities of heat, sound or light, exposure meters
902750	Other instruments and apparatus using optical radiations (UV, visible, IR)

902780	Other instruments and apparatus for physical or chemical analysis
902810	Gas meters
902820	Liquid meters
902830	Electricity meters
902890	Parts for gas, liquid or electricity supply or production meters, including calibrating meters therefor
902910	Revolution counters, production counters, taximeters, mileometers, pedometers and the like
902920	Speed indicators and tachometers; stroboscopes
902990	Parts and accessories for revolution counters, production counters, taximeters, mileometers, pedometers and the like; speed indicators and tachometers, other than those of heading No. 90.14 or 90.15; stroboscopes
903010	Instruments and apparatus for measuring or detecting ionising radiations
903020	Cathode-ray oscilloscopes and cathode-ray oscillographs
903031	Multimeters without a recording device
903039	Other instruments and apparatus for measuring or checking voltage, current, etc. without a recording device
903040	Other instruments and apparatus, specially designed for telecommunications (for example, cross-talk meters, gain measuring instruments, distortion factor meters, psophometers)
903082	Other instruments for measuring or checking semiconductor wafers or devices
903083	Other instruments for measuring or checking semiconductor wafers or devices with a recording device
903110	Measuring or checking instruments, appliances and machines n.e.s, machines for balancing mechanical parts
903120	Measuring or checking instruments, appliances and machines n.e.s, test benches
903130	Measuring or checking instruments, appliances and machines n.e.s, profile projectors
903141	Other optical instruments and appliances, for inspecting semiconductor wafers or devices or for inspecting photomasks or reticles used in manufacturing semiconductor devices
903180	Other measuring or checking instruments, appliances and machines, n.e.s.
903190	Parts and accessories for measuring or checking instruments, appliances and machines, n.e.s.
903210	Thermostats
903220	Manostats
903289	Other automatic regulating or controlling instruments and apparatus, n.e.s.
903290	Parts and accessories for automatic regulating or controlling instruments and apparatus

Notes

1. Titles are according to the 2002 Harmonized System. Some have been changed slightly in the interests of clarity and space.
2. Industry of origin not in the OECD ICT sector.
3. HS 1996 and HS 2002 codes differ.

Annex IV

Core list of ICT indicators

Agreed at the WSIS Thematic Meeting on Measuring the Information Society (Geneva, 7–9 February 2005)

Core indicators on infrastructure and access

Basic core	
A-1	Fixed telephone lines per 100 inhabitants
A-2	Mobile cellular subscribers per 100 inhabitants
A-3	Computers per 100 inhabitants
A-4	Internet subscribers per 100 inhabitants
A-5	Broadband Internet subscribers per 100 inhabitants
A-6	International Internet bandwidth per inhabitant
A-7	Percentage of population covered by mobile cellular telephony
A-8	Internet access tariffs (20 hours per month), in US$, and as a percentage of per capita income
A-9	Mobile cellular tariffs (100 minutes of use per month), in US$, and as a percentage of per capita income
A-10	Percentage of localities with public Internet access centres (PIACs) by number of inhabitants (rural/urban)
Extended core	
A-11	Radio sets per 100 inhabitants
A-12	Television sets per 100 inhabitants

Core indicators on access and use of ICTs by households and individuals

Basic core	
HH-1	Proportion of households with a radio
HH-2	Proportion of households with a TV
HH-3	Proportion of households with a fixed line telephone
HH-4	Proportion of households with a mobile cellular telephone
HH-5	Proportion of households with a computer
HH-6	Proportion of individuals that used a computer (from any location) in the last 12 months
HH-7	Proportion of households with Internet access at home
HH-8	Proportion of individuals that used the Internet (from any location) in the last 12 months
HH-9	Location of individual use of the Internet in the last 12 months *Response categories:* • At home • At work • Place of education • At another person's home • Community Internet access facility (specific denomination depends on national practices) • Commercial Internet access facility (specific denomination depends on national practices) • Others

HH-10	Internet activities undertaken by individuals in the last 12 months:
	Response categories:
	• Getting information
	❏ About goods or services
	❏ Related to health or health services
	❏ From government organisations/public authorities via websites or e-mail
	❏ Other information or general Web browsing
	• Communicating
	• Purchasing or ordering goods or services
	• Internet banking
	• Formal education or training activities
	• Dealing with government organisations/public authorities
	• Leisure activities
	❏ Playing/downloading video or computer games
	❏ Downloading movies, music or software
	❏ Reading/downloading electronic books, newspapers or magazines
	❏ Other leisure activities

Extended core	
HH-11	Proportion of individuals with use of a mobile telephone
HH-12	Proportion of households with access to the Internet by type of access
	• Response categories should allow an aggregation to narrowband and broadband, where broadband excludes slower speed technologies, such as dial-up modem, ISDN and most 2G mobile phone access. Broadband will usually have an advertised download speed of at least 256 Kbps.
HH-13	Frequency of individual access to the Internet in the last 12 months (from any location)
	Response categories:
	• At least once a day
	• At least once a week but not every day
	• At least once a month but not every week
	• Less than once a month

Reference indicator	
HH-R1	Proportion of households with electricity*

* Electricity is not specifically an ICT commodity, but is an important prerequisite for developing countries to use ICTs therefore it is not included in the core list, but it is a reference indicator, just like the number of households, population, GDP etc.

Core indicators on use of ICTs by businesses

Basic core	
B-1	Proportion of businesses using computers
B-2	Proportion of employees using computers
B-3	Proportion of businesses using the Internet
B-4	Proportion of employees using the Internet
B-5	Proportion of businesses with a web presence
B-6	Proportion of businesses with an intranet
B-7	Proportion of businesses receiving orders over the Internet
B-8	Proportion of businesses placing orders over the Internet

Extended core	
B-9	Proportion of businesses using the Internet by type of access • Response categories should allow an aggregation to narrowband and broadband, where broadband excludes slower speed technologies, such as dial-up modem, Integrated Services Digital Network (ISDN) and most second generation (2G) mobile phone access. Broadband will usually have an advertised download speed of at least 256 kbps.
B-10	Proportion of businesses with a Local Area Network (LAN)
B-11	Proportion of businesses with an extranet

B-12	Proportion of businesses using the Internet by type of activity
	
	Response categories:
	Proportion of businesses using the Internet by type of activity
	• Sending and receiving email
	• Getting information
	    ❏ About goods or services
	    ❏ From government organisations/public authorities via websites or email
	    ❏ Other information searches or research activities
	• Performing Internet banking or accessing other financial services
	• Dealing (interacting) with government organisations/public authorities
	• Providing customer services
	• Delivering products online

Core indicators on the ICT sector and trade in ICT goods

ICT sector and trade basic core	
ICT-1	Proportion of total business sector workforce involved in the ICT sector
ICT-2	Value added in the ICT sector (as a percentage of total business sector value added)
ICT-3	ICT goods imports as percentage of total imports
ICT-4	ICT goods exports as percentage of total exports

References

Departamento Administrativo Nacional de Estadística (DANE) (2003). *Modelo de la medición de las tecnologías de la información y las comunicaciones –TIC, Resumen ejecutivo*, http://www.dane.gov.co/inf_est/tics/Diciembre2003/resumen_ ejecutivo.pdf.

European Commission (2005). eEurope 2005 Action Plan.

Eurostat (2005). *Statistics in focus : Industry, trade and services - population and social conditions - science and technology*, 18/2005.

Infocomm Development Authority of Singapore (IDA) (2001). *Summary of findings and follow-up to industry consultation: A framework on building trust and confidence in electronic commerce*, http://www.ida.gov.sg/idaweb/doc/download/I888/ Rel_of_findg_Trust_&_Confidence_in_EC_(final).pdf.

Infocomm Development Authority of Singapore (IDA) (2002a). *Survey on Broadband and Wireless Usage in Singapore 2002, Summary Report*, http://www.ida.gov.sg/idaweb/doc/download/I2389/Survey_on_BB_and_wireless_usage_in_ Spore_2002.pdf.

Infocomm Development Authority of Singapore (IDA) (2002b). *Survey on Infocomm Literacy for 2002, Executive Summary*, http:/ /www.ida.gov.sg/idaweb/doc/download/I2533/Survey_on_InfocommLiteracy_for_2002.pdf.

Infocomm Development Authority of Singapore (IDA) (2003a). *Annual Survey on Infocomm Manpower for 2003, Executive Summary*, http://www.ida.gov.sg/idaweb/doc/download/I3015/2003_MPExecSummaryFinalv1_1.pdf.

Infocomm Development Authority of Singapore (IDA) (2003b). *Annual Survey on Infocomm Usage in Businesses for 2003, Executive Summary*, http://www.ida.gov.sg/idaweb/doc/download/I3018/Annual_Survey_on_Infocomm_Usage_in_ Businesses_for_2003_Executive_Summary_.pdf.

Infocomm Development Authority of Singapore (IDA) (2003c). *Singapore: A snapshot of the Infocomm sector*, http:// www.ida.gov.sg/idaweb/doc/download/I2235/Snapshot.pdf.

ITU (2001). *The e city: Singapore Internet case study*, http://www.itu.int/ITU-D/ict/cs/singapore/material/Singapore.pdf.

ITU (2003). *World Telecommunications Development Report*.

ITU (2004). *The fifth pillar: Republic of Mauritius ICT case study*, http://www.itu.int/ITU-D/ict/cs/mauritius/material/ CS_MUS.pdf.

Ministry of Public Administration and Information of Trinidad and Tobago (2003a). *National ICT Benchmarking Study: Trinidad and Tobago versus Selected Comparator Countries*, http://www.nict.gov.tt/downloads/ National_ICT_Benchmarking_Study-Full_Report.pdf.

Ministry of Public Administration and Information of Trinidad and Tobago (2003b). *National ICT Strategy Development: Draft E-readiness Assessment Examining Trinidad and Tobago's Current State of ICT Development*, http://www.nict.gov.tt/downloads/National_e-Readiness_Assessment-FullReport.pdf.

National Computer Board of Mauritius (2001). *ICT Usage Survey 2001: A survey on the ICT adoption of businesses in Mauritius*, http://ncb.intnet.mu/ncb/downloads/Downloads/Reports%20and%20surveys/ ictusagesurvey2001.pdf.

National Computer Board of Mauritius (2002). *Information and Communications Technology (ICT) Outlook: ICT Indicators For Mauritius*. Request for proposal for assessment (tender), http://ncb.intnet.mu/ncb/ downloads/Downloads/Reports%20and%20surveys/ICT%20Outlook2002.pdf.

OECD (2004). *Information Technology Outlook*, 2004.

OECD (2005). *Methodologies and Model Questions: Business Core ICT Use Indicators*. Paper presented at the WSIS Thematic Meeting held from 7 to 9 February 2005 in Geneva.

Partnership on Measuring ICT for Development (2005a). Core ICT indicators.

Partnership on Measuring ICT for Development (2005b). Measuring ICT: the global status of ICT indicators.

Sridhar KS and V Sridhar (2004). Telecommunications infrastructure and economic growth: Evidence from developing countries. Working paper, National Institute of Public Finance and Policy, New Delhi.

Torero M, S Chowdhury and V Galdo (2002). Telecommunications infrastructure and economic growth: A cross-country analysis. Mimeo.

UNCTAD (2003a). Information society measurements: The case of e-business. Background paper for Expert Meeting on Measuring Electronic Commerce as an Instrument for the Development of the Digital Economy, Geneva, 8–10 September 2003.

UNCTAD (2002), *E-Commerce and Development Report 2002*.

UNCTAD (2003b), *E-Commerce and Development Report 2003*.

UNCTAD (2004), *E-Commerce and Development Report 2004*.

UNCTAD (2005). Stocktaking of ICT business indicators. Paper prepared for the WSIS Thematic Meeting on Measuring the Information Society, Geneva, 7–9 February 2005.

Waverman L, Meschi M and M Fuss (2005). The impact of telecoms on economic growth in developing countries, in Vodaphone Policy Paper Series, Number 2, March 2005, pp. 10–23, http://www.vodafone.com/assets/files/en/GPP%20SIM%20paper.pdf.

World Bank (2005). *Financing Information and Communication Infrastructure Needs in the Developing World: Public and Private Roles*, draft prepared for the WSIS Task Force on Financing ICT, February 2005.

World Trade Organization (2004). *International Trade Statistics 2004*.

Notes

1. According to the ITU definition, broadband refers to connections with a speed of at least 256 Kbps covering both fixed and wireless access. See http://www.itu.int/ITU-D/ict/material/Top50_e-WTIM-2005-8June.doc

2. Shipment data generally include laptops. However, they do not include mobile devices.

3. There are some comparability issues related to the reporting of mobile subscribers. These arise primarily from the fact that in some countries, inactive prepaid subscribers or prepaid double subscribers are included. This may occur in countries with a relatively large number of prepaid subscribers (mainly in Asia).

4. Shyam Telecom as reported at http://news.bbc.co.uk/2/hi/technology/3256516.stm.

5. See chapter 7 of UNCTAD (2004).

6. *Economist,* The real digital divide, 12 March 2005. The article describes Coca-Cola vendors in a market in Zambia being paid by mobile phone.

7. In 2004, 23 countries were surveyed, and this resulted in limited comparable data for 10 countries. In 2005, 39 countries were surveyed, the survey resulting in limited comparable data for 19 countries.

8. Broadband refers to speeds equal to, or greater than, 256 Kbps. ADSL broadband will carry over 512 Kbps, while SDSL can carry from 256 Kbps to 2 Mbps. ISDN can carry up to 128 Kbps (two high-speed lines capable of running at 64 Kbps each), which can be sufficient for most home users and small enterprises. For comparison, a standard analog modem's speed is 56 Kbps.

9. For a definition of e-commerce, see OECD (2004).

10. This information is available in the website of the US Bureau of Census. See http://www.census.gov/eos/www/ebusiness614.htm.

11. This information is available in the website of Statistics Canada. See http://www.statcan.ca/Daily/English/050420/d050420b.htm.

12. Data available only for Denmark, Germany, Greece, Spain, Italy, Luxembourg, Portugal, Finland, the United Kingdom and Norway as at 16 June 2005. See http://epp.eurostat.cec.eu.int/.

13. Singapore and Trinidad and Tobago data are from 2003. Colombia data are from 2001.

14. Full electronic case handling: public service dealt with entirely via the website, including decision and delivery.

15. An intranet is a network using the same protocol as the Internet and allowing communication within an organization. It is typically set up behind a firewall to control access.

16. An extranet is a private, secure extension of the intranet running on Internet protocol that allows external users to access some parts of an organization's intranet.

17. A draft classification of trade in ICT services is currently under discussion in the OECD Working Party on Indicators for the Information Society (WPIIS). For further information, see OECD (2004).

18. In 2003, exports of ICT goods amounted to $1126 billion, while exports of agriculture ($674 billion), textiles ($169 billion) and clothing ($226 billion) amounted to $1069 billion (WTO, 2004).

19. It is worth noting that the above figures are based on current prices and, as ICT goods have experienced declining prices, do not fully reflect the changes in terms-of-trade volume.

20. Both Malaysia and Singapore experienced in 2001 a fall in their level of ICT goods exports and, while during 2002 and 2003 exports of ICT goods grew again, they have not reached their 2000 levels.

21. A detailed description of these indicators and their calculation is provided in chapter nine of the *E-Commerce and Development Report 2002* (UNCTAD, 2002). The revealed comparative advantage (RCA) index, defined as a country's share of world exports of ICT goods divided by its share of total world trade, measures the relative export performance of a country in the ICT manufacturing industry. Countries with RCA indices above one and positive RCA growth rates are

those most competitive in exporting ICT goods. On the other hand, the study of the world market shares in ICT goods of individual countries over time highlights which are the countries that are gaining ground in the international ICT market. As in the case of the RCA index, a WMS index above one and a positive WMS growth rate shows that a country is expanding its market share in the global ICT goods market.

22.   Data cover only the 15 LDCs that reported their exports of ICT goods for 2003.

23.   Data cover only the 18 LDCs that reported their imports of ICT goods for 2003.

24.   A detailed list of the ICT goods covered under each category is provided in annex III.

25.   A number of regional meetings on ICT statistics were held in the second part of 2004 for Western Asia (Beirut, October 2004), Africa (Gaborone, October 2004), and Latin America and the Caribbean (Santiago, November 2004). There was also an ICT statistics meeting in Wellington, New Zealand (December 2004) for some of the Asia-Pacific countries. Each of these meetings resulted in a regional core list of ICT indicators. These lists, together with the results of the stocktaking inventory and the experience of the Partners working with NSOs in both developed and developing countries, were used as an input into the finalization of an initial core list of ICT indicators.

26.   The model surveys can be downloaded from the OECD website on "Measuring the Information Economy" at http:// www.oecd.org/document/22/0,2340,en_2649_34449_34508886_1_1_1_1,00.html.

27.   Within the framework of the Partnership on "Measuring ICT for Development", a global stocktaking exercise was carried out to measure the availability of official information society statistics. In July 2004, a metadata questionnaire on ICT statistics was sent by ECA, ECLAC, ESCAP, ESCWA and UNCTAD/ECE to NSOs of all developing countries and a number of Central and Eastern European countries. The questionnaire aimed to provide an overview of the types of surveys that NSOs have in place to collect data and statistics on ICTs and the actual indicators collected. It consisted of four sections covering general aspects of ICT statistics and surveys, household statistics, business statistics and other areas of ICT statistics. In the business statistics section, NSOs were asked to respond to questions about which indicators they already collect, which they are planning to collect in the next year or three years and those which they do not plan to collect at this stage. They were also asked to indicate the type of collections used to gather this information and the level of demand for ICT business indicators in their countries.

28.   For a complete presentation of the results, see UNCTAD (2005).

29.   While the stocktaking survey was carried out only in non-OECD countries, OECD members, in a separate exercise, were asked to provide information on the list of 20 household and business indicators.

30.   For further information on WPIIS, see http://www.oecd.org/document/22/0,2340,en_2649_37441_34508886_1_1_1_37441,00.html.

31.   See http://www.fastforward.tt, http://vision2020.info.tt/about/, and http://nict.gov.tt/.

32.   The survey also fed into an e-Readiness Assessment (Ministry of Public Administration and Informatio of Trinidad and Tobago, 2003b) that was an integral part of Trinidad & Tobago's National ICT Strategy development.

33.   2003 National Survey of E-Commerce Usage and Awareness among Businesses.

34.   The corresponding International Standard Industrial Classification (ISIC) tabulation category is H (Hotels and Restaurants).

35.   See http://nict.gov.tt/plan/documents/Chapter_Four.pdf.

36.   Its 1998 E-Commerce Master Plan had a target of 50 per cent of businesses conducting e-commerce by the year 2003 (ITU, 2001). IDA reported achieving 42 per cent (IDA, 2003b).

37.   Singapore has a decentralized statistical system, and official statistics are collected and compiled by the DOS as well as by other research and statistical units, government departments and statutory boards.

38.   The "Collaborative High-Tech Manufacturing Plan" was launched in 2004. See http://www.ida.gov.sg/idaweb/ ebusiness/infopage.jsp?infopagecategory=&infopageid=I2852&versionid=1.

39.   A consultation sought feedback from the industry and public as to the level of trust in e-commerce in order to raise the level of such activities. See IDA (2001).

40.   Singapore also periodically collects more in-depth information on ICT "manpower", i.e. employees that work with ICTs, by occupational groups and by sector (ICT-related or end-user), and ICT literacy or savvy among the workforce. See http://www.ida.gov.sg/idaweb/manpower/ and IDA (2002b, 2003a).

41.   See http://www.e-cybercity.mu/bpml.asp. See also the ITU case study on Mauritius (ITU, 2004).

42.   "L'Etat mènera le progrès des Tics", article in the *Express* newspaper of Mauritius, 5 April 2005, http://www.lexpress.mu/display_search_result.php?news_id=39181.

43.   The tender background document includes a detailed description of the comprehensive set of indicators to be collected and their rationale.

44.   See http://www.agenda.gov.co/.

45.   http://www.agenda.gov.co/documents/files/ComparativoIndices.PDF.

46.   Presentation by Colombia's Minister of Communications, April 2005, available at http://www.agenda.gov.co/.

Chapter 2

INTERNATIONAL INTERNET BACKBONE CONNECTIVITY: ISSUES FOR DEVELOPING COUNTRIES

A. Introduction

Are Internet users in developing countries subsidizing users in the industrialized world? If so, is this the result of unfair, anti-competitive practices? Could this be making Internet access less affordable for developing countries than it needs to be? Is there any practical way to redress such a situation? These are some of the questions that arise from the criticisms being made of current arrangements for the access of developing countries to the services of major international Internet backbone providers.

When international telecommunications were largely a matter of interconnection of national telephony networks, developing countries were net recipients of financial flows as a result of the operation of the mechanisms that historically have regulated international telephony in the framework of the ITU (the so-called accounting rate system). The evolution of telecommunications technology, and profound changes in the organization of the global telecommunications industry, put these mechanisms under severe pressure as more and more traffic flows outside the accounting rate system (using the Internet) or is re-routed to take advantage of lower-cost routes that are not necessarily the most direct ones.

The largely unregulated Internet international connectivity arrangements in place between global Internet backbone providers and lower-tier developing country providers represent a radical departure from the traditional telecom model in which the general principle applied to international interconnection was that the operators shared the costs of calls terminated in each other's networks. In the case of Internet backbone connectivity, the arrangements between the concerned parties can theoretically take different forms, which will be described later in this chapter, but in practice the most frequent case is the one in which the operator in the developing country pays the full cost of the connection between its network and that of the backbone service provider, regardless of the fact that the connection is actually used to carry traffic in both directions.

Criticism of these arrangements has been heard in a number of international forums, most recently in the context of the World Summit on the Information Society, or during the cycle of regional conferences on ICT, competitiveness and development organized by UNCTAD in 2002–2003.[1] Critics among developing countries' Governments and civil society entities have argued that the resulting payments may be draining scarce resources away from developing countries, raising costs to local Internet users and hindering the emergence of information societies in the developing world. Critics consider them to be inequitable and to result sometimes from anti-competitive practices. Some claim that the arrangements amount to a reverse subsidy that is being paid by developing country Internet service providers (ISPs) to international backbone service providers and to their customers in developed countries, who benefit from cost-free access to the networks of developing countries.[2]

While a return to traditional, regulated compensation mechanisms is not generally considered to be a viable option, there are doubts about the possibility of a laissez-faire attitude resulting in a satisfactory solution to the perceived inequities of the system. Because of the impact that international backbone connectivity costs are claimed to have on overall Internet connectivity costs in some developing countries, and hence on the access of their population to the Internet, the question of the need for alternative arrangements has featured among those proposed for inclusion in the global Internet governance agenda.

The purpose of this chapter is to look into the effects of the arrangements under which ISPs in developing countries have access to the Internet backbone, including the effects of conditions that are determined at the domestic level, with the focus on their consequences for the affordability of Internet access for businesses and households, and to explore the options that are available to counter any negative effects that may be identified. In order to do so, the chapter will first briefly describe the economic foundations of the various modes of operation of the market for Internet backbone interconnection, and the aspects in respect of which they may be different from traditional telecommunications markets. This will be followed by an account of recent developments in the global markets for bandwidth and interconnection services, with a particular focus on the availability of backbone connectivity in the developing regions of the world, the extent to which connectivity is being provided under competitive conditions, and the way in which this has affected the cost of connecting to the global backbone for lower-tier operators from developing countries. There then follows a presentation of the international debate about the imbalances and inequities that are said to prevail in the international arrangements for Internet traffic exchange between the developed world and developing countries, and possible remedies that could be identified. The chapter ends with the presentation of a number of policy options and proposals that may be envisaged both at the domestic and international levels in order to reduce the costs that the ISPs of developing countries face in accessing international backbone as well as the overall cost of Internet use in those countries.

B.   Economic aspects of backbone connectivity

1.   The Internet backbones

The Internet can be defined, with some simplification, as an open, worldwide network that interconnects computer networks using a number of standardized protocols in order to allow the exchange of data among them. There are fundamental differences between the Internet and older global telecommunications networks, some of which are more than a hundred years old; such differences play an important role in making the conditions of competition in Internet services significantly different from those in telephony. The first one relates to the different functions that protocols and infrastructure perform in the Internet and in telephony networks. While the Internet protocols are what constitute the essence of the Internet and have enabled its emergence and explosive growth (see chart 2.1, which shows how the number of Internet hosts grew from slightly over 4.8

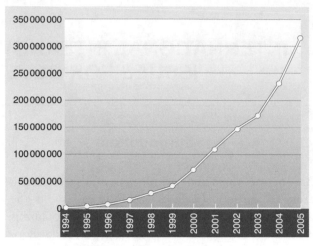

Chart 2.1

Number of hosts advertised in the DNS

Source: Internet Systems Consortium (2005).

million to more than 317.million in the last decade),[3] the hardware of the Internet, the physical networks of cables and the computers they interconnect, are not conceptually different from those that existed prior to the emergence of the Internet.

The second differentiating factor to keep in mind when comparing the Internet with older telecommunications networks is the fact that in the Internet the intelligence lies at the periphery of the network and the core is relatively dumb – and thus subject to a trend of commoditization and declining prices – whereas in telephony networks the opposite is true.

Several explanations have been proposed for the fact that structural differences between telephony and the Internet can translate into differences in the financial arrangements of interconnection (see box 2.1). These explanations refer to aspects such as the following: the different role that networks play in the determination of the service provided – in telephony the network determines the services provided, while in the Internet these are determined by the end systems and remain transparent to the network; the different transactional units ("call minutes" and "data packets") that are not comparable because the requirements they impose on the network are rather different; the different network reliability requirements; and the fact that while network paths in transmissions are not necessarily symmetrical in the Internet, they must be so in telephony.[4]

In order to connect to the Internet any computer must be part of a network. In the most basic example, a private user connecting from home or a small busi-

Box 2.1

A comparison between settlement mechanisms
in telephony and Internet services

Traditional telephony networks are based on the switched-circuit model. In this model a single channel (circuit) connects the two ends of the communication and is reserved for the transmission of the message for the whole duration of the transmission. No other traffic can use that particular circuit while the communication takes place and the message is exchanged intact over the dedicated circuit. This contrasts with the packet-switched approach used by the Internet, in which the information to be communicated is broken up into smaller "packets" that may travel to their destination using different routes over the most efficient circuits available at any point during the transmission.

Historically, the framework for the relations between telephone operators of different countries – which typically were State-owned monopolies – was based on agreed accounting rates to be charged for carrying one minute of international voice traffic from the originating network to the destination network. In theory, accounting rates were fixed at levels that covered the total cost of carrying the voice traffic from one end of the call to the other. Operators shared the costs by paying each other a share of the accounting rate (normally 50 per cent) for the termination of the call on the other operator's network. At the end of the agreed period the operators settled their accounts and the operator with a net inflow of traffic received an amount equal to the agreed accounting share multiplied by the net incoming minutes of traffic.[1] Because of traffic patterns, in the case of links between developed and developing countries the receiving operator normally tended to be the one from the developing country. In 1998, the ITU agreed on three new procedures for remunerating the party that terminates international traffic. These were "termination charge procedure" – the operator that terminates a call can make a single charge for this, under agreed conditions; the "settlement rate procedure" – using negotiated cost-oriented and asymmetrical settlement rates; and the "commercial arrangement", which in countries that have liberalized telephony services allows operators to agree bilaterally on the remuneration regime that is best suited to their requirements.

The logic that underpins the settlement system outlined above is not as different from the one operating in the compensation systems in place for Internet interconnection as it is often said to be. In general, both respond to the volume of traffic that one network passes on to another, although in the case of telephony traffic volume is measured in minutes and in the case of the Internet the unit of measure is megabytes of data. In both cases, if traffic flows more or less equally in both directions, the net financial exchange tends to be zero, either by virtue of peering agreements or through net payments made.

The divergences between the two systems appear in the treatment of the relationship between two dissimilar networks or in the case that traffic flows are asymmetrical. In this case, in the telephony system, financial flows follow the same direction as the net traffic flows: the network originating most of the calls pays a fee to the network that terminates the calls. In the case of the Internet, the net flow of payments tends to go in the opposite direction to the net traffic flow. Smaller ISPs with less traffic pay larger ISPs with more traffic (customers) for the right to send their traffic through the larger network (transit). As a result, while traditionally the international telephony regime has resulted in financial flows going from developed countries to less developed ones, (in large part because developed countries make more calls to poorer ones than viceversa), in the case of the Internet, the financial flow is reversed: ISPs from developing countries tend to make net financial payments to NSPs, which are generally headquartered in developed countries.

---

[1] See a description of the accounting rate system at ww.itu.int/osg/spu/intset/whatare/howwork.html.

ness must use a modem and a telephone line to dial up to an ISP, which can be either a commercial operator or a government, research or educational institution. The user may also connect to the ISP using any of a variety of broadband technologies (DSL, cable, wireless) that are increasingly being adopted in most developed and some developing countries, as indicated by the data provided in chapter 1 of this Report. In any case, regardless of the technology used for the connection, the previously isolated domestic computer becomes, for the duration of the connection, part of the ISP's network. Many business users access the Internet from the local area networks of their enterprises, but in most cases they will still need to connect to the Internet through an ISP. If the ISP itself is not a large operator, it may aggregate traffic from its cus-

tomers and buy direct Internet access to a larger ISP, often a telecommunications operator. In either case, routers and switches owned by the ISP will direct the data packets (the traffic) it receives from its customers to a local Point of Presence (PoP).[5] Through these PoPs, traffic is passed on to high-speed hubs, which are in turn connected to other hubs at considerable distances using high-speed circuits that are generally owned by major telecommunications operators.[6] These hubs and the long-haul, high-speed circuits that connect them constitute an "Internet backbone network". Internet backbone networks connect to each other into the global Internet.

Thus, a hierarchy of tiered networks emerges: tier 1 consists of very large network service providers

Chart 2.2

Three tiers of network/Internet service providers

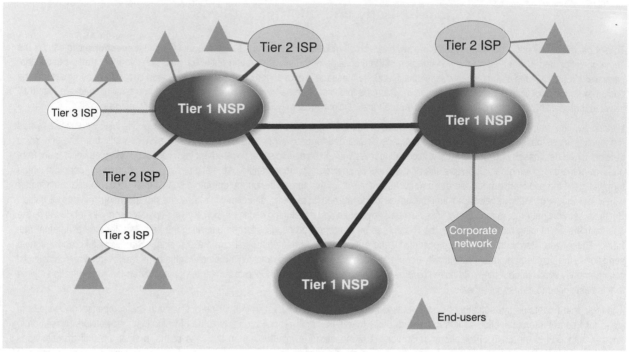

(NSPs) that own their own fibre optic or satellite links across nations and around the world, for example those of companies such as AT&T, Cable & Wireless and BT. Many operate also as ISPs, selling services to final users; others focus exclusively on the wholesale market, selling bandwidth to tier 2 and tier 3 providers. Tier 1 providers can also be defined as ISPs that have access to the global Internet routing table but do not purchase transit from anyone.[7] Tier 2 ISPs buy capacity from tier 1 providers for resale. They have networks with a more limited geographical coverage (there are some 100 in the United States, for example) and they have to rely on tier 1 NSPs to carry their traffic outside their region. However, they own their own PoPs and backbone nodes. The customers of tier 2 ISPs tend to be final users (businesses and households), but also include tier 3 operators. Tier 3 consists of the small ISPs, providing services exclusively to end users and usually active within a small geographical area. They must connect to either tier 2 or tier 1 providers in order to access the Internet through the latter's backbones; they may also have to lease their PoP facilities. Chart 2.2 provides a graphic representation of this model.

During the earliest phases of the development of the Internet there was a single Internet backbone network, the ARPANET (Advanced Research Projects

Agency Network of the Department of Defense of the United States), which originally (1969) consisted of four nodes, all located in the continental territory of the United States. In 1989 the NSFNet (National Science Foundation Network) backbone was established and ARPANET ceased to operate. By mid-1995, as the Internet began its phase of explosive growth and globalization, a new architecture replaced the NSFNet and commercial networks, interconnected at network access points (NAPs) and later at Internet exchange points (IXPs), emerged as the providers of backbone services for the global Internet.[8] To a large extent, the fast rate of growth of the Internet was made possible by the inherent characteristics of the Transmission Control Protocol/Internet Protocol (TCP/IP) as a public domain standard: its cross-compatibility and the protection against obsolescence that openness provides. This facilitated investment in Internet technologies and the growth of the network. The public domain nature of TCP/IP, as will be explained later, also constitutes an important consideration in securing lower barriers of access in Internet interconnection services as opposed to other telecommunications technologies.

The meaning of the term "Internet backbone" has changed significantly since the time when ARPANET and NSFNet were created. These networks were true

Table 2.1

Largest NSPs by number of autonomous Systems Connections (2004 and 2000)

Provider	Rank 2004	Number of autonomous systems connections 2004	Rank 2000	Number of AS connections 2000	% change in AS connections
MCI	1	3 034	1	2 242	35
AT&T	2	1 966	4	695	183
Sprint	3	1 842	3	1 036	78
Level 3	4	1 167	5	658	77
Qwest	35	1 074	6	418	157
Intermap	6	668	11	211	217
Savvis	7	664	12	210	216
NTT	8	636	8	379	68
Global Crossing	9	616	10	217	184
AboveNet	10	590	13	207	185

Source: Analysys Consulting Limited (2005), quoting Telegeography Research Global Internet Geography 2004.

backbone networks in the sense that they connected all the elements of the Internet as it existed then. Today the term "Internet backbone" has taken a different meaning and is generally used to designate, in a rather general way, the core physical infrastructure that carries IP traffic. In this regard, it is important to stress that the Border Gateway Protocol (BGP), a major Internet protocol that is used for routing traffic, ensures that the Internet operates without the need for any single "central" network. Over 300 operators provided commercial backbone services as of the end of 2004 and the broader network services industry sales are estimated at about $1.3 trillion worldwide.[9, 10] The failure, or even the disappearance of any of these backbone networks, would therefore have no significant impact on the overall functioning of the global Internet. Of course, backbone networks offer a widely varying level of capacity and geographical coverage, and consequently their market shares vary considerably, with a process of consolidation taking place in the industry among operators of all three tiers. Of the 300 backbone networks mentioned before, the top 50 carry nearly 95 per cent of all IP traffic, and only five of them can be considered to have a truly global presence.[11, 12] AT&T Corp. (currently in the process of a merger with SBC Communications Inc.), MCI Inc. (which has a merger agreement with Verizon Communications Inc.) and Sprint Corp. (which announced a merger agreement with Nextel Communications Inc. in December 2004) own the three most-connected backbone networks (based on autonomous system connectivity).[13, 14] Table 2.1

lists the largest NSPs ranked by number of connected autonomous systems in 2004 and 2000.

The predominance of operators headquartered in the United States (all of them except NTT) is clear, in spite of the growing decentralization of the Internet. Another notable feature of the ranking is its stability between 2000 and 2004. Only three providers that were among the top ten in 2000 do not show up in the 2004 ranking. Of the top ten in 2004 only half are traditional telecommunications operators. Finally, the top five providers have significantly more connections than the others, but their growth is slower. This could indicate that as smaller ISPs increasingly establish peering interconnections among themselves, their need to obtain transit from major backbone providers decreases.

Chart 2.3 shows how different backbones interconnect at IXPs.

For ISPs to be able to provide their end users with the service they demand – the possibility of sending traffic to and receiving traffic from, any other computer connected to the Internet – they need to ensure that they can exchange traffic with other ISPs. This exchange happens at so-called peering points. Networks can interconnect in several ways: (a) through private bilateral interconnection; (b) through a public NAP or IXP; or (c) peering in a customer–provider relationship. In any event, peering will require three elements: the facility where the physical connection

Chart 2.3

Three tiers of network/Internet service providers

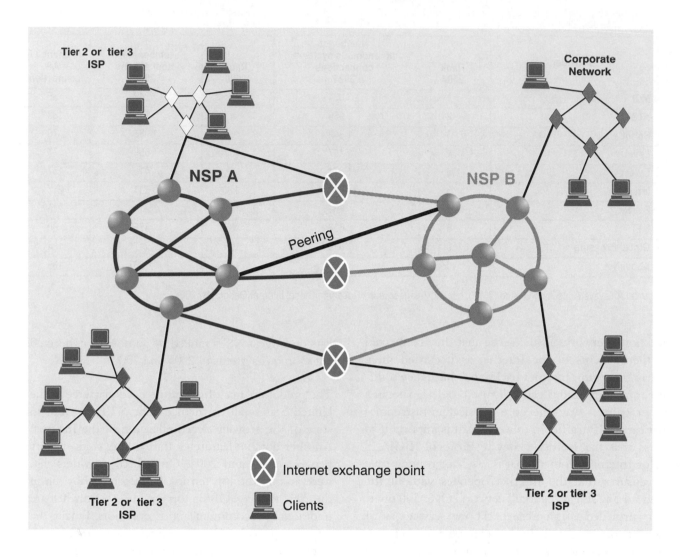

between the networks takes place, the technical linkage between the networks to allow for the routing of traffic and the contractual (commercial or otherwise) arrangements that regulate how traffic is going to be exchanged among the networks.

Tier 1 providers tend to peer among themselves without charging each other (on the basis that traffic flows roughly equally from and into each network), in "bill and keep" agreements. Since these providers tend to charge for peering with smaller ISPs, the latter tend to converge into IXPs, which allow them to exchange traffic in a more balanced way. An IXP is a facility that several ISPs can jointly own and run in order to exchange traffic between their networks using peering agreements and thus reduce their dependence on higher-tier providers. IXPs also improve quality of

service, notably through significant reductions in network latency.[16] As for the customer–provider relationship, which is more prevalent in the lower tiers, it cannot be considered a proper peering relationship (participants are not equals), as the customer is paying for his traffic to transit through his upstream ISP.

Interconnection at IXPs is governed by bilateral agreements between the parties involved. The negotiation of such agreements is sometimes facilitated by the publishing of a set of rules and standards adopted by the IXP itself.[17] In other cases the IXP does not impose any conditions or norms on the contracts made by third-party networks using it. As mentioned above, some contracts do not require financial payments between the networks exchanging traffic; in this case, the payment takes place in kind (by mutually accepting traffic from the other network), and this is what some consider to be "true peering".[18] Other arrangements require financial payments in exchange for connectivity, a mode of relationship between networks called "transit".

The choice between peering and transit as an interconnection modality is a commercial one.[19] Peering will be chosen if both participating networks expect to see their cost equally affected as a result of the traffic flowing between them. The determining factor in the decision to peer or to transit is the impact on cost, and not the relative size or traffic volumes of each of the participating networks. Two networks very dissimilar in terms of size may generate symmetrical traffic flows provided that their respective customers (ISPs or end customers) are similar.[20] However, similarity between the networks is not sufficient to ensure that peering will take place. Even if traffic volumes are symmetrical, one network may incur higher costs than the other per unit of traffic carried – mainly for geographical reasons – and may therefore refuse to peer with the lower-cost network. Under these circumstances, whether the exchange of traffic between networks takes place on a barter basis (peering) or a monetary one (transit) does not provide an indication of the intensity or otherwise of competition prevailing among networks, but merely of the similarity or disparity between the cost structures of the various players. It cannot be ruled out therefore that the refusal to enter into peering agreements, rather than being an anti-competitive practice, may represent a legitimate commercial choice in view of the differences between the proposed participants.

Beltrán (2004) includes an interesting study of the forces at play in the case of the interconnection agreements in IXPs in several Latin American countries. The author finds that in that region interconnection at IXPs takes place almost exclusively on a peering base, even though participating ISPs can be rather dissimilar by any conventional measure, which would be contrary to the literature, which generally considers these to be the requirements for peering.[21] Although these peering agreements between large and small ISPs tend to be limited to the exchange of national traffic and do not necessarily include international traffic, the study finds that such arrangements may render the IXPs unstable.

Another important factor in the peering versus transit decision-making process is the history of the relationship between the networks. Norton (2002) examines the experience of a large number of ISPs and con-

cludes that even in circumstances that, according to the consensus of the literature, should not lead to a peering agreement, this has been possible. He distinguishes 19 "honest" and "less honest or not honest at all" tactics that ISPs can adopt and observes that peering decisions are heavily influenced by an ISP's record of peering/transit decisions: it is nearly impossible to transform a transit relationship into a peering one.

3. Competition

Because of the technological environment in which backbone providers operate, low barriers to access and cheap expansion of supply capacity can be safely assumed.[22] Customers of NSPs rarely have to settle for exclusive or long-term deals. When ISPs buy the amounts of bandwidth that they need in order to connect to the global Internet (through transit agreements as described above), available information about the prices for ranges of bandwidth capacity points to a healthy level of competition among NSPs.[23] For example, Economides (2004b) includes a comparison of the prices charged by AT&T and UUNET for various bandwidth capacities in early 1999, showing them to be identical for all of them except in the range of burstable 21.01-45 Mbps, where the difference was less than 1 per cent. When bandwidth demand fell behind the expectations generated during the years of the Internet boom and the concurrent growth in bandwidth available from backbone providers, prices started on a downward spiral. Another indication can be seen in Giovannetti et al. (2004). They looked at the prices posted by six major transit providers between July 2003 and July 2004 in the London-based X-Band online bandwidth market,[24] and found that both the highest and the lowest prices had fallen by about a third, that prices had consistently declined during the observation period and that all providers follow the general trend and respond to price falls. They conclude that the scenario corresponds to that of a competitive market.

In developed markets lock-in effects are rare and ISPs can change providers in response to price stimuli without having to bear significant switching costs. The situation is less clear in the case of developing countries, and the theoretical possibility of market failure exists, particularly in the case of regions with very limited physical availability of alternative backbones, such as some landlocked countries in Africa and Asia, or some small island developing States. However, the existence of significant spare capacity and the emergence of virtual NSPs should facilitate an improvement in the variety of connectivity options available to ISPs in those regions.[25] As mentioned before, it is common for ISPs to have agreements with more than one backbone provider, and multi-homing allows them the possibility of controlling how their traffic is routed.[26] As in the case of other ICT goods, the price of the routers needed for ISP multihoming has declined significantly over recent years. As a consequence, ISPs increasingly have the possibility of changing the capacity with which they access the Internet by transiting through a given backbone provider, for example in response to changes in prices.[27] This of course limits the capacity of backbone providers to raise their prices. Similarly, the customers of ISPs have the possibility to use "customer multihoming", with similar effects on their capacity to react to price increases by ISPs. Caching, mirroring and intelligent content distribution help reduce demand for backbone carriage for a given amount of content flows.[28]

An interesting question is the extent to which the network externalities of the Internet could facilitate the emergence of a backbone provider that enjoyed monopolistic power. However, considering the conditions that should be met for a provider to be able to exploit network externalities as a way to gain monopolistic power, this appears to be an unlikely occurrence. Those conditions are the following:

- The operator should be able to have exclusive control over the protocols and standards used in the network.

- Its customers should have no incentive to reach the customers and services of more than one network provider.

- Customers should face a high cost if they wished to switch to another network.[29]

The Internet, of course, provides an excellent example of network externalities, since with any new Internet user or computer node connected to the network, or any new network that gets connected, the value of an Internet connection increases for every other user and network connected: there are more websites to visit, more people with whom e-mail can be exchanged, more e-commerce opportunities, and so forth. However, the magnitude of this effect is the subject of some debate. While many assume that Metcalfe's law, which states that the value of a communications network is proportional to the square of the size of the network, applies to the Internet, others

argue that this is an overestimation and that the value of a communications network of n members grows like $n \log (n)$.[30] In this case, network effects are not as strong as Metcalfe's law implies. In a network in which Metcalfe's law holds, the value of interconnection is the same for both interconnecting networks, regardless of their relative size. In a network in which the value for participants grows as $n \log (n)$ the smaller network would gain significantly more from interconnection than the larger one. Therefore, there would be a justification for the larger network to demand payment for interconnection, and a refusal to peer would not necessarily represent anti-competitive behaviour.

Technological reasons also support the consideration that the conditions prevailing in the market for backbone connectivity are different from the ones in which network externalities could support the development of monopolies. The Internet is based on the use of open, public standards, and the mechanisms through which these standards and protocols are defined and extended make it highly unlikely that proprietary standards would be imposed in the future by any operator.[31]

Another point of view to consider is the behaviour of Internet users. Given the nature of the content available on the Internet, users require universal connectivity: they do not know in advance the location of specific information or service that may interest them. And conversely, users cannot calculate the cost of the loss of opportunities that they would suffer if customers of other backbone providers were unable to access them. Thus, a backbone provider that refuses to provide universal connectivity would be unlikely to succeed. The fact that, in developed markets at least, no backbone operator has exclusive coverage of any extended region and that most ISPs can connect to more than one backbone without major switching costs further adds to the difficulties of the would-be monopolist backbone provider. The influence of users' behaviour can be felt in another way: as the Internet becomes culturally and linguistically more diverse, content and the traffic it generates become less concentrated, thus eroding the market power of established operators.

A large backbone provider could, however, attempt to impose its power on the markets in ways that would be detrimental to its customers. It could, for example, increase the prices of its services, replacing peering with transit agreements at high prices; it could practise price discrimination, charging some networks

Chart 2.4a

Traffic flows before NSP increase prices

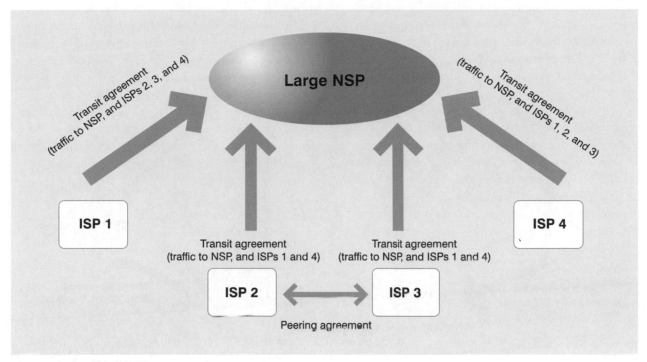

Source: Economides (2004b).

more than others for the same services; or it could deliberately provide interconnection services of lower quality to rival networks in order to divert traffic towards its own network. It would, however, face considerable difficulties in achieving its objectives.

Let us consider the price rise first. The first effect of an increase in price would be to create profit opportunities for its rivals (to which at least some of its customers would switch) and provide an incentive for new operators to enter the market. As explained before, in developed markets it is very common for ISPs to be connected to several backbone providers; ISPs that use multihoming can easily reduce the amount of bandwidth they buy from a given backbone provider. A large backbone provider that attempts to impose increases in transport costs will see other providers and ISPs divert traffic from its network and reroute it using more of the others' capacity.[32] Only traffic destined for ISPs with exclusive connection to the large backbone provider would not be bypassing its network. Chart 2.4, taken from Economides (2004b), shows the situation before and after a price increase in the case of four ISPs that purchase transit from a large provider, two of which peer with each other and buy transit for their traffic to the large provider and the other small ISPs, and the remaining two buy transit from the large provider for

all their traffic. As a result of the price increase, all of the ISPs will buy from the large provider only bandwidth sufficient to carry traffic with destined for the provider's own network, which would lead to a significant decrease in revenue for it. The beneficiaries would be the ISPs that had a peering agreement and that would have been able to sell capacity to the other ISPs, and whose networks would have grown bigger.

Price discrimination against rival networks would also be unlikely to be undertaken, as rivals are better placed than any other customers to avoid use of the network of the provider that raises prices. Another option available for an operator attempting to displace rivals could be to deliberately degrade the quality of service it makes available to other networks that interconnect with it. However, this strategy would be very counterproductive, as it would harm the perpetrator as much as any victim. A refusal to deal with other networks would also be a self-defeating option, as customers demand connectivity to be as far-reaching as possible – ideally, universal. A refusal to establish interconnection agreements with other networks would therefore amount to a deliberate reduction of the quality of service provided to its own customers, and would benefit those rivals that would receive the traffic originating from the network to which a deal had been refused. Network externalities in all these

Chart 2.4b

Traffic flows after NSP increases prices

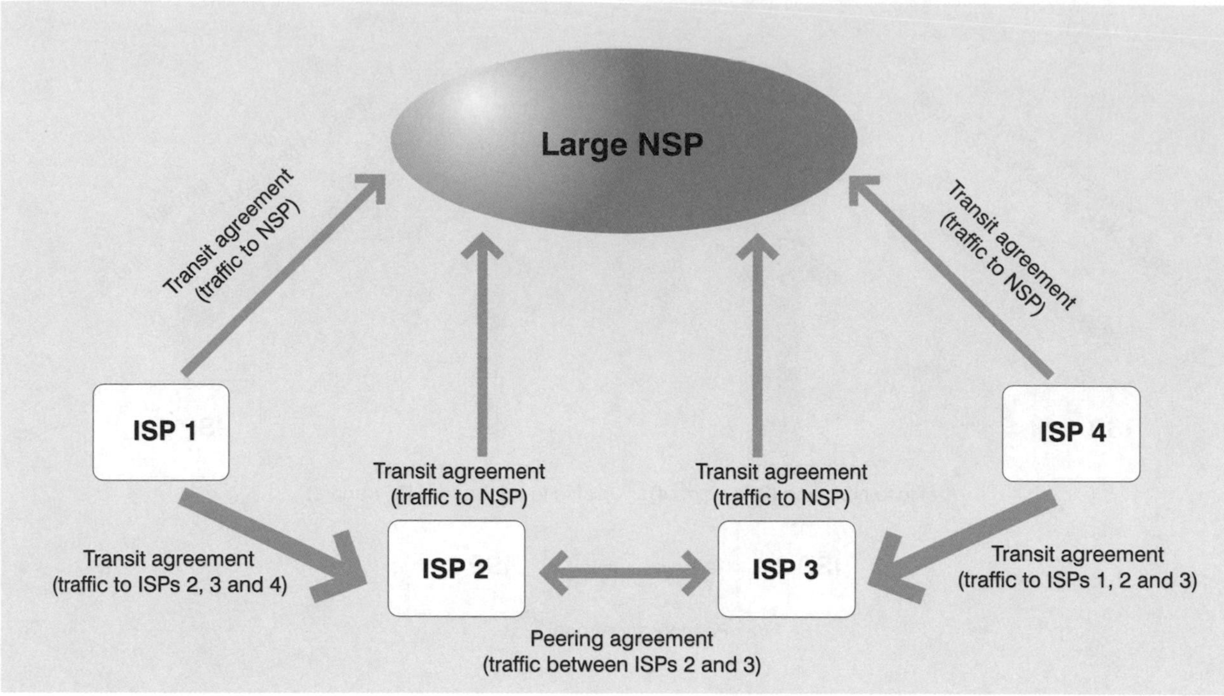

Source: Economides (2004b).

cases seem to be working in favour of greater competition.

The reasoning outlined in the preceding paragraphs seems to support the view that effective competition can be expected to be normally present in the market for Internet backbone services. There seem to be few theoretical reasons to expect the emergence of conditions under which a dominant operator could successfully impose its standards and/or refuse to interconnect other networks as an anti-competitive strategy. This should not be understood as implying that in practice backbone operators could or should be left wholly unsupervised, but merely as a suggestion that the fact that a NSP refuses to peer with a lower-tier operator does not by itself constitute evidence of anti-competitive behaviour. As pointed out by Economides (2004a), inequality is natural in the market structure of network industries. And, as noted before, networks of different sizes face different incentives to interconnect: they are much more significant for smaller networks, and a refusal to peer on the part of the larger ones would not necessarily constitute anti-competitive behaviour.[33]

In spite of the above considerations, even if the theoretical conditions for competition are present in the Internet backbone services market, as in any other market the vigilance of regulators is necessary in order to ensure that the larger operators do not undermine the conditions of competition. After all, the larger the network of an Internet backbone provider, the more tempted it may be to try to impose access terms on downstream networks. And as networks gain financial capacity to buy their potential competitors, barriers to entry for newcomers may become higher.

In these circumstances, regulators in both the United States and the European Union have had to intervene in order to prevent possible anti-competitive behaviour on the part of tier 1 backbone providers. For example, the market for local Internet access remains, even in many developed countries, largely in the hands of telecoms incumbents and there is clear justification for regulatory obligations being imposed on them in order to prevent discriminatory practices that may bottleneck certain facilities and functionalities for rent-seeking. This is the approach followed, for example, by the regulatory framework of the European Union adopted in 2002. In the United States, although the general position of successive administrations has been that when no dominant player was present there was no need for government involvement in the operation of the Internet's privately owned global infrastructure, regulators have sometimes shown hesitation about the impact on the Internet of fully unrestricted market forces: for example, in 2000, when the Department of Justice went to court to block the merger of America's two largest Internet backbone providers (WorldCom and Sprint), because a combined company would control 53 per cent of US Internet traffic – five times that of the next largest competitor. The position of the Department of Justice was that the merger might give the resulting company the capacity to restrict competition through rises in costs and deterioration in the quality of service.

Similar considerations would clearly be applicable to the situation of developing countries with regard to the practical implications of the market power of the largest international backbone providers. An important matter of concern to ISPs of developing countries is the practical actions that could be undertaken in order to prevent global backbone providers exercising excessive market power to shift the investment and operation costs of international access onto the smaller network operators. In order to address this question it is first necessary to look briefly at the evolution of the global market for Internet backbone services.

C. The evolution of the global market for Internet backbone services

1. The developed countries

The analysis in the previous section is based on the experience of the United States, where the first commercial backbone providers started to operate in the early 1990s, and is now applicable in large part to the situation in the rest of the developed world. As the Internet expanded into other regions of the world somewhat later than in the United States – mostly in the second half of the 1990s – ISPs outside that country needed to get connected to North American backbone networks. At that time, in most countries the infrastructure required for that purpose was still owned by monopolies or by the former monopoly, as the liberalization of telecommunications services was

relatively recent (or in some cases had not even been completed). ISPs had to use leased lines to get connected to NAPs (originally) or IXPs (later) in the United States. The reason for them to do this was not only that the United States was where the initial backbones and a very large part of the Internet content were located, but also the fact that because more advanced liberalization in that market had brought down the prices of international circuits originating in the United States, a link there provided the most economical way to exchange traffic at the global level. Foreign ISPs could minimize the cost of exchanging traffic by doing so in the United States.

It soon became clear, however, that the situation that was developing was far from optimal from the networking point of view: traffic between neighbouring countries in Europe or Asia was using transcontinental lines to the United States. ISPs thus became interested in setting up national and regional IXPs so that non-US traffic did not have to be carried over United States backbones. Another reason for this interest was the commercial requirement of improving the quality of service provided to end-users, for example reduced latency. As liberalization advanced in most developed countries, the cost of the domestic and regional links to the non-US IXPs fell considerably.

An important force for change was the move by traditional telecommunications operators, the former monopolies, into the Internet services arena in the second half of the 1990s. The infrastructure with which they provided these services, however, had been built under the rules of the circuit-switched model, which meant that they only owned the capacity they needed up to a theoretical mid-way point. In order to serve their customers, most telecommunication operators had to turn to providers with backbones in the United States. This entailed a shift of financial flows between telecommunications operators in favour of those based in the United States, which were already advanced in the building of privately owned, commercially operated international infrastructure. While the incumbent operators – monopolies or former monopolies – still had to buy foreign half-circuits, backbone providers in the United States were already able to carry traffic end to end on their networks.[34]

Since the policy environment in most developed countries was particularly favourable to liberalization, deregulation and privatization of telecommunications services, operators were unable to obtain from their Governments the traditional remedies they would have sought for this kind of imbalance in the relationship with operators from the United States, namely government intervention to regulate prices, and were forced to develop commercial solutions. Regulatory developments on both sides of the Atlantic facilitated the process. In the United States, the 1996 Telecommunication Act encouraged new participants to enter all market segments. European markets were also mostly open for the provision of end-to-end facilities as liberalization moved forward.

Backbone capacity in the United States and international routes linking that country to the rest of the world expanded at a phenomenal rate, giving operators from outside the United States increased options in their commercial dealings with United States backbone providers. In the process prices fell, buyers were able to negotiate better deals and, in spite of some complaints by foreign operators, the backbone market was considered to have moved in the direction of increased competitiveness.[35] Foreign operators were also able to add their own backbone networks through the United States (Cable and Wireless, Telia, France Telecom, NTT, Telecom Italia, Telefonica, among others), which gave them the ability to carry traffic end to end. Indeed, studies seem to indicate that the United States is the most competitive backbone market in the OECD.[36]

The larger operators have in front of them a rather long menu when deciding the kind of relationship they wish to establish with other networks. They can establish partnership agreements with operators that complement their geographical coverage, they can buy spare capacity or dark fibre from other operators, they can swap capacity, or they can simply buy up a company. In line with the description in section B above they can also agree to peer so that they exchange traffic without monetary payments, or conclude transit agreements for all or part of their traffic, with either one or several backbone providers. For most of the large operators from outside the United States, the deployment or acquisition of their United States backbones is part of a worldwide strategy that involves the presence of their own backbones in other regions outside their home country – and sometimes even their own region. This trend, of course, has been reciprocated by United States-based carriers that have also built their end-to-end networks in other parts of the world, particularly in Europe and Asia.

These trends are reinforced by the evolution of technology. Drawing a comparison with the historical evolution of the transport industry, Odlyzko (2004)

points out the role of technology in reducing costs in the core of the Internet and how the logical and economically efficient outcome of the process for NSPs is to become suppliers of a commodity with a uniformly high-quality service. This trend is strongly reinforced by the degree of competition on major long-distance routes and the lack of a player that might have a chance to monopolize fibre optic cable supplies. When operators decide whether to exchange traffic on a peering or transit basis, this does not happen because of regulatory mandate, or because of lack of infrastructure. Rather, such deals are concluded if and when a valid business case can be made for them. Equally important is the fact that operators enjoy greater control over the factors that determine the level of quality of the service they deliver to their customers.

2.   The developing world

The decline in bandwidth prices and the increase of international bandwidth availability in recent years and in all regions of the world are two major features of the environment in which the question of the international Internet connectivity of developing countries should be considered (see chart 2.5 and table 2.2) Although these trends cannot by themselves be taken as evidence of the existence of a perfectly competitive market for international Internet connectivity services, not least because of the secrecy in which commercial connectivity arrangements are shrouded, they seem to indicate that, at least in the heavier traffic routes, the most evident signs of lack of competition are absent. As some players find themselves unable to survive in such an environment, a consolidation process is under way and some providers may withdraw from the Internet transit market in certain areas, or even leave the business. In 2004 and 2005 this has combined with a strong increase in bandwidth demand, resulting in a slowing down in the fall of bandwidth prices.[37]

However, one should not overlook the fact that the smaller, low-income Internet markets in developing countries, particularly in Africa, have been unable to attract sufficient investment in infrastructure, which – combined with lack of competition – results in bandwidth cost that can be up to 100 times higher than in developed countries.[38] In most cases, these countries remain outside the reach of fibre optic cables, and must turn to satellites for international – and sometimes even domestic – connectivity. In spite of the significant improvements brought about by technolo-

Chart 2.5

International bandwith prices and growth

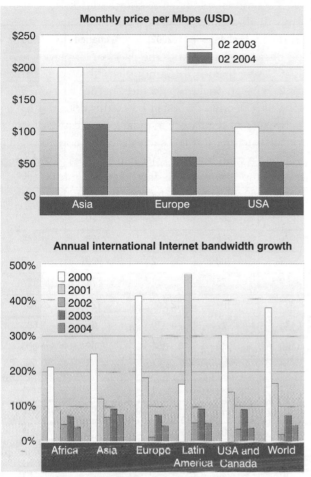

Source: OECD (2005), quoting Primetrica

gies such as Very Small Aperture Terminal (VSAT) satellites, the costs of satellite capacity is in an order of magnitude higher than that of fibre optic cable

A key consideration for developing countries is the extent to which the experience of operators in developed countries, which was outlined in the preceding section, is relevant to the conditions under which developing countries connect to the global Internet. On the one hand, it can be reasonably argued that operators from developing countries may find it difficult, or even impossible, to implement the kind of strategies that were followed by their counterparts in developed countries in order to enhance their connectivity, for example capacity swapping. It may also be the case that the conditions under which the backbone market was considered to be a competitive one are not present in developing countries because of the existence of market failures that may justify regulatory

intervention in the market for international backbone connectivity.

On the other hand, one should consider whether the removal of restrictions on Internet access markets would not provide incentives for operators in developing countries that would be comparable to those that have driven the changes in commercial arrangements and infrastructure deployment in the more developed markets. The experience of a number of developing countries indicates that by lifting restrictions on the provision of Internet backbone services, connectivity costs may be cut down and infrastructure deployment accelerated. For example, in India, where liberalization has already progressed, international backbone connectivity has exploded – and this has had positive effects for the development of Internet-based activity in that country. In other countries restrictions affecting the provision of international connectivity, such as making it compulsory for ISPs to use the international gateway of the incumbent operator, or restrictions on the availability of international leased lines, have been said to partially account for differences in bandwidth costs among countries in the same region:[39] for example, in May 2003 the monthly cost of 1 Mbps of international bandwidth in Singapore was of $1,300, while in Thailand it was $4,500.[40] Another example is provided by South Africa, where in a document released in March 2005, an association representing the country's ISPs complained that "at present, Telkom's monopoly over the SAT-3 cable, and the high prices Telkom currently charges to other telecommunications service providers for access to this cable are perhaps the single greatest contributor to the high costs of Internet access in South Africa".[41]

The comments of the South African ISPs point to an important consideration. In the final analysis, the cost of international connectivity matters insofar as it is reflected in the total cost of Internet access, and is the variable that will have an impact on Internet take-up and on the development of an information economy in developing countries. One should therefore pay attention to the breakdown of total end-user costs. In the most common case, these can be divided in two parts: ISP charges and telecommunication charges. Total ISP charges will partly reflect the ISP's international costs and partly reflect other costs (licence fees, capital costs, salaries and profit). Global Internet connectivity cost will be only one of the components of the international costs of the ISP, the other one being the cost of any international private leased circuit it uses. A comparative study of six African and Asian

Table 2.2

International bandwidth availability in selected developing countries/economies (2000–2003)

Country/economy	2000	% change	2001	% change	2002	% change	2003
Benin	2	0	2	5	2	2138	47
Bhutan	1	100	2	0	2	182	6
Cambodia	4	71	6	100	12	50	18
Cape Verde	1	100	2	50	3	167	8
China	2 799	171	7 598	23	9 380	190	27 216
Côte d'Ivoire	3	106	7	194	20	105	40
Cuba	17	206	52	48	77	13	87
Djibouti	0	300	1	300	2	0	2
Egypt	31	797	275	168	735	56	1 148
Eritrea	1	96	1	100	2	0	2
French Polynesia	8	7	8	75	14	71	24
Hong Kong (China)	4 180	51	6 308	101	12 668	127	28 737
India	840	76	1 475	27	1 870	60	3 000
Iran (Islamic Rep. of)	36	344	160	244	550	82	1 000
Lao PDR	2	0	2	-10	2	0	2
Lesotho	1	95	1	2	1	-2	1
Macao (China)	106	13	120	113	255	99	509
Marshall Islands	1	0	1	202	2	0	2
Mauritania	1	0	1	1134	10	0	10
Mauritius	6	67	10	240	34	79	61
Micronesia	1	95	2	0	2	0	2
Mongolia	8	25	10	70	17	29	22
Myanmar	1	300	4	20	5	88	9
Pakistan	50	350	225	82	410	38	567
Paraguay	10	5	10	877	100	0	100
Rep. of Korea	2 268	332	9 800	76	17 207	144	42 000
Samoa	0	781	2	33	3	0	3
Seychelles	2	200	6	0	6	0	6
Solomon Islands	0	100	1	0	1	0	1
Somalia	0	0	0	1103	1	30	1
Sri Lanka	10	150	25	270	93	0	93
Suriname	3	33	4	200	12	275	45
Taiwan PC	2 136	238	7 228	105	14 790	204	44 923
Thailand	268	140	642	57	1 011	42	1 438
Turkey	578	7	620	83	1 132	94	2 200
Uganda	2	207	5	82	10	5	10
Viet Nam	24	42	34	321	143	626	1 038
Average change		152		175		135	

developing countries found that the share of global Internet connectivity in total end-user Internet access costs ranged from 39 per cent in the case of Cambodia, mainly owing to the small size of the market and the consequently low levels of bandwidth supplied, to 4 per cent in India, which has a large market with significant levels of competition. The average value was 15 per cent.[42]

One should not expect the paths followed by carriers in developing countries as they build their Internet business to be identical to those taken by their counterparts in developed countries. For instance, developing national infrastructure will probably have a higher priority than international links – and it is likely that increased competition will also bring about positive results in this area too. However, these two goals should not necessarily be regarded as being mutually exclusive. As competitive pressures drive down the cost of international bandwidth, some developing country operators may find themselves increasingly able to provide end-to-end services in those routes that are strategically more important for them. Furthermore, such ability is not merely a function of bandwidth prices. In a radical departure from the switched-circuit model of the past, in which capacity was available on a point-to-point basis, in today's more flexible environment some major international backbone providers can sell amounts of capacity that can later be allocated to various routes.

Lack of competition in domestic Internet markets often makes it difficult for developing countries to benefit fully from the possibilities offered by the changes in the international environment in terms of better international connectivity. For example, when ISPs in developing countries can create national or regional IXPs, they are able to aggregate traffic and thus give global backbone networks a greater incentive to interconnect their infrastructure. Transit arrangements can be negotiated under better conditions for carriers from developing countries and there are more possibilities for peering. In addition, technology now allows even distant ISPs to benefit from participation in IXPs.[43] However, in a repetition of the experience of the more advanced countries in the earlier phase of the development of the Internet, monopolies often oppose the creation of domestic and regional IXPs in developing countries. Where incumbents do not enjoy a legal or de facto monopoly over Internet services, they may succeed in their opposition to the establishment of IXPs by controlling basic telecommunications infrastructure in such a way that independent ISPs do not stand a chance as

far as developing their business is concerned. For example, in many developing countries monopolies impose high prices on leased lines, this being a key component in ensuring that ISPs and large business users are able to connect to global and domestic backbones. The number of leased lines permanently connected to the Internet has been found to be strongly correlated with the number of ISPs, for some of which the cost of leased lines may represent up to 70 per cent of the total cost of services to their customers.[44] In other cases, unreasonable delays in the provision of the service are reported, and in the worst cases leased lines may simply not be offered by the incumbent.

In a more competitive environment new entrants into the ISP market, which would not have the option of extracting monopoly rents from international connectivity, should have strong incentives to make commercial arrangements that suit their interests and those of their customers. This is borne out by the fact that the majority of the developing countries first connected to the Internet when the commercialization of the Internet was already well under way. Unlike earlier entrants from developed countries, developing countries did not always use the services of providers based in the United States or connect in the first place to backbones located in that country. The results of an OECD study published in 2002 and covering the 110 countries which had fewer than five ISPs at that time showed that the companies that advertised the greatest number of routes to networks in those countries were headquartered in a variety of countries. First in the ranking was France Telecom, which provided connectivity to 29 networks. The second provider was Cable and Wireless, which connected networks in 23 countries, followed by Teleglobe, which connected networks in 15 countries. About one third of the countries had ISPs that were connected via more than one foreign backbone provider. Arguably, the structure of the Internet is no longer centred on the United States. Western Europe, and increasingly East Asia and the Pacific, tend to have more capacity for intraregional links than for connections with the North American region. These regional hubs replicate, on a smaller scale, the hub-and-spoke structure of the early, US-centred Internet.

In other words, the international Internet connectivity of developing countries is less and less dependent on links to one single country, and the geographical layout of networks is less and less a function of the country in which the network operator is headquartered. Because the global environment is one of increasing flexibility and more options, developing countries have an opportunity to facilitate Internet deployment – and consequently the development of Internet-supported business opportunities – by empowering their ISPs to make their own choices about the infrastructure and commercial modalities that are best suited to their business needs. Some will prefer to buy transit services from regional or global networks. Others may decide to cooperate with operators of similar size to aggregate traffic and thus gain leverage in their dealings with global providers. Yet others may find that there is a solid business case for building or buying their own end-to-end capacity.

This said, concerns remain about the situation in those developing countries, particularly the least developed countries and landlocked developing countries – most of which are also LDCs – that face bottlenecks due to very limited access to international backbone networks. For reasons both of the small size of their markets and the resulting limited opportunities for benefiting from economies of scale, and of geographical difficulties, it is unrealistic to expect that domestic liberalization on its own will be enough to bring the cost of Internet interconnection down to levels that enable a significant increase in Internet access by people and companies. International cooperation has therefore an important role to play in accompanying and supporting the commercial development of Internet connectivity in these countries.

Another aspect that will require further consideration is the development of mechanisms to protect smaller developing country operators from potential anti-competitive behaviour by large international NSPs. As noted before, the regulatory authorities in developed countries have at different times felt the need to look into the level of competition prevailing in the markets for Internet backbone services. Developing countries may need to strengthen their capacity to assess developments in this area and to explore ways to develop effective response mechanisms – including through international cooperation – should the need arise.

Developing country policymakers should also take into account the fact that the outcome, in terms of broader diffusion of the Internet, of the introduction of increased competition in the different segments of the Internet services sector is not indifferent to the timing and pace of the opening process, or to the level of competition in the upstream segment of the telecommunications sector. For instance, there is little

possibility for new ISPs to start operating unless they have access to reasonably priced telephone lines.

D.   The international dimension

1.   In the ITU context: Recommendation D.50

The debate about the consequences for developing countries of the commercial arrangements concerning international Internet traffic has, to a large extent, centred on ITU-T Recommendation D.50, work on which has been carried out within ITU-T Study Group 3 since 1998. The first draft of the Recommendation, which was adopted in Geneva in April 2000, read as follows: "It is recommended that administrations negotiate and agree to bilateral commercial arrangements applying to direct international Internet connection whereby each administration will be compensated for the costs that it incurs in carrying traffic that is generated by the other administration."[45] Although the language of the Recommendation does not amount to anything more than a call for the sharing of the costs of bilateral international interconnection among the parties involved, substantial divergences emerged among ITU member States about its meaning and consequences.

Some developed countries and major international operators, who also tend to be major ISPs in developed markets, saw in the Recommendation an attempt to impose on the Internet a traffic-based settlement system that would replicate the accounting rate regime used for international telephony – of which they were also critical. It was argued that this would entail excessive regulation of the Internet, which by restricting the freedom of ISPs to negotiate interconnection agreements on the basis of their own commercial considerations would interfere with private investment decisions and result in non-optimal allocation of resources that would slow down the deployment of global bandwidth and the growth of global Internet connectivity.

Other countries, mostly developing countries from the Asia-Pacific region, but also including some developed countries such as Australia, whose position later evolved, took the view that what was needed was not to transpose the telephony model onto the Internet but merely to ensure that unobjectionable principles such as non-discrimination, transparency and cost-based be applied to all services. According to this interpretation, the Recommendation was not calling for government intervention but relied on commercial negotiations; it was also pro-competitive and supportive of the emergence of new ISPs worldwide because, under the arrangements in place, non-US operators were in fact subsidizing tier 1 NSPs, which at that time were mostly US companies. The subsidy appeared because the non-US operator had to pay the full cost of the international transmission capacity to the United States even though the capacity was made available – without charge – to US-based ISPs to send Internet traffic in the opposite direction. As a result, non-US ISPs faced unfairly high international interconnection costs, which in turn had an impact on the cost of Internet access for their customers.

The response from the other side was that although it was true that US backbone providers required ISPs from the rest of the world to acquire their own transmission facilities if they wished to connect in the United States, many of the US backbone providers had PoPs outside the United States. And non-US ISPs were free to build or buy their own US backbones if they wished, as the market for backbone services was open. It was also argued that the Recommendation was insufficiently inclusive as it considered only international leased line costs but failed to address the cost-sharing of more general aspects of Internet facilities (for example, the costs of domestic links or hubs).

The debate continued in May 2000 at the Cancún (Mexico) meeting of ministers from the Asia-Pacific Economic Cooperation (APEC) group. The discussions resulted in proposing to the meeting of APEC's finance ministers at their November 2000 meeting in Brunei an action programme that included language to the effect that:

(1) Government intervention was not needed in private business agreements concerning charging for international Internet services if they were concluded in a competitive environment. However, when there are dominant players or de facto monopolies, Governments should promote fair competition.

(2) Internet charging agreements between providers of network services should be commercially negotiated and, among other issues, reflect the contribution of each network to the communication, the use by each party of the interconnected network resources and the end-to-end costs of international transport link capacity.

In October of the same year, the ITU's World Telecommunication Standardization Assembly (WTSA), held in Montreal, adopted a compromise version of Recommendation D.50. The new text was adopted by consensus, although the United States and Greece formulated reservations. The revised text read as follows: "It is recommended that administrations involved in the provision of international Internet connections negotiate and agree to bilateral commercial arrangements enabling direct international Internet connections that take into account the possible need for compensation between them for the value of elements such as traffic flow, number of routes, geographical coverage and cost of international transmission among others."

Following WTSA-2000, Study Group 3 undertook additional analysis of the technical and economic aspects of international Internet connectivity and considered the possible development of general principles that could be applicable to commercial relationships in this field. Two Rapporteur Groups were created. The first one, on international Internet connectivity, was to work on the establishment of guidelines that could facilitate the implementation of Recommendation D.50. The task of the second Rapporteur Group was to investigate the possibility of using traffic flows as a main negotiating factor in the field of international Internet connectivity.

On the basis of proposals by those Rapporteur Groups, guidelines to complement Recommendation D.50 were adopted in June 2004[47]. However, the study on the traffic flow methodology has not concluded and work continues.

Study Group 3 has recognized that the high cost of the international connectivity between the least developed countries and the Internet backbone networks remains a serious problem. It has recommended that the donor community undertake special actions in this respect. These could include, for example, supporting and facilitating traffic aggregation and exchange at the local, national and regional levels so that less traffic has to be sent over intercontinental satellite or cable links between least developed countries and Europe or North America. The retention of local and national traffic would reduce the dependence of developing countries on international communications links.

The Study Group also pointed to the importance of supporting the development and use of the Internet as a means of bringing about economic growth and development in developing countries, and in particular in the least developed countries. The scarcity of human resources capable of using and producing local Internet content was recognized by the Group as another very important problem. Addressing the human resource problem was identified as a priority for existing or new economic and social development programmes.

2. Interconnection and peering in the WSIS process

Different matters related to the question of Internet interconnection costs were brought up by some developing countries in the context of the discussions on Internet governance that took place during the first phase of the World Summit on the Information Society (WSIS), which was held in Geneva in December 2003. The final text of the Plan of Action refers to the question in paragraphs 9 j) and k) with language calling for the reduction of interconnection costs through the creation of regional backbones and facilitation of the creation of IXPs, and for commercially negotiated Internet transit and interconnection costs to be "oriented towards objective, transparent and non-discriminatory parameters".

The Summit decided that discussions on the question of Internet governance should continue, so as to prepare the ground for decisions that should be taken the second phase of the WSIS, scheduled for Tunis in November 2005. The Summit also requested the Secretary-General of the United Nations to create a Working Group on Internet Governance (WGIG), which should present the results of its work in a report "for consideration and appropriate action for the second phase of the WSIS in Tunis 2005". The tasks of the Working Group include developing a working definition of Internet governance, identifying the public policy issues that are relevant to Internet governance, and developing a common understanding of the respective roles and responsibilities of Governments, international organizations and other forums, as well as the private sector and civil society of both developing and developed countries.

The WGIG prepared a number of working papers in order to develop a common understanding of the issues and to facilitate its work. The papers were made public for comment at the WGIG's site. One of them, entitled "Peering and interconnection", addressed international backbone connectivity.[48] The paper, which for the most part is a factual account of the international discussions held so far on the matter, elicited less comment than for questions such as the governance of the domain name system, the reform of ICANN and control over the root servers. The question of interconnection costs was nonetheless identified in the group's final report as one of the priority public policy issues relevant to Internet governance.[49] The report includes a number of recommendations with regard to (a) the need to conduct research into possible alternative solutions; (b) a call for WSIS principles of multilateralism, transparency and democratic process to be reflected in the treatment of the problem; (c) an invitation to international organizations to report on the issue in the framework of whatever body, forum or mechanism for Internet governance and coordination that may be established by the WSIS; (d) a call for funding for initiatives to enhance connectivity, IXPs and content creation in developing countries; and (e) "building on international agreements", with interested parties being encouraged to "continue and intensify work in relevant international organizations on international Internet connectivity issues". The majority of these recommendations address more the need to build regional backbones, and the role of IXPs in reducing Internet access costs, than the establishment of international corrective mechanisms to the central issue of interconnection agreements between NSPs and developing countries' providers. This outcome is a reflection of the variety of views held on this question by different countries and other stakeholders, and could indicate that the status of the question of Internet interconnection, and in particular the implementation of ITU Recommendation D.50, may not undergo significant changes in the near future.

E. Policy options and proposals

The previous paragraphs show the difficulty of settling, in a general way and for all developing countries, the question of whether the commercial arrangements that currently determine the financing of the cost of international backbone connectivity are biased against developing countries. A related question to be addressed, and probably a more important one from the point of view of development, is the extent to which action at the international and national levels can be undertaken to effectively enhance access to the Internet in developing countries through interventions aimed at changing the results of the commercial decisions that now define international backbone connectivity.

The need to monitor competition in markets

Because those commercial decisions can reasonably be assumed to have been taken in a competitive environment – with the important qualification that in the case of some LDCs and small developing economies market failure may indeed be a problem[50] – it can be argued that *ex-ante* regulatory intervention in the market for international backbone connectivity would not be likely to bring about significant improvements in terms of the cost of access to the Internet in developing countries. This said, it would appear to be important that vigilance be exercised so that market structures do not evolve in a direction in which powerful market players can engage in anti-competitive practices. Regulators in developing and developed countries should also explore ways to cooperate in order to promote greater transparency concerning the dealings between developing country operators and global backbone providers, so as to prevent anti-competitive practices in the establishment of peering and transit arrangements. Requiring NSPs to make public the criteria they apply in order to decide whether to peer with other operators – as many already do – could be a useful measure in this regard. Greater transparency concerning prices and other aspects of the commercial transit arrangements reached between backbone providers and ISPs should also be facilitated. This would be particularly important in respect of their dealings with players from developing countries. Furthermore, efforts should be made to improve the availability of information about the quality of service provided by NSPs, as this can be used as an anti-competitive weapon. The identification and development of adequate grievance redress procedures that could be used in response to potential anti-competitive behaviour in the market for Internet backbone services could also be useful.

Domestic factors affecting international connectivity

Research indicates that ISP costs generally account for less than half of total Internet use cost in most developing countries, with the greater portion corresponding to telecommunications costs. As previously noted, not more than 20 to 35 per cent of total ISP costs have been found to correspond to international connectivity (with exceptional situations in some landlocked and LDC countries).[51] The most impor-

tant factor that affects this international element of the cost of connectivity is probably the size of the market, as this determines whether investment in fibre optic infrastructure is economically viable or not – although general considerations about the attractiveness of the country or region for international investment may also play a role. As noted, economies of scale imply that the amount of capacity that is bought from international NSPs also plays an important role, hence the usefulness of traffic aggregation. Neither of these two factors is susceptible to change through direct policy action at the national level. This is not always the case of other factors that influence international cost, such as whether ISPs are allowed to buy international capacity directly, the price of international leased circuits and the relationship between ISP and international capacity providers – for example, whether the incumbent telecommunications operator also controls the ISP market, or whether independent ISPs are required to use the incumbent's international Internet gateway.

At the same time it cannot be denied that the organization of Internet traffic in many developing countries, insofar as it often requires unnecessary international segments, does impose wasteful costs on Internet users. There are real benefits to be gained by addressing these issues.

Developing countries have at their disposal a number of policy options that would allow them to significantly lower Internet access costs through national measures. Lack of competition in the market for Internet services among ISPs, and, where these exist, domestic restrictions that ISPs must overcome in order to access the Internet backbone, represent a potentially highly productive area for policy intervention. The costs imposed on Internet users by monopolies or dominant operators, because of last-mile issues and of obligations to use their services for international interconnection, may be more significant than those derived from the international segment of connectivity. The Halfway Proposition, outlined in box 2.2, offers a good inventory of policy measures (developed by developing country ISPs themselves) that developing countries could consider adopting without the need to wait for regulatory developments at the international level.

Supporting traffic aggregation and exchange

An instrument that needs to be fully exploited is the development of local and/or national IXPs, where these do not exist yet or have only a limited reach.

Box 2.2

The Halfway Proposition

The Halfway Proposition was formulated by the African Internet Service Providers Association (AfrISPA) and presented to the Conference of African Ministers of Finance, Planning and Economic Development held in Johannesburg, South Africa, in October 2002.[1]

The aim of the proposal was to "articulate the root causes of high connectivity costs in Africa and to map out a strategy of how to tackle the problem". The paper argues that the current burden of international Internet connectivity is unfairly placed on countries in Africa and that the existence of these reverse subsidies is the single largest factor contributing to high bandwidth costs. It estimated reverse subsidies to amount to between $250 and 500 million per year. The authors considered that redressing the balance through regulation by the ITU was not the way forward and that it would be preferable to allow the process to be driven by the private sector.

According to the document, the requirements for a private-sector-driven process included the aggregation of traffic within Africa (through the creation of Internet exchange points and the emergence of regional carriers facilitating regional peering), the creation of "Digital Arteries" that would carry the traffic regionally (through regional fibre optic infrastructure that would reduce the costs of regional peering) and internationally (through international fibre optic infrastructure to reduce the costs for backbone providers of establishing PoPs in Africa).

The document identified a number of players that should be involved in the implementation of this initiative: ISPs, grouped in AfrISPA, would ensure that domestic traffic stays at that level through cooperation in the creation of effective national IXPs; national regulators and policymakers should provide the required enabling environment. The African Telecommunications Union, the African Union and the New Partnership for Africa's Development (NEPAD) would ensure that governments provide the necessary enabling environment to allow national and regional peering to evolve quickly. They would also play a role in awareness raising and sensitization about the cost of international connectivity in Africa. Finally, the donor Governments were called on to provide financial support for the initiative.

---

[1] See http://www.afrispa.org/Initiatives.htm

Chart 2.6 provides an image of the uneven level of development of IXPs across the various regions of the world. IXPs offer significant gains for developing country Internet connectivity in several regards, of which quality of service and the reduction of cost are perhaps the most outstanding ones as they refer to the two most commonly reported factors impeding the development of local Internet content and use. The establishment of IXPs in developing countries faces regulatory obstacles (limitations on non-regulated telecommunications infrastructure and on facilities, restrictive licensing, taxation issues), and the opposition of telecommunications incumbents and large ISPs (often also owned by the incumbent telecom), which fear the increased competition.

Policies to facilitate the creation of IXPs in developing countries should first create awareness among the Internet community – ISPs, large Internet users, universities, and so forth – so as to identify the relevant obstacles and the strategies to remove them. Associative efforts among ISPs aimed at the creation of the IXP should be supported, so that the IXP can be run efficiently and neutrally on behalf of participating ISPs. Also, it is important to bring on board the rele-

vant government officials whose support will be necessary in order to address the legal and regulatory obstacles. Regulators should be particularly attentive to attempts by telecommunications incumbents to prevent the creation of new IXPs or suffocate those that already exist.

Chart 2.6

Number of IXPs per region, October 2004

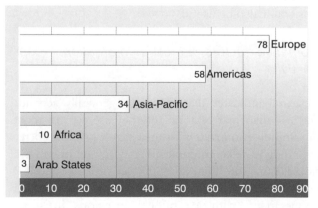

Source: ITU (2004)

Where IXPs exist, policies should be put in place to facilitate their operation at the national level, and to promote cooperation agreements at the regional level. The reasons that make it advisable to support the development of national IXPs also apply to the creation of regional IXPs, which can help developing country operators to improve their bargaining power in their negotiations with global NSPs, and eventually aggregate enough traffic to be able to establish peering agreements rather than buying transit from them. The more serious difficulty for the creation of such regional IXPs is of course the varying levels of Internet development even among countries in the same region. Because of economies of scale, countries in which Internet markets are more developed tend to enjoy lower international access costs. These are sometimes even lower than the price that they would have to pay for the use of a common connection shared with a country with a smaller market. Countries with larger Internet markets therefore do not have an incentive to participate in a regional IXP, although the benefits of this in terms of quality of service (for example, reduced latency) could be significant. An alternative to regional IXPs may be the establishment of interconnection agreements between national IXPs of developing countries in the same region.

A competitive environment for ISPs

At the domestic level, it is important that Governments establish the conditions in which ISPs can operate in a competitive environment, thus reducing access cost and supporting the development of Internet markets. In such an environment, ISPs should be able to identify and negotiate the best commercial arrangements for international connectivity. In many cases, this process may be facilitated by helping ISPs to better understand the full range of international connectivity options open to them.[52] Assessing the appropriateness of each of them for their specific circumstances already represents a significant burden for many developing country ISPs, and capacity-building in this area could be a fruitful initiative for the international community to support.

Regulators in developing countries need to pay particular attention to ISP interconnection issues at the domestic level. For instance, it is important to ensure that new entrants are able to interconnect with other operators, particularly with the incumbent, quickly and at reasonable cost. It is also important that access to content be non-discriminatory regardless of the network access provider involved, and that network

providers are free to choose their hosting providers. Quality is another aspect in respect of which interconnection among ISPs should take place on a non-discriminatory basis.

Another aspect in respect of which action taken at the national level can reduce Internet access costs concerns ISP licensing, which in many developing countries are subject to arrangements that represent an objective impediment to the development of Internet markets. Research suggests that countries requiring formal regulatory approval for ISPs have fewer Internet users and hosts than countries that do not require such approval.[53] Licence fees in particular should be examined. It is not uncommon that licence fees of ISPs are levied on the basis of the latter's turnover, this being equivalent to imposing a tax on the use of the Internet. Regulators should consider setting licensing fees at a level commensurate with the cost of regulatory activity, rather than regard such fees as a source of government revenue.

International and domestic leased circuits are another aspect in respect of which telecommunications policies should promote effective competition. In extreme cases the incumbent telecommunications operator may not even offer business users the possibility of leasing lines. In general, international leased circuits represent by far the largest component of the total international Internet connectivity cost faced by ISPs. The price for this is in the majority of cases determined or significantly influenced by the telecommunications incumbent, particularly if there is not long experience of competition in this segment of the market. In some cases, ISPs must buy international leased circuits and global backbone connectivity in a single package provided by the incumbent, normally at prices that are a multiple of cost. Giving ISPs more options for the purchase of international leased circuit capacity and eventually unbundling this from the purchase of backbone connectivity (transit capacity) should result in increased competition and lower prices. However, the fact remains that if ISPs of developing countries do not aggregate their traffic, the relatively low amounts of bandwidth they demand will mean that they will not be able to benefit from the more attractive prices available to those that buy higher-capacity volumes.

The role of VSAT satellites

While still considerably more expensive than fibre optic cable, VSAT satellites may offer another possibility of dramatically increasing the availability of bandwidth and reducing its cost, particularly in remote or sparsely populated areas. The cost of some of these terminals is now less than $2,000 and the monthly charges for Internet access could be as low as $150.[54] Potentially economies of scale could bring these figures down to $750 and $100 respectively. However, in many developing countries regulatory restrictions and high licensing fees (which can be as high as $15,000 per year/terminal for a 128 Kbps link) are inhibiting the deployment of VSAT.[55] Another obstacle preventing developing countries from fully benefiting from the cost-reducing effects of VSAT is the heterogeneity of applicable policies across neighbouring developing countries. Since many of these are small markets, investors may find it difficult to offer satellite services in just one or two countries, but the high costs involved in securing regulatory approval in several countries and the associated complexity introduce delays in the deployment of VSAT, add to the risk of the investment and increase the cost of deployment. The development of policy consensus among developing countries at the regional level concerning the regulatory requirements for VSAT operation would provide an incentive for the deployment of VSAT, bring down barriers to access for new entrants and thus result in increased competition in Internet access services and its attendant cost reductions and quality improvements.

These and other obstacles to the emergence of efficient ISPs may push companies to host their content overseas, as was documented in a number of cases in UNCTAD (2001). This has a cost in terms of lost e-business opportunities (for instance in the area of outsourcing), reduces the quality of service provided to domestic users and generally hampers Internet take-up among businesses. It also makes it difficult to implement strategies to cut connectivity costs such as the promotion of local hosting of local content and the caching of frequently demanded foreign content.

Regulatory capacity-building

The policy arsenal available to the developing countries in order to reduce Internet access costs seems therefore to offer significant possibilities for action at the national level. In addition to regulatory actions, in many developing countries policymakers could consider addressing institutional regulatory issues. Developing countries face severe shortages in regulatory capacity in a sector such as telecommunications in general and the Internet in particular, which is complex and fast-changing and in which the market conditions prevailing in developing countries often differ significantly from those in which the more widespread regulatory models and approaches evolved. These models often require levels of expertise and resources that are scarce in developing countries. Support for capacity-building in this area is therefore crucial. From the internal point of view, it is important that the regulatory authorities enjoy the political support that is needed to enable them to check the potential effects on market competition of the power that incumbents still wield as a result of their historical pre-eminence in the country's public sector.

The preceding considerations have stressed the importance of creating a pro-competitive environment in the market for Internet access in developing countries. Commercial arrangements, provided that abuses of dominant positions are prevented and traffic exchange is facilitated, should offer Internet operators the right set of incentives to invest in infrastructure, deliver lower-cost and higher-quality services, and increase connectivity in developing countries. However, in the final analysis, the fundamental reason why higher access Internet costs prevail in the developing world compared with the developed countries has more to do with low Internet penetration combined with the high costs of setting up terrestrial infrastructure from scratch, than with the concrete modality in which international backbone access costs are shared between ISPs and backbone providers. Small Internet markets make it difficult to generate economies of scale that could result in lower costs. Policy intervention in a number of other areas – the domestic Internet market, telecommunications, and other economic and social aspects of Internet access – stands a greater chance of starting a virtuous circle (higher use level generating economies of scale leading to reduced access cost and thus higher use) than *ex-ante* regulatory intervention in the market for international backbone connectivity.

References

African Internet Service Providers Association (AfrISPA) (2002). The Halfway Proposition. Background Paper on Reverse Subsidy of G8 Countries by African ISPs. October, www.afrispa.org/initiatives.htm.

Analysys Consulting Limited (2005). Comparison of the EU-US Internet Connectivity Structures. Revision 1, www.cocombine.org/deliverables.htm.

Antelope Consulting (2001). DFID Internet Costs Study. The Costs of Internet Access in Developing Countries: Overview Report. 15 October, www.antelope.org.uk/internet_costs.htm#internet_costs

Beltrán F (2003). Effects of Interconnection Agreements on Internet Competition: The Case of the Network Access Point as a Cooperative Agreement for Internet Traffic Exchange. NET Institute Working Paper #03-01, October, www.netinst.org.

Economides N (2004a). Competition Policy in Network Industries: An Introduction. NET Institute Working Paper # 04-23, www.netinst.org.

Economides, N (2004b). The Economics of the Internet Backbone. NET Institute Working Paper #04-23, www.netinst.org.

Gartner Inc. (2004). *Gartner's 2004 Network Service Providers Magic Quadrants.* 10 December 2004, www.gartner.com/resources/124900/124915/gartners_2004_n.pdf.

Gartner Inc. (2005) *The AT&T And MCI Acquisitions Will Shape the Future of the U.S. Network Services Markets* 28 April, www.gartner.com/resources/127200/127262/the_att_and_mci.pdf.

Giovanetti E et al. (2004). Initial Data Set on Data Prices and Quality. Revision 1,

www.cocombine.org/deliverables.htm.

Giovannetti E and D'Inazio A (2004) Report on the Economic Literature on Internet Bilateral Peering and Transit Decisions. Revision 1, www.cocombine.org/deliverables.htm.

Huston G (2005). Where's the Money? – Internet Interconnection and Financial Settlements. Available at ispcolumn.isoc.org/200-01/interconns.txt.

International Development Research Centre of Canada (IDRC) (2004). Open and Closed Skies. Satellite Access in Africa, www.gvf.org/database/regulatoryDB/africaskiesindex.cfm.

International Telecommunication Union (ITU) (2004). Trends in Telecommunication Reform 2004/05. Licensing in an Era of Convergence. Summary.

www.itu.int/ITU-D/treg/publications/Trends04_summary.pdf.

Internet Systems Consortium (2005). Internet Domain Survey Host Count, www.isc.org/index.pl?/ops/ds.

Lightreading.com (2004). *Better News on Internet Backbones.* 26 August, www.lightreading.com.

Norton WB (2001). Internet Service Providers and Peering. Draft 2.4, www-2.cs.cmu.edu/~srini/15-744/F04/readings/Nor01.pdf.

Norton WB (2002). The Art of Peering: The Peering Playbook. Draft 1.2, www.nanog.org/papers/playbook.doc.

Odlyzko, A (2004). The Evolution of Price Discrimination in Transportation and its Implications for the Internet. *Review of Networks Economics,* vol. 3, issue 3. September, www.rnejournal.com/articles/odlyzko_RNE_sept_2004.pdf.

Odlyzko, A and Tilly, B (2005). A Refutation of Metcalfe's Law and a Better Estimate for the Value of Networks and Networks Interconnections. Preliminary version, 2 March 2005, www.dtc.umn.edu/~odlyzko/doc/metcalfe.pdf.

OECD (2002). Internet Traffic Exchange and the Development of End-to-End International Telecommunication Competition. 13 March, Paris, www.oecd.org.

OECD (2005). OECD Input to the United Nations Working Group on Internet Governance. Paris, www.oecd.org/dataoecd/34/9/34727842.pdf.

Telegeography (2005). Bandwidth Demand Outpaces Price Declines. Press release dated 7 April, www.telegeography.com/press/releases/2005-04-07.php.

UNCTAD (2001). *E-commerce and Development Report 2001*. UNCTAD/SDTE/ECB/1. United Nations publication, sales no. E.0.II.D.30. New York and Geneva, www.unctad.org/ecommerce.

UNCTAD (2003). *E-commerce and Development Report 2003*. UNCTAD /SDTE/ECB/2003/1. United Nations publication, sales no. E.03.II.D.30. New York and Geneva. www.unctad.org/ecommerce.

United States General Accounting Office (2001) Telecommunications: Characteristics and Competitiveness of the Internet Backbone Market. Washington DC, www.gao.gov/new.items/d0216.pdf.

Working Group on Internet Governance (2005a). Draft issues paper on international Internet connections. February, http://www.wgig.org/docs/WP-Peering.pdf.

Working Group on Internet Governance (2005b). Report of the Working Group. June, http://www.wgig.org/docs/WGIGREPORT.pdf.

Notes

1.   See www.unctad.org/ecommerce/ecommerce_en/events_en.htm.

2.   A good summary of the critics' arguments can be found in the issues paper on peering and interconnection that was prepared for the first meeting of the Working Group on Internet Governance, convened by the Secretary-General of the United Nations as part of the preparation for the second phase of the World Summit on the Information Society. See www.wgig.org/docs/WP-Peering.pdf.

3.   See the Internet Systems Consortium's Domain Survey, available at www.isc.org.

4.   See Huston (2005) for an summary presentation of the implications of these differences for the possible financial arrangements for Internet interconnections.

5.   Routers are specialized computers that forward data packets to their destination. Switches connect network segments.

6.   Normally backbones use fibre optic cables that can carry between 155 Mbps and 9.6 Gbps.

7.   Norton (2001).

8.   There are no major functional differences between NAPs and IXPs. The term "NAP" originally referred to facilities in the United States designated by the National Science Foundation in order to provide for traffic exchange during the earlier phase of the commercialization of the Internet. NAPs were originally operated by telecommunications carriers. While in the United States NAPs are now generally operated by neutral, for-profit specialized operators or by non-neutral telecommunications operators, in many other countries the facilities performing traffic exchange functions are called IXPs, and tend to be operated by cooperative, non-profit organizations created by ISPs.

9.   Telegeography Inc. (2005).

10.   Gartner Inc. (2005).

11.   According to research by Telegeography Inc. See Lightreading.com (2004).

12.   Gartner Inc. (2004).

13.   Lightreading.com (2004).

14.   An autonomous system, in Internet terminology, is a group of networks controlled by the same entity (normally an ISP or a large organization), using a common internal gateway protocol for routing packets among them and a common external gateway protocol for routing packets to the rest of the Internet.

15.   A rich literature has developed around the issues of peering, transit and interconnection. See, for example, Giovannetti and D'Ignazio (2004).

16.   Bandwidth and latency are the two main determinants of the performance of a network. Bandwidth indicates the amount of data that can flow over the network by unit of time. Latency is the average time it takes for a data packet to travel across the network. While some latency is unavoidable, factors such as slow servers or complex routing can result in longer delays that seriously degrade network performance.

17.   See, for example, the site of the London Internet Exchange at www.linx.net.

18.   It should be noted that although no monetary payments are made, the exchange of traffic is not costless. Peering implies that the cost incurred by the two participating networks in carrying traffic from one network to the other and vice versa is approximately the same, but certainly not zero.

19.   See Norton (2001) for an analysis of the conditions in which an ISP may choose to peer with another ISP.

20.   Economides (2004b) illustrates this point with a simple numerical example: Network A has 20 ISPs with 5 websites and 500 users each. Network B has 1 ISP with 5 websites and 500 users. If all users have the same surfing habits and

all visit all websites, traffic from A to B will be 20 x 500 x 5 = 50,000 visits, while traffic from B to A will be 500 x 5 x 20 = 50,000 visits.

21.   Various criteria may be used to assess similarity between networks, such as geographical coverage, network capacity, traffic volume, size of the customer base or position in the market.

22.   Significant amounts of fibre optic remain "dark" as a consequence of past overinvestment, although some recent forecasts indicate that the "bandwidth glut" may start being absorbed in 2005. At the same time, technological development seems to ensure that the technical transport possibilities offered by fibre optic networks will continue to grow at a considerably faster pace than demand.

23.   See, for instance, sites such as www.telegeography.com or www.itquotes.com.

24.   See www.band-x.com.

25.   Virtual NSPs do not own their own physical infrastructure, but buy unused capacity from other NSPs and market it under their own name.

26.   The term "multihoming" refers to a computer host that has multiple IP addresses to connected networks. Addresses with different prefixes can be used to force traffic to be routed through different carriers.

27.   Reliability and quality of service are other reasons for the increased popularity of multihoming.

28.   Caching is the local storage of frequently accessed data, which reduces the need for data transfer over networks; mirroring consists in creating and maintaining multiple copies of websites or pages, often on different servers in different geographical locations; and intelligent content distribution technologies optimize data delivery by routing data-heavy web traffic using criteria such as bandwidth availability, distance and others.

29.   See Economides (2004b).

30.   See Odlyzko and Tilly (2005).

31.   See www.isoc.org/standards for an explanation of the process of development and adoption of Internet standards and protocols.

32.   If necessary, fibre optic not being used for Internet transport can easily be leased from other operators, and routers and switches are readily available at reasonable costs.

33.   See Odlyzko (2004).

34.   It should be noted that even today, and in spite of the large number of IXPs operating in Europe, some intra-European traffic may still be exchanged in the United States. Sometimes even traffic between ISPs in the same European country goes through US backbones. However, the reasons for this are purely commercial, as Internet traffic flows among developed countries are exclusively determined by commercial considerations and not by any infrastructure deficiency.

35.   See United States General Accounting Office (2001).

36.   See OECD (2002).

37.   See Telegeography (2005).

38.   See IDRC (2004).

39.   The economies of scale generated by factors such as the numbers of Internet users or the geographical concentration of users also influence bandwidth costs.

40.   See chart 1.5 of UNCTAD (2003).

41.   See www.ispa.org.za/regcom/submissions/ispa-sub-proposed-interconnection-facilities-leasing-regulations.doc, p. 6.

42.   See Antelope Consulting (2001). The countries involved were Cambodia, India, Nepal, South Africa, Uganda and Zambia.

43.   An example of this is provided by the "Linx anywhere" system of the London Internet Exchange.

44.   See OECD (2002).

45.   In the language of ITU texts, the term "administration" refers to a telecommunications operator or Recognized Operating Agency (ROA).

46.   See www.itu.int/ITU-T/studygroups/com03/iic/rapp.html.

47.   See www.itu.int/ITU-T/studygroups/com03/iic/docs/TRECD50-0406Amd1E.pdf.

48.   See Working Group on Internet Governance (2005a),. www.wgig.org/docs/WP-Peering.pdf.

49.   See Working Group on Internet Governance (2005b), www.wgig.org/docs/WGIGREPORT.pdf.

50.   This could refer to countries that remain beyond the reach of fibre optic cables and whose small Internet markets make infrastructure investment extremely difficult to sustain.

51.   See Antelope Consulting (2001).

52.   See Antelope Consulting (2001).

53.   ITU (2004).

54.   See IRDC (2004).

55.   Ibid.

Chapter 3

E-Credit Information, Trade Finance and E-Finance: Overcoming Information Asymmetries

A. Introduction

In most developing countries financial service providers are not yet in a position to use modern credit risk management techniques to provide short-term working capital and trade finance to local enterprises at competitive terms. An important reason for such a situation is the lack of credit reporting systems. Many developing countries still need to establish functional credit information systems in order to improve the quality of financial information on enterprises and rate them as credit risks.

The inability of creditors to assess borrowers' risk owing to a paucity of credit information flows – regularly updated information on the financial state and payment record of borrowers – is the root cause of information asymmetry between these two principal economic agents. Weak and fragmented public record systems, laxity in disclosure of companies' financials and the nascent state of both public and private credit information entities are among the reasons for deficient credit risk management in many developing and transition economies.

Enterprises in the formal economy may not have access to credit partly owing to their own weaknesses and partly owing to structural and institutional deficiencies. These may include inefficient public records systems, inadequate credit reporting and a lack of sharing and pooling, by financial service providers, of information on borrowers. The situation is further aggravated by the fact that many companies still operate in the informal economy. They are not officially registered and they do not pay taxes. Such firms mainly transact with cash and are subject to usurious terms of credit, and they are excluded from the formal financial intermediation.

Payment systems have been using proprietary electronic networks since the beginning of 1970s and were based on private telecom infrastructures and networks belonging to the banking industry. Nowadays the e-payment systems are increasingly networks, based on the public network infrastructure of the Internet (UNCTAD, 2001, 2002). In spite of concerns about security and interoperability, the financial services sector is continuing its adoption of Internet technologies and Internet-based applications for e-credit information, e-credit scoring and e-rating of enterprises, thus permitting a wider use of e-payments and e-finance techniques.

In developing and transition economies the problems of transparency and information sharing in the formal sector and the persistence of the informal economy are the main obstacles to introducing innovative electronic credit information and risk management techniques. As a result, many of them are forgoing the opportunity for considerable improvements in access to trade-related finance and e-finance. Internet-based information and communication technologies (ICTs) permit firms to communicate, network and transact at much lower costs, and are improving the quality of information flows. In particular, managing trade-related credit risks and payments online greatly reduces the costs of financial intermediation (see UNCTAD 2001 and 2002). Therefore, actively using the Internet and ICTs to build modern credit information services has the potential for leapfrogging towards the latest and most efficient e-credit information technologies and systems and thus embracing the information economy by considerably diminishing information asymmetries in creditor–borrower relations.

Enterprises in developing and transition economies are becoming increasingly aware that successful international, regional and domestic trade requires access to trade finance and e-finance on competitive terms. For such access they need to be assessed using procedures that are increasingly technology-enabled, such as e-scoring and e-rating. That implies a respect for accuracy and transparency in information flows concerning their finance and payment records.

The international banking regulatory capital standards known as Basel II make the rating of enterprises a necessary condition for providing credit. The regulatory challenge of Basel II may motivate countries and their financial service providers and enterprises to move towards modern e-credit, e-rating and e-financing techniques. Alternatively, not meeting the requirements of Basel II – scheduled to come to force in 2007 – will further complicate developing country enterprises' access to trade finance and e-finance. Non-bank trade finance sources that will compete with banks burdened by Basel II rules will also need to carry out e-rating in order to adequately assess risks while providing trading enterprises with short-term finance and e-finance.

In response to the problems outlined UNCTAD XI initiated a discourse on the prospects of development of e-credit information systems and trade finance and e-finance for enterprises in developing countries. Major credit information and credit insurance agencies, banks and others exchanged information on their achievements and problems and shared ideas on the ways forward in this new and promising domain. Further details of this dialogue are provided in the Annex.

This chapter suggests that an important avenue for improving developing countries' access to trade-related finance and e-finance and leading them towards the information economy is the use of opportunities provided by the Internet to help overcome information asymmetries between creditors and borrowers. Part B underscores the importance of credit information, the need to meet the challenge of the Basel II framework and the need to move away from an informal economy. It underlines the importance of creating business-friendly and transparent conditions for collecting credit information on developing countries' enterprises, establishing e-credit information infrastructures and using e-credit scoring and e-rating techniques. It also addresses further challenges arising from IT security and interoperability in progressing towards paperless trade and e-trade finance. Part C considers credit insurance as a financial service that relies heavily on credit information, and its migration towards greater use of Internet-based technologies. Part D reviews the progress in trade-related e-banking, integrated e-trade finance platforms and other e-trade finance related techniques, and presents selected examples from devel-

oped and developing countries. Part E, in conclusion, discusses the conditions that developing countries should create to introduce improvements in their e-credit information capacities that will permit enterprises to have better access to trade finance and e-finance.

B. Information economy for accelerated development: The case for credit and e-credit information

The existence of information asymmetry in the markets has been at the centre of economic debate for quite some time (see Arrow, 1963; Akerlof, 1970; Stiglitz and Weiss, 1981; and Stiglitz 2000 and 2001). Although an extended discussion of this debate lies outside the scope of this chapter, it should still be stressed that in the context of lender–borrower relations information asymmetries raise the problems of adverse selection and moral hazard, in particular in developing countries. Information asymmetry refers to a situation in which transacting parties do not have access to the same information and as a result one party can take advantage at the expense of the other. The intervention of a third party (say banks in creditor–borrower intermediation) may provide a remedy to this problem. Adverse selection in the case of credit consists in financing a borrower without much concern for the probability of default. That creates the problem of moral hazard, as in the case of default the costs will normally be borne by the debtors rather than by the creditors who made the mistake in the first place.

Overcoming as much as possible information asymmetries between economic agents is one of the main features of the emerging information economy. The latter is characterized by instantaneous and networked electronic communications and drastically decreased transaction costs for all information-intensive operations (including those of collecting credit information), which thus increase labour productivity and make possible major efficiency gains and improved organization. Such communications are valuable tools for overcoming information asymmetries and can become one of the building blocks of the emerging information economy in those countries.

The regulatory and institutional environment, and a culture that is conducive to accumulation and updating of information, in a standardized electronic format, on enterprises and households as credit risks, are among the key characteristics differentiating a developed economy from a developing one. The quality of credit information here is of primordial importance. First, public record infrastructure and accounting and audit standards stipulate accurate general and financial statements and their issuance by enterprises. Second, credit information can be collected not only from the public sector and enterprises, but also from third parties and independent sources; this makes it possible to have an additional check on the quality of information. The regulatory and institutional back-up for credit information should ensure that it is provided at low cost. By definition, credit information services are limited to enterprises operating in a formal economy.

The high level of information asymmetry in creditor–borrower relations in the developing countries can be explained by weak credit information infrastructure, ineffective public records, lack of credit management skills and underdeveloped financial intermediation. A generally restrictive and cumbersome regulatory environment and a large informal cash-based economy, make the matter worse. Those and other obstacles make it difficult for financial intermediaries to build up objective and verifiable databases on credit risks

1. The importance of credit information

Credit information is a set of data used by creditors to verify the financial status and payments record of borrowers. Limited research on this subject suggests that there is a strong positive correlation between the availability and cost of credit and the level of development of credit information (Miller, 2003). Thus, according to Japelli and Pagano (1993), the exchange of information on borrowers between financial service providers decreases default rates and average interest rates. Some available analysis also suggests that it is important for creditors to share not only negative information (state of arrears on credits) on borrowers but also positive information (volume and terms of credits paid on time). As suggested by recent research by the World Bank (Majnoni et al., 2004), combining negative and positive information on borrowers gives creditors more predictive power and permits more borrowers to have access to credit than would be the case if only negative information had been shared.

Credit information enables the creditor to assess more adequately the creditworthiness of the bor-

rower. The difficulty involved in obtaining that information remains substantial in the majority of developing countries and in many economies in transition. In granting credit, finance or credit insurance the decision maker looks for two main elements: "ability to pay" and "willingness to pay". The latter is sometimes referred to as "commercial morality" or "reputation collateral". In developed countries firms pay because if they fail to do so they will be put out of business. This is because the laws and courts permit the creditor to pursue the debtor. In many developing countries this infrastructure is still not very effective and therefore there is no compelling reason for a buyer to pay. Foreign suppliers can still rely on larger enterprises that want to purchase from abroad and are aware that damaging their reputation can inhibit their ability to import. However, if the importer is an SME the case is less compelling. Hence, for the successful functioning of credit and e-credit information systems, developing countries have first to address adequately the above issues of fundamental commercial law and enforcement and adequate accounting and auditing standards.

In developed economies businesses and consumers have relatively easy access to finance. One of the reasons for this is the ability of the financier to assess the credit risk of the applicant rapidly and efficiently. This ability stems from the highly developed, electronic systems of formatted and standardized information on the financial state and behaviour of companies and households (primarily as borrowers but also as suppliers, trustees etc.) in the hands of specialized information companies. These include public credit registries (PCRs), private credit bureaux, credit insurers, banks, credit card companies and other creditors. Another important characteristic is that this commoditized credit information is available instantaneously and at low cost. Moreover, the existence of PCRs permits central banks to gauge the debt outstanding of the banking industry and hence its financial robustness, while individual banks can evaluate a potential debtor's exposure with other banks. The credit bureaux collect more extensive information from a variety of sources on companies' financials, credit history, current state of debt repayments, and so forth, before extending any credit opinion, scoring, or rating on a particular debtor. Tradition and adequate regulatory requirements for the disclosure of financial state and payments records of corporate and individual debtors contributed to the creation of a highly sophisticated and commoditized credit information industry, particularly in the United States. The scoring given to companies by Dun & Bradstreet (D&B), as well as by other major US credit bureaux (Equifax, Experian and TransUnion) are considered sufficient by US banks for taking decisions to extend credit to those companies. At the same time the bulk of credit information in continental Europe is produced by major credit insurers that use credit information as an input into their business model of credit insurance (Atradius, Coface and Euler-Hermes; for more details see box 3.2). To produce credit information major credit insurers also maintain an ownership position in credit information companies (Graydon and SCRL). They also purchase credit information from other credit bureaux.

The US banks while relying on D&B and similar scorings are assuming the risk of borrower's default by themselves. Similarly, the credit scoring services of US credit bureaux are actively supporting credit managers of US firms while the latter are deciding whether to supply goods and services on credit. In fact, credit scoring and management services are becoming a more important part of services provided by European credit insurers. At the same time in Europe credit information on buyers permits credit insurers to issue a credit insurance policy covering sellers against default risks of buyers. Banks assume a lower risk since in the case of a credit request from a seller for, say, working capital financing, the credit insurance policy is assigned as collateral to the creditor bank and in the case of default of a buyer the credit insurer reimburses the bank directly.

It is also important to stress that in developed countries banks, credit bureaux and credit insurers generally trust the quality of the financial reporting of the borrower companies. However, one of the main challenges in the developing and transition countries is the quality of financial information provided – the accounting is frequently not up to international standards and the audits are not always reliable. Therefore, accurate periodic financial statements of the borrowers are as important as the parts of credit reports on their payments record and commercial morality. The need to improve the quality of accounting and audit in these countries is one of the most important factors for credit reporting systems to operate effectively and for permitting better access of enterprises to trade finance (and to finance in general).

Since 1999, the World Bank has conducted several global periodic surveys of PCRs and private credit bureaux. An important systemic consideration of the financial supervisory authorities while creating PCRs was to measure the debt outstanding to the banking

industry and the rate of delinquency among borrowers. Credit reporting by banks to supervisory authorities is compulsory, as the system should at least have negative information on borrowers. PCRs are helping bank regulators to strengthen supervision, promote competition, examine monetary and financial aggregates and improve other aspects of regulation. PCRs exist in more than 60 countries and are continuing to proliferate in developing and transition economies.

Private credit bureaux could be independent entities or closely related to banks or credit insurers, or corporate rating agencies. While PCRs cover mainly bank-related credit risks, private credit bureaux accumulate information on borrowers from both the public and the private sector. An important part of credit information collected by credit bureaux is public sector information, such as company registers, court records and collateral filings. These are then verified by means of extensive information collection from the companies (financial statements, trade data, publications, annual reports and payments records) and third parties (specialized press, chambers of commerce, partners etc.). Moreover, credit bureaux help major suppliers of goods and services to develop databases on their buyers. The sellers either apply credit scoring software to better manage their customer-related risks or outsource such credit management to credit bureaux and other financial service providers (for more details see section B4).

In other words, there are complementarities in the nature of credit information collected by PCRs and credit bureaux. Such complementarities should normally generate efficient communication lines between both institutions, but this is not the case in the majority of developing countries as observed by the World Bank. PCRs by and large do not share data with credit bureaux. While the main users of information provided by the former are the central banks and commercial banks, the latter sell credit information to non-bank users such as credit insurers, factors and lessors, as well as to companies selling and buying goods and services. The existence of both types of credit bureaux has a very important disciplinary effect on the borrowers, as no company or consumer would like to be blacklisted as delinquent and thus lose its "reputation capital".

In developed countries other than the United States, the availability and the transparency requirements for credit information vary from country to country in line with their legislations. In Europe and Japan credit reporting systems are well developed. In the United

States, however, an extensive credit information industry exists in its own right, while in Europe credit information supply is mainly in the hands of major credit insurers. For the latter their large credit information databases are primarily an input that makes it possible to run credit insurance business (for more details see section C). In developed countries the applicants (corporates and countries alike) with a good credit profile are beneficiaries of the credit reporting system and have access to credit on time. The credit information providers and financial institutions put on notice those applicants whose borrowings have earned them a poor reputation. Many of them possess not only information about the payments behaviour of individuals and companies but also comprehensive ratings for companies and countries that help to assess respectively their commercial and political risks.

Domestic providers of credit information apart from PRCs and credit bureaux could include other public entities, banks, credit insurers, debt collectors, specialized information companies, utilities, and so forth. Foreign entities such as international specialized information companies, credit insurers, banks and credit card companies could also be information providers for local commercial and political risks. Those involved in the creation of local credit information facilities should be able to collect information at low cost from the commerce registry, pension fund, tax, statistical and other information-related public offices. They should also have an authority (given by clients) to make inquiries using banks' and other private information providers' databases. Local debt collectors and credit insurers (if any) would be the parties most naturally interested in the creation of national credit information facilities.

In the majority of developing and transition economies the system of organized credit information is still at an embryonic stage. The main problem is the lack of uniform, reliable and accurate public sector information, lack of disclosure requirements and lack of willingness to disclose voluntarily. The absence of standardized and detailed credit reporting is one (though not the only) limiting factor for the development of a modern financial sector. Simple bank lending or financing of SMEs is still problematic in most cases. The absence of trade finance hinders exports, and such commonplace instruments in developed countries as credit insurance and factoring are currently used by only a handful of developing and transition countries that export manufactures. However, some of those countries have already developed quite

elaborate credit information, credit insurance and export-import financing systems. One of the best examples of credit information is to be found in Brazil (see box 3.1). The Asian financial crisis was a "wake-up call" for those countries in terms of the creation of credit information services. In fact, it was part of the Bretton Woods institutions' conditionality for bailing out those countries. As a result, credit bureaux started to spread in the late 1990s and the banking communities in the region started to accept the idea of pooling information on their debtors. Gathering information on SMEs and other companies is also emerging (Bartels 2003).

An example of an early stage in the development of credit information infrastructure is the Russian Federation. In the command economy, with its rigid quantities and administrative prices, the planners and enterprise managers used to know and could predict the reciprocal products and payments flows between public enterprises. However, the poor quality of products, shortages, increasingly phantom reporting and the emerging grey economy signalled the weaknesses of the system. After the liberalization of prices, which started the replacement of the command system, the emerging quasi-privatized enterprises found themselves trapped in huge payment arrears owing to the collapse of old inter-enterprise relations and the precarious state of new business linkages. Although the situation has since improved, there are still virtually no market-based systems supporting the dissemination of credit information. Creation of credit bureaux, including a non-profit organisation under the auspices of the Russian Bankers Association (RBA), restarting of the Russian Eximbank and the emergence of factoring operations are the first steps in that direction. However, as the RBA is a voluntary organization and not a credit registry under the Central Bank, the commercial banks belonging to the credit bureau might be reluctant to share positive information on their good clients. At the same time the improvements in the tax regime, the need to access bank credits and the rapid dissemination of Internet-based solutions are improving prospects for acceptance of modern methods of trade-related credit information and debt collection. Meanwhile, some transition economies in Eastern Europe have already managed to develop credit information, credit insurance and factoring, and have started rapidly to introduce e-finance services, considerably filling the gap in that critical domain.

More transparent and equitable banking and data protection legislation, debtor and creditor-related laws

Box 3.1

Basel II ratings and changes in capital requirements for a trade finance risk

Basel I considered short-term bank-guaranteed trade finance to be a good, tier 1 bank risk (letters of credit, other bank-guaranteed negotiable instruments), assigning only 20 per cent capital weighting for OECD bank assets with both OECD and non-OECD banks. Thus the Basel I risk weight for, say $100 million of such assets was 20 per cent, and with a minimum capital ratio of 8 per cent, this demands regulatory capital to the tune of $1.6 million (8 per cent of 20 million). As the table below shows, for all Basel II options the demand for regulatory capital is higher and in the case of Standardised option 1 and Foundation IRB uncalibrated (specific default characteristics of trade finance product) it is much higher.

Basel I	Basel II					
	Standardised Option 1	Standardised option 2	Foundation IRB Uncalibrated	Foundation IRB Calibrated	Advanced IRB Uncalibrated	Advanced IRB Calibrated
1.6	7.6	4.7	8.7	4.3	4.3	2.6
	+375%	+194%	+444%	+169%	+169%	+63%

Source: LTP Trade in Global Trade Review, September/October 2004, p. 3.

permitting enforcement of bankruptcy, and other regulatory requirements are prerequisites for the creation of effective credit information systems. Such a regulatory system should include in particular:

- Effective commercial legal and judiciary systems, including registration laws, bankruptcy laws, and public and court registers;

- Standards for adequate and timely reporting and disclosure by private sector operators;

- Adoption of international accounting standards and standards for auditors;

- Adequate public data dissemination and publishing requirements;

- Possibility of collecting, processing and disseminating public records, suits and judgements;

- Permission to access companies' track records with banks for authorized institutions and other creditors.

2. Facing the Basel II challenge

One of the challenges that underscores the need to build up modern credit information and risk management systems, thus making it possible to develop the rating of enterprises as credit risks, is the emerging new international banking regulation known as Basel II. Rating the credit risks of potential borrow-

ers is becoming a condition for their access to bank loans. Moreover, Basel II recommends new, more differentiated and stricter regulatory capital criteria for various types of ratings. Already the majority of more than 100 central banks from developing and transition economies that applied capital standards and other regulations based on existing Basel I have announced their commitment to adopt Basel II (Bank for International Settlements, 2004b).

To improve financial sector stability and banks' management of their credit portfolios the Basel Committee on Banking Supervision (comprising the central banks of 13 leading developed economies) has recommended a move from the Basel I to the Basel II regulation starting in 2007. The latest June 2004 framework for Basel II entitled "International Convergence of Capital Measurement and Capital Standards: a Revised Framework" comprises three Pillars. The first Pillar is about minimum capital requirements, the second the supervisory review process and the third market discipline.[1] While Basel II maintains the minimum capital requirement of Basel I at 8 per cent it introduces a much more differentiated and complex assignment of weights based on the credit profile of borrowers.

Another innovation related to capital requirement is regulatory capital provisioning for so-called operational risks (failures due to internal and external errors and attacks; see chapter 5). Banks basically can choose two approaches for calculating the regulatory capital for credit risk: the standardised approach or the internal rating based (IRB) approach. In the standardised approach the ratings for corporate, sovereign and banking borrowers are based on ratings as given by external credit assessment institutions approved by the national regulator. Those institutions include well-known credit rating agencies such as Standard & Poor's, Moody's and Fitch,[2] major credit insurers such as Coface, Atradius and Euler-Hermes (for smaller companies) and national rating agencies approved by a country's regulator (which will raise the problem of comparability between national agencies' credit assessments). Major credit information suppliers such as Dun & Bradstreet, Experian and others might also play a similar role especially for SME ratings, while public credit registries run by central banks could also provide data to develop the latter.

The most important issue from the trade finance perspective is the differentiation of credit risks in Basel II (see box 3.1). In a way Basel I was less stringent regarding borrowers with higher risks, as the regulatory capital requirements were the same for lending to a blue chip company or a company from a developing country (although in the case of higher risks the banks could keep more economic capital, depending on their internal procedures).[3]

In other words, Basel II explicitly gives a competitive advantage to sophisticated banks by allowing them to assign less capital for the same portfolio of credits than to those obliged to use the Standardised approach. To retain their customer base the latter might resort to selling their trade credit risks to, for example, institutional investors that can operate with less capital since they are not subject to Basel II regulations or using other capital market techniques while structuring their trade finance portfolio (Bayliss and Parsons, 2004).

To help manage the challenges that developing and transition economies are facing with the advent of the complex system of Basel II, a team led by World Bank experts proposed that the calibrated IRB approach be changed into a centralized-rating-based approach (CRB). In such an approach while banks will continue to rate their clients, the regulator will determine the rating scale and default probabilities. They also proposed that credit risk be estimated by a homogeneous methodology of direct sampling as it makes it possible to produce comparable statistics across emerging economies and their banks. According to the team, it will need time for regulators and banks in emerging

economies to acquire resources and enough sophistication to adequately implement the IRB approach (Majnoni, Miller and Powell, 2004).

Apart from the need for further sophistication of their banks, many developing countries that have agreed to implement the Basel II recommendations might face a situation where the lack of credit information and hence possibilities for credit scoring and rating of enterprises might compromise their willingness to follow them. Thus, in a way, Basel II is serving as a catalyst for the creation of credit bureaux in developing countries. Such bureaux might facilitate the provision of trade finance not only by banks but also by financial companies and funds that may arise as a competitive response to the Basel II straitjacket on the banks. These future challenges and opportunities also underscore the need to create incentives for enterprises that are still operating in the informal market and are being cut off from formal finance and e-finance to start considering moving towards the formal economy and eventually have opportunities to benefit from innovations and better terms of e-finance that financial service providers may eventually propose.

3. From informal to information economy

While addressing the need to modernize the credit information systems and face the future challenges of Basel II in developing economies, one should not forget that major parts of these economies are still represented by an informal sector, in which enterprises lack track records and are hence excluded from the above process. The discussion on the formal and informal sectors is part of the long-standing development economics debate (Hart, 1973). While companies in the formal sector pay taxes, more or less follow labour and other regulations and show their financials for various kinds of assessments, those in the informal sector tend to work with less capital, not to pay taxes, provide precarious and unstable employment, and operate in an environment of cash-based transactions and usurious terms of credit.[4] In the majority of countries this is tolerated because it addresses the problem of high rural and urban unemployment. In one of the first articles on the dual economy model Lewis (1954) forecast that the traditional sector in developing countries, which was the reservoir of surplus labour, would with time give way to the modern sector. However, as this did not occur in the majority of developing countries owing to the continuing pressure of surplus labour, other views, stressing the important role of the informal sector in providing employment and income to large masses of the population, including through efficient SME and microenterprise operations, also gained importance (Schneider and Klinglmair, 2004).[5]

The median assessment for the informal sector of the US economy is around 10 per cent (Edgcomb and Thetford, 2004). It is higher, and sometimes considerably so, in other OECD countries. In parts of the economy where credit is not important or is managed differently, the informal sector might persist. This is the case for, say, household and rural individual work (even in the OECD area) or for microenterprise activities.

Research shows that the informal sector in developing countries is an important economic feature. For example, according to the Government of Kenya, in 2002 two thirds of urban employees were in the informal sector (in the manufacturing sector the share of informal enterprises was even higher, reaching 83 per cent) (Bigsten et al., 2004). In many countries the estimated growth of the informal sector is higher than that of the formal sector, a fact that reflects the high labour absorptive capacity of the former in the urbanization process of many countries. In rural economies the informal sector is much larger and prospects for its formalization are even worse. According to the same study on informality in Kenya the appropriate development policy should encourage informal firms to be absorbed by the formal sector. In particular, it was stressed that uncertain legal status and absence of proper accounts result in lack of credit rating. Meanwhile, microfinance, owing to its limited scale (it only accounts for a small percentage of financial sector operations), scope (one-man shops) and methods of risk management (peer pressure) cannot be a substitute for a lack of credit information on larger enterprises, as in such cases the latter are merely deprived of access to modern working capital and trade finance. At the same time it should also be recognized that even microfinance institutions are increasingly moving towards more automated and quantitative credit evaluation methods, including credit scoring, and are building a credit information / credit bureau type of database.

Paradoxically, even in a country with highly developed credit information services such as Brazil, the informal sector continues to endure. According to *The McKinsey Quarterly* (2005a), this situation in Brazil was due to the heavy regulatory burden on enterprises. By

saving money while avoiding taxes and regulations, the informal economy companies can survive with productivity equal to half of that of formal economy firms. While in agriculture informality is very high (90 per cent), those migrating to cities normally also end up entering the urban informal sector. As a result, between 1992 and 2002 the informal employment did not change, remaining at a level of 55 per cent of overall employment. The high level of corporate taxes and administrative costs incurred in paying them, inefficiency and irregularities in the judiciary system were some of the examples of regulatory burdens. In comparison, the low level of informality in relatively advanced market economies in South-East Asia could be explained by the combining of reasonable tax and regulatory arrangements with strong law and law enforcement systems. Moreover, the dynamic increase in the use of ICT makes information flows more transparent and is driving those countries faster towards the information economy.

There are conflicting views on the role of the informal economy and the nature of the formal economy in China. Thus *The McKinsey Quarterly* (2005a) believes that in China the level of the grey economy is low, while other sources, depending on the methodology used for measurement, consider it relatively high. At the same time according to Bartels (2004), the formal part of the Chinese economy is still characterized by a lack of transparency and opaque information flows (poor accounting standards, lack of willingness to voluntarily disclose the accurate financial position of an enterprise), while credit information is highly fragmented and consumer information is not permitted to be used by private information companies.[6] At the same time China has launched its credit information and credit insurance services. Thus its credit bureau in the Shanghai area achieved a coverage that is quite high by international standards. Its credit insurer, Sinosure, is a member of the Berne Union and is actively cooperating with other credit insurers.

India still continues to have a large informal sector in spite of relatively high growth rates and economic dynamism over the last years. The most comprehensive and official report on unorganized labour is the NSSO (National Sample Survey Organization) Survey of 1999–2000. According to the survey, by the end of last century the main part of the total workforce in the country was still employed in the unorganized sector.[7] The contribution of the unorganized sector to the net domestic product and its share in total GDP at current prices has been estimated to be over 60 per cent. Presumably, part of this unorganized labour are working in SMEs and larger companies that are reporting financial information and paying corporate taxes. Hence, they cannot really be considered to be a part of the informal sector. Further research is needed to identify the real share of the latter and the degree of its contribution to GDP growth as compared with the formal sector. According to one estimate, India's informal economy accounts for 40 per cent of the total economy (Bartels, 2004). At the same time, highly successful national strategies to support the development of the ICT services sector in India are opening up new prospects for information flows in the economy and might empower policymakers and market participants to address the problems of the informal sector more adequately. Thus, being able to develop sophisticated software at affordable costs, Indian IT companies could contribute to the development of credit information services in India and other developing countries. There is thus a need for further business-friendly regulatory changes and improvements in government functioning, which might contribute to the expansion of the formal sector and make possible the access of Indian enterprises to competitive trade finance and e finance provided by banks and other financial service providers. It should also be mentioned that the Indian Export Import Bank and the Export Credit Guarantee Corporation have been supporting Indian trade for quite some time, while in the late 1990s the Indian Central Bank created a PCR to develop credit information services.

As ICTs and the Internet are helping to decrease the transaction costs of information and financial flows, the opportunity cost for enterprises from both the formal and the informal sectors entailed by staying away from this emerging world might eventually be quite high. In their turn the improvements in the regulatory framework and in the development of credit information systems will encourage more enterprises to move to the formal sector and thus contribute to widening the tax base and improving the tax collection situation.

4. E-credit information and related online scoring and rating systems

As noted above, credit information systems can develop only if an adequate regulatory and institutional framework encouraging financial reporting and data disclosure is in place. That should give rise to well-developed public records, including public and court registers, availability of data from independent sources, and a readiness on the part of enterprises and financial service providers to share and pool credit information. Maintaining and even refining these conditions are equally important for launching and developing their modern variant e-credit information. The main functionalities of e-credit information providers include credit information databases presented in a highly standardized and commoditized manner. It is possible to construct such databases as a result of the regular inflow of detailed information on companies. While rules and regulations requiring company data disclosure provided credit bureaux with opportunities to accumulate detailed information on trading companies, the advent of ICT made unit costs of collecting and updating of such data lower, thus making it possible to widen the scope and depth of information collection. Normally, each company has a reference number in major databases and should be able to update its files with new proven records. The databases provide such information as companies' details, financial health and payments record. Nowadays all major credit bureaux in developed and in some developing countries have functional websites permitting companies that are registered in their databases to provide inputs directly on the web into their respective files. On the basis of that and other independent information and analysis accumulated in the databases the credit bureaux are automatically assigning a credit rating or a scoring to companies. Major credit bureaux are able to do that thanks to advanced mathematical methods and statistical tools that determine the probability of a company's default (mainly default on paying a short-term trade-related debt). With time, successful ratings are becoming powerful tools to help the credit bureaux attract more enterprises seeking access to trade finance and e-finance.

One of the important services of credit information suppliers is to provide software credit management decision tools (frequently online) to companies to improve the latter's cash flow through better management of their accounts receivable and payable (money that companies should receive or pay as a result of selling or buying on credit). Major sellers need to predict the payment behaviour of their buyers. Providing solutions with software on predictive scoring of buyers' extended payment risk is the main part of services that credit bureaux try to sell to suppliers. In this service credit bureaux compete with banks, and credit insurers (see subsequent sections). In the United States major credit bureaux, such as Dun and Bradstreet (D&B), Experian, Equifax and Transunion, developed such tools in cooperation with major decision software producers, such as Fair Isaac Corporation (FICO). For companies supplying to a large number of buyers credit scoring software might help in taking quick credit decisions that is, whether to accept an extended payment from a buyer or not. Using software to find out the borrower's profile is increasingly considered a competitive advantage, accelerating the cash flow of the businesses and preventing excessive paperwork and delays. Major credit bureaux are leveraging such software, trying to per-

suade companies to outsource the whole credit management process to them. For middle-sized companies that might be an optimal solution given that they are not trapped in cartel prices for those services.

Box 3.2 describes two examples of best practices (one in a developed country and another in a developing country) of a pure credit bureau model with a focus on enterprise-related e-credit information.

Box 3.2

E-credit information: The cases of Dun and Bradstreet (D&B), United States, and Serasa, Brazil

D&B is a publicly quoted company with sales of around of $1.4 billion, in which credit reports represent the bulk of the business. It is the largest credit information supplier on enterprise risks, claiming that it keeps online databases on more than 92 million companies worldwide, of which 66 million are active companies.[1] Although historically a US-centric company, it actually has more foreign companies in its databases. The credit information in those databases is presented in a highly standardized and commoditized manner. Each of the companies in D&B online databases is identified by its individual D-U-N-S® number. D&B indicates that it undertakes massive (more than a million a day) updating of the elements of databases it possesses. Customers, including sellers, creditors, and other private and public institutions, can obtain updated information for a fee; this enables them to take informed business decisions, primarily those about extending various forms of short-term trade credit of reasonable volumes (known also as credit limits) to different types of borrowers. To help customers better read such information and identify risks, D&B also gives various types of credit scores to companies mainly as payers. Through a quality process known as DUNSRight, D&B not only tries to give its customers the possibility of making informed decisions about their credit risks, but also provides information on suppliers (McKinsey, 2005b).

D&B considers credit management services rendered to enterprises to be one its important business lines. One of its credit management products is the Global Decision Maker, which is an Internet application for immediate use by SMEs, hosted and managed directly by D&B. To leverage core competences, D&B entered into cooperation with FICO in providing online analytics to help SMEs take credit decisions vis-a-vis their buyers. It is estimated that 90 per cent of top US small business lenders use FICO software to approve loans (*DMReview*, 2005). Similar solutions are available also for larger enterprises and especially for major suppliers of consumer durables that prefer to embed such scoring techniques in their in-house credit management rules and systems (see further discussion in B.5).

Serasa of Brazil is the first major credit bureau in a developing country that can currently be considered a best practice example not only for developing countries but also for some OECD countries. More than 35 years ago the Brazilian banks that became its shareholders established the company called Serasa. It is now the leading credit bureau in the developing world and has the largest database in Latin America on the financial state and payments behaviour of companies (in fact, D&B relies on Serasa reports for information on Brazilian companies). Serasa is a profitable company and is paying dividends to its shareholders, namely banks.[2] It has developed a quite sophisticated system of information gathering on companies, which comes from different sources such as banks, chambers of commerce and notaries. Currently, Serasa has a nationwide presence in 140 cities in Brazil and maintains a relationship with over 300,000 enterprises, including data collection and information consulting. The Serasa database serves three million consultations daily, related mainly to SMEs. Brazilian SMEs number approximately four million, representing 98 per cent of Brazilian companies, producing 20 per cent of the country's GDP and employing 45 per cent of formal labour force.

Serasa has developed a credit risk scoring system on the basis of an advanced statistical tool, which indicates the probability of default by a firm for a given period of time. The Serasa database allows for constant updating of information on firms and their constituent parts. Based on reference files and behavioural information that are available in the market, the system makes it possible to classify the credit risks of Brazilian SMEs. During the transaction cycle Serasa helps companies make credit decisions, monitor risks and manage portfolios. Serasa also monitors firms at the level of conglomerates and consortia. Analysing the situation of whole industries or warning firms against various forms of fraud practices is also a part of Serasa's services.[3]

---

[1] See: www.dnb.com.

[2] www.serasa.com.br.

[3] Serasa presentation at the e-finance event of UNCTAD XI, São Paulo, 16 June 2004.

The above example of Serasa shows that determination on the part of commercial banks in a developing country to establish a private credit bureau was enough to develop an elaborate credit information pooling and sharing system. While banks and other financial service providers are the driving forces behind the credit information industry its development is becoming a multistakeholder process whereby suppliers of goods and services and Governments are equally trying to reap the new benefits coming from ICTs and the Internet, which are greatly facilitating the developments in this field.

The proliferation of credit bureaux in developing countries is gaining momentum. An impetus for their proliferation in Asia was the severe financial crisis in the late 1990s. For example, in 1999, the Thai Ministry of Finance initiated with the Government Housing Bank and a local technical partner the creation of Thai Credit Bureau Company Ltd. In 2001 the State Bank of India established a PCR, Credit Information Bureau India Ltd, in cooperation with D&B and Trans Union as technical partners.[8] Meanwhile, Serasa took the lead in cooperating with other credit bureaux in Latin America and recently initiated the establishment of an association of the Latin American credit bureaux. The existing and emerging credit bureaux develop websites with various levels of functionalities and are actively trying to promote their web-based operations at national and regional levels.

5. Emerging e-credit management and scoring systems for sellers

In domestic and increasingly in international trade sellers themselves provide the bulk of short-term supplier credit. Normally it represents an extension of payment from 30 to 90 days. In many cases, companies still base their credit decisions on traditional confidence-building methods. However, they are often not able to analyse the previous payment behaviour of new customers as they do not have access to formal credit information. As mentioned above, the software and credit risk management firms (credit information and insurance providers) offer a variety of software tools to help companies automate their credit analysis and management processes, which frequently involve internal credit scoring of their customers. Such programs collect and aggregate data throughout the organization and make it available for all departments of companies and especially for those taking decisions to sell on credit. While many SMEs may not be able to afford in-house sophisticated

credit decision systems, large companies may be able to use modern software tools to support their credit decisions and improve the efficiency of their credit and collection functions. Instead of screening each customer manually, the new software programs make it possible to focus only on those that manifest abnormal payment behaviour. Such systems normally make it possible to identify individual delinquent borrowers and treat them on a case-by-case basis (see example of SMEloan in section D.6). In some cases, companies take credit decisions directly while relying on the support of software providers and specialist management consultancies, which help to absorb those programs and adapt them to company internal structures. In other cases companies prefer to outsource the credit management functions to specialist firms or even to banks with which they keep their main accounts.

Financial service providers may also rely on each other's services. The scoring system Scorex is used by some US banks to identify on a daily basis the delinquent borrowers in commercial and retail lending operations, and hence brings about efficiency gains in collection operations. Credit insurers such as Coface, Atradius and Euler Hermes have also developed their own scoring systems (for further details see box 3.3). Another trade finance service provider, the United Kingdom's LTP Trade, has developed an online solution called Trade Edge, which helps companies by hosting an online sales management system that is adaptable to the individual requirements of each company. According to LTP Trade, the system permits companies to adopt electronic documentation and end-to-end solutions, interface with bank settlement systems and integrate with a company's internal or customer systems.

Using credit scoring techniques helps a well-trained and experienced credit manager to predict the behaviour of a client. Managers add to the automatic extrapolation of clients' past behaviour his or her intuition and hopefully knowledge of clients' current status, and thus predict future risks more accurately. Some credit managers believe that a thorough risk assessment with appropriate payment terms and/or financing arrangements might make it possible to forgo, for example, additional costs of insurance policies and/or discounting schemes often loaded on the seller's price.

This underscores the importance of devoting more resources to training professional international credit and risk managers in enterprises as well as in trade finance departments of banks and in credit insurance and factoring companies. They are the pivots of timely and successful settlement of a trade or financing transaction provided that they have access to up-to-date e-credit information and e-scoring tools. In the firm's strategy, payment terms are part of the marketing approach.

While simplification of the credit managers' tasks in defining buyers' behaviour has increased their productivity, they continue to cover a wide array of tasks, including verification and approving of credit applications, credit limit management, fraud and identity theft mitigation, dispute resolution, document management, deduction and charge-back processing, measuring, monitoring, and reporting on their department's performance.

6. Issues of security and interoperability

As will be shown in the following sections, it is not possible to achieve a meaningful level of automation of the trade process if the online credit information and credit risk management systems are not in place. However, even if the trading parties and their financial intermediaries have enough confidence to run open-account or documentary-collection-based e-payments, they still might be concerned about exogenous risks such as the security and interoperability of IT systems that they use in their everyday operations.

The story of the credit insurer Euler Hermes (see section C), which needed much time and effort to create an integrated system out of three proprietary IT systems, suggests that this is a major issue. According to *The McKinsey Quarterly* (2003), the traditional build-to-order mindset of companies' IT divisions results in too many application silos and hence an expensive IT surplus capacity. With the increasing need to manage web-centred architectures, the IT infrastructure management should be keener to use off-the-shelf, open and interoperable software applications and environments.

Traders, and especially SMEs, have received many proposals by major financial service providers to host their credit information and management operations and provide e-trade finance on a selective basis. Major players, such as e-trade platform specialists Bolero, tried initially to introduce industry standards. However, banks, including even Bolero's major shareholders, were lukewarm towards such an idea. Instead, multiple standards and fierce competition among the

main players for dominant position have characterized the market for quite some time. This forces decisions and gives rise to dilemmas about selecting a platform that is more promising in terms of interoperability with hopefully less risk of making IT investments a sunk cost in a few years' time.

Concerns about security in the case of card-based and other modes of e-payments that need to be protected from cyber attacks (for more details on issues of security and cybercrime see chapters 5 and 6) sometimes bring about a wait-and-see approach by traders and their financial service providers, thus postponing the removal of expensive and error-prone paper-based trade and trade finance.

Among the major concerns of bank regulators when adding new regulatory capital requirements for an operational risk under the Basel II regime were the risks related to securing smooth operation of the banks' IT systems. That involves not only the issues of human errors or cyber attacks, but also those of standardization and interoperability of electronic documents. One of the best examples of such standardization is the SWIFnet, the interbank e-payment system that has proved to be robust and fairly error-free.

Various forums, including those within the UN, have been discussing the issues that relate to achieving paperless trade, with e-trade finance being an important part of the agenda. Thus, in April 2005 the United Nations Centre for Trade Facilitation and Electronic Business (UN/CEFACT) launched a new initiative based on international standards and best business practices to replace paper documents with electronic alternatives. It takes the UNeDocs project as the basis for a new global standard. Based on the latest Internet technologies, the UNeDocs standard is supposed to facilitate exchange of fewer but better data, and to simplify trade procedures and increase security. This concept also allows the conversion of e-documents into paper ones in the event that local regulations so require.[9]

The standardization and unification of credit information documents and formats are important for ensuring their interoperability while migrating from one electronic system to another. Those documents should normally conform to such standards as UN/EDIFACT or EbXML (electronic business using eXtensible Markup Language). Further work at the international level might be needed to help develop best practice on the format and contents of credit information data.

C. Extensive use of credit and e-credit information: The case of credit insurance

1. Insuring buyer's risk based on extensive e-credit information databases

Many countries that developed sophisticated credit information infrastructures also built up related credit insurance systems. In fact, the latter cannot exist without the former. Credit insurance is mainly a method of protecting sellers from the risk of non-payment by buyers. The credit insurer needs information on a maximum number of companies in order to extend the geography of risks coverage as much as possible and thus increase the share of so-called general (i.e. not buyer-specific) insurance policies. That makes it possible to expand the business of short-term export credit insurance. Sometimes traders associate export credit with a purely bank credit to an exporter. Meantime, in countries where banks accept the quality of credit insurers, the credit insurance policy issued by the latter frequently serves as collateral while extending bank credit to a seller in the form of pre-export working capital or post-shipment finance. The literature on the subject is not particularly extensive and only a few books have been written on credit insurance.[10] Recently, the Berne Union (International Union of Credit and Investment Insurers), which includes nearly all OECD and some developing and transition countries' export credit agencies (ECAs), has started to publish a yearbook, devoted to the problems of export credit, project finance and investment insurance.[11]

Currently, the bulk of credit insurance is concentrated in the OECD area and protects sellers from buyer's risk through mainly short-term credit insurance policies. Generally, these policies protect against political risks related mainly to exchange restrictions, war and social conflicts and natural disasters (normally issued by credit insurers but mainly covered by Governments), and commercial risks, including protracted buyer's default to pay due to financial difficulties or outright bankruptcy (risks covered by credit insurers themselves). In trying to issue a general credit insurance policy for a seller the credit insurer is interested in covering as many buyers as he can. But to cover the risk, the insurer needs to have credit information on buyers. Normally, a general credit insurance policy

stipulates that the seller should seek an authorization for the cover for each buyer. If a credit insurer has no credit information on a buyer, he might be reluctant to extend the cover for that individual transaction. Hence, to insure supplier credit the credit insurer needs to construct his own credit information database or buy credit information from credit bureaux. Major credit insurers have already transformed their credit information files into e-credit information databases and as a result can give automatic authorization for a cover if the seller so requests.

It is hard to quantify the exact volume of short-term trade credits extended by exporters themselves. However, it is known that open-account trade constitutes around two thirds of world trade, which is nearing the figure of $9 trillion.[12] While banks mitigate through letter-of-credit (LC) arrangements the payments risks related to the remaining one third of world trade, the exporters manage themselves the risks related to the bulk of extended, mainly open-account payments by importers. They also mitigate a part of these risks by resorting to such instruments as export credit insurance and factoring (see D.4). Demanding prepayments from importers is recommended for a very few high-risk countries, such payments representing only a very small share of trade-related payments.[13]

It is interesting to note that the short-term credit insurance provided by members of the Berne Union accounts around 7 per cent of world trade. These highly repetitive and automated operations of insuring buyers' risks mainly cover intra-OECD, short-term, open-account trade. In 2003 the volume of short-term export credit insurance was $570 billion, representing 90 per cent of all credit insurance business (Berne Union, 2005).

The short-term insurance covering risks of importers from many developing countries might be either very expensive or non-existent mainly owing to a lack of credit information on corporate risks in those countries. E-credit information on reliable companies located in relatively risky countries might permit the credit insurer to overrule country limits based on political risk and extend cover for a trade on credit to those companies.

Hence, the important role that credit information plays in credit insurance. It is symptomatic that Atradius, Coface and Euler Hermes, the three dominant players in the short-term credit insurance market, are at the same time the main producers and users of online credit information. Each of them has access to online credit information on more than 40 million companies (see box 3.3). While credit information is globally available in those companies' intranets, the credit decision on existing buyers that are in the database is normally taken by a branch of the credit insurer that is in geographical proximity to a buyer. Credit insurers collect information themselves as well as sourcing it from credit bureaux (D&B, Graydon,), rating agencies (Moody's, S&P) and other sources. For example, when Atradius processes a credit limit application, it has access to information on 45 million companies, while its own database has a capacity of around 10 million companies (Berne Union, 2005, p. 150). Maintaining, upgrading and integrating such sophisticated databases require major investments in IT systems. That is one of the explanations for fierce competition and consolidation of the market for short-term credit insurance, which is so dependent on a wealth of e-credit information.

2. The main features of e-credit insurance

As was noted above, all main credit insurance companies have developed their in-house e-credit information databases on credit risks. They also buy credit information on the market. Both sources help them to overcome information asymmetry and extend credit insurance coverage, issue bonds and guarantees, develop e-credit rating and scoring, and provide credit management services for enterprises. Like credit bureaux, credit insurers update e-credit information on a daily basis. Credit rating or credit scoring

is provided on the basis of analysis of the risks of enterprises present in their e-credit information databases. If the buyers of an insured are not present in the database of a credit insurer it acquires missing credit information from credit bureaux or other credit insurers. In the event of a lack of credit information, the decision to insure a supplier against a given risk is at the discretion of the credit insurer and is determined by various factors, including the risk appetite of the credit insurer. When working with other credit insurers, major credit insurers might also propose a reinsurance capacity.

Typically, the e-credit insurance platforms insure online sellers against the risk of buyers' non-payment. They also provide such services as e-credit opinion and/or e-credit rating. When an enterprise visits the website of a credit insurer it can choose between getting a credit opinion on an individual buyer or subscribing to various credit insurance policies, including the one covering the default risks of all buyers. If those buyers receive a credit rating from a credit insurer, the seller automatically gets the insurance coverage on the former. If that is not the case, the seller can still subscribe to a general insurance policy online, but the cover extension on each buyer would be on a case-by-case basis. Apart from online credit insurance, credit information and rating, major credit insurers can provide electronic receivables (credit) management and factoring services (see section D.4).

The biggest global players in the short-term credit insurance market with a strong presence on the Internet are Coface, Atradius and Euler Hermes.[14] A summary of their business models is presented in box 3.3.

Box 3.3

E-credit insurance: The cases of Atradius, Coface Group and Euler Hermes

Atradius is a renamed version of Gerling NCM, itself the result of a major merger in late 2001. The rebranding of the group was a result of the need to separate credit insurance from other insurance activities of the Gerling group. As a result, Atradius emerged in January 2004 (Atradius, 2004, p. 11) with Deutsche Bank and Swiss Re as its major shareholders.

Having also a major database on buyers and business conditions, Atradius provides e-credit insurance as its main service. At the same time it puts emphasis on diversification into such services as bonding and guarantees, and credit management for enterprises. In addition to online underwriting of credit risks for sellers, Atradius is trying to provide the latter with services to help diminish pressures on working capital and collect debts.

Consecutive mergers of its constituent parts raised the problem of integrating three different IT platforms. The fact that it took two and half years for Atradius to integrate those platforms shows the complexity of this process (Atradius, 2004, p. 98). By the end of 2004 customers and underwriters were able to plug into an online platform with access to information on more than 45 million companies. Access to the new platform is through an interface called Serv@net, which makes it possible to give online credit opinions, get information on claims and perform many other operations. Like COFACE, Atradius extends, if requested, an e-credit insurance coverage for companies that received its e-credit opinion.

Box 3.3 *(continued)*

One of the successful online solutions launched by Gerling in 2000 was the so-called Trusted Shops Services (UNCTAD, 2002, pp. 143–144). The idea was to give the label of Trusted Shops to reliable e-commerce operators and collect premiums as a percentage of purchase from customers preferring to buy from such shops. Given the problems of reliability and security of B2C e-commerce and e-payments, the project started successfully and by the end of 2004 it had handled risks totalling 250 million euros, covering the increasing number of consumers that are purchasing online. So far, the subscription of online shops to that service continues to double every year and since 2003 the Trusted Shops have been making a profit.[2]

Coface Group is a leading provider of e-credit insurance, e-credit information and e-credit management services. It is active in developing and transition economies and has set up branches and subsidiaries in 58 countries in Europe, the Americas, Asia and Africa. It has also entered into cooperation agreements with more than 40 local credit information and credit insurance companies. Currently, all Coface branches and partners are hosted together on an electronic intranet in the framework of a network called CreditAlliance. The latter can provide services to customers in 93 developed and developing countries (accounting for more than three quarters of world trade). By running the network Coface and its partners are updating their databases on commercial as well as country risks. Coface backstops network partners if needed by proposing reinsurance: while giving positive credit advice within the network, it automatically extends cover limits. As a global player, Coface tries to be active in the main credit management activities such as information and ratings on businesses, credit insurance, receivables management and factoring.

The Internet-based global product that Coface proposes is known as @rating solution. It is based on an e-credit information database of more than 40 million companies, and bundles both credit information and credit insurance products. The @rating solution is delivered through different products:

> ➤ rating "at-a-click" is available on partners' websites (such as banks, factors, institutions, marketplaces), where customers can get a snapshot view of the risk on any trading partner. The service covers 56 countries.

> ➤ rating Line is a subscription product which allows customers to manage all their buyers within a portfolio and get ongoing information on the evolution of the credit risk. A specific version of @rating Line has been designed per market segment, from SMEs to MNCs, in respect of which customers can decide whether to get information or insurance services on the portfolio. @rating Line is available in 17 countries.

> ➤ Integrated @rating services are embedded in a customer system, and monitor @rating credit opinion so that customers can easily manage their credit risk within their own IT infrastructure.

The above solutions are distributed in the web through Coface's entities' portals, partners' portals and its client extranet called "Cofanet". The latter can be accessed from 50 countries and is available in 16 languages. In addition, with @rating line available through Cofanet the customer companies can manage their contracts online and get the credit rating of their whole portfolio (buyers, debtors, partners). Coface also gives its customers access to the underwriters who monitor risks. That makes it possible to overcome the limitations of country risk considerations when analysing the quality of the corporate risk.[1]

Euler Hermes is also one of three major players in the short-term credit insurance market. It was formed as a result of a merger between the French Euler and the German Hermes, and is one of the companies in a leading insurance conglomerate, Allianz Group. It is a market leader with 34 per cent of market share, with a presence in 40 countries and with 40 million companies monitored in its risk database. The bulk of its turnover of nearly 2 billion euros comes from credit insurance. Like its competitors, it provides trade receivables management services to companies, insures sellers against the commercial and political risk of buyers or helps them prevent non-payment risk through credit opinion or credit information services. It also helps customers to collect debts. It has a distinct e-trade finance service whereby its online tool, Eolis, permits insured companies to inform banks that they have credit insurance coverage, and on that basis get a bank credit. Other services include commercial trade debt collection services for companies without a credit insurance policy and a wide range of guarantees and bonding for national contracts or exports.

One of its programmes evaluates the risk of diversified trade receivable portfolios of companies on the basis of its risk database and its own rating programme that gives "grades" to those portfolios. The aim is to propose to banks tools to evaluate trade receivable portfolios and assess suppliers' credit risks when extending a further credit. Like Atradius, Euler Hermes had to face the challenge of reconciling two major IT systems and business cultures. It took some time for the firm to streamline its online communications and in-house IT architecture.

Recently, Euler Hermes established partnerships in Asia to meet the dynamic increase in demand for credit insurance products. Thus, it increased its sales through its local partners such as SGIC in the Republic of Korea, Sinsure in China and the Allianz Mumbai branch in India (Euler Hermes, 2005).[3]

---

[1] See www.atradius.com.

[2] See www.coface.com.

[3] See www.euler-hermes.com

Normally, when a major European export credit insurer provides positive credit information to credit insurers from developing or transition economies it also tries to offer a reinsurance capacity to the latter. Some of them are building up their databases on debtors by accumulating in-house information and buying the missing parts in the credit information market. They also join various international networks or cooperative arrangements of credit insurers such as Credit Alliance.

The major e-credit insurance companies' best practices do not preclude the possibility of starting to develop local e-credit information and e-credit insurance capacities based on such advantages as local knowledge and proximity to clients. The example of early transition economies in Eastern Europe, which successfully managed to develop from scratch rather elaborate systems, including in some cases a twin system of local export-import bank and national credit insurer (Czech Republic, Hungary), is a striking one.[15] It is symptomatic that the new Berne Union members and other credit insurers from the emerging economies have organized their own subgroup called the Prague Group. The latter is a conduit for transferring the best practices of the leading members of the Berne Union to those that are at the beginning of the learning curve.

Another striking example was the development of credit insurance in Asia. Thus, India, China, Thailand, Malaysia and other countries have developed national export credit agencies focusing on insuring national exporters against possible defaults of foreign buyers.[16] All of them are building up online services locally and are trying to join various regional and global networks. While the Indian Export Credit Guarantee Corporation (ECGC) and Malaysia Export Credit Insurance Berhad (MECIB) are already established institutions and are instrumental in supporting exports of goods and services especially by SMEs, the China Export and Credit Insurance Corporation (Sinosure) was created only in December 2001 and took over the nascent export credit insurance businesses of the People's Insurance Company of China and the Export and Import Bank of China. Meanwhile the Thai model of credit insurance continues to develop under the roof of the Export Import Bank of Thailand. Interestingly, Thai banks in cooperation with the Eximbank extend credit insurance policy to their clients that cover not only buyers' risks but also buyers' banks' risks.

The process of creation and development of credit insurance and credit information in other countries of Eastern Europe, the CIS, Asia and Latin America is also under way. However, the situation is worse in that respect in Africa, and especially its sub-Saharan region. To mitigate political risks of countries in that region the World Bank helped to create in 2001 the African Trade Insurance Agency (ATI). With the financial backstopping of the World Bank, ATI increases reinsurance capacity through Lloyds in the reinsurance market.[17]

Unfortunately, the majority of developing and transition countries do not yet have credit insurance facilities. PCR frameworks are also still at a nascent stage in those countries and they dispose of only limited information on bank borrowers. Many countries are just starting to take steps in building credit information, credit insurance and other trade-finance-related facilities. Others already engaged on that path might still need a real impetus to make those institutions truly operative. Well-functioning national credit information systems and efficient linkages with sources of information on foreign risks are crucial for managing financial risks and, in particular, creating credit insurance facilities.

Given the lack of legacy electronic systems for both credit information and credit insurance in many developing countries, it is quite feasible for them to start from the outset using Internet-based electronic platforms to accumulate information on credit risks or to extend e-credit insurance. Such platforms are easier to link to major ones, as small credit insurers need the reinsurance capacity of major credit insurance or reinsurance companies. By joining such major e-credit information databases they may start getting online reinsurance cover for their insurance policies. Initially, that would be policies issued for local traders selling to OECD or other low-risk markets. With more positive experience the appetite for higher risks will increase.

D. Trade-related e-banking and other e-finance

1. E-payments and trade

E-credit information and e-credit insurance are the means to improve asymmetrical information on enterprises as credit risks, and hence their access to suppliers' credit or trade-related finance and e-finance provided by financial intermediaries. Banks are continuing to play a decisive role in trade-related payments and finance and will probably try to maintain a similar role in the emerging world of e-payments and e-finance. They are the main users of credit information and credit insurance products when deciding whether to extend a trade credit to an enterprise. They also have their internal credit reporting systems, accumulating information on the creditworthiness of borrowers. In the event of a lack of trust in respect of buyers, banks replace the buyer's risk by switching it to a bank's risk, for example by introducing documentary credit (letter of credits or L/Cs) as a method of financing international trade (this mode competes with credit insurers who support open-account payments in international trade). Trade finance providers and facilitators are moving online not only to overcome information asymmetry at lower costs, but also to actually provide finance at less cost through the more extensive use of e-payments, e-banking and e-trade finance techniques. According to Visa, a 10 per cent increase in e-payments in the United States might be translated into economic growth of a half per cent.

According to the Boston Consulting Group (2004), competition among banks and between banking and non-banking institutions in capturing increasing domestic and international payment traffic will further squeeze transaction margins and force further innovation and active use of online payments. The payments will become more customer-driven, with customers demanding a more holistic approach to their payment needs. To stay competitive, the banks will be forced to further participate in multibank e-payments models or engage in those run by third parties. In that respect, it is interesting to note that in spite of initial difficulties at the beginning of this century with the migration of SWIFT (Society for Worldwide Interbank Financial Telecommunication), the biggest interbank payment system, to the Internet-based SWIFTNet e-payments network, the process is well under way now. Ninety-five per cent of banks belonging to SWIFT have migrated to SWIFTNet and applied to SWIFTNet Link, a mandatory software product providing minimal functionality and interoperability to the members of the network. The Link offers to SWIFT users single-window access to SWIFTNet.

This section will consider progress in e-trade finance by reviewing leading bank-based and specialized e-trade finance platforms, factoring and e-factoring services and card-based solutions, with a focus on SMEs. It will also review several examples of best practices in developing countries.

2. Bank-based e-trade finance platforms

The bank-based e-trade finance platforms (see below) and so-called integrated trade finance platforms (see next subsection) are basically competing models. While the latter stress that they can provide services to major companies that prefer to work with several banks, the major banks also try to provide technology support to other banks or to banks of their major clients, so as to overcome the limitations of the monobank model.

Leading banks in trade finance such as ABN AMRO, BNP Paribas, Citibank, HSBC, JP Morgan, Standard Chartered and others have created their own electronic platforms for documentary credit and open-account e-payments to meet the emerging requirements of their corporate clients, including both large companies and SMEs. While major banks tried to persuade their clients to concentrate all their trade finance operations on their bank's platform (the so-called monobank solution), they realized that they had to adapt to their major clients' desire to work with several banks, that is through multibank channels. While developing their own e-trade finance platforms, banks tried also to develop interfaces to fit in the automated corporate supply channels of transnational corporations and primarily those of their payables, receivables and cash flows. To follow those major companies, banks try to make sure that their platforms are interoperable with those of their clients and hence are able to enter into collaboration with them. Alternatively, the banks have entered into collaboration among themselves to create such platforms as Identrus and Bolero (see next subsection), trying to present ready-made multibank platforms to the corporates.

It is still early to predict which model will prevail. It is probable that they will coexist, as all major banks specializing in trade finance have very strong and long-standing brand names and will try as much as possible to retain customers, especially local and regional companies, within their systems, while trying to collaborate with major ones on the margins of their systems. Moreover, some banks try to leverage on their leading position and render online services to other banks and financial institutions. Thus, JP Morgan, the leader in clearing arrangements, launched in 2004 a Global Payments Infrastructure (GPI) hosting a clearing processing solution for other banks and claiming to help reduce unit costs per transaction and increase capabilities, while maintaining regulatory compliance and mitigating risk.[18]

A typical major bank-based e-trade finance platform would include functions such as documentary and open-account e-trade finance and payments, e-credit protection, e-discounting and others, regardless of their proprietary structure (monobank or multibank or other). Web-based solutions of banks include transaction initiation, shipping document preparation and outsourcing, supply chain e-financing (i.e. discounting of payables and receivables), information on progress of transaction and payments, and linkages with logistics providers (Tagart, 2004). Some of them try also to provide e-credit protection. Storing the most important data in electronic templates helps to generate various trade-transaction-related e-documents and e-mail it to counterparties. As a result, common electronic data reduce discrepancies. For example, banks help exporters sell on open account to prepare online collections orders, invoices, packing lists and bills of exchange. Viewing online the delivery status of trade-related documents includes examination of the state of documentary credit (DC) and that of outstanding trade bills. Saving the templates of commonly issued DC types make it possible to reuse them, thus saving time for future applications. According to the banks, the automated document preparation and compliance, straight-through processing (STP) and integration with the back office improve the level of data integrity and lead to significant cost savings and efficiency gains for both parts of the trade transaction.

Box 3.4 presents two quite typical examples of major bank-based online trade finance platforms.

Box 3.4

Bank-based e-trade finance platforms: The cases of JPMorgan and Standard Chartered

JPMorgan Chase is one of the leaders in the banking industry and especially in trade finance. It has developed a major e-trade finance platform providing e-payments and e-finance services not only to traders but also to other banks, thus trying to overcome the limitations of the monobank solution.

When the client is another bank, hosting of e-payment technology can be provided on a private label basis. The client bank then offers the service onwards to its corporate clients. The JPMorgan service is thus "seamless" and the client bank does not consider it a competitive threat. Alternatively, solutions can be provided directly to corporate clients.

An example of a JPMorgan product is the so-called TradeDoc, which prepares online commercial trade documents, including presentation and negotiation of L/Cs on behalf of the client. Thus, in the case of L/Cs, while the customer provides information related to documentary credit and shipment, the bank prepares those and other documents, including the third party documents. Documents are available for viewing in a so-called Trade Information Exchange. According to JPMorgan, that makes it possible to undertake end-to-end solutions, identify through a built-in comparison engine potential discrepancies, improve cash flow, negotiate L/Cs through JPMorgan global interfaces, and allow for remote printing and for transmitting to Bolero-compatible documents.[1]

Standard Chartered set up an elaborate e-trade finance platform called B2BeX solution. The platform is an integrated system permitting customers to transact with all their buyers, suppliers and service providers.

Customers can create and submit electronic applications, communicate deal messages and keep accurate records. The Hong Kong Monetary Authority, the regulator overseeing the implementation of the platform, stipulates that all transactions be kept secure and confidential using the latest Internet technologies.

In addition to trade finance documents such as L/Cs, export documentary collection, orders and guarantees, the platform prepares the other documents related to the trade chain, thus also playing the role of a trade facilitator.

The client can retrieve L/C data from its back office and e-mail it to the B2BeX Trade Banking system. The latter will have entered the data into L/Cs, prepared for the client's review. The "Transaction in Process" and "Signature Required" pages allow clients to download and print selected documents in the PDF format. The bank encourages trading companies to assign a system administrator, overseeing the whole process of trade and e-trade finance transactions related to their companies. The bank also provides them with real-time reporting on the status of the e-trade finance process and that of other trade-related documents. The e-banking capabilities permit to follow that process from any point in the world.

According to the bank, the B2BeX is aiming to halve for its users the cost of managing international trade associated with the paperwork. It is believed to have actual savings of 25 to 50 per cent in trade processing and documentation costs. B2BeX is currently available in Singapore, Hong Kong (China), the United Kingdom and the United States, with plans to make it a global network.[2]

---

[1] See www.jpmorgan.com.
[2] See: www.scb2bex.com.

The above-mentioned solutions are typical ones for major banks active in e-trade finance. After the first wave of major investments before the dot com crisis and difficulties with moving clients online, the major banks are starting to reconsider e-trade finance platforms as a means of retaining corporate and especially SME clients, and creating an interface of collaboration with major companies. Another service that banks also propose, and in respect of which they compete with credit bureaus and credit insurers, is the credit management services to companies and especially SMEs. They host on their websites various predictive credit scoring techniques and permit SMEs managers to assess their buyers' creditworthiness and to take credit decisions.

Also, banks try to upgrade and improve their e-trade finance platforms by responding to the challenges of specialized e-trade finance platforms that stress the usefulness for major enterprises to work with several banks while undertaking trade operations on credit. As the following subsection will show, the banks' platforms have several features in common with those platforms and are competing with them to attract the attention of companies seeking e-trade finance.

3. Specialized e-trade finance platforms

Attempts to get rid of paperwork in international trade have been ongoing for some time, but success rates still fall short of initial expectations. Hundreds of billions of dollars are still spent on paper related to trade contracts, invoices, payments, transportation, customs, and so forth. For some years now, integrated e-trade finance electronic platforms such as Bolero, Tradecard and Global Trade Corporation (GTC, formerly CCEweb) have been trying with mixed results to contribute to that end (see *E-Commerce and Development Report, 2002*, chapter 6). The main reasons for their difficulties are overoptimistic expectations that companies would move swiftly from trusted and legally tested paper-based trade finance documents to electronic ones. The latter initially look complex and raise questions for companies as far as their security and legality are concerned. Lack of industry standards, complex workflows of online e-trade finance transactions, the need for major investments in new models, uncertain volumes of future operations and the hesitant behaviour of banks are also among the reasons explaining the difficulties in this process.

Meantime, the above integrators realized that they have to work for quite some time in markets characterized by multiple standards of market players and various client preferences. The initial investments, say by Bolero and its shareholders, in overambitious models such as electronic bills of lading did not translate into the emergence of standards for the international trade community. This became partly a sunk cost and partly helped architects to update designs, permitting more adequate assessment this time of the perceived behaviour and needs of potential customers.

The common feature of such integrated e-trade finance platforms was that e-documentary credit or open-account e-payments are reconciled on an electronic platform with other key standardized documents of international trade, including contracts, invoices, packing lists, bills of lading, cargo insurance, customs clearance, and so forth. Automated compliance checking and e-credit management are supposed to be a part of the process. The standards of messaging and their security should have also played a primordial role here. These platforms tried to create a workflow of the above documents in a smooth and quick manner and achieve savings resulting from a lack of delays in goods and services delivery and prompt payments through electronic means. Some of them even try to integrate with the traders' enterprise resource planning (ERP) systems. Given the fact that the majority of documents in the L/C payments have to be prepared by the exporter and that it is in the interest of the latter to speed up the e-payments, some of those platforms try to focus on the needs of the exporter. In particular, they provide tools for collaboration with all parties in transactions and inform them regularly of the status of the flow of goods and payments. Preparing a master document reflecting a maximum amount information on the transaction in the case of open-account payments also helps them facilitate the creation of documents for third-party trade service providers. As box 3.5 shows, all of them are multibank platforms, that is they permit companies and their banks to work together on the same platform.

As the e-trade finance technology platforms have not yet matured, there are concerns about interoperability between platforms. Hence, a wait-and-see attitude prevails among banks and corporations. Nevertheless the platforms described above are trying to adapt their business models to the challenges of online markets. At the same time it is difficult to make any judgement about the rate of their success, as they

Box 3.5

Integrated e-trade finance platforms:
Bolero, GTC, Tradecard and Visa Commerce

Bolero (Bill of Lading Electronic Registry Organisation) of the United Kingdom was created in 1998 by SWIFT (the leading interbank payment cooperative) and TT Club (the leading transport and logistics industry association). Bolero's value added was supposed to be improvements in operational efficiencies, better cash flow management and optimization of the working capital needs of clients. However, its initial investments aiming to make its electronic bill of lading an industry standard have not yet achieved the initial aim. Its so called Trusted Trade Platform is hosted and operated by SWIFT, which processes e-trade and e-trade finance electronic documents issued by banks for companies that have agreed to work through Bolero. The Platform functionalities include security of messaging, standards of messaging, rule book (legal standards), title registry, reconciliation and compliance engine, and workflow management. While its back-office layer ensures connectivity, gateways and integration tools, the web access layer hosts Bolero applications, configures user experience and defines workflow parameters. According to Bolero, its financial supply chains provide cover from procurement to payment for the buyer and from order to cash for the seller.

The Bolero e-trade finance applications are mainly presented as neutral, that is multibank automated solutions, and have suites for open-account and documentary credit operations. In the case of documentary credit it provides a bank-neutral documentary credit applications and standards, permitting traders to use those L/C applications with many of their banks that can issue and advise e-L/Cs on the Bolero platform. The Bolero suite also permits automated compliance checking and credit management in a mode of seamless multibank use. Apparently, it is also able to provide its web application for individual bank-offered solutions.

As there are no data on the volume of Bolero operations and number of its clients, it is hard to assess the real growth and volume of its operations. It is worth mentioning the intention of Cargill, a major trader, to process through Bolero eL/Cs and other e-documentary collection.

GTC (Global Trade Corporation) of Canada, formerly known as CCEWeb (see UNCTAD, 2002), has changed its business model during the last two years and now competes more with Bolero than with TradeCard. Here also one might observe a trial-and-error process.

While Bolero still tries to promote its own model and at the same time accepts documents in eUCP of ICC, GTC adopted the strategy of accompanying eUCP documents by providing multibank solutions of e-trade finance document workflow centred on the interest of the exporter.

According to GTC, eUCP is not yet a common instrument, since owing to customs and legal requirements (for example, to legalize the document), importers continue to ask banks to issue mainly traditional UCP-based L/Cs. Thus, it is the exporter who should be more driven to make eUCP-based eL/C and other e-payments an industry standard, as the cost effects due to diminished lags in payments and risks of discrepancies might be promising ones. Exporters have to produce six out of eight types of papers in the L/C-based trade chain as soon as they get acceptance from their advising bank of the letter of credit issued by the bank of the importer.

GTC launched last year its GlobalTrade eLC Delivery and Document Preparation and Collaboration systems, which according to it represent a multibank and multicompany electronic platform permitting collaboration between different parties in both open-account and L/C workflows. The eLC here could be issued in structured MT700 format, whereby data could be instantaneously captured and monitored and where third-party paper documents are usually not required. In an open-account workflow parties use a master template from which the information migrates to other documents, including those related to trade service providers (freight forwarder, insurance, inspection) and to the buyer's bank. In eL/C workflow the information from the L/C is automatically mapped into the master template and from there to all other document templates (certificate of origin, bill of lading, etc.). The eLCs are available online for review by seller's departments worldwide. The GTC platform also provides tools for collaboration between the relevant department of the seller and third-party documents issuers such as freight forwarders and chambers of commerce. GTC is monitoring the state of eLCs and alerting parties by e-mails about their status. The possibility of converting documents from Word to PDF and XML and printing documents in PDF format is important for countries that have the habit of legalizing paper documents. As a result, according to GTC its platform makes it possible to reduce operational risk owing to compliant electronic documents, on-time presentation and improved monitoring and control. Reducing the number of days sales outstanding (DSO) makes it possible to achieve costs savings for a client. The GTC systems have been live since October 2004 with four banks and large corporate clients such as Daimler, Siemens and Chevron Texaco.

Tradecard Inc. of the United States also started in the late 1990s by providing online e-trade finance to buyers, sellers, and financial and logistics service providers in an environment of a centrally managed system. TradeCard created and copyrighted analogues of L/C and other trade finance instruments, trying to provide them in a bundled manner and to host on its platform all parties involved in trade transactions. Tradecard claims that it creates trading communities and thus achieves an economy of scale effect.

According to TradeCard, it integrates automated financial services for buyers, sellers and partners, making processes visible, mitigating risk and improving cash flow. Having a platform that is integrated with financial service and third-party trade service providers, it connects traders from procurement to completion of payment online.

Connecting trading partners through a web browser, TradeCard can also integrate with ERP back-end systems, which implies that there is no need to change technology or business processes.

Box 3.5 *(continued)*

All parties apparently have access to view and amend documents as the transaction progresses and thus customize their workflow. As each step of a transaction progresses, TradeCard automatically alerts the next party via e-mail. Its three online modular services, which build upon each other, include trading partner management purchase order management, electronic invoicing, ERP connectivity), accounts payable/accounts receivable management (electronic checking of patented document compliance, online discrepancy resolution, payment decisions and schedules, warehouse reconciliation and chargeback management) and financial management (money movement, online credit protection, online export financing, early payment programme).[1]

Visa Commerce is an open, Internet-based B2B non-card e-payment solution developed by Visa International, a major card and e-payments solutions provider. It permits buyers and sellers via their banks to initiate and request e-payments, access all related transaction details and "store and forward" payments. Development of the Visa Commerce platform was completed in late 2003. Several domestic and cross-border programs are currently in pilot.

In essence, Visa Commerce addresses the companies' and public entities' need for a large-value, global business-to-business payment solution. Buyers and sellers utilize the Internet either to access the graphical user interface (GUI) in order to initiate payments, or perform file transfers directly from an organization's enterprise system for multiple payments. The system supports straight-through processing and provides visibility into payables and receivables for improved working capital management. This straight-through processing, combined with enhanced data and controls, provides a new solution not currently available with traditional methods of payment such as cheques, ACH/EFT and wires.[2]

---

[1] For further details see www.bolero.net, www.globaltradecorp.com and www.tradecard.com.

[2] See www.corporate.visa.com.

---

have not yet released data that make it possible to assess their operative and financial results.

Mention should be made of the differences in financial management between GTC and Tradecard. While GTC is concentrating on automating the flow of accepted e-LC models, Tradecard is replacing them by creating the analogues of credit insurance, export financing and factoring services on its platform. In the case of seller's paper discounting it also transfers the discount to the buyer if it was actually the latter (and not the factor) that made the early payment. Also while GTC is targeting exporters as a driving force in its model, Tradecard actually tries to persuade major companies to have at their disposal an automated financial supply chain to source products and services from a variety of mainly SME suppliers by taking all of them on its platform. At the same time trying to lock in all parties on one platform inhibits the flexibility of traders and banks and could serve as a barrier to participants when deciding between flexibility and lock-in scenarios.

As was mentioned above, in international trade documentary credit-based payments still capture around 30 per cent of all payments, with the rest going to mainly open-account operations. The platforms described above are trying to make e-documentary credit a prevailing mode in L/C business. There are also some other smaller entities trying to make inroads into this relatively new area. At the same time major changes and more realistic approaches to the standardization of the market suggest that the process is not an easy one and that further time is needed to assess the longer-term implications of the above models and others.

4. Factoring and e-factoring

One of the rapidly developing industries in trade finance is factoring. It is based on the principle of discounting sellers' accounts receivables without recourse. In other words, the factors are buying at discount the sellers' claims on buyers and then through their own network make sure that they will collect the totality of debt from the buyers. If a buyer defaults, the risk is assumed by the factors. The viability of this business model is based on minimizing the problem of information asymmetry for buyers. For that to happen, factors build up credit information on buyers to make sure that their credit risks are well managed and that they can propose to sellers the service of discounting their commercial paper. The status of factors is interpreted differently in various countries. In some they are considered part of banking that is subject to Basel II capital requirements and supervision, while in others they are considered receivables financiers and hence are not subject to the restrictions of Basel II (World Factoring Yearbook, 2004, p. 5)

When "factoring" accounts receivables for a seller of goods, a factor (export factor in international trade), through a network of its peers, normally has a counterpart factor (import factor), normally in the buyer's location (or country), responsible for the collection of debt from the buyer. Factors try to render the service of secure payment in the shortest possible time. Their closest competitors are credit insurance and L/C business. The fees paid to a factor represent a service charge for the risk protection service and for the collection service and an interest rate covering the post-shipment period from financing date until the time of actual collection.   The biggest international association of factors is Factors Chain International (FCI), capturing globally more than half of the market that in 2004 stood at $438 billion (of which only 44 billion was export factoring with the FCI share reaching 64 per cent). Nearly 200 factors (and banks offering a factoring service) have joined the organization, which covers 59 countries.[19]

FCI has developed for its members a centralized Internet-based system of electronic communications, obligatory for the members of FCI and reminiscent of SWIFT in banking. The system is called "edifactoring.com" and is run through FCI servers with central processing, reporting, message validation and delivery. It can afford an unlimited number of simultaneous users and is available to members at no charge. Members need only a browser to use it. While in the past information has been exchanged by mail or fax, it is now exchanged exclusively through EDI format. Information about all the factored invoices and cooperation with a multitude of correspondent factors are all reflected in edifactoring.

It is interesting to note that factors are combining the functions of risk protection, financing and collection and as such they have first-hand information about the buyer's payment behaviour. According to FCI, since they exposed to the trade transaction, factors know about a buyer's payment problems before that information reaches credit bureaux. At the same time it is quite difficult to persuade factors to share their credit information databases on buyers as they consider this knowledge to be their know-how and competitive advantage.

The number of factors, be they a branch of a bank or an independent factor, is proliferating in developing

and transition countries, with some of them ready to join the ranks of FCI.

5. Using payment cards as e-trade finance solutions

Company managers as well as government employees are using payment cards more frequently to meet their office and other working capital requirements. The credit limit of the cards could be interpreted for the purposes of our analysis as a short-term trade-financing device for relatively small purchases. The purchase credit cards provided to company managers reflect the trust of banks issuing cards in the creditworthiness of their clients. In the case of government employees it is more an issue of government's controlling office expenses. Card purchases simplify the procurement process by combining in one card operation such functions as purchase order, receipt, accounting and payment.[20] For example, on average US officials have a limit of $25,000 per card. However, in exceptional cases some government offices and high-level officials are authorized to make much larger purchases by payment cards. All main card companies, such as Visa, Mastercard, American Express and others, have various levels of involvement in this type of card-based small ticket financing.

For example, Visa, one of the major card and other e-payment solutions provider, has recently developed several projects for businesses and Governments to facilitate the above-mentioned card-based small ticket e-payments such as purchase cards for Governments and businesses. The Visa government cards are issued in the United States, the United Kingdom and some other countries. While US-based purchase cards have rather high credit limits those accepted in other countries could have considerably lower ones.

Visa also cooperates with the US Small Business Administration in extending through Wells Fargo Bank purchase cards to US SMEs. Wells Fargo has developed with the help of Fair Isaac a proprietary credit scoring system tracing the payment behaviour and reliability of SME cardholder managers. The latter can also use the payment card to meet some of their working capital needs on a recurrent basis. Similar programmes for financing SMEs supported by development or commercial banks in the United States and developing countries could be categorized as short-term e-trade financing programmes. Thus, Visa-card-related programs involve such banks as the Puerto Rico Economic Development Bank (see below), the Brazilian BNDES, the Indian ICICI bank and some others. Other card-based projects include that of Banco do Brasil.

It is interesting to note that enterprises in developing countries that operate in the informal economy and still keep bank accounts might have access to debit cards. Some of the banks that issue debit cards for such SME businesses trace their payment behaviour through the use of those debit cards. By then applying behavioural credit scoring methods the banks might even take eventually decisions to issue credit cards to businesses with good behavioural patterns, thus permitting the latter to use those cards and meet a part of their working capital financing needs.

Card-based e-trade finance project: The case of the Puerto Rico Economic Development Bank

Established in 1985 as a government bank, the Puerto Rico Economic Development Bank (EDB) re-engineered itself in 2002 to meet the borrowing requirements of SMEs through the use of modern card-based e trade finance tools. Using Visa payment cards, EDB established unusually high credit limits of $25,000 for SMEs, permitting expenditures on working capital and general expenses. Thus, it created so-called enterprise and agricultural business cards, permitting SMEs to use these cards as an important instrument to borrow and to buy inputs, including small-scale machinery. The card-based payments were decreasing the bank's costs related to the renewal and disbursement process of an ordinary credit. As EDB was not a commercial bank and could not be a direct issuer, it hired Banco Popular of Puerto Rico as a servicing bank. Visa agreed to accept EDB business card as a co-branded card. In the first year of the pilot the EDB issued 529 cards to SMEs. Thus, the new system whereby EDB approves or refuses the credit within 48 hours has replaced the old cumbersome and lengthy process of credit disbursement. After approving a credit application EDB notifies the servicing bank that issues the card. In two business days the SME receives the card from the servicing bank, and it can be activated by a toll-free call with a credit line advance embedded in the card. In other words, it takes five working days from approval to disbursement of the credit limit on the card. To centralize the credit process, manage good credit and achieve low delinquency rates, EDB was using the Fair Isaac Liquid Credit Desk scoring system, maintaining ongoing communications with customers and performing

monthly reviews of portfolio to quickly detect behavioural patterns. As a result, EDB increased its clientele and efficiency, saved $300,000 in overhead costs and greatly improved its image. To backstop the venture, EDB had obtained the support of public guarantee funds, which however have barely been used.[21]

Given the fact that Puerto Rico is in geographical proximity to the Central and Latin American region, its experience can be adapted for developing countries with a strong presence of local development banks. The following subsection considers several examples of e-trade finance platforms in developing countries.

6.   Selected e-trade finance platforms of developing countries

Developing and transition economies, and especially so-called emerging economies, are quite active in e-banking services and many of them have developed online services in payments and trade finance to support national exporters or to provide high-quality services to importers. In large countries online services exist also in domestic trade finance. The examples below show some of the best practices in various regions.

ICICI Bank (India)

One of the most advanced banks in terms of online financial services in Asia is ICICI Bank of India. It has developed quite elaborate e-trade finance services for corporates with a special suite devoted to SMEs. Its e-business suite includes such services as Internet banking, forex online, debt online, bill payment, cash management and trade services. Its online trade services make it possible to submit an online application for a L/C, view details of e-L/Cs, or e-bank guarantees, bills outstanding, forward contracts and other e-payment and e-trade finance documents prepared by ICICI on behalf of its customers. ICICI Bank tries to provide a full range of financial services for Indian exporters, including pre-shipment finance such as export packing credit; negotiating L/Cs with issuing banks, despite discrepancies in the document, to accelerate approval and payment; taking part of payment risk by discounting against sanctioned credit limits of the exporter's invoice in an open-account operation; advancing rupees against export bills; collecting payments within documentary collection activities; arranging for forfeiting export   bills without recourse; and issuing bank guarantees. Having a wide network of corresponding bank relationships, ICICI Bank also supports Indian importers by issuing L/Cs, providing import collection bill services, advance payment towards imports, and so forth. It also claims that it can arrange for Indian importers a supplier or a buyer credit from an exporter or its bank at competitive interest rates.[22]

Development Bank of the Philippines and Smetrix

The Development Bank of the Philippines (DBP) in a partnership with a local company called Smetrix proposed an online trading system for SMEs. The Securities and Exchange Commission has approved the system. This online e-trade finance marketplace is intended to provide the possibility of raising capital for companies by selling their receivables to banks and other major financial institutions. The time required for confirmations and authentication among trading partners is intended to be minimal and the lending to SMEs will mainly come from an electronic financing facility. DBP has already launched several projects to boost the use of information technology for local SMEs. The bank has chosen educational institutions to provide assistance to SMEs and specifically those in rural areas.[23]

This interesting initiative is based on an earlier Smetrix B2B trade and e-trade finance clearing-house proposal, which was aimed at addressing the problem of more rapid and less costly access by SMEs to trade finance through the creation of a global e-supply chain in which a central clearing house handles the problems of authentication and risk assessment of SMEs. Central to this approach was the proprietary Implementation Document Hub system, which enables the creation of legally enforceable trade documents in a digital form. The clearing house permits SMEs to have their online receivables discounted, or to receive structured finance (handling the risk of a given transaction) from a participating bank, or to securitize those receivables, capitalizing on the higher corporate rating grades of their major trading partners.

A major technology provider has been selected to support digital warehousing of the trade documents as well as interfaces with payment systems, while an international bank plays the role of the central registry for the originated trade receivables/securities. A major Philippine multinational has also agreed to be the first user by bringing its trading community into the marketplace. It was anticipated that when the transaction history of the SMEs is built up, the information could be the starting basis for the online credit evaluation system for the SME receivables.

SMEloan of Hong Kong (China)

SMEloan of Hong Kong (China) and its technology solution company called Maveo Systems Ltd created a web-based software and its operating model called Maveo Regulator, which captures in real time the cash flow and business performance of the borrower SMEs. That permitted SMEloan to lend directly to Hong Kong (China) SMEs using its cash-flow-capturing method. To start lending, SMEloan requires information from a borrower, such as its bank statement, sales and debtor details, current loan obligations, and ID card information of all owners and directors. The credit risks of borrowers are evaluated online on the basis of the ongoing submission of sales, receivable and buyer collection. Borrowers performing out of the norm will be flagged and followed up, with creditors thus being able to adopt a more proactive risk management approach.

The success of the method attracted the attention of the International Finance Corporation, which provided a loan for this business model development. The new element in SMEloan activities is that after the initial success of lending it started to insource the SME lending services of major banks. Thus, one of its first turnkey loan services is provided to SME clients of Standard Chartered Bank (Hong Kong). The OCBC bank of Singapore also selected this lending model, which complemented its approach to lending to SMEs. By offering cash flow lending called "business cash financing" in Singapore, OCBC hopes to expand its ability to service the SME market segment.

The experience of these e-trade finance platforms from developing countries shows that they are able to compete with major providers of similar services in terms of the use of sophisticated web-based technologies, which make it possible for example to undertake e-trade finance operations (the case of ICICI bank or SMEloan) or to replicate an integrated platform to reconcile various online trade operations, including e-trade finance (DBP and Smetrix). That proves the ability of many developing countries' operators to apply state-of-the-art technologies provided that they have enough resources to access them. At the same time in some cases they might need to be supported by well-targeted technical assistance in the initial stages.

E.   Conclusions

The rapid dissemination of ICTs and the Internet are opening up new prospects for diminishing information asymmetries between creditors and borrowers. In the context of the developing and transition countries this opens a new window of opportunity for local companies to improve their access to trade finance and e-finance by developing credit and e-credit information infrastructures. To achieve this end, regulatory and business environments in developing countries should quickly adjust to the requirements of such systems. The following are the major considerations that should be the central elements of this agenda.

➤ Potential of ICT tools and the Internet

The potential impact of Internet technologies should motivate policymakers in those countries to accelerate improvements in the regulatory and institutional environment and encourage enterprises to report on financial data, as well as financial institutions to share data on customers. As a result, a culture of credit information sharing and pooling might emerge. That in its turn should improve transparency and underpin the development credit infrastructures. Coupling the benefits of ICT with the requisite institutional changes in the developing countries will not only improve access to modern finance and e-finance for many enterprises in the formal sector, but also encourage migration of enterprises from the informal to the formal economy.

➤ Establishing credit information institutions and improving the quality of credit information

Building up e-credit information as part of local financial services and greatly improving the supervision practices would be essential steps in the right direction. In that respect, a good start would be the establishment of private credit bureaux by financial service providers such as banks, but also local credit insurers or debt collectors. Establishment of public credit registries by central banks, obliging commercial banks to share at least among themselves both positive and negative information on borrowers, could

also be a part of that process. At the same time developing such institutions as company registries, independent arbitrage with publicly available court decisions, and legal, accounting and audit services of international standard, would be the elements necessary for ensuring the required level of credit reporting and improved quality of credit information. As a result of the creation of credible and verifiable electronic credit information databases on corporate financials and their current payments behaviour, local and foreign banks and other financiers will be able to express a clear interest in providing local enterprises with trade finance and e-finance as well as such specialized forms of finance as credit insurance, bonding, factoring and leasing.

➤ Leapfrogging to modern know-how and technology

Without the existence of highly developed systems of credit reporting and information, the credit industry in developed countries would probably have been of a smaller size, and given the importance of credit in creating an effective demand, one could argue that without access to credit it is doubtful whether those economies would have enjoyed such dynamic development and have been as mature as they are today. The challenge is to replicate in a historically shorter period the value generation functionalities of credit and credit information in developing and transition economies by using the qualitatively higher level of technologies of modern ICTs and the Internet as offered by e-credit and e-credit information applications and platforms.

➤ International support

To achieve that end, many countries considered as acceptable risks should link the mobilization of internal resources devoted to the development of credit infrastructure with a wide array of arrangements involving foreign specialized financial service providers and other investors. In the case of countries considered to be high investment risks by the latter, major efforts, including international public–private partnerships, technical assistance and other capacity-building, should not be spared.

Annex I

Discussing e-trade finance at UNCTAD XI

One of the parallel events of UNCTAD XI in São Paulo, Brazil, in June 2004 was devoted to the prospects of development of e-credit information systems and trade finance and e-finance for SMEs.[24] Participants from leading credit information and credit insurance agencies, banks and others exchanged information on their achievements and problems, and ideas about the ways forward in this new and promising domain. One of the main discussion topics was the issue of better risk-sharing arrangements between banks, credit insurers and credit bureaux in providing trade finance and e-finance to enterprises. Participants agreed that ICT and the Internet being per se concepts of networking and collaboration can become a platform for collaborative credit risk management and e-trade finance systems, in particular involving four groups of actors in international trade: (i) creditor banks; (ii) credit information, rating or credit insurance agencies; (iii) trading enterprises; (iv) and their associations.

At the same time participants stressed that risk-sharing arrangements can work only if there is accurate, timely and reliable information to assess credit risk, whether the assessment is by banks, credit insurers or others. To overcome these information asymmetry problems, targeted efforts, including steps to improve data, such as corporate registry data, data on collateral and court data, and to achieve good credit reporting were suggested.

While a bank offers a trade credit to a rated enterprise it still assumes the borrower's risk of default. Only when a borrower is a seller and has a credit insurance policy can a bank transfer the risk to the credit insurer. At the same time credit rating agencies do not normally assume financial responsibilities for rated companies.

To overcome the reluctance of banks as sole risk takers to finance trading companies, the idea of a collaborative risk-sharing arrangement was discussed in detail. An arrangement combining the virtues of credit rating with those of risk cover was proposed. The main idea was that the bulk of risks related to a rated enterprise might be shared between creditor banks, credit insurers (or credit bureaux) and enterprise associations in proportions agreed among those parties. Creditor banks could enhance their credit portfolio by accepting partial risk coverage or a sort of "borrower's bonding" issued by a rating or scoring agency and by a special mutual insurance scheme established by enterprise association for that purpose.

The collaborative risk-sharing arrangement would relieve banks of full risk coverage of trade finance and working capital loans. At the same time banks could charge slightly higher interest to retrocede to a credit insurer or bureau an agreed premium for a part covered by the latter. Equally, enterprise associations might charge members annual premiums to fund mutual insurance schemes.

Banks and credit insurers considered enterprise associations' participation important since these associations might have first-hand updated information on their members and would inform partner financial service providers on a confidential basis concerning current or potential risks of rated enterprises of which the rating agency or bank may not be aware.

Participants also stressed the importance of avoiding adverse selection in the arrangement so that neither enterprises nor each of its supporters would abuse the arrangement to the detriment of partners.

A proposal for backstopping such an arrangement in the event of financial crises through co-guarantee funds of international financial institutions was also made.

Participants agreed that the shares of risk to be covered should reflect local circumstances and preferences of the partners and could be decided on a case-by-case basis. Banks and credit insurers or credit bureaux would be responsible for the adequate selection of clients, on the basis of credit ratings, and should share credit risk accordingly. Enterprise and especially SME associations would provide partial coverage through the mutual insurance schemes mentioned above, and SMEs enjoying a favourable credit rating could be asked to offer a partial asset-based collateral to creditor banks.

The success of such an arrangement would motivate enterprises, especially in developing and transition econo-mies, to provide online credit information on their financials and payment record in order to get e-rating. To deal with large numbers of SMEs, major credit information and credit insurance agencies will need to extend the net-works of suppliers of credit information for their databases. Those suppliers in developing and transition econo-mies would include local credit insurers and credit bureaux. However, in the majority of countries their number and their capacity to collect information are still limited. In this context it is hard to overestimate the value of technical assistance that global development agencies might render to help to establish e-credit information and e-credit insurance services in those countries.

Finally, wide acceptance of collaborative risk-sharing arrangements by financial service providers could lead rated borrowers to become members of card-based or similar e-payment schemes. Those e-payment schemes used for trade or working capital e-finance will register incoming and outgoing payments, thus permitting banks to moni-tor the flow of accounts payable and receivable. The credit limits of payment cards would correspond to limits advised in e-credit rating. E-payments might also allow enterprises to participate in online supply chains and other e-business arrangements.

Given high domestic interest rates in the majority of those economies, it is important to stress the potential bene-fits from access via such schemes and others to international trade finance and credit insurance facilities at a rela-tively reasonable cost for reliable local exporters as well as importers.

References and bibliography

Arrow KJ (1963). Uncertainty and the Welfare Economics of Medical Care. *American Economic Review* 53(5): 941–973

Akerlof GA (1970). The Market for Lemons. *Quarterly Journal of Economics* 84(3): 488–500

Atradius (2004). *New Worlds: The Global Credit Management 2004*. Published by Newdesk Communications Ltd on Behalf of Atradius NV, London.

Bank for International Settlements (2004a). *International Convergence of Capital Measurement and Capital Standards: A Revised Framework*. Basel Committee on Banking Supervision, June.

Bank for International Settlements (2004b). Implementation of the new capital adequacy framework in non-Basel Committee member countries. Financial Stability Institute Occasional Paper No. 4, July.

Barral G (1987). *L'assurance des crédits à l'exportation*. Paris Coface-Nathan.

Bartels JC (2001). Customer Risk Assessment: The Role of Information in Risk Assessment. Chapter 7 in the *Handbook of International Credit Management,* 3rd edition, Gower Publications.

Bartels JC (2003). The State of Information. *Global Trade Review,* May/June.

Bartels JC (2004). China Discovers the Gains and Pains of Credit. Electronic Publishing Services, 1 December, www.epsltd.com/clients/search/archiveSearch.asp.

Bastin J (1993). *La défaillance de paiement et sa protection, l'assurance-crédit*. Paris, L.G.D.J.

Bayliss P and J Parsons (2004). *What Will Your Trade Finance Business Be After Basel II? Global Trade Review,* September/October.

Berne Union (International Union of Credit and Investment Insurers) (2005). *The Berne Union Yearbook 2005*. Newdesk Communications Ltd, on behalf of the Berne Union, London.

Bigsten A, P Kimuyu and K Lundwall (2004). What to Do with the Informal Sector. *Development Policy Review,* January, 22(6): 701–715.

Boston Consulting Group (2004). *Preparing the Endgame: Global Payments 2004*. By N Viner, C Rutstein, N Storz and S Sarma. London.

Buehler SK, V D'Silva and G Prisch (2004). The Business Case for Basel II. *McKinsey Quarterly,* no. 1

Cornford A (2004a). Basel II: The Revised Framework of June 2004. November.

Cornford A (2004b). The banking capital of Basel II in non-standard contexts. November.

DMReview (2005). They Do the Math. May.

Economist, The (2005). Who Rates the Raters 26 March.

Edgcomb E and T Thetford (2004). The Informal Economy: Making it in Rural America. Microenterprise Fund for Innovation Effectiveness, Learning and Dissemination (FIELD), Aspen Institute, Washington, DC, February.

Euler Hermes (2005). Activity and Results 2004, www.euler-hermes.com.

Hart K (1973). Informal Income: Opportunities and Urban Employment in Ghana. *Journal of Modern African Studies* 11(1): 61–89.

International Monetary Fund (2003). Trade Finance in Financial Crises: Assessment of Key Issues. Prepared by the Policy Development and Review Department, Official Finance Division, 9 December.

Japelli T and M Pagano (1993). Information Sharing in Credit Markets. *Journal of Finance,* vol. 43(5), December: 1639–1718.

Japelli T and M Pagano (2003). Public Credit Information: A European Perspective. In: Miller M. (ed.), *Credit Reporting Systems and the International Economy*, Boston, MIT Press: 81-115.

Katsman J (2003). How Close is the Market to Paperless Trading? Paper presented to Containerisation International 6th Annual Liner Shipping Conference, April.

Kaufman Daniel (2004). Corruption, Governance and Security: Challenges for the Rich Countries and the World. In: *Global Competitiveness Report 2004/2005,* World Economic Forum: 83-102

Lewis WA (1954). Economic Development with Unlimited Supply of Labour. *Manchester School of Economic and Social Studies,* 22: 130–191.

Love I and N Mylenko (2003). Credit Reporting and Financing Constraints. Policy Research Working Paper 3142, World Bank, October.

LTP Trade (2003). How are Modern Corporations Harnessing the Internet to Address Their Sales Financing Needs, www.ltptrade.com.

Luoto J, C McIntosh and B Wydick (2004). Credit Information in Less-Developed Countries: Recent History and a Test. Universities of California and Berkeley and San Diego, and University of San Francisco, September.

Majnoni G, M Miller, N Mylenko and A Powell (2004). Improving Credit Information, Bank Regulation and Supervision. Policy Research Working Paper 3437, World Bank, November.

Majnoni G, M Miller and A Powell (2004). Bank Capital and Loan Loss Reserves under Basel II: Implications for Emerging Countries. Policy Research Working Paper 3437, World Bank, October.

Miller M (ed.) (2003) *Credit Reporting Systems and the International Economy.* Boston, MIT Press.

McKinsey Quarterly (2005a). *Reining in Brazil's Informal Economy.* No. 1

McKinsey Quarterly (2005b). *Leading a Turnaround: An Interview with the Chairman of D&B.* No. 2.

McKinsey Quarterly (2004a). *The Business Case for Basel II.* No. 1.

McKinsey Quarterly (2004b). *Managing next Business Case for Basel II.* No 3

McKinsey Quarterly (2003). *Designing IT for Businesse.* No. 3

OECD (2005). *Arrangement on Officially Supported Export Credit.* TD/PG (2004) 12/REV, 27 January.

Olegario R (2003). Credit Reporting Agencies: A Historical Perspective. In: Miller M. (ed.), *Credit Reporting Systems and the International Economy,* Boston, MIT Press: 115-161.

Schneider F and R Klinglmair (2004). Shadow Economies Around the World: What Do We Know? Working Paper No. 0403, University of Linz, April.

Stephens M (1999). *The Changing Role of Export Credit Agencies.* IMF, Washington, DC.

Stiglitz JE (2000). The Contributions of the Economics of Information to Twentieth Century Economics. *Quarterly Journal of Economics,* November: 1441–1478.

Stiglitz JE (2001). Information and the Change in the Paradigm in Economics. Nobel Prize Lecture, 8 December, Columbia University, New York.

Stiglitz JE and A Weiss (1981). Credit Rationing in Markets with Imperfect Information. *American Economic Review*

Tagart A (2004). *Cutting the Costs of Trade Processes. Trade and Forfaiting Review,* November.

Trade & Forfaiting Review (2004). EBRD Trade Finance Awards: and the Winners are…29 April.

UNCTAD (2001). Managing Payment and Credit Risks Online: New Challenges for Financial Service Providers. Chapter 7, *E-Commerce and Development Report 2001*, New York and Geneva.

UNCTAD (2002). E-Finance for Development: Global Trends, National Experiences and SMEs. Chapter 6, *E-Commerce and Development Report 2002*, New York and Geneva.

UNCTAD, ITC, COTUNACE, AIO, Dakar Union and Jean Bastin Foundation (2000). Proceedings of the First International Conference on Developing Credit Insurance in Africa and Mediterranean, Tunis.

World Bank (2004). Financing Developing Countries Trade. Chapter 5, *Global Development Finance 2004*.

World Factoring Yearbook 2004 (2004). FCI and BCR publishing. London.

WTO (2004). Improving the Availability of Trade Financing: Report of Preliminary Work. Note by Secretariat, Working Group on Trade, Debt and Finance, WT/WGTDF/W23, 25 March.

Selected Internet sites of e-credit information and e-trade finance providers and experts:

www.atradius.com; www.bndes.com.br; www.bolero.net; www.citigroup.com; www.coface.com; www.dmreview.com; www.dnb.com; www.euler-hermes.com; www.experian.com; www.gdb-pur.com; www.globaltradecorp.com;   www.gtreview.com;   www.icici.com;   www.ltptrade.com;   www.scb2bex.com; www.serasa.com.br; www.smeloan.com; www.smetrix.com www.tradecard.com; www.transunionadvantage.com; www.visa.com

Notes

1   For more details see: http://www.bis.org/publ/bcbs107.htm.

2   To anticipate Basel II, those rating agencies are starting to provide predictive default ratios (PDs) for banks not only on large companies but also on medium-sized ones.

3   Economic capital is a discretionary decision of a bank to keep an excess over regulatory capital, reflecting the bank's own assessment of risk exposure.

4   In economic literature the terms "informal", "traditional", "grey" and "parallel" with regard to an economy are used more or less interchangeably. The similar term "unorganized" refers more to labour. Informal economic activities should not be confused with criminal activities such as drug trafficking and money laundering.

5.   ILO has created an Informal Economy Resource Database containing many papers on the subject matter. While some of those materials analyse the way out from the informal sector, others consider possibilities for improving the situation within that sector.

6.   See also "The State of Information in World Markets", presentation by Joachim C. Bartels at the FCIB International Credit Executive Conference, Chicago, April 2005 (www.intrepidex.com).

7.   See http//www.labour.nic.in.

8.   See www.tcb.co.th; www.rbi.org.in.

9.   See Press Release ECE/TRADE/05/P04, Geneva, 20 April 2005.

10.   See, for example, Malcolm Stephens, *The Changing Role of Export Credit Agencies*. IMF, Washington, DC, 1999; Jean Bastin, *La défaillance de paiment et sa protection, l'assurance-crédit*. Paris, L.G.D.J, 1993; Geneviève Barral, *L'assurance des crédits à l'exportation*. Paris Coface-Nathan, 1987.

11.   Berne Union. *The Berne Union Yearbooks London* 1998–2005.

13.   Estimate of UNCTAD Time Series Database.

14.   Recommended modes of trade-related payments with individual countries are given by specialized periodicals. Prepayments are recommended for five to six small countries. See, for example, *Trade Finance*, no. 2005

14.   Coface and Atradius (formerly Gerling NCM) models were discussed in chapter 6 of the *Electronic Commerce and Development Report 2002*.

15.   See www.mehib.hu; www.egap.cz.

16.   See www.ecgcindia.com, www.sinosure.com.cn; www.exim.go.th; www.mecib.com.my.

17.   See www.ati-aca.com.

18.   See www.jpmorgan.com.

19.   See www.factors-chain.com.

20.   See www.international.visa.com/fb/vgs/purchasing_benefits.jsp.

21.   Puerto Rico EDB presentation at UNCTAD XI, São Paulo, Brazil, 16 June 2004.

22.   http://ebusiness.icicibank.com.

23.   *The Manila Times*, 30 November 2004 (www.dbp-ats.com.ph).

24.   See www.unctadxi.org.

Chapter 4

TAKING OFF: E-TOURISM OPPORTUNITIES
FOR DEVELOPING COUNTRIES

A. Introduction

How can Governments and tourism providers together make use of the Internet to successfully reach online consumers and improve their relative position in tourism markets? What policies and strategies should they adopt to create value by promoting online their tourism offer? What are the best practices for developing an effective destination management system (DMS)?[1] This chapter attempts to respond to those questions by focusing on e-tourism policies and strategies that could help developing countries tap the opportunities offered by ICTs in this sector.

In 2001, the *E-Commerce and Development Report (ECDR)* analysed e-commerce and tourism with a view to exploring how the tourism industry was starting to benefit from information technologies and the Internet, as well as the effects on developing countries' competitiveness in tourism markets. The *ECDR* noted that one of the main changes brought about by e-tourism was the disintermediation of the tourism value chain driving revenue directly to tourism providers. This chapter further examines this issue, arguing that the online distribution of tourism products and services by developing countries' tourism providers can give the latter an opportunity to access international tourism markets on an equal footing, targeting potential tourists directly. Over the years, the demand for tourism products and services on the Internet has been growing, like the number of Internet users and the speed of access to the Internet.[2] Recent studies released in the United States show that 56 per cent of Internet users are planning their vacations online (in particular making their hotel and airline bookings), whereas 23 per cent consult both travel agents and the Internet, and 10 per cent rely exclusively on travel agents.[3] If most consumers are more likely to use the Internet to search for tourism-related information, this means that online travel purchasing is gaining ground in the United States. In about four years the number of Internet users in the

United States who have booked their travel online has reached 50 per cent, compared with 30 per cent in 2000.[4] Travel is the largest source of business-to-consumer (B2C) revenues with $52.4 billion in 2004, and is predicted to reach over $119 billion by 2010.[5] The European online travel market grew by 51 per cent to reach $ 23.3 billion in 2004 and is estimated to grow to $ 49.9 billion in 2006.[6] Most of the information relating to tourism opportunities is generated and maintained by developed country service providers and naturally reflects their interests. Most of the tourism sales are made through those overseas tourism providers.

The growing number of Internet users that want to obtain tourism-related information and prepare their itineraries, and the growing demand for new travel experiences[7] respectful of environmental preservation and involving cultural, natural and social resources, open up huge opportunities for developing countries. ICTs also help destinations and national tourism providers to develop, manage and sell their offerings worldwide. The reorganization of the tourism market together with effective use of ICTs could allow developing countries to build their own brand images, develop new products, promote their tourism resources and expand their customer base to ultimately increase tourism foreign earnings and contribute to local development. The application of ICTs to this information-intensive industry, as a key business driver to organize and market destinations in developing countries, is an illustration of ICTs' potential for economic and social development and can contribute to the realization of the Millennium Development Goals (MDGs).

More and more destination management organizations (DMOs)[8] in developing countries are using the Internet to market their tourism offerings. Their websites are mainly an information window and only a small share of DMOs have been able to offer fully fledged services in the form of a sophisticated DMS. In addition to using the Internet to market their offers, tourism policies and strategies should be based on effective tourism innovations (new tourism products and services, technology).[9]

In view of the constraints faced by developing countries, in terms of infrastructure, human capacity and low level of adoption of e-business by local tourism providers, Governments and DMOs should play a central role in encouraging the participation and inclusion of tourism enterprises in global tourism markets. This chapter firstly considers the status of developing countries in the international tourism market and reviews ICT-related trends in the online segment of the tourism industry Then, it discusses how DMS can support the management and marketing of destinations by creating an integrated tourism product and a cooperation network among tourism providers. It provides an overview of e-tourism websites developed by national tourism offices, the national DMOs in the LDCs. The experiences of Tunisia, Thailand, Quebec (Canada), and the ASEAN and the Caribbean regions in developing a DMS will illustrate key elements of e-tourism strategies and common challenges, possible options and best practices to build an effective DMS. In conclusion, the chapter proposes some recommendations for policymakers and enterprises to develop effective e-tourism strategies.

B.　Global trends in the tourism industry

The purpose of this section is to present key data on and trends in tourism, including its online segment, and to describe who is benefiting and who can further benefit from tourism flows and revenue. In 2003, tourism accounted for about 11 per cent of the world's gross domestic product (GDP) and foreign tourism earnings amounted to $523 billion with 691 million international tourism arrivals.[10] This industry supported over 200 million jobs, representing about 9 per cent of the global workforce. [11]

1.　Tourism and developing countries

Despite the large share of tourism in many developing countries' export revenues, and particularly the LDCs,[12] the majority of developing countries have not been able to capture a significant share of the value created by tourism activities. Charts 4.1 and 4.2

illustrate the evolution of international tourism arrivals by region from 1950 to 2004, as well as the distribution of international tourism receipts by region.[13] Over that period, international tourism arrivals[14] increased by a factor of 30, reaching 760 million travellers in 2004.[15] International tourist flows and receipts[16] have been largely dominated by Western Europe and North America, although the latter's market share has declined over the years. These two regions are simultaneously the main destinations and tourist suppliers. Europe itself regularly absorbs more than half of international tourists and receipts. This concentration of flows in Europe and North America reflects the importance of intraregional tourism within these two regions.[17] In comparison, developing countries, albeit starting with very low levels of arrivals (about 8 per cent of international tourism arrivals in 1960), have attracted a growing number of travellers over the years totalling 34.5 per cent in 2004,[18] out of which East Asia and the Pacific accounted for more than 19 per cent.

The number of international tourism arrivals has constantly increased over the period in Asia and the Pacific, reaching 147 million in 2004, and has recorded higher growth than in Europe and North America. Tourism in Asia is mainly intraregional (78 per cent of international tourism arrivals)[19] and the rapid economic development of this region[20] contributes to the growth of tourism. The spectacular growth of China in terms of international tourism arrivals and receipts is the key factor in the rise of tourism in East Asia. A few years ago, China joined the top ten world tourism receivers, and in 2004 took over Italy's position as the fourth most visited destination worldwide with over 41 million international tourists. According to the World Tourism Organization (WTO), China will establish itself as the first tourism destination by 2020.

However, apart from East Asia and the Pacific, developing countries have not been able to significantly increase their tourism foreign earnings during the same period, and thus have not benefited in the same way from the spectacular development of international tourism receipts, which increased by a factor of 250, reaching 523 billion in 2003.

In 2003, developing countries attracted over 242 million tourists of which over 148 million were concentrated in 12 countries.[21] Therefore, for the large majority of developing countries, their share in the

Chart 4.1

Share of international tourism arrivals by region (1950-2004)

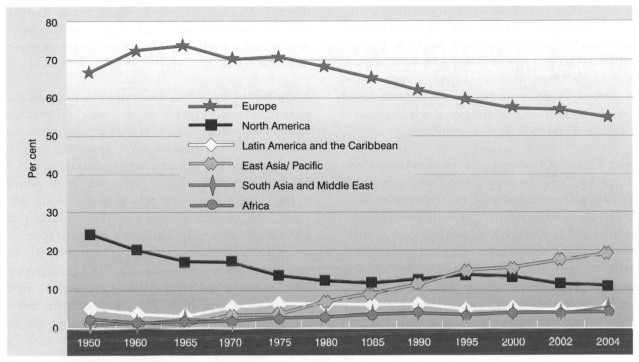

Source: UNCTAD elaboration of data from the World Tourism Organization.

Chart 4.2

Distribution of international tourism receipts by region (1950-2002)

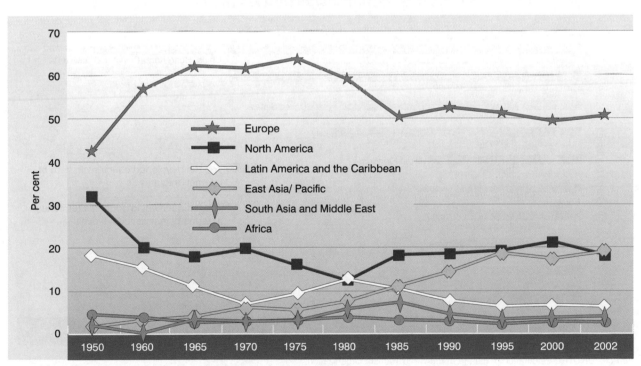

Source: UNCTAD elaboration of data from the World Tourism Organization.

international tourism market, in terms of both international tourism arrivals and receipts, is still small. Latin America, Central and Eastern Europe, Africa and the Middle East represent a small share of the world tourism flows and are dependent on tourists from other regions, in particular Western Europe, North America and Japan.[22] Despite the rise of tourism in South Africa, Morocco, Egypt, Tunisia, Kenya and Senegal, Africa attracted only 4 per cent of all international tourists and accounted for less than 3 per cent of world tourism receipts in 2003.

Charts 4.3 and 4.4 compare the top ten destinations in developed and developing countries in terms of international tourism arrivals and receipts in 2003. The top ten tourism destinations in developed countries attracted 323 million international tourism arrivals and totalled about $263 billion in international tourism receipts, jointly accounting for almost half of international tourism arrivals and receipts. In comparison, for the top ten destinations in developing countries, international tourism arrivals totalled 138 million and tourism foreign earnings amounted to $85

billion. Destinations such as India, Morocco and Indonesia are generating more tourism foreign earnings than others such as Tunisia and South Africa, which have attracted in comparison more tourists. The way in which, tourism has developed in these destinations contributes to explaining this situation (see section C.3).

According to the WTO, the number of international tourism arrivals is expected to increase by 4.1 per cent annually to reach close to 1.6 billion international arrivals by 2020. Long–haul travel is expected to grow by 5.4 per cent per year and intraregional travel by 3.8 per cent over the period.[24] The steady development of the tourism demand, as well as its complexity, has driven the growth of new tourism products that address specific market segments and in respect of which developing countries have a competitive advantage. As in other sectors, the effects of globalization have led to the appearance of new forms of tourism directed to sustainable tourism.[25] Such tourism niches could help destinations in developing countries in diversifying their offer. The online promotion of

Chart 4.3

International tourism arrivals for top ten developed and developing countries/territories (2003)[23]

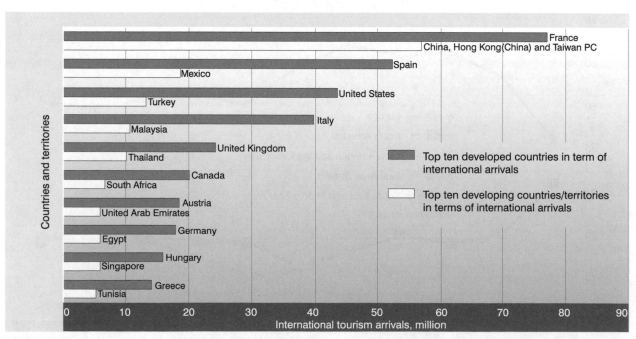

Source: UNCTAD elaboration of data from the World Tourism Organization.

Chart 4.4

International tourism receipts for top ten developed and developing countries (2003)

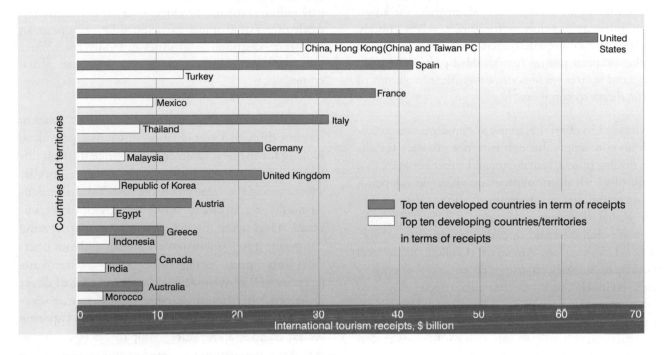

Source: UNCTAD elaboration of data from the World Tourism Organization.

tourism niches by the destinations complements the tourism product offering of online travel distributors from developed countries, which is still rather uniform. The latter mainly propose accommodation offered by international hotel chains and "static" tour packages.

Consumers are more and more looking for tailor-made vacations, exotic destinations and authentic experiences,[26] and expect to obtain related information online. Travelling is increasingly linked to the discovery of cultures and people, such as staying in a longhouse in the forests of Borneo, learning belly-dancing in Cairo, relaxing with an Ayurveda treatment in Kerala or learning how to prepare local cuisine in Marrakesh. Consumers are favouring the appearance of niche tourism markets offering thematic or personalized travel experiences, and are expecting to obtain related information online. Ecotourism, for instance, is looked at by many Governments in developing countries and LDCs with a growing interest, as it promises direct financial benefits and empowerment for local communities, thus improving their welfare

while protecting natural and cultural resources. In that sense, eco-tourism could complement national policies to address Millennium Development Goal 7, whose aim is to ensure environmental sustainability and target human welfare and ecosystem health. It is one of the fastest-growing tourism segments,[27] and received great attention in 2002 with the United Nations International Year of Ecotourism, which contributed to promoting global recognition of the important role of sustainable tourism within the global framework of sustainable development.

2. Tourism in the Internet age

The heterogeneous, intangible and perishable[28] nature of tourism products distinguishes them from other industrial sectors and explains the importance of information in this industry and the relevance of ICTs. The international dimensions of tourism and the fact that tourism is a service industry also contribute to the central role of information in the tourism industry.

The Internet has provided consumers with an increasing number of options for obtaining information and organizing their trips, more travel choices, and price transparency in an online highly competitive environment (see section B.3). Meanwhile, the Internet represents a solution for direct sellers (hotels, transportation companies) enabling them to enter the market without paying fees to third-party intermediaries, and search engines drive significant volumes of traffic direct to suppliers.[29]

As detailed in chart 4.5, many systems are now accessible to consumers through Internet gateways for airline tickets, hotels, rental cars and other services, as a result of which distribution channels are less dependent on traditional customer reservation systems (CRS) and global distribution systems (GDS). CRS were originally designed and operated by airlines, and further GDS such as Amadeus, Galileo, Sabre and Worldspan have been extended to travel agents as sales channels such as Expedia, Travelocity and Orbitz (see section B.3). The first GDS, Sabre, appeared in the United States in 1976 at the initiative of American Airlines to automate information systems related to flight reservations, schedules, prices and availability. For online pioneers in air transport, electronic distribution systems such as CRS and GDS have boosted competitiveness and productivity by automating processes and integrating new systems to improve business functions and reduce operating costs through yield management.[30] Today, GDS display airline company products over an extensive network of 500,000 travel agencies. GDS represent an important distribution channel not only for airlines but also increasingly for hotels and car rental companies.

Potential tourists may aggregate different tourism services through a combination of tourism providers, looking for the best value or lowest price through different channels. Each distribution channel has specific advantages in the value chain and responds to particular needs of consumers. While the advice of a traditional travel agent is still valuable when preparing composite travel, online travel agencies and tour operators offer great facilities for travel arrangements (static as well as dynamic packages); websites of direct producers offer brand guarantee and customer services; and search engines and emerging travel-specific search engines allow price comparison (see section B.3). Price competition is manifest across the tourism industry and consumers are attentive to price (see chart 4.6) when they are preparing their travel.

Chart 4.5

Tourism distribution systems

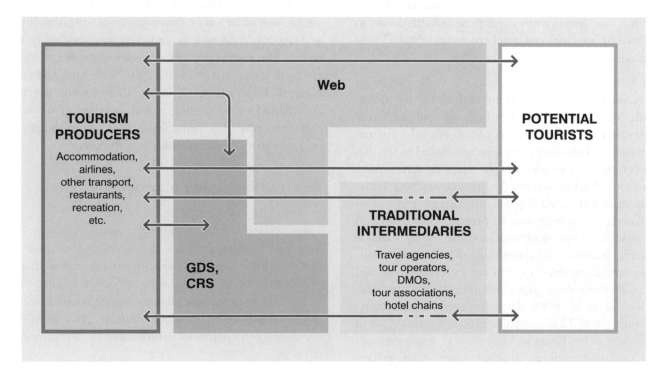

Online tourism markets have regional or country-specific attributes that is, behaviour/activities that might be somewhat different depending on the way in which tourism has developed (such as the greater prevalence of package holidays in Europe compared with the United States). As noted in the previous section, tourism in North America and in Europe is mainly intraregional, and therefore the majority of online bookings are done through tourism providers from developed countries. Tourism in the United States is mainly domestic and 90 per cent of tourism sales are made through online US airlines and travel agencies, as shown in chart 4.8. The United States is the largest Internet users' market (23 per cent of worldwide Internet users and a penetration rate of 55.58 per cent).[31] In 2005, over 32 million US households are expected to use the Internet to buy leisure trips, on which they will spend $63.6 billion. This figure is expected to be over 46 million households by 2009, spending $111 billion according to Forrester Research[32] Confidence about online payment systems offered by US-based tourism enterprises explains the growing number of consumers who purchase products and services online. Internet travel-related behaviour presented in this section, based on US consumers, reflects the facilities offered by tourism providers in developed countries (online bookings, travel agents, etc.).

Tourism-related Internet use has engendered a customer profile that reflects particular habits, expectations and requirements. It provides useful indications for policymakers and tourism enterprises when they are preparing their online e-tourism strategy. Consumers are increasingly mastering the online research and purchase processes. They expect to find high-quality and reliable information enabling them to organize and purchase the best product offering for each occasion, and receive comprehensive feedback and confirmation. The Internet also allows consumers to share their travel experience and provides useful peer-to-peer evaluation of tourism providers.

Chart 4.6 shows the main reasons why US consumers use search engines for online travel. While information on destinations is at the top list, pricing and best offers/deals attract a great deal of consumers' attention. Suggestions about what to do and where to go are among the information that consumers look for on search engines. The increasing popularity of Internet search engines over the years accounts for part of

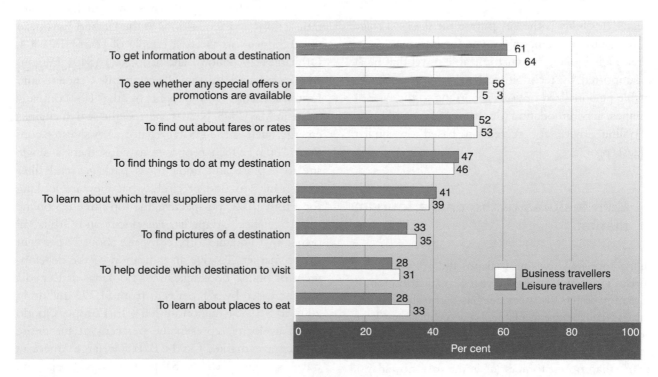

Chart 4.6

Use of online search engines for tourism in the United States (2004)

Source: Forrester's Consumer Technographics® December 2004 North American Study.

the growth of online bookings. More consumers are encouraged to visit travel sites as a result of searches than through any other media source[33]. Leading search engines among US consumers used to obtain travel-related information are the largest web page indexers: Google (with about 33 per cent of leisure travellers and 22 per cent of business travellers according to Forrester Research, Inc.),[34] followed by Yahoo!,[35] MSN and AOL according to different surveys in 2005. More recently meta-search engines[36] aimed at providing the lowest prices, such as Fare-Chase, Kayak.com and Mobissimo Travel Search, are gaining ground, but most of them are newcomers and represent a low percentage of traffic.

While the Internet is currently used widely to search for tourism information, a large portion of world travel sales still takes place offline. Many consumers do not feel confident about the modalities of payment and data privacy, or simply prefer talking to someone to make a reservation.[37] However, several factors will continue to boost the growth in online bookings, the first of which is the increasing number of people connected to the Internet at work and/or at home. Also, the improvement of technology, in particular broadband availability, significantly facilitates access to information, as does the appearance of new online marketing tools, including videos, interactive maps, virtual tours or visits.

Greater flexibility is the key phrase for the next stage of consumers' empowerment. Consumers are increasingly looking for customizable travel that must be supported by technological innovations, such as flexible personalized options according to the type of activities, accommodation, duration of stay and price, or online advice for recreation based on similar request/profile.[38]

3. Main features of the online tourism market

Online tourism drives and shapes the growth of the tourism industry.[39] Over the years, the distribution of tourism products and services has had to be adapted to the infrastructure available. New technologies have help to support the changing needs of the industry, focusing more on transactions ("transaction-centric")[40] than on customers (as is the case nowadays). In developed countries, large resources are being

invested by tourism providers to design user-friendly DMS based on innovative ICT-based tools offering various functionalities to meet their customers' expectations. At the same time ICTs are reducing operating costs, improving business processes and providing tourism producers with additional opportunities to present and sell their products, as well as to establish partnerships with carriers, GDS, tour operators, travel agencies and national tourism offices. The growing adoption of the Open Travel Alliance (OTA) standard based on Extensible Markup Language (XML)[41] by the tourism business community greatly facilitates the exchange of information among tourism enterprises such as airlines, hotels, car rental enterprises and travel integrators such as Cendant, Sabre, Expedia, Orbitz and SITA.[42] The OTA XML standard serves to improve the ability of consumers to search and book in a single online operation, and to increase aggregation processes among the industry. However, only a few large tourism players in developed countries are benefiting from technological innovations. The majority of developing countries are mainly concerned with setting up informative e-tourism websites to market their destinations (see section C).

Over the years, the number of online tourism providers, both generalists and niche players, has increased, and the market has experienced a gradual consolidation into the hands of the larger and better-funded companies. There have been some notable merger transactions and acquisitions in the US and European travel industry in the past couple of years. In 2004, Orbitz ($1.25 billion), and Ebookers ($404 million) were purchased by the US company Cendant, and Lastminute.com was bought by the US company Sabre in May 2005. New travel-specific search engines emerge, such as the US aggregator www.sidestep.com (May 2005), which proposes to consumers a single site to explore and book travel packages and filter their results to find precisely what they are looking for. From a B2C perspective, the top three US online travel agencies[43], Expedia, Travelocity and Orbitz, all owned by Cendant Corp., comprise about 77 per cent of the market. To give an indication of the development of online bookings, gross bookings at Expedia Inc. increased by 578 per cent from $1,793 million in 2002 to $10,364 million in 2004. In Europe, Opodo and Travelocity represent 60 per cent of the entire online travel market. On the B2B side, large American travel groups such as Sabre Holdings Corp. and Cendant Corp. dominate the online market.

The emergence of travel-specific search engines has also amplified the aggregation of the travel industry and competition among the players. As previously noted, they allow customers to find the best value or lowest price for air tickets and hotels by browsing the databases of a large number of distributors which are often promising the lowest fare.

Today's distribution systems (see annex V) have reduced the market share of traditional travel agents. However, the latter have proved to be more resilient than predicted and high-street travel agents still dominate the market in terms of distribution. Human contact remains important particularly when the travel is complex, and the security of online transactions remains an issue for consumers. Additionally, major traditional tour operators have joined leading suppliers of e-business solutions to the travel industry that are often powering a large number of websites. For example, Thomas Cook, one of the biggest global high-street travel brands, is expecting to reach a similar level in the online travel sector by setting up an e-business platform which enables travellers to build tailor-made deals online by combining flights and hotels.

Another important feature of the online market is the move towards direct sellers (branded websites), such as airlines, hotels and transportation companies. Direct sellers in the United States, particularly airlines and hotels, have managed over time to increase their revenues online by avoiding third-party distributors, as is the case for airlines and hotels which capture the largest share of the online travel market, as indicated in chart 4.7.[44] As explained earlier, only 10 per cent of travel sales are made through non-US tourism providers.

Chart 4.7

Use of online travel market per segment in 2003

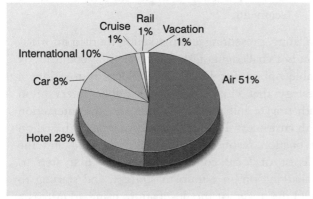

Source: PhoCusWright Inc. (2004).

Chart 4.8 details online travel distribution estimates by major travel categories from 2003 to 2008. The compound annual growth rate (CAGR) over the period is estimated at 22.9 per cent, and strong growth is expected for all travel categories. Cruises and all inclusive vacation packages lead the way with about 34 per cent CAGR, albeit starting from a relatively small base, followed by hotels (25.4 per cent) and airlines (21.2 per cent).

Chart 4.8

Online travel volume forecasts by travel category in the United States 2001-2008E

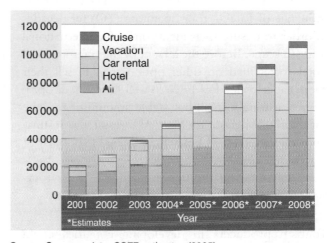

Source: Company data, CSFB estimates (2005).

For tourism players, the Internet has become an essential and growing channel of distribution where they seek to both cooperate and compete. For instance, an airline or a hotel will make profits by selling its products directly to consumers, but also by participating in other distribution networks to reach more consumers and sell available seats or rooms until the last minute.

4. Destination management systems

The growth of tourist flows, and the variety of consumers' motivations and requirements, lead destinations to organize their tourism industry to better respond to consumers' expectations. DMS are strategic ICT tools that can help DMOs and tourism enterprises in developing countries integrate, promote and distribute tourism products and services. The two primary functions of a DMS are to provide consumers with comprehensive and accurate information for the preparation of their vacations, and with booking facilities for tourism services and products. It also provides tourism enterprises with the means to be better integrated into the tourism supply chain by organizing and promoting personalized and enriched tourism experiences.

In developing countries, the tourism industry tends to be fragmented and heterogeneous, encompassing a wealth of tourism SMEs that could be better organized and promoted. For example, WTO estimates that 85 per cent of accommodation enterprises in developing countries are small or medium-sized. Small businesses such as hotels in developing countries have often been excluded from global tourism distribution channels. Some of them have been under the influence of foreign tour operators (TO) for decades in order to ensure their inclusion in the international tourism scene. Before the advent of the Internet, local hotels often had no other option than to sell their room capacity at a low price to well-known tour operators, ensuring a small but stable amount of revenue for them throughout the year. As a result, the destinations marketed by TO may have gained in popularity, increasingly in the form of low-price package vacations, encouraging the development of "mass tourism" (see section C.3), but earned very low returns.

Tourism producers in developing countries could achieve autonomy and save costs by promoting and selling products directly to consumers provided that they have an effective website. The Internet enables tourism producers to manage their assets, make decisions on yield management and reduce commissions to third-party distributors. However, the Internet should be regarded as a distribution channel complementary to other offline and online distribution channels that attract a large number of consumers worldwide.

Tourism involves many different actors from the public and private sectors. The involvement of the public sector is necessary for the development of a brand image, the integration of tourism enterprises into the DMS and the contribution of initial funds. However, the operations of the DMS can be subcontracted to private companies. The cases presented in section C show that the public sector is the best interlocutor to coordinate the various interests of the stakeholders and to strategically support local tourism enterprises, while the private sector is better prepared to exploit the system in a commercial way.

The main beneficiaries of a DMS are:

  (i) Potential travellers;

  (ii) Providers of tourism products and services such as hospitality, restaurants, and leisure and transportation companies;

  (iii) National travel agents and outbound travel agents;

  (iv) Public sector: ministry in charge of tourism, national tourism offices, regional administrations, municipalities, ministries of economy, foreign affairs, environment, etc.;

  (v) IT providers;

  (vi) Investors.

The main objectives of a DMS are the following:

- To efficiently integrate and facilitate interaction among all stakeholders;

- To optimize the relationships with targeted groups;

- To collect, manage and distribute information on tourism products to a larger proportion of consumers and tourism distributors throughout the world;

- To develop an integrated tourism product and service offerings;

- To provide up-to-date and attractive tourism information and products according to the country's interests;

- To allow consumers to easily make a reservation and quickly receive a confirmation;

- To reduce marketing costs compared with traditional channels (such as printed material);

- To collect information on customers and to design marketing strategies for different market segments.

Collating, presenting and marketing tourism information is a challenging task for developing countries. A viable option for DMS stakeholders is to adopt a strategy that closely associates public intervention with private initiative, and optimizes the interaction with customers. Defining a tourism strategy based on destination resources, consumers' demand and the interest of local communities is the first step to embarking on an e-tourism strategy, and starting to build the image of the destination, using a DMS as a promotional tool and eventually as an online reservation system. The establishment of a DMS depends on the costs involved and the capacity of DMOs to run different functionalities, depending on the technological, human and financial resources available, and the capacity of the various stakeholders. Success in the development of a DMS is mainly associated with its organizational structure and the cooperation mechanisms established between the Government and the private sector.

DMS can have different forms and functionalities depending on financial, human capacity and organizational characteristics of DMOs. They can be divided into four categories depending on their different functionalities, as shown in chart 4.9.

Chart 4.9

Various levels of services provided by DMS

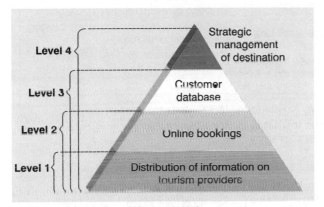

Source: Adapted from O'Connor (1999)

Level 1 is the most basic function and level 4 the most complex.[45] A new function is being added from one level to the next:

- Level 1 includes the distribution of information on tourism products and services (like an electronic brochure);

- Level 2 includes the functions of level 1 plus online reservation facilities;

- Level 3 includes the functions of levels 1 and 2 plus customer database management to improve the marketing of the destination globally;

- Level 4 includes the functions of levels 1, 2 and 3 plus the strategic management of the destination.

The large majority of DMS in developing countries have only reached level 1 (see section C). Table 4.1 details some of the main services and functions that a DMS should include in order to meet the expecta-

tions of stakeholders, in particular consumers and tourism sellers. The two sub-level categories, "informative" and "strategic", are intended to reflect the degree of information that DMOs can gradually offer when building up their DMS. Depending on the degree of requirements and the availability of resources of destinations in developing countries, DMS can be gradually implemented in four stages as noted above.

From a consumer's perspective, the primary functions of a DMS are to provide information and manage customers' relationships by offering dynamic services. When creating the website, it is important to focus on the following key principles that contribute to their effectiveness:

- Maximize the ease of use, and make sure that the layout and site navigation are clear and straightforward;

- Integrate all tourism products and services, and provide accurate information;

- Offer activity selection/what to do?

- Differentiate your offer: niche markets, customized ("do it yourself" approach) products and dynamic packaging;

- Optimize interaction with customers, offering timely responsiveness;

- Propose content in the languages of targeted tourism markets and customize the layout and content on the basis of the targeted market;

- Find out how to improve service and product offerings;

- Ensure quality assurance of service and product offerings;

- Link up with outbound and inbound tourism distributors and ensure search engine optimization;

- Ensure and communicate on the security of transactions.

In order to promote e-tourism development, UNCTAD has developed a DMS as part of the E-Tourism Initiative (ETI), a technical assistance package aimed at promoting the application of ICTs in tourism so as to enable developing countries to exploit their tourism resources and benefit from greater autonomy in developing and promoting their own brand (see box 4.1).

Table 4.1

Key services and functions of a DMS

Services and functions of a DMS	Informative	Strategic
General information	– Information on destination: history, culture, natural assets, geography, main tourist attractions; – Practical information: visa requirements, international and national companies flying to the country, maps, pictures, specific events (festivals, fairs, markets...), weather forecasts, entertainment...), foreign consulates within the country, embassies abroad, vaccinations, hospitals, currency and foreign exchange, etc.	– Content available in the languages of destinations' main existing and potential tourism markets; – Depending on the language chosen, the content and its presentation can differ to match different targeted tou-rism markets.
Management of information on tourism products and services	– Accurate description (including photos) of the products and services (accommodation, restaurants, museums, cultural centres, boutiques, etc.), including information about surrounding areas; links to their websites if available; – Information on cultural or leisure activities;- Excursions and guided tours; – Contacts of national travel agencies, transport companies (airlines, train, car, boats, etc).	– Suggestion ideas for holidays: places to go and things to do (adventure, nature, sports, art and culture, gastronomy, etc.); – Itinerary planning; – Real-time dynamic/customized packages; – Information search by key word, category, geographical location, etc;- – Market optimization and yield management.
Customer management functions	– Customer database management; – Communication with customers by e-mail, telephone or fax, via a call centre, or direct contact with tourism providers.	– Market research and impact analysis; – Marketing campaigns.
Reservation functions	- Bookings are made by e-mail, telephone or fax, via a call centre, or by contacting directly the suppliers.	– Online payment; – Security of transactions.

Box 4.1

E-Tourism Initiative: A comprehensive capacity-building package for destinations in developing countries

Destination marketing and management are key strategies for emerging destinations. Launched at UNCTAD XI in São Paulo, Brazil, in June 2004, the ETI offers business value for all stakeholders in the tourism industry. The ETI is the electronic component of UNCTAD's Task Force on Sustainable Tourism for Development, established in June 2003. The E-Tourism Initiative (ETI) is structured around a comprehensive package that includes ICT-based tools and a methodology, based on a steady partnership-building approach. Its main goals are to support the personalized traveller decision process and to allow developing and least developed countries to organize, market and distribute online aggregated tourism services from small and medium-sized enterprises, which are traditionally kept out of the market. The objective is to increase their inbound tourism flow, maximize the linkages between stakeholders, and increase their autonomy in the management of their destination.

For more information, see http://etourism.unctad.org.

C. E-tourism: Learning from experience

ICTs are one of the most effective tools allowing public authorities and tourism enterprises to take charge of the organization and promotion of their tourism, as well as for encouraging the adoption of e-business practices among national tourism providers and improving their competitiveness in tourism markets. However, the development of e-tourism is often hampered by a number of persistent issues. These include the lack of ICT infrastructure, of human capacity and vision about e-business-based strategies and policies that policymakers and enterprises in developing countries could adopt to develop and maintain competitive advantages in tourism markets. Most national tourism providers in developing countries continue with traditional operational practices and are not yet taking advantage of ICTs for conducting their business operations. The lack of awareness of ICT potentialities, knowledge of ICT tools and resources is preventing them from changing their work practices.

The diffusion of ICTs enables tourism producers to make tourism information available to a large number of people at relatively low cost, and to interact with consumers, other tourism producers and distributors. In developing countries, e-tourism websites reflect various levels of maturity, from very basic websites to a limited number of sophisticated DMS (for example, South Africa, Thailand and the Caribbean). Some developing countries, and LDCs, have started to develop and promote new and innovative tourism products online, such as ecotourism,[46] taking advantage of their tourism potentialities and consumers' needs and wants.

Destinations have their own priorities in terms of tourism development (domestic, regional, international), such as to increase market share or income, or to develop innovative products and services. They have to focus on their natural and cultural assets and development objectives in order to decide on adequate tourism strategies. Mass tourism and niche tourism have to be considered taking into account their advantages and value added for the individual country. In all cases, developing countries should integrate the principles of sustainable development into country policies and tourism programmes, and ensure that tourism is sustainable.

1. E-tourism in least developed countries

As noted in section B.1, the participation of LDCs in international tourism markets is progressing but still remains insignificant. International tourism arrivals in the LDCs have increased by 6.5 per cent annually since 1988, compared with world growth of 3.7 per cent. Tourism is a prominent economic sector in some LDCs, ranking first,[47] second or third among all export sectors in 19 LDCs, and is a less prominent but fast-growing sector for another 10 LDCs.[48] However, their overall share in international tourism is small, accounting for less than 1 per cent of international tourism receipts with a total of 6.4 million international tourism arrivals in 2003.[49]

To assess the level of development of e-tourism in the LDCs, UNCTAD has conducted a survey with national DMOs that have developed a dedicated e-tourism website. The purpose of the survey was twofold: to evaluate the level of development of the e-tourism websites and to identify the challenges faced in the successful development of e-tourism.

Out of 50 DMOs, 17 do not have an e-tourism website.[50] Tourism in these countries is insignificant, owing to instability, structural disadvantages (including poverty), the absence of tourism policies or a lack of demand. Among the 33 NTOs that promote their tourism online, 24 have a dedicated e-tourism website[51] and 9 use government websites. This figure reflects a growing understanding among public authorities of the important role that e-tourism can play in development. Of the 24 questionnaires sent out to DMOs with dedicated e-tourism websites, 10 were completed and returned.

In addition to the questionnaire, the presentation, content and technical functionalities of the websites were evaluated according to their user-friendliness and the number/level of services proposed.[52]

The location of the servers hosting the websites (including those with no dedicated e-tourism website), the companies that developed the websites, and the operating systems used, provide a good indication of the technical facilities and human capacities in LDCs. As shown in table 4.2, the large number of websites that are still dependent on the infrastructure of developed countries for worldwide access, high bandwidth and uninterrupted service reflects the lack of ICT availability in the LDCs. However, a large majority of

Table 4.2

DMO websites in 24 selected LDCs (2005) *— Server location, website development and operating systems

Technical specificities specific	Websites	Information available
Server location	16 DMOs use servers in developed countries;9 in the United States (Benin, Nepal, Rwanda, Samoa, Senegal, Solomon Islands, Tuvalu, Vanuatu, Yemen);6 in Europe (Djibouti, tiopía, Madagascar, Mali, Togo, Uganda);1 in Australia (Timor-Leste).	21/24 LDCs
	3 have their own servers (Gambia, Guinea, Maldives).	
	2 have a server in their region (Bangladesh, Burkina Faso).	
Website development	The majority of DMO websites (18) are being developed locally, with the exception of Senegal (United States) Timor-Leste (Portugal), Togo (Belgium), Tuvalu (Fiji) and Uganda (Ireland).	23/24 LDCs
Operating systems	A total of 11 DMOs use FOSS (GNU/Linux - Server Apache), and 13 operate under proprietary systems (UNIX, Windows).	24/24 LDCs

* LDCs with dedicated e-tourism websites

websites were developed by local companies. In addition, FOSS[53] tends to be used by nearly half of DMOs.

The main messages drawn from the questionnaires and the research into the 24 e-tourism websites are the following:

- Websites are mostly purely informative, corresponding to level 1 of DMS functions, as presented in chart 4.9. Online bookings are not available for any of the websites, but 18 of them provide links to local hotels, national travel agents and tour operators.[54] According to DMOs, the lack of both financial and human resources, together with a lack of dynamism on the part of tourism providers, prevents them from proposing this service.

- The majority of the websites provide rich information on the destinations (history, traditions, culture and geography, as well as accommodation, restaurants and entertainment, mainly in the form of tourism provider contacts or links to major hotel chain websites). The information is presented graphically in an attractive way and documented with photographs. Moreover, some websites propose specific activities, mainly related to the country's ecosystem, such as ecotourism. Regarding the 24 DMOs' websites, ecotourism is proposed by 15 countries.[55] Activities such as bird or gorilla watching, safaris and scuba diving are the main activities proposed. In some cases, activities based on cultural and natural resources are also offered.

- A couple of DMO websites offer poor-quality content, which could have a negative effect. In general, for promotional websites, the rule is not "something is better than nothing", because the website is a critical asset, but rather "no website is better than a bad one". Having an e-tourism website is an operational requirement, but it has to be supported by high-quality content and functionalities as discussed in section B.4. However, as described earlier, a DMS can be built gradually. At each level, the content must be of high quality and meet consumers' needs.

- The number of visits per website serves as a benchmarking indicator for NTOs, and a few of them, for instance the DMO of Nepal,[56] also identify the country of origin of visitors to their website.

- Of the 10 DMOs that responded to the survey, 4 indicated[57] that they had redesigned their e-tourism websites in 2004 and 2005, mainly to facilitate the ease of use and introduce new languages with a view to improving their effectiveness. In most cases, this was done by a local communication company or by the DMOs themselves (as shown in table 4.2). Several DMOs are planning to make their site more dynamic and user friendly.

- Out of 24 DMO e-tourism websites, 11 are multilingual,[58] with a maximum of six languages for Nepal, four for Senegal and three for Maldives. Eleven websites are available only in English and two only in French.

- One of the main tasks of the DMOs is to include all tourism providers, especially when existing databases are flawed and incomplete. They have all put in place different business models, some free of charge and some subject to an annual registration fee.

- Among the constraints the DMOs face, they reported a lack of knowledge, skills and human resources for web design, maintenance (includ-

ing the update of data) and database management. Some DMOs have received international or regional support to build their websites (UNDP, the EU, South Pacific Tourism Organisation and Portuguese Cooperation).

- The DMOs indicated that international support is essential, in particular in terms of capacity-building. They also stated their views on the benefit of sharing information among DMOs in order to learn from the experience of others.

Overall, the DMOs reported that the Internet has become the cheapest and quickest form of promoting their tourism offer. However, the technology in itself represents both an opportunity and a challenge for developing countries, notably the LDCs. The lack of knowledge of ICT tools and resources places developing countries at a severe disadvantage in competing in the international online tourism market.

One of the major challenges involved in setting up a DMS (see box 4.2) is to foster the support and commitment of all the tourism providers, and it is crucial to create awareness at an early stage among tourism producers about the creation and benefits of a DMS.

Box 4.2

The main challenges to the development of an effective DMS

- Lack of strategic orientation;

- Inability to strengthen the competitiveness of the local industry;

- Technology-leading project rather than a project that follows appropriate marketing and management strategies;

- Poor integrated approach;

- Inability to provide total services for tourism demand and supply;

- Limited geographical basis, which makes the system unfeasible;

- Premature innovation in a traditionally reserved industry;

- Lack of standardization and compatibility;

- Withdrawal of public sector interest and funding;

- Product rather than demand orientation.

Source: Buhalis (2003).

To illustrate the obstacles encountered by national DMOs, the case of Cambodia is presented in box 4.3.

Box 4.3

www.tourismcambodia.com

Since 1994, the number of international tourism arrivals in Cambodia has increased sixfold, reaching over one million tourists in 2004 according to Cambodia's official statistics. Tourism is a leading economic sector for Cambodia, ranking third (after sawn timber and logs) in 1998 of all export sectors with 9.5 per cent of total export of goods and services. In 2005, its tourism industry is expected to generate 7.3 per cent of GDP and close to 400,000 direct jobs.[1] As part of its development strategy, the NTO launched in 2001 www.tourismcambodia.com, and since then the website has received over 230,000 visits. In addition, the Government of Cambodia is preparing a number of legal instruments related to electronic commerce that will favour the development of e-tourism. The promotion of the tourism industry is also beginning to diversify from its traditional focus on city-based cultural and heritage sites to turn to tour packages along the Mekong, beach activities, boating and diving.

Cambodia is poorly marketed by major online travel agents at the international level. Of the six main online travel agencies in the United States (Expedia, Orbitz, Travelocity, Lastminute.com, eBookers.com and Opodo), only Expedia, Orbitz and Opodo promote this destination, proposing a maximum of 10 hotels from international chains. In this context, it is essential for Cambodia to promote online its tourism products and services according to its interests and to ensure extensive participation by local tourism SMEs.

One of the major challenges for the DMO is the collection of information and data on tourism providers throughout the country. Very few local hotels have a website, and therefore could benefit from the DMO website to increase their promotion. According to the DMO business plan, it will cost annually $100 for five-star hotels and $70 for four-star hotel and below, and $40 for travel agents to be referenced on the website. However, most of the tourism providers are not familiar with the NTOs' website, and this emphasizes the need for an awareness campaign. This is, for instance, the case of the Bopha-Angkor, a 22-room hotel in Siam Reap. The hotel set up www.bopha-angkor.com in 2001, using the Internet as an additional distribution channel, complementary to the information available in other media sources (tourism guides, articles, etc.). The hotel claims to generate 70 per cent of its revenues online and to receive an average of 20 online bookings a day by electronic mail. The website was reviewed in June 2005 to improve its presentation, as shown below, and to propose new products such as promotional seasonal packages.

---

[1] http://www.wttc.org/

www.bopha-angkor.com: before and after

May 2005   **June 2005**

2. National e-tourism strategies: Best practices

In view of all the public and private actors directly and indirectly involved, tourism growth depends largely on the interrelationships among its various components. ICTs can help all tourism stakeholders to create or reinforce their cooperation. E-tourism offers a collaborative space for public authorities (at the national, regional and local levels) and private providers.

The formulation of a national e-tourism strategy is a precondition for the establishment of a DMS that will support the promotion of a destination. Within the framework of a national e-tourism strategy, the role of the Government is to stimulate the tourism industry by supporting the adoption of e-business practices by enterprises for their integration into global tourism markets, and by coordinating the various interests, acting as a facilitator, and to build trust among consumers. In recent years there have been several national e-tourism initiatives by destinations, from which lessons can be drawn and best practices shared with regard in particular to public–private partnerships. In order to illustrate the diversity of the initiatives, this section will look at three case studies based on three DMS at different levels of development: www.tunisietourisme.com.tn, www.tourismthailand org and www.bonjourquebec.com. The latter have received several national and international awards for the quality of its website, its web marketing and online services. The experience of www.bonjourquebec.com generates a great deal of interest in other countries, and was presented at a national seminar in Tunisia, which is currently setting up a DMS.

www.tunisietourisme.com.tn

(i) Context

Tunisia was the third tourism destination in Africa and the Middle East in 2003, with over 5.1 million international tourism arrivals, tourism representing 18.4 per cent of its exports and 5.85 per cent of its GDP.[59] However, in terms of tourism foreign earnings, Tunisia received only $1,475 million, which represents an average of about $288 per arrival, compared with $625 per arrival in Morocco. The low level of foreign tourism earnings in Tunisia can be partly explained by the development of seaside resorts and wellness tourism[60] in the form of mass tourism pro-

moted as "all-inclusive" packages (including transport and accommodation). The natural and cultural resources of Tunisia, together with low wages, and attractive prices and offers, have significantly contributed to the development of mass tourism in Tunisia.

The tourism market in Tunisia is mainly supplied by Western Europe (about 50 per cent, of which 17 per cent from France, Germany, Italy and the United Kingdom) and the Maghreb (with the Libyan Arab Jamahiriya accounting for 25 per cent and Algeria for 16 per cent).[61] Its promotion is primarily ensured by foreign tour operators, mainly European,[62] both offline and online. For example, in France, one of the top three online travel agencies selling vacation packages[63] offers a week in Tunisia for $215, including the flight and half-board accommodation.

Analysis of the main European tourism markets in terms of Internet use sheds light on the importance of this tool in the distribution of tourism products. France, Germany, Italy and the United Kingdom benefit from high Internet penetration rates.[64] In 2004, 47 per cent of French tourists searched for information on the Internet to prepare their vacation one month in advance.[65] In 2004, 62 per cent of Internet users in Germany searched for information to plan their holidays. In Italy, the proportion reached 54 per cent in 2004.[66] A recent study[67] reveals that 68 per cent of British travellers use the Internet to obtain information on their travel and accommodation, and it is estimated that 50 per cent will be purchasing their travel online within the next two years. With regard to the people travelling from the Maghreb to Tunisia, the web marketing of the destination does not constitute a priority in view of the low Internet connectivity rate in those countries.[68]

(ii) Objectives and strategy

In the last few years, Tunisia has incorporated access to new technologies, and in particular to the Internet, into its development strategy, as a precondition for the participation of businesses and consumers in the digital economy (UNCTAD, 2004).

Since 1995, the Tunisian Government has set up several structures and consultative groups on tourism,[69] and the National Tourism Office has been holding seminars and workshops to foster dialogue with and among all the stakeholders of the tourism industry and to associate them in the definition of the national strategy in this sector.

Over the last few years the Ministry of Tourism has carried out a number of studies with a view to defining priority action for its strategy based on tourism innovation (products, services, ICTs). The first priority aims at improving the existing offer (such as wellness tourism), developing new products and services, and involving the private sector. New products could include thematic forms of tourism based on Tunisia's natural resources such as cultural tourism, ecotourism, desert excursions and golf. The second priority consists in promoting effective institutions in the tourism sector, developing solid partnerships between the public sector at the national, regional, local levels, and the private sector. The third priority focuses on the competitiveness of the sector, which could be improved by investment incentives and revision of taxation. The fourth priority consists in elaborating a strategic marketing plan, recognizing the need to better target consumers and diversifying distribution channels. In addition, the development of human capacity in ICTs has been recognized as essential.

In support of its tourism strategy and as part of its national e-strategy aimed at creating an enabling environment for the development of e-business, the Government of Tunisia has decided to build a DMS. The objectives are twofold: through the use of ICTs, to reach consumers in existing and potential tourism markets, and therefore increase foreign exchange earnings; and to stimulate the adoption of e-business practices by tourism enterprises.

(iii)   Challenges and opportunities

Seaside resort tourism which is currently the main type of offer in Tunisia is seasonal. For Tunisia, e-tourism will help to promote innovative tourism products and to target new tourism markets such as China, Malaysia, Serbia and Montenegro, South Africa, Turkey and also Latin American countries.[70] In that regard, and considering the growing importance of Chinese outbound tourism, Tunisia signed a cooperation agreement on tourism with China in June 2004.[71]

The Government of Tunisia organized in 2004 a national consultation on ICT and tourism in order to reach a consensus on the options available in terms of policies and strategies for development of the sector, and to identify the concerns of the professionals, encouraging them to take part in the process at an early stage (in order to be more committed in the implementation phase of the strategies). The main outcomes of the consultation include the creation of::

- A national DMS to enhance the promotion of tourism products in association with all stakeholders ;

- Regional commissions responsible for ensuring the follow-up and the coordination of the actions with the stakeholders in the tourist sector on a regional scale;

- A committee to follow up on the recommendations of the national consultation.

In addition, the workshop agreed on capacitybuilding actions, as well as the development of a communication strategy adapted to consumers' needs and wants.

As at June 2005, www.tunisietourisme.com.tn had not yet been entirely finalized. The website is available in three languages (French, German and English). Online bookings and payment are not yet available. The website offers a "tourist guide", brochures in PDF format, photos, information on 11 cities around the country, the directory of Tunisian tourism offices worldwide, and some information on the history of Tunisia over the centuries. The "tourist guide" includes information on accommodation (searchable by town, type and category), transport, activities, events, restaurants and attractions.

In order to develop all the functionalities to make its DMS effective (estimated at $2 million), Tunisia should identify technical partners that could help cover the related costs. One of the main priorities of the Government of Tunisia is to encourage the participation of local tourism enterprises in the DMS through an awareness campaign on the benefits of ICTs.

www.tourismthailand.org

(i) Context

In 2003, tourism in Thailand represented 5.47 per cent of GDP and 9.71 per cent of the country's exports.[72] According to the Tourism Authority of Thailand (TAT), domestic tourism[73] represented in 2004 about 73 million tourists, who on average travel for two to three days, and spend an average of $46 per person per day. Sixty per cent of international tourists that went to Thailand in 2004 came from

East Asia (about 7 million) and 22 per cent from Europe.[74] The length of stay of international tourists is about 8 days for which they spend $ 98 per person per day.[75]

Thailand has devoted great efforts and financial resources to marketing its destination in both domestic (Travel Thailand-Can Go Every Month, Unseen Thailand, One Day Fun Trip, etc.) and foreign markets ("Visit Thailand Year", "The World Our Guest",[76] "Amazing Thailand",[77] "Happiness on Earth") through promotional campaigns via newspapers, radio, television programmes and the Internet. Thailand has also developed subregional cooperation to jointly promote multi-destination packages such as the Heritage Necklace of South-East Asia, connecting cultural tourism places such as Phukam in Myanmar, Nan in Thailand, Luang Prabang in the Lao People's Democratic Republic, Hue in VietNam and Siem Riep in Cambodia.

The first step in the development of tourism in Thailand (1960–1980) consisted in developing tourist facilities for Thais, and in building knowledge about the importance of tourism among the public and private actors, including in provincial areas, through seminars, training and the media. Between 1965 and 1973, the Thai tourism industry experienced rapid growth and represented the third largest foreign exchange revenue after exports of rubber and rice. A National Tourism Development Plan was formulated (1979–1991) and included for the first time in the National Economic and Social Development Plan.

However, tourism planning in the initial stages did not feature much local community involvement. Most government policies focused on increasing markets and tourism numbers. This led to rapid growth in arrivals and income, but also to negative effects on society and the environment. The Thai tourism industry fell into a "low price trap" cycle, which eventually led to the deterioration of tourism products. To remedy this situation, the strategy adopted was to move to quality products through a greater balance between marketing and development by focusing on the tourism providers rather than the demand as a driving force. The concept of sustainable tourism development was introduced with a view to adding value to tourism products and services and as a means of building and strengthening local communities, combining economy, ecology and society. An eco-tourism-based plan was formulated, and led to the promotion of community-based tourism, home

stay programmes, agro-tourism and adventure tourism. In addition, shopping, sports, food, culture, cultural heritage and cooperation with neighbouring countries to increase the length of stay and average expenditure were promoted.

(ii) Objectives and strategy

As a result of its tourism strategy, Thailand received over 10 million international tourism arrivals in 2003. In order to achieve the goal of 20 million tourism arrivals by 2008, the TAT has set e-tourism as one of the main priorities of the Thailand Tourism Promotion Policies for 2003–2006. To that end, TAT proposed to accelerate the development of an information technology system that facilitates e-tourism, including online business transactions as well as IT-based marketing operations and provision of security systems. The main objectives of enhancing the use of ICTs are to increase competitive advantage in the tourism sector, to generate income, to satisfy the needs of international tourists, and to maximize the efficiency and the effectiveness of tourism operations within TAT. www.tourismthailand.org was officially launched in 2003. The website provides information about the country and is supported by www.thailandebookings.com, which offers a selection of hotels, thematic tour packages searchable by key word, location and price, transport facilities and a booking system (provided by the Bank of Asia in partnership with Verisign). The website is available in 13 languages.[78]

The role of TAT is twofold: to centralize tourism information, public relations and tourism promotion into one database, including information on public and private tourism agencies locally and globally; and to use ICT to stimulate and support online business transactions to meet the needs of consumers and tourism enterprises. TAT focuses on the adoption of e-business practices by tourism providers, and encourages them to make use of the Internet in their businesses through many different initiatives. These include training courses to enhance the capacity of tourism providers to learn more about the Internet and e-commerce, and also their integration into www.thailandebookings.com (B2C) as well as the B2B trade portal www.thaitravelmart.com. This portal helps Thai sellers, in particular SMEs, and overseas buyers, of tourism products and services to identify trading partners. At present, a total of 530 Thai operators and 371 overseas tourism travel agents have registered; they belong to nine major tourism categories (travel agents, hotel and resort, restaurant, spa, golf, theme park, diving, health care and rental transportation). In order to foster the participation of tourism providers, the membership is free of charge for both buyers and sellers who register themselves on www.thaitravelmart.com. Search can be made by product or by company (overseas and Thai tourism directories are available).

In 2004, the number of Internet hits on www.thailandebooking.com was about 150,000 per month, and 3,000 and 5,000 e-mails were sent by consumers to get information on particular hotels and tours. About 1,000 online bookings were received every month. The website is linked with http://www.asean-tourism.com in order to help promote destinations among ASEAN countries.[79]

(iii)   Challenges, opportunities and lessons learned

The main challenges encountered are lack of IT and English skills, lack of online marketing knowledge among tourism providers and limited access to telecommunication systems. According to TAT, the main benefit of the Internet is that tourism providers have been able to reach more consumers and business partners globally, in a more efficient way and at relatively low costs. Thai tourism enterprises, especially the SMEs, can become more autonomous by broadening their market and targeting directly consumers, and by creating direct relationships with tourism distributors.

Thailand has a long tradition in marketing its destination to worldwide consumers and to its tourism enterprises. With the rapid development of tourism, partnerships with overseas travel agents have developed over the years, and those partners are already registered on www.thaitravelmart.com. TAT intends to further ensure the promotion of Thailand through global online travel agencies (Cheap Tickets and Orbitz) in order to enlarge its customer base.

In addition, a new version of www.tourismthailand.org should be launched before the end of 2005. The website, which uses the HTML format, will adopt in its new version XML standards to better enable the interchange and update of data with other websites in a more effective way.

www.bonjourquebec.com

(i)   Context

Tourism in Quebec is mainly domestic. Out of the 26.8 million tourists in 2003, only 9.3 per cent came from the United States and 3.6 per cent from other countries. www.bonjourquebec.com (BQC) is the official tourism DMS of the Government of Quebec and was launched in 2000. Its mission is to enhance the promotion of Quebec's tourism industry globally in order to attract new markets.

BQC is a sophisticated but easy to use DMS resulting from a successful public and private partnership between the Quebec Ministry of Tourism, the Destination Management Organisation of Quebec, and Bell Canada for the technological realization. Several development steps were necessary over the years in order to conceive and develop the various functionalities of the portal. Resources and efforts focused on the steady coordination between the Government and the private sector, as well as on the development of tourism products and the online promotion of the destination.

(ii)   Objectives and functionalities

The main objectives of BQC are twofold: to provide travellers worldwide with accurate and attractive information on the destination; and to facilitate interaction among public and private initiatives. To this end, www.bonjourquebec.com integrates 39 functionalities addressing four main user categories:

(a)   Customers

It provides worldwide customers who plan to visit Quebec with a unique information/documentation/booking window in French, English and Spanish (and partially in German, Italian and Japanese):

–   Information on tourism products and services, including vacation suggestions (more than 250 packages are offered), product descriptions, photos, dynamic mapping, guides, brochures that can be downloaded in PDF format, and a search engine;

–   Reservation system with searchable directories cross-referenced by regions for accommodation, cultural events such as theatre and sporting manifestations through a "ticket office". Partnership agreements have been concluded with Travel-

Picture 1

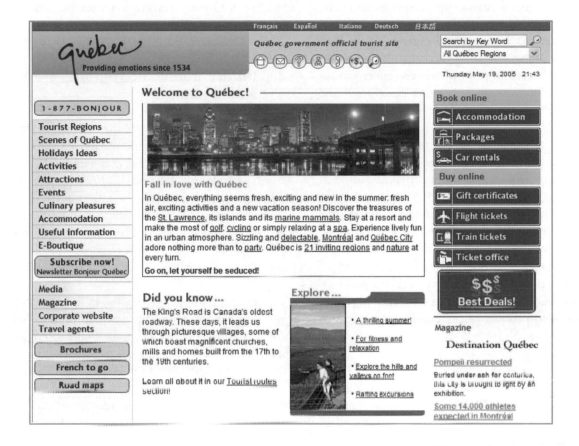

price for the online sale of air and train tickets, and car rental reservation;

– Customer service functions that rely on a customer relationship management (CRM) approach, available seven days a week through e-mail, telephone, fax, national tourist offices and travel agencies in Quebec.

(b) Tourism enterprises

To date, over 13,000 information files give a very detailed description of attractions and tourist establishments. The registration and update of these files are free of charge. Of the 5,000 hotel properties classified by the Quebec Ministry of Tourism, more than 700 are transactional members, fulfilling the requirements of credit card acceptance and Internet connection at their property. The transactional members give a percentage to BQC for each online transaction. They benefit from an inventory management and Internet reservation service through a secure extranet on Bell's Resources Centre, which allows them to receive information on transactions. Businesses are invited to provide a description and photos to be displayed on the website to market and sell their prod-

ucts. In 2004, 72,000 transactions were processed online through www.bonjourquebec.com with payment by credit card.

(c) The Quebec Ministry of Tourism's staff, which update and manage databases as well as all functions related to marketing initiatives, the booking process and an internal electronic bulletin;

(d) Bell Canada's staff, which manage the reservation and billing system.

Since 1999, BQC has experienced a growth rate of 470 per cent in the number of customers, reaching in 2004 over nine million customers, of whom 69 per cent were located outside Quebec (mainly in the United States).

(iii) Challenges, opportunities, and lessons learned

The implementation of this DMS, even in a technologically advanced country, took nearly eight years from its theoretical inception based on several studies on the administrative and technological aspects of the

DMS and bid (to select the partner) to the gradual implementation of the functionalities for testing purposes and to ensure high-quality services and adequate training of the staff. In 2004, two additional functions were added to collect customers' data for targeted marketing purposes (allowing customers to keep abreast of current promotions and package deals by receiving electronically a monthly newsletter); and to create an electronic bulletin for enterprises.

The constraints faced by Quebec regarding the adoption of the DMS are similar to those faced traditionally by developing countries, to a different degree of intensity. To overcome them, BQC devoted great attention to the management of changes, the training and support of staff, and the definition and follow-up of the working process. One of the main challenges was to reduce the scepticism and conservatism of tourism enterprises with regard to new technologies. Hotels are still facing difficulties in applying yield management to product prices owing to their lack of expertise.

BQC represents a major change in the promotion and distribution of tourism services in Quebec. It allowed the Quebec Ministry of Tourism to be more competitive and to offer more comprehensive services to an increased number of clients with approximately the same number of staff, with a reduction in the costs related in particular to promotional mailing and transactional costs.

Key success factors include the partnership with Bell Canada, which enabled the whole project to materialize. Joining complementary skills and resources, and sharing the financial cost and risk, were essential to the success of the initiative. The Quebec Ministry of Tourism bore the costs related to the technological development and exploitation linked to its tourist information services, and to the exploitation of the DMS customers' database. It also ensured the promotion of BQC on global markets and the operationalization of its call centre. Bell Canada supplies the technology for BQC, and bears the risks and costs of the development and operation of the reservation system and e-commerce services.

The free-of-charge registration of tourism enterprises have guaranteed a high level of participation in the DMS. BQC ensured the accuracy and uniformity of the information provided by tourism enterprises by standardizing it and entering the data. The complementarities between the Internet, the tourist information offices and the call centres have ensured the suc-

cess of the initiative. BQC also intends to multiply access points by offering to regional tourism organizations in Quebec reservation sites (as well as databases) to increase its impact.

3. Intraregional and regional e-tourism strategies

Travellers may want to combine multiple destinations and organize thematic expeditions based on natural or cultural resources such as cruises, temples, imperial cities and safaris. Beyond destination competition, this represents one of the incentives for countries to jointly promote their destinations and mutually benefit from tourism flows. The existence of regional, intraregional and/or sub-regional tourism also encourages destinations to develop joint brands.

There are a number of advantages in promoting several destinations under the same umbrella, including considerable economies of scale that can be expected and, thanks to the operational gains brought about by sharing resources (IT and linguistic, online marketing, for example), efficiency, management structures, developments and technological innovation. There are also many challenges to overcome. Regional DMS are being developed by regional institutions such as ASEAN (www.asean-tourism.com) and the Caribbean Tourism Organization (www.doitcaribbean.com) to encourage the development of B2C and B2B tourism. Their main goal is to build economic growth through cooperation among destinations to increase intra-regional or international tourism. Other objectives include developing regional innovative and dynamic packages, entering new markets or building on tourism's potential.

www.asean-tourism.com

As noted in section B.1, tourism in Asia is mainly intraregional. International tourism arrivals in ASEAN countries totalled over 37.4 million by the end of 2003,[80] of which intra-ASEAN tourism represented 44 per cent. Out of the 15 million ASEAN arrivals, Singapore (5.6 million), Indonesia (1.8 million), Thailand (1.6 million) and Malaysia (1.3 million) had the largest shares. Furthermore, Asia as a whole represented a total of 74 per cent of arrivals in ASEAN countries,[81] with the main tourism arrivals being from China (2 million), Japan (1.9 million) and the Republic of Korea (1.2). The growth of intraregional tourism in particular in South-East Asia led

ASEAN member countries to focus on developing strategies in order to foster such tourism.

In the 1990s, ASEAN members agreed to increase cooperative efforts in tourism promotion. During the "Visit ASEAN year" (1992) ASEAN member countries were invited to work together to promote the area as one destination. The ASEAN Bangkok Summit (1995) established the notion of promoting sustainable tourism.

In 1998, the ASEAN member countries set up an intraregional Plan of Action for tourism. One of the primary objectives was to abandon the traditional competitive approach to tourism growth in favour of a complementary relationship with other member countries and the building of a common brand image for the region as one vast and attractive destination that would provide a wide range of experiences for potential tourists.

In 2002, ASEAN member countries signed a tourism cooperation and promotion agreement to give a major boost to facilitation of intra-ASEAN travel, market access, safety and security, marketing campaigns, sustainable development and human resources development. As part of the actions conducted to increase intra-ASEAN travel, the "Visit ASEAN Campaign" (VAC) was launched in 2001 and introduced into national policies and actions in ASEAN member countries through related programmes, festivals and special events.

The website www.asean-tourism.com and the ASEAN Tourism Association's website, www.aseanta.org[82], were established in 2001 to support the VAC. The main objective of the campaign was to build a strong branding of the ASEAN region as a single tourism destination, building on its unique strengths and diversities, as well as the strong unity and complementation of the individual member countries. www.asean-tourism.com reflects that objective by presenting "Asia's Perfect 10 Paradise" through the world cultural and natural heritage sites of the region as a whole. The website provides information on each country, including direct links to the official DMO websites, information on common heritage, events, attractions (sailing and canoeing, diving, forest tracking and hiking, and beaches), and tourism guides that can be purchased online at http://www.barnesandnoble.com.[83] The information on tourism products such as accommodation and each country's entry formalities is available on each national website. ASEAN DMOs are encouraged to update the content of their pages by, for example, amending the text and putting in new pictures, and so forth, and can update it directly.

www.asean-tourism.com is an information window and contains mainly photos. It does not provide tourism products. A link to www.aseanta.org gives access to two air and hotel passes directed at travellers outside ASEAN (the "ASEAN Air and Hotel Pass"[84]), and the "ASEAN Hip-Hop Pass", only available to ASEAN citizens. These travel packages are being offered in cooperation with participating airlines, hotels and travel agents, and propose competitive prices for international and intraregional travel. They include three components, namely air, hotel and city tour passes.

The "ASEAN Hip Hop Pass" sold 15,500 coupons worth $2.1 million to 5,000 ASEAN residents in 2004. Considering the size of the ASEAN market for the region, these results are still low. In order to further promote this Pass, a marketing budget of $300,000 was given to ASEANTA in 2004. More marketing actions and time will be needed to get the ASEAN market used to flying to two or more destinations on one trip. On the occasion of the ASEAN Tourism Forum (Malaysia, January 2005), the ASEAN task force on marketing concluded that a study of the Pass was needed in order to define whether it was the best model or whether there were other options such as more targeted marketing for ASEAN.

www.doitcaribbean.com

The Caribbean is considered the most tourism-dependent region in the world since tourism accounts for about 25 per cent of its GDP and is a significant contributor to the income, employment and development of the region.[85] In 2004, the Caribbean attracted over 42 million tourists, of whom 20 million were cruise passengers, and generated $21 billion.[86]

The Caribbean set an example with its regional e-tourism strategy. In late 2000, the Caribbean Tourism Organization (CTO) developed a DMS to collectively promote the 33 destinations of the Caribbean (www.doitcaribbean.com; see picture 2). The objective was to offer the region an online body to market its diversity, culture and heritage, as well as to facilitate the marketing of small islands that are offering similar tourism products. A regional strategy was established to guarantee to member countries, in particular the smaller ones, equal competition.

"Places to go", "things to do" and "special deals" are at the forefront of the website. The website proposes about 20 different activities, including eco-tourism. A choice of hotels (according to their size) is provided, together with a description and a link to hotel websites whenever available.

The website is available in six languages, which correspond to the Caribbean main markets, namely Germany, the United Kingdom and the United States, Spain, France, Italy and the Netherlands. According to the language chosen, the presentation of the website slightly differs,[87] taking advantage of web segment marketing. Technically, sub-sites were developed for each main tourism market. They provide to consumers an overview of a particular destination or special interest activity, linking directly to detailed information and booking links on the national websites of the member countries themselves.

The information provided by each sub-site is tailored to the particular interests and needs of each country (e.g. for the Spanish version a list of Spanish travel agents, airlines flying from Spain to the Caribbean and visa requirements). In order to update and maximize the content of the websites, a user-friendly content management system was put in place for CTO's international offices, for which a high level of coordination is required.

www.doitcaribbean.com is based on user-friendly web-management tools that include advanced functionalities providing value-added services to consumers, such as an interactive trip planner that offers information on selected areas of interest and hotels

and travel agents' contacts. An interactive map allows consumers to identify tourism-related activities for each destination. Online booking and payment facilities are available, and in order to address security and confidence issues, payment goes directly into a trust account supervised by Barclay Card merchant services. No money is released to the operator of the website until the client has arrived at the resort. In 2004, a new version of the booking engine used by many hotels and guesthouses was launched (powered by UK-based Escape2Travel, ltd,[88] using the latest available technologies net and XML to facilitate communication and transfer of data). The main objective was to facilitate the online promotion of small hotels. Over 400 hotels have signed up so far for the booking engine. The booking system is available to both tourism distributors (who get a commission per booking of about 10 per cent) and consumers (the same price applies whether the booking is made online or through a travel agent), and offers the same rates for all users. According to the CTO, the booking engine offers higher commissions to travel agents and gives tour operators the ability to purchase a large inventory of rooms.

In support of the B2C website doitcaribbean.com, a B2B portal, www.onecaribbean.org, features prospects for businesses and individuals eager to develop their share of the Caribbean tourism business, including business seeking business, employment, investment, goods and services, and tender opportunities. It also includes a B2B directory with Caribbean accommodation, Caribbean specialist travel agents in the United States, Canada and Europe, tour operators, international and intra-Caribbean carriers, Caribbean ground operators and attractions, golf courses, yacht charters, and so forth. To better serve the tourism providers, Onecaribbean.org is offering various reports and publications, tourism statistics, market intelligence and research, and the like. It also provides several private forums for various groups (e.g. for Directors of Tourism, Directors of Marketing, HRD specialists, etc.) where members can "meet" and share information. Recently, it has been used to provide online training for travel agents, and this activity is expected to develop in the future. The site receives about 20,000 visits a month from both within and outside the region. The CTO plans to upgrade the system in the near future in order to improve its structure and navigation so that it becomes easier to find information.

www.doitcaribbean.com receives over two million visitors a year. Capitalizing on its success, the CTO intends to offer to Caribbean member countries and tourism providers online marketing opportunities and global reach by proposing that website banner advertisements be added on the individual websites. To that end, a partnership agreement with International Travel Communications (ITC), a US-based marketing and communication enterprise, was signed in May 2005 for the production of various banner advertising options.[89]

D. Conclusions and recommendations

Greater ICT availability and awareness of the potentialities of the Internet have led developing countries, including LDCs, to develop e-tourism websites. However, the large majority are still unable to exploit the potential of the Internet to the full, although they have a tremendous opportunity to reach a growing number of consumers who want their tourism products, which are not widely marketed and distributed by overseas operators. While the latter may be good at providing an overview of a country (and perhaps not even that much in the case of LDCs), they usually do not provide the level of detail that a focused or niche tourism DMS could offer.

Destinations and tourism providers must now fully embrace the use of ICTs to be able to meet consumers' needs and help tourism providers distribute their products and services on a global scale. The challenge is not so much the technology as the adoption of new business models based on tourism innovation by all

the stakeholders. Public authorities, DMOs and tourism providers (at the national, regional and local levels) all have an important role to play in order to ensure effective and successful promotion of their destinations and improve their competitiveness in tourism markets. The use of ICTs should assist them in their efforts to market their tourism offer globally and at the same time to organize their tourism market and build a solid partnering industry that could capitalize on the benefits brought about by the Internet.

The following indicative elements should be considered when elaborating an ICT strategy for tourism development in developing countries.

Facilitate an enabling environment for e-tourism

Taking into account the multisector dimension of tourism, e-tourism strategies should be based on a holistic approach involving all stakeholders and combining local action in a sound national framework. Governments have a central role to play, particularly in terms of tourism planning and policy. E-tourism strategies should be integrated within the broader framework of national ICT policies addressing ICT access and liberalization of telecommunication infrastructure, capacity-building issues and the adaptation of the legal and regulatory framework, together with trust-building issues related to online payment.

Governments should support ICT use by SMEs and consumers, in particular in remote areas, by facilitating the provision of easy and low-cost access to broadband solutions to encourage their participation in the tourism industry. They should create awareness of the potential of e-tourism and provide incentives for the development of tourism enterprises' websites (for hotels, for instance) that could be referenced to the DMO e-tourism website. They should develop capacity-building through education programmes and training in relevant fields (including IT, web management, marketing, language abilities and cultural understanding in the curricula of tourism institutes).

In order to set up a DMS, Governments and DMOs should organize consultative meetings with relevant partners (including customs, immigration and finance officials, for whom ICTs can also be used to improve processes in official tourism-related functions). They should share knowledge with other destinations that have implemented an e-tourism strategy to identify the challenges and available options. Feasibility studies should be conducted to determine the strategic, administrative and technological aspects of the DMS, and a consensus on objectives, targets and relevant actions should be reached by all stakeholders.

Form solid public and private partnerships

Partnerships can be developed on a global, regional, national and/or local level, depending on the scope of activities and the extent of cooperation agreed upon. Partners can contribute to the technical development of the DMS, the development of new products and services, marketing actions, information technology and funding, as illustrated in the case studies.

Partnerships are particularly relevant as they enable all concerned, whether private or public stakeholders, to coordinate their resources and objectives, creating economies of scale by pooling human, financial and technical resources as in the case of regional or intraregional e-tourism promotion. The DMS gradually set up in both developed and developing countries demonstrate the importance of coordinating public policy and private initiatives and forming solid partnerships.

Adopt new business models

ICTs provide effective tools for DMOs and tourism providers to conduct their operations, from the organization of their tourism resources (databases, data processing) and networking with business partners to the distribution and web marketing of products. ICTs also help them identify consumers' needs, competitors and partners. Since the Internet is creating opportunities for cross-selling tourism products, B2B platforms should be implemented to help tourism buyers and sellers to identify partners in a simple and effective way. The examples of B2B travel trade portals www.thaitravelmart.com and www.onecaribbean.org have emphasized the importance for DMOs of creating awareness of the DMS among all tourism providers at the national, regional and local levels, and facilitating their participation by providing them free-of-charge registration.

DMOs and tourism enterprises should engage in process innovation and strengthen IT literacy, use and ownership, as well as adopt XML standards to improve connectivity between business partners and the packaging of tourism products, and to lower distribution costs. They should incorporate ICTs into their business operations, integrating yield manage-

ment to better manage their inventory online, taking into account the options available for cross-selling their tourism products and services. They should define cost-revenue models and differentiate them according to the different categories of tourism providers that have joined DMS and to end-users. To that end, DMOs should establish the cost plan (fixed and variable costs), define the main revenue streams and carry out revenue analysis. Business models should be adapted to the conditions of each country to ensure DMS durability.

Be customer-centred

E-tourism websites and services must be truly customer-centred. Early in the chapter, we observed that building an effective DMS supposes that DMOs (at national, regional and local levels) present tourism products in ways that respond to consumers' expectations for unbiased and high-quality information and dynamic services, including reservation and booking systems, as shown in the example of www.bonjourquebec.com or www.doitcaribbean.com. DMOs should guarantee the credibility of the system by providing unbiased information, offering an easy-to-use, attractive presentation of the website. They can target specific tourism markets in offering sub-sites in different languages, and customize their presentation and content accordingly.

The risk in promoting a destination is that the offer will not match the consumer in the end. Therefore, DMOs need to have a comprehensive vision of existing and potential market segments, tourism evolution and prospects, consumers' tourism-related Internet use and tourism behaviour to be able to translate those into web-based technologies and adequate services (languages, presentation, content) and marketing campaigns. To that end, several methods and types of information can be used. This includes the collection and analysis of statistics on national and international tourism flows, the classification of consumers according to socio-economic factors and type of vacations, and the definition of behavioural patterns.

The ability to use technology innovations will be essential for DMOs. Proposing innovative quality products in the form of self-tailored packages and product-centric specifics will meet the expectations of tomorrow's traveller. DMOs should present dynamically tourism products by travel experience (activities) or preferences (duration of stay, type of accommodation, price). In this regard, developing countries could make use of ICT tools, such as the E-Tourism Platform developed as part of the UNCTAD e-tourism initiative, which integrates this functionality.

Identify the most valuable products and services

A challenging task for destinations and tourism enterprises is to offer new products and services that are most likely to increase their attractiveness and competitiveness. Eco-tourism, cultural and natural heritage tourism, health and medical tourism and adventure tourism are some of the strategies used by destinations and tourism enterprises in developing countries. Niche tourism must be supported by the delivery of high-quality services. For instance, the destinations that have developed eco-tourism must be able to provide a sufficient number of qualified or experienced guides, and rural accommodation.

In order to online market niche tourism, destination and tourism providers should keep abreast of technological developments, standards, and consumers' travel behaviour, so as to adapt whenever necessary their tourism offerings and distribution.

Build trust

Building a dynamic DMS with comprehensive packaging is essential for meeting consumers' need for information, purchase, care and security. Security issues, in particular related to the transmission of credit card information, have to be addressed at the national level. In the end, the lack of confidence, security and user-friendly and high-quality frameworks remains influential in customers' decisions. This is an issue of particular relevance for the majority of developing countries, and particularly LDCs. Most of them do not have transaction capabilities or legal instruments to protect both businesses and consumers, or do not have the capacity to develop an

effective DMS, and cannot only rely on uncertain online revenues. For this reason, it is essential to propose different and complementary traditional distribution channels (travel agents, national tourism offices, tourism producers, call centres, etc.). DMS should work with certification authorities, building alliances with local bodies if they exist or international providers that offer the "stamp of approval" that consumers in developed countries now expect from online merchants (i.e. VeriSign, etc.). Privacy and security policies should be highly developed and prominently stated on the website. Transparency in these two areas is of paramount importance for building confidence.

Market e-tourism websites

As part of the actions to build a brand image, developing countries could take the lead in setting up the ".travel" domain, available since 2005. Provided that consumers easily associate country.travel or cities.travel, and find websites that meet their expectations, the ".travel" domain could support the branding efforts of destinations in developing countries. The ".travel" could be useful, but only if it is actually used; ensuring such use is something which the other special-interest top level domains (TLDs) have unfortunately not been very successful in doing so far.

The promotion of e-tourism websites must be supported by adequate marketing budgets and promotional actions. According to their tourism development objectives (domestic, intraregional or international), destinations and DMOs should organize tailor-made promotional campaigns. As emphasized in this chapter, they should use all channels and technology available, such as tourist guides, brochures, fairs, TV, radio, newspapers, direct marketing via e-mail, search optimization on major Internet search engines such as Google and Yahoo!,[90] and cross-linking to traditional and online travel distributors to increase their worldwide visibility.

Annex I

Table 1 — Evolution of international tourism arrivals by region

Per cent	1950	1960	1965	1970	1975	1980	1985	1990	1995	2000	2002	2004
Europe North America	66.48 24.44	72.32 20.20	73.67 17.17	70.14 17.16	70.73 13.70	67.97 12.42	64.90 12.01	61.97 12.40	59.47 13.85	57.13 13.26	56.47 11.8	54.6 11.1
Sub-total	90.92	90.52	90.84	87.30	84.43	80.39	76.91	74.31	73.32	70.39	68.27	65.7
Latin America and The Caribbean	5.17	3.91	3.43	5.79	6.34	6.43	6.30	6.39	5.37	5.33	4.83	5.3
East Asia/Pacific	0.75	0.98	1.42	3.04	3.64	7.02	9.17	11.53	14.74	15.8	17.8	19.3
South Asia and Middle East	1.09	1.10	2.57	2.09	2.94	3.19	4.10	3.72	3.26	4.37	4.83	5.6
Africa	2.07	1.49	1.74	1.78	2.65	2.97	3.52	3.99	3.31	3.98	4.56	4.3
Sub-total	9.08	7.48	9.16	12.70	15.57	19.61	23.09	25.63	26.14	29.48	32.03	34.5
World total	100	100	100	100	100	100	100	100	100	100	100	100
World (total in thousands)	25 282	69 296	112 729	159 690	214 357	284 841	321 240	443 866	567 033	687 300	702 600	760 000

Source: UNCTAD elaboration of data from the World Tourism Organization.

Table 2 — Distribution of international tourism receipts by region

Per cent	1950	1960	1965	1970	1975	1980	1985	1990	1995	2000	2002
Europe North America	42.14 31.81	56.56 20.21	62.04 17.85	61.58 19.66	63.52 15.75	58.83 12.06	50.12 18.11	52.59 18.43	51.07 19.23	49.16 21.17	50.71 17.94
Sub-total	73.95	76.77	79.89	81.24	79.27	70.89	68.23	71.02	70.30	70.33	68.65
Latin America and The Caribbean	18.67	15.50	11.11	7.16	9.36	12.85	10.57	7.66	6.38	6.64	6.15
East Asia/Pacific	1.43	2.84	3.54	6.15	5.32	7.32	11.08	14.39	4.65	17.19	18.89
South Asia and Middle East	1.76	1.35	3.05	2.76	2.93	5.49	7.10	4.26	2.81	3.54	3.81
Africa	4.19	3.54	2.41	2.69	3.12	3.45	3.02	2.67	1.86	2.26	2.48
Sub-total	26.05	23.23	20.11	18.76	20.73	29.11	31.77	28.98	29.70	29.63	31.35
World total	100	100	100	100	100	100	100	100	100	100	100
World (total $ million)	2 100	6 867	11 604	17 900	40 702	102 372	116 158	254 816	371 682	477 00	474 200

Source: UNCTAD elaboration of data from the World Tourism Organization.

Annex II

Differences between developing countries/territories in international tourism arrivals in 2003 (from 1 to > 10 million arrivals)

	Countries with> 10 million arrivals	5 to 10 million arrivals	5 to 10 million arrivals	Total of arrivals in thousands
Asia and the Pacific		Macao (China), Singapore	Indonesia, India, Kazakhstan, Philippines, Republic of Korea, Taiwan Province of China, VietNam	103 124
Latin America and the Caribbean	China, Hong Kong (China), Malaysia, Thailand		Argentina, Brazil, Bahamas, Dominican Republic, Chile, Costa Rica, Cuba, Jamaica, Puerto Rico, Uruguay	41 322
Africa	Mexico	South Africa, Tunisia	Botswana, Morocco, Zimbabwe	19 410
Middle East		United Arab Emirates, Saudi Arabia	Bahrain, Egypt, Islamic Republic of Iran, Jordan, Lebanon, Syrian Arab Republic	30 349
Europe	Turkey		Cyprus	15 644

Source: UNCTAD elaboration of data from the World Tourism Organization.

Annex III

International tourism arrivals (million) and receipts ($ billion) for top ten developed countries / top ten developing countries in 2003

International tourism arrivals (millions) and receipts ($ billions) for top ten developed countries / top ten developing countries/territories in 2003										
Top ten developed countries	France	Spain	United States	Italy	United Kingdom	Canada	Austria	Germany	Hungary	Greece
International arrivals	77	52.3	43.5	39.5	24.2	20.1	18.6	18	15.9	14.2
Top ten developing countries/ territories	(China (including Taiwan PC and Hong Kong (China))	Mexico	Turkey	Malaysia	Thailand	South Africa	United Arab Emriates	Egyt	Singapore	Tunisia
International arrivals	57.1	18.7	13.3	10.6	10.1	6.6	5.9	5.7	5.7	5.1
Top ten developed countries	United States	Spain	France	Italy	Germany	United Kingdom	Austria	Greece	Canada	Australia
International receipts	64.5	41.8	37	31.2	23	22.8	14.1	10.7	9.7	8.1
Top ten developing countries/ territories	(China (including Taiwan PC and Hong Kong (China))	Turkey	Mexico	Thailad	Malaysia	Republic of Korea	Egypt	Indonesia	India	Morocco
International receipts	28.0	13.2	9.5	7.8	5.9	5.3	4.6	4.0	3.5	3.2

Source: UNCTAD elaboration of data from the World Tourism Organization.

Annex IV

Search engine optimization on Google and Yahoo!

Google is a fully automated search engine, which employs robots known as "spiders" to crawl the web on a monthly basis and find sites for inclusion in the Google index. Since this process does not involve human editors, it is not necessary to submit one's e-tourism website to Google in order to be included in its index. In fact, the vast majority of sites listed are not manually submitted for inclusion.

Google's engine ranks pages largely on the basis of how many other sites link to them, sending the most popular pages to the top. Therefore, the best way to ensure that Google finds and ranks e-tourism websites is to ensure that it is linked to a large number of other sites (regional tourism portals, NGOs, partners, etc.). For more information, see at: http://www.google.com/webmasters/.

Yahoo! offers several ways for content providers to submit web pages and content directly to the Yahoo! Search Index and the Yahoo! Directory. The Yahoo! Directory is organized by subject. Sites are placed in categories by the Yahoo! Directory team to ensure that the Directory is organized in the best possible way, so that it is easy to use, intuitive and helpful to everyone. Websites need to be submitted and registered manually on Yahoo!, as it is more an index than a real search engine. For more information, see at: http://search.yahoo.com/info/submit.html.

Annex V

Evolution of Travel Distribution

	Early Stages	Core Development	Growth of Traditional intermediaries	Emergence of Online Distribution Channels
Timeframe	1920's - 1950's	1960's - 1970's	1980's - Early 1990's	Mid 1990's - Present
Suppliers	Airlines	Airlines	• Car Rentals • Airlines • Lodging	• Airlines • Cruise • Lodging • Rail • Car Rental • Package • Tours
Industry Needs	• Reduce time and costs necessary to process ticket • Increase productivity of airline reservation agents • Immediately determine what flights/Seats are for sale • Modify inventory • Automating the recording of passenger record (PNR)	• Improve speed in accessing passenger records (PNR) • Improve reservation processing time from three hours to seconds • Reduce reservation error rate • Reduce staffing and training cost	• Increase productivity and capability for handling large amounts of information • Travel agents seek immediate access to airline flight schedules and fares • Ability o serve new business travel marketplace • Meet the demand of global airline alliances • Globalization of CRSs • Online booking	• Provide consumers with direct access to suppliers' inventory • Capture confidence in internet security • Capture and leverage consumer insight • Provide complex travel products • Enable customer self-service • Meet needs of small and large industry suppliers, intermediaries, and consumers

System Capacities	• Electromagnetic Systems – electronic signal between agents terminal and main control room
	• Magnetronic Reservisor – giant aluminium wheel that recorded millions of small electric charges
		Sabre
		• Two IBM 7090 computers used for data storage and processing
			Sabre
			– easySabre (provides online booking to consumers in 1985)
			• Worldspan
			• Amadeus
			• Galileo
			• Corporate travel agencies
				• Online agencies
				  – Travelocity.com
				• Supllier Websites
				  – Delta.com
				• GDS Web-based booking services
				  – Plante Sabre

Annex V *(continued)*

	Early Stages	Core Development	Growth of Traditional intermediaries	Emergence of Online Distribution Channels
	• Data Organizing Translator – machine readable card system			
System Deficiencies	• Still experience time delay in information processing • unable to accurately assign PNR information to a seat	Adequate system reliability due to thousands of agency locations	• GDSs are text only, inflexible and require complex commands • Legacy systems are outdated, expensive to maintain, require significant training time and have limited search capacity	• Customer data is fragmented • Lack standardized communication between suppliers and intermediataries • Unable to provide complex products • Unable to tailor info to individual needs

Source: Accenture/World Travel and Tourism Council (WTTC), May 2002.

References and bibliography

Buhalis D (2003). *E-Tourism: Information technology for strategic tourism management*. Pearson Education, UK.

Caribbean Tourism Organization (2005). *CTO News -February 2005 issue*. See http://www.onecaribbean.org/information/documentview.php?rowid=3060.

Caribbean Tourism Statistical Report 2002–2003, see at http://www.onecaribbean.org.

Center for Excellence in Service at the Robert H. Smith School of Business, University of Maryland, Rockbridge Associates, Inc. (2005). Reported by http://www.emarketer.com.

Credit Suisse First Boston (2005). *A white paper on the emergence of the home-based agency channel*. See http://www.performancemediainc.com/HomeBasedAgentWhitePaper.pdf.

Ebusiness Watch (2004). *The European E-Business Report 2004*. See http://www.ebusiness-watch.org/resources/documents/eBusiness-Report-2004.pdf.

Economist, printed edition (7 October 2004) *Medical tourism to India*.

eMarketer (2005). *Travel Agencies Online*. See http://www.emarketer.com/.

eMarketer (2004). *Online Travel: Marketing and selling*. See http://www.emarketer.com/.

Embassy of the Tunisian Republic in France (2004). *Marchés touristiques: Miser sur de nouvelles catégories de touristes plus aisées et plus dépensières*. See http://www.amb-tunisie.fr/info/article.php3?id_article=438.

Forrester Research (2004*). Web Travel Continues its Skyward Climb*. See http://www.forrester.com.

Forrester Research (2005). *The Search Engines Web Travelers Use*. See http://www.forrester.com/Research/Document/0,7211,36633,00.html.

Forrester Research(2004), Online Leisure Travel Forecast 2004-2009. See http://www.forrester.com.

Forrester Research (2004), *Trends 2005: Travel Web Sites*. See http://www.forrester.com.

Keynote Systems (2004). See http://www.keynote.com/.

Marketing British Tourism (2004). *Leisure market profile: Germany: Getting the best from the market*. See http://www.tourismtrade.org.uk/uktrade/Docs/Original/42_10699.doc.

Mintel International Group Ltd. (2004). *Emerging Destinations International*. See http://www.marketresearch.com/map/prod/1055200.html.

Mintel Reports (2005). *European Leisure Travel Industry   Europe*. See http://reports.mintel.com/sinatra/reports/search_results/show&&type=RCItem&page=0&noaccess_page=0/display/id=144742.

NetStrategic LLC (2004). *Customer Focused Online Travel Distribution for the 21stCentury*. See http://www.netstrategic.com

O'Connor P (1999). Electroic Information Distribution in Tourism and Hospitality. Wallingford, UK, CAB International.

OECD (2003), *Innovation and Growth in Tourism*. See http://www.oecd.org/document/22/0,2340,en_2649_34389_12980694_1_1_1_1,00.html.

Papatheodorou A and Song H *International Tourism Forecasts: A Time Series Analysis of World and Regional Data*.

PhoCusWright (2005), *German Online Travel Market Powers up as European Market Continues to Move Online*. See http://www.phocuswright.com/fyi/fyi_174.php.

Pollock (2001). *Destination manage*ment systems, reported by Travel Daily News (March 2003). See

Trans Africa Forum (2000). *the impact of tourism on the Caribbean*. See http://www.transafricaforum.org/reports/tourism_issuebrief0700.pdf.

UNCTAD (2000). *Building Confidence, Electronic Commerce and Development.*

See http://r0.unctad.org/ecommerce/docs/edr00_en.htm

UNCTAD (2001). *E-Commerce and Development Report.* See http://www.unctad.org/ecommerce.

UNCTAD (2001). *Tourism and Development in the Least Developed Countries.* See http://www.unctad.org/en/docs/ poldcm64.en.pdf

UNCTAD (2004). *E-Commerce and Development Report.* See http://www.unctad.org/ecommerce.

UNDESA (2003). A *New Approach to Sustainable Tourism Development: Moving beyond Environmental Protection.* See http:// www.un.org/esa/esa03dp29.pdf.

World Tourism Organization (1999). *Global Code of Ethics for Tourism.* See   http://www.world-tourism.org/code_ethics/ eng.html.

World Tourism Organization (2002). *Tourism and Poverty Alleviation: Background Information.* See *http://world-tourism.org/ liberaliz- ation/poverty_alleviation.htm.*

World Tourism Organization (2003/2004). *Tourism Highlights.* See http://www.world-tourism.org/facts/highlights/HIGH- LIGHTS%20INGLES%2020041.pdf.

World Tourism Organization (2004). *Compendium of Tourism Statistics.* See http://www.world-tourism.org/cgi-bin/infos- hop.storefront/EN/product/1352-1.

World Tourism Organization (2004/2005). *World Tourism Barometer.* See http://www.world-tourism.org/facts/wtb.html.

World Tourism Organization (2004). *Tourism 2020 Vision.* See http://www.world-tourism.org/facts/2020/2020.htm.

World Travel and Tourism Council (2003). *Blueprint for New Tourism.* See http://www.wttc.org/.

World Travel and Tourism Council (2005). *Travel &Tourism Economic Research.* See http://www.wttc.org/

WTTC IT/eCommerce Task Force (2002). *Customer-Centric Systems for the Travel and Tourism Industry.* See http://www.eyefor- travel.com/papers/Customer_Centric_Transformation_WTTC_White_Paper.doc.

Yesawich, Pepperdine, Brown & Russell (2005), *Leisure travel hits six year high. Outlook positive for leisure travel in the year ahead according to 2005 national leisure travel monitor results.* See http://www.ypbr.com/page_ loader.php?tid=v4&sid=news&pid=pressrelease&cid=25.

Notes

1. Pollock (2001) defines a DMS as "the IT infrastructure used by a DMO for the collection, storage, manipulation and distribution of information in all its forms, and for the transaction of reservations and other commercial activities"

2. See *Information Economy Report 2005*, chapter 1.

3. http://www.ypbr.com/page_loader.php?tid=v4&sid=news&pid=pressrelease&id=25.

4. Source: Center for Excellence in Service at the Robert H. Smith School of Business, University of Maryland, Rockbridge Associates, Inc. (February 2005), reported by http://www.emarketer.com.

5. Source: Forrester Research, August 2004, reported by http://www.emarketer.com/.

6. PhoCusWright, see at http://www.netimperative.com/2005/05/17/Allcheckin_travel/view.

7. Buhalis (2003).

8. A DMO is a public or private organization responsible for the promotion and coordination of tourism.

9. OECD (2003).

10. See http://www.world-tourism.org/facts/highlights/HIGHLIGHTS%20INGLES%2020041.pdf.

11. See World Travel and Tourism Council (2005).

12. According to UNCTAD ("Tourism and development in the least developed countries", UNCTAD/LDC/Misc.64, Geneva, 23 February 2001), the combined tourism export receipts of all LDCs in 1998 accounted for 16.2 per cent of their total non-oil export receipts. Tourism was the leading service export sector in 24 LDCs and the first source of foreign exchange earnings in 7 of them.

13. See annex I.

14. According to WTO, international tourism consists of both inbound tourism (tourism of non-resident visitors within the economic territory of the country of reference) and outbound tourism (tourism of resident visitors outside the economic territory of the country of reference).

15. WTO *World Tourism Barometer*, January 2005.

16. According to WTO, international tourism receipts earned by a destination country from inbound tourism cover all tourism receipts resulting from expenditure by visitors from abroad on, for instance, lodging, food and drinks, fuel, transport in the country, entertainment and shopping, etc.

17. WTO, *Tourism Highlights*, 2003.

18. *Compendium of Tourism Statistics*, WTO, edition 2004.

19. WTO, *Tourism Highlights*, 2003.

20. According to the World Bank, emerging economies in Asia and the Pacific are projected to grow by 6 per cent in 2005.

21. Developing countries which receive over 5 million international tourists in annex II.

22. In the Middle East, 45 per cent of the tourism is intraregional. In Africa, this proportion falls to 40 per cent and in South Asia to 35 per cent.

23. See annex III.

24. WTO, *Tourism 2020 Vision*, http://www.world-tourism.org/facts/2020/2020.htm.

25. According to UNEP, sustainability, for tourism as for other industries, has three interconnected aspects: environmental, socio-cultural and economic. Sustainability implies permanence, and so sustainable tourism includes optimum use of resources, including biological diversity; minimization of ecological, cultural and social impacts; and maximization of benefits to conservation and local communities. It also refers to the management structures that are needed to achieve this. See at http://www.uneptie.org/pc/tourism/sust-tourism/about.htm.

26. Buhalis (2003).

27. UNDESA (2003).

28. When a seat on a plane or a room in a hotel is not sold for a particular day, its revenue is lost for ever.

29. Online Travel: Marketing and selling, eMarketer, November 2004.

30. Yield management is an economic method that allows the comparison between supply and demand through differenti-ated pricing and systematic control of the inventory. Based on real-time demand forecasting by market micro-segment and an optimization model, yield management, which began in the United States in the 1980s, enables suppliers to increase their revenue, and customers to benefit from lower prices for the same quality of service, by calculating the best pricing policy for the sale of a product or service. For more information, see http://www.optims.com/UK/hight_profits.html.

31. See *Information Economy Report 2005*, chapter 1.

32. Forrester Research Inc, Online Leisure Travel Forecast 2004–2009 (March 2004), at http://www.forrester.com.

33. Marketer, Travel Agencies online, March 2005.

34. Forrester Research Inc, The search engines web travelers use (March 2005), at http://www.forrester.com/.

35. See annex IV for details of search engine optimization on Google and Yahoo!

36. A meta-search engine transmits one's search simultaneously to several individual search engines and their databases of web pages. See at http://www.lib.berkeley.edu/TeachingLib/Guides/Internet/MetaSearch.html.

37. See *Information Economy Report 2005*, chapters 5 and 6.

38. Buhalis (2003).

39. http://www.eyefortravel.com/papers/Customer Centric Transformation_WTTC_White_Paper.doc.

40. See annex V.

41. For a discussion on OTA and XML, see the *E Commerce and Development Report 2001*. A list of OTA members is available at http://www.opentravel.org/members.cfm#.

42. SITA is the world's leading provider of integrated information and telecommunications solutions for the air transport industry, and provides services to airlines, airports, travel distribution and computer reservation systems, governmental organizations, aerospace companies and airfreight companies. For more information, see at http://www.sita.aero/default.htm.

43. Keynote Systems (2004).

44. Marketer (2005).

45. See UNCTAD (2000).

46. The International Ecotourism Society defines ecotourism as "responsible travel to natural areas that conserves the environment and improves the well-being of local people". See at http://www.uneptie.org/pc/tourism/sust-tourism/about.htm.

47. First for Comoros, Gambia, Maldives, Samoa, Tuvalu, United Republic of Tanzania and Vanuatu.

48. See http://www.unctad.org/en/docs/poldcm64.en.pdf.

49. See WTO (2004). Calculations based on reported figures from 30 LDCs.

50. Afghanistan, Cape Verde, Central African Republic, Chad, Comoros, Democratic Republic of the Congo, Equatorial Guinea, Eritrea, Guinea-Bissau, Kiribati, Lao People's Democratic Republic, Liberia, Niger, Sao Tome and Principe, Sierra Leone, Somalia and Sudan.

51. Bangladesh, Benin, Burkina Faso, Cambodia, Djibouti, Ethiopia, Gambia, Guinea, Madagascar, Maldives, Mali, Nepal, Rwanda, Samoa, Senegal, Solomon Islands, Timor-Leste, Togo, Tuvalu, Uganda, United Republic of Tanzania, Vanuatu, Yemen and Zambia.

52.   The WTO has defined benchmarking criteria of e-tourism websites from a consumer perspective: accessibility, consistency, content usability, credibility, customization and interactivity, navigation, and technical performance.

53.   For a detailed discussion on FOSS, see the *E-Commerce and Development Report 2004*.

54.   Benin, Burkina Faso, Cambodia, Ethiopia, Gambia, Madagascar, Maldives, Mali, Nepal, Rwanda, Senegal, Solomon Islands, Timor-Leste, Togo, Uganda, Vanuatu, Yemen and Zambia

55.   Benin, Burkina Faso, Gambia, Maldives, Nepal, Rwanda, Samoa, Senegal, Timor-Leste, Togo, Uganda, United Republic of Tanzania, Vanuatu, Yemen and Zambia.

56.   The NTO website of Nepal has attracted visitors from the United States, India, the United Kingdom, Japan, Hong Kong SAR, Germany, France, China, Australia and Canada.

57.   Maldives, Nepal, Mali and Uganda.

58.   Benin, Maldives, Mali, Nepal, Rwanda, Samoa, Senegal, Timor, Togo, Vanuatu and Zambia.

59.   Source: UNCTAD *Handbook of Statistics*, 2004.

60.   After about 10 years, Tunisia occupies the second position after France for wellness tourism (thalassotherapy).

61.   http://www.ins.nat.tn/html/page01133.htm.

62.   The main ones are Neckermann, with 13 per cent of the market share in terms of nights; TUI (10.2 per cent); ITS (6 per cent); and Étapes Nouvelles (5 per cent). See http://www.webmanagercenter.com/telecharge/mr_tourisme_072004.pdf.

63.   http://www.promovacances.com.

64.   See the *Information Economy Report 2005*, chapter 1.

65.   TNS Sofres, 2004. See http://www.tns-sofres.com.

66.   Marketing British Tourism (2004).

67.   See http://www.abtamembers.org/research/abtastatstrends2004.pdf.

68.   See chapter 1.

69.   The structures and consultative groups created are the following: the National Commission on Electronic Commerce (1997) in charge of implementing the e-commerce strategy and the infrastructure in Tunisia; the National Council of Tourism (1997); the National Observatory of Tourism (1995); and the management board of the competitiveness funds.

70.   See http://www.amb-tunisie.fr/info/article.php3?id_article=438.

71.   The growth of Chinese outbound tourism (16 million in 2004 according to the China National Tourism Administration) encourages not only Tunisia but also an increasing number of destinations in Europe, Latin America and Africa to sign cooperation agreements to develop joint-venture arrangements with travel agencies, facilitating the procedures for Chinese travellers.

72.   Source: UNCTAD *Handbook of Statistics*, 2004.

73.   According to WTO, domestic tourism is the tourism of resident visitors within the economic territory of the country of reference.

74.   http://www2.tat.or.th/stat/download/1204/res-1-12.xls.

75.   http://www2.tat.or.th/stat/web/static_index.php.

76.   The World Our Guest"(1992) was a collaboration between the public and the private sector, inviting foreign tour operators and media to visit Thailand.

77.   Amazing Thailand" (1998–1999) was launched after the Asian economic crisis and focused on value-added tourism products and services: Amazing Shopping Paradise, Amazing Taste of Thailand, Amazing Cultural Heritage, Amazing Arts and Lifestyle , Amazing World Heritage, Amazing Natural Heritage, Amazing Gateways, Amazing Sport & Entertainment and Amazing Agricultural Heritage.

78.   www.tourismthailand.org is available in the following languages: Thai, English, Korean, German, Japanese, French, Italian, Portuguese, Spanish, Singaporian, Greek, Romanian and Chinese.

79.   The ASEAN member countries are Brunei Darussalam, Cambodia, Indonesia, the Lao People's Democratic Republic, Malaysia, Myanmar, the Philippines, Singapore, Thailand and VietNam.

80.   See http://www.aseansec.org/17091.htm.

81.   See http://www.aseansec.org/tour_stat/Major%20Market%20Share%20by%20Region-2003.htm.

82.   The ASEAN Tourism Association is a non-profit association comprising both public and private tourism organizations from ASEAN such as NTOs, hotel associations, travel agents' associations and national airlines. Its mission is to undertake marketing and relevant programmes to promote the growth of tourism, to form public and private partnerships to ensure a long-term perspective for tourism growth, and to develop new services and operational benchmarks for the tourism industry through certification programmes.

83.   http://www.barnesandnoble.com is one of the largest online book distributors in the United States.

84.   The ASEAN Air and Hotel Pass covers seven countries: Brunei, Indonesia, Malaysia, the Philippines, Singapore, Thailand and VietNam. See www.aseanta.org.

85.   Caribbean Tourism Statistical Report 2002–2003; see at http://www.onecaribbean.org; http://www.transafricaforum.org/reports/tourism_issuebrief0700.pdf.

86.   Caribbean Tourism Organization (2005).

87.   See http://www.doitcaribbean.nl/ and http://www.caribbean.co.uk/homepage/index.html.en-GB.

88.   Escape2Travel, ltd (ET2) is a wholly owned subsidiary of the Morris Kevan International group, which has been marketing and selling the Caribbean for the past 35 years.

89.   The banner advertising options are available at www.itrgo.com/cto.

90.   See annex IV.

Chapter 5

INFORMATION TECHNOLOGY AND SECURITY: RISK MANAGEMENT AND POLICY IMPLICATIONS

A. Introduction

Information security is the sum of the processes and technologies used to protect information assets from unauthorized acquisition, disclosure, manipulation, modification, or damage and loss.[1] Information security underlines the importance of trust and trust-building in everyday economic and civic life. Economic activities, such as trade or financial transactions, may be critically dependent on information security, as globalization encourages and directs remote or mutually unfamiliar firms and individuals to interact. As e-business becomes part of the everyday experience of large numbers of firms, who will on average tend to be more risk-averse than early adopters of technology, security in all its dimensions becomes crucially important (UNCTAD, 2003).[2]

The innovative use of information and communication technologies (ICTs) is often seen as a means for making improvements in productivity and efficiency, but in practice it is not all "strengths and opportunities". The "challenges and threats" part of the equation is mission-critical for realizing these improvements, and they can largely be seen as involving a process of active risk management of perils and hazards encountered in the application of ICTs.

Understanding information security and using a risk management approach is equally important for Governments and firms from developed and developing countries. However, developing countries may need to promote information security awareness and risk management more actively because of their relatively larger proportion of recent ICT adopters, be they firms, public bodies or individuals. Fast progress from minor ICT usage to full connectivity and access can complicate information security.

Information security also raises questions as to what combination of technical, management, regulatory and legal solutions works best. Here too, knowledge and awareness of the basic technology landscape can

be an advantage, while a strategic approach built around a core of risk management notions can be a decisive asset. Proactive and strategic information security has become indispensable from a regulatory perspective as well. The international community has arrived at a common approach to information security practice and has recognized the threat of cyber-crime to information economy development.[3] International forums and national regulatory bodies are formulating and advising on minimum information security standards for international commercial partners. As a result, firms from developing countries can be affected and may risk marginalization if they cannot meet the information security requirements of their counterparts in the developed world. This can be of particular importance for countries seeking to develop business process outsourcing activities, in particular in the areas of financial services, ICT services and software export.

In order to elucidate the relevant issues, this chapter will start with an overview of basic concepts and notions that explain why information security matters. It will then describe the information security business sector. It will briefly describe the chronological development of cryptographic and security technologies. This is more than academic. Newness and hype often go hand-in-hand, and an appreciation of the origins and continuity of security technology developments can be invaluable when confronted with the latest paradigm-shifting cure-all security solution. Following this, the discussion will focus on security issues from a risk management perspective. It will note the diversity of information security threats, as well as the needs of Governments as users and also as enablers of e-business and e-governance. Particular technologies will also be discussed within a risk management framework, and this will serve to highlight the need for a management-centric, as opposed to technology-centric, approach to information security. This will, in turn, permit a discussion of notions related to human resource capacity and development, as well as to the changing regulatory environments resulting from increased information security needs.

The chapter will go on to present an overview of international policy discussions on information security. It will, however, avoid a discussion of legal issues of information security, often considered under the collective term of cybercrime, as these are covered in chapter 6 of this report. The chapter will close with a discussion of policy recommendations for Governments and some reflections as to future developments and relevance for intergovernmental processes and the international community.

B. Concepts and context

1. Definition and objectives

Information security consists of processes and controls that aim to protect information and data, and their underlying infrastructures. The mission of information security is to establish trust in technologies that make possible various positive societal and commercial activities, including e-commerce, e-business and e-government. This mission is achieved by simultaneously working towards a number of objectives, including maintaining the confidentiality of ICT users, securing data integrity, securing the availability of data and information, and assuring authentication and providing non-repudiation (Menezes, van Oorschot and Vanstone, 1997). These objectives branch out into a more diverse range of goals and corresponding activities that are described in table 5.1.

The implementation of information security can focus on particular technologies that address critical issues from a problem-response or reactive perspective. As many information security threats fall into the category of cybercrime, their analysis from a legal perspective has much to offer as well, and indeed chapter 6 of this report provides just that. This chapter will however propose that information security has much to gain from using a risk management framework for information security, as it involves planning, foresight and focus on human resources, policy and process issues, as well as on actual security technologies.

Table 5.1

Information security goals and activities

Goals	Activity
Privacy and confidentiality	Information and data are rendered secret to all entities without an authorization.
Data integrity	Information and data cannot be altered by entities without an authorization.
Entity authentication	The identity of an entity is verified.
Message authentication	The source or origin of the information or data is verified.
Signature	An entity is bound to a particular message or data.
Authorization	An entity is given an official sanction to perform predefined activities using specified resources and for specified information and data.
Validation	An entity is given a time scope for performing on its authorization.
Access control	Access and privileges to data and information vary according to preset policies.
Certification	A trusted third party endorses information.
Time stamping	The time of creation, expiry or duration of validity of specified information or data is established.
Witnessing	A third party verifies the creation or existence of specified data.
Receipt	An acknowledgment is produced establishing that certain data or information have been received.
Confirmation	An acknowledgment is produced establishing that certain services have been provided.
Ownership	The legal right of an entity to use specified resources, data and information is established.
Anonymity	The identity of an entity using specified resources, data or information is concealed.
Non-repudiation	The denial of established and agreed commitments or activities is prevented.
Revocation	A specific certification or authorization is retracted

Source: based on Menezes, van Oorschot and Vanstone (1997).

2. Information security and communication

In order to fully appreciate the importance of information security, it can be useful to revisit our understanding of how our communications environment changes as we increase our use of technology.

The most basic form of human communication – spoken language among physically present persons – is endowed with a default level of security that we often take for granted. We usually know if our counterpart is a perfect stranger, a business partner or an old friend, and we habitually judge what level of confidence and trust to expect from the exchange. We will easily recognize a previous acquaintance by their appearance, behaviour and speech, and will seek and receive some indication that our counterpart has recognized us as well. Mutual authentication provides a platform of trust from which we can carry on with exchanges and discussions of substance.[4] Our physiological vocal limitations and conversational habits will limit the physical range in which a discussion can be heard and understood, and therefore guards its privacy to some degree. We would also consciously choose the level of privacy of our conversation.[5] Finally, unless it is recorded, the substance of the discussion evaporates and, at best, is committed to imperfect memory. A simple move to using written messages introduces new issues. It requires trust in the paper media to keep the message coherent, as well as confidence that the carrier transporting the message will carry out its function. The recipient needs to trust the authenticity of the message through recognizable handwriting, signatures, or a variety of stamps, envelopes and seals. Still, there is little to guarantee that a message will not be intercepted and perhaps altered, and the content copied and used beyond the scope of the author's knowledge, control or intent.

A fast-forward to modern digital communication technologies involves substantial adjustments in our behaviour, because these technologies make compromising the privacy and security of communication ever easier. Whether using the telephone or e-mail or simply browsing an interactive website, as opposed to receiving a letter or meeting in person, our confidence in who the other conversant is and the information they request or give, as well as the privacy of our exchange, may drop dramatically.

The use of digital communication technologies, while resolving the limitations of time and space, pushes to the extreme four fundamental problems. The first is that our capacity to authenticate – to be certain of the identity of our counterpart – can be severely reduced. The second is that using a communications infrastructure may compromise the privacy of the content of our exchange. The third is that it can be difficult, or nearly impossible, to establish whether the communicated files have been altered or tampered with during transmission. Finally, using digital technologies often leaves traces and trails pointing to the nature and substance of our exchanges, sometimes even lodging their full content on computer systems that are increasingly networked and accessed by many entities.

3. Why does it matter?

From a privacy and human rights perspective, information security issues matter and are being increasingly addressed through policy as well as through technology. Indeed, Article 12 of the Universal Declaration of Human Rights states: "No one shall be subjected to arbitrary interference with his privacy, family, home or correspondence, nor to attacks upon his honour and reputation. Everyone has the right to the protection of the law against such interference or attacks."[6] More recently, United Nations General Assembly resolutions 55/63 and 56/121 specifically addressed the issues of endangering information security through cybercrime and framed the problem through the perspective of the UN Millennium Declaration and the role of information technologies in economic and social development, education and democratic governance.[7]

From a business perspective, information security issues are just as acute. Entrepreneurs or employees frequently enter into remote communications that require an appropriate level of trust that corresponds to the value of the underlying business and any associated risks and liabilities. Firms are public entities, and their public personalities are easily knowable. Firms also have exploitable assets whose value is often public knowledge. Thus, targeting their information security can be a fundamentally premeditated exercise – more so than in the case of individuals.

Governments have concerns similar to those of firms but with an overarching mandate and a fundamental responsibility towards citizens and organizations, since they administer data related to civil, fiscal, social security and other issues. Governments are often deeply involved in ICT infrastructures, at the very least from a policy and regulatory perspective, and more often in developing countries as owners and administrators of communications and network infrastructures. While individuals and firms may be free to strike a balance between acceptable risk and investment in security technology and risk management, Governments may have absolute public policy and accountability considerations, in particular when they engage in a positive ICT development strategy and aim to support the development of e-commerce activities. Thus, understanding the security issues and the role of technology in creating trustworthy digital environments, conducive to e-business activity and benefiting the efficiency and quality of governance, matters.

A common problem for individuals, firms and public bodies occurs when the realization sets in that "something needs to be done". At this point advice may be sought on possible solutions. Individuals will struggle with off-the-shelf firewall and anti-virus software and decide to use encryption for their e-mail. They may even adventure to change their computer desktop environment and use free and open-source software (FOSS) in the hope that it will be more secure because its source code has been inspected and corrected by thousands of users and programmers. However, neither FOSS nor proprietary software provides any guarantees, much like a car manufacturer that cannot guarantee against car accidents. Nevertheless, there is an active debate about security and the openness of software and part E.2 of the chapter attempts to addresses more specifically the issue of risk avoidance through the use of FOSS.

Firms and public bodies will be approached by vendors, each touting its own cryptographic tools and security solutions, but what will ensure that the right choices are made? Furthermore, who can predict whether the technologies will be used correctly or perhaps in an unpredictable, harmful or even negligent way and thus compromise both security and security investments? Headlines announcing "Government ICT security shows worrying lapses" or "Survey finds 81% of computer users have a common password and almost 30% note their passwords down…"[8] may worry some but hardly surprise anyone. Good decisions will be assisted by a general appreciation of security technologies as they advance together with the development of the information society. Even better choices will be exercised by embracing a risk management framework, rather than simply dealing with threats on an ad hoc basis, often when some ICT catastrophe is looming.

4. Economic incentive

Every person, firm or institution will weigh their incentives for investing effort and resources in information security. Whether intuitively, on the back of an envelope, or using formal microeconomic or risk management analysis or methods, technology users will evaluate their assets, assess their environment and explore their expectations. The level of information security achieved will be a function of the incentives faced, rather than the available scope of technologies (Anderson 2001).

Incentive failure can lead to poor security. Varian (2000) pointed out that denial-of-service attacks on commercial websites could be stopped by users operating the thousands of zombie computers used in the attacks or by their ISPs.[9] However, incentives are lacking, as the asset under attack does not belong to the computer users and, in a tragedy of the commons scenario, there is no guarantee that any of the other zombie computers would be sanitized anyway.[10] Security can never be airtight and will cost real money and it takes just one discovery of a serious flaw by any one of half a billion Internet users to cause a major security breakdown and losses. When we consider this in the context of the digital divide, we see that firms and institutions from developed countries, as well as developing countries with strategic interest in technology development, will have incentives for using and developing security technologies. For developing countries that have only recently made progress in ICT adoption, disincentives may need to be counteracted with a positive policy approach whereby e-strategy frameworks need to be supported by domestic political commitment and through international policy and technical cooperation.

Moving to the supply side, the amount of security built into technology products may be suboptimal because of network externalities. First-mover advantages in markets that have high network externalities provide incentives for early if buggy releases. Compounding the problem is the conventional wisdom that security strength and usability are almost in contradiction with each other when it comes to desktop platforms and programmes that need to focus on being user-friendly. In other cases, where security is specifically required as a primary product feature, producers may have an incentive to go with proprietary solutions, rather than with tested public standards, in order to differentiate their product and lock-in consumers. Finally, software producers typically decline any liability beyond the amount paid for the software, or its repair or replacement.[11]

Disincentives to reveal critical information abound and are yet another cause of suboptimal investment in information security (Cashell et al, 2004). Financial markets may react very negatively to news of security breaches, in particular those affecting financial services companies. A loss of reputation and consumer confidence can be detrimental. Firms that have suffered security breaches may fear litigation and will not have much motivation to release any details of the event. Security breaches may indicate that a firm is in violation of information security regulations or laws. A publicized breach of security may invite further attacks, as it could signal that defenses are weak in the firm and perhaps in the sector or region. Finally, technical personnel can be reluctant to report security failures if it may lead to getting fired.

A risk management approach to information security involves the economic assessment of the information assets at risk before looking at possible solutions. Thus, while it will not provide any additional incentives, it should clearly outline and define existing incentives and juxtapose them against the investment needed and the value of the proposed improvement of security. Once this has been done, policy processes at the level of a firm, an industry association or a Government, at the national or international level, may consider possible action to improve incentives for better information security.

C.   The information security industry

The global information security market is estimated at around $40 billion, half of which is represented by the United States.[12] The corresponding estimates of economic damage caused by security breaches in 2003 vary from $12.5 billion for viruses only to over $200 billion for all forms of digital attack. While damage from viruses is likely to decrease because of better and broader deployment of anti-virus software, total digital damage is likely to rise if only because of the continuously expanding use of Internet-based technologies.[13]

While demand for information security may be sticky as spending on security technology increases, a decrease in such spending can be related to an overall decrease in information technology budgets. In this sense, the economic slump of 2001-2002 cooled all expectations of strong growth for the beginning of the decade. Sales of security technology accelerated after 2003 and are expected to account for 5 to 6 per cent of ICT budgets, which should reach $1 trillion before the end of the decade.[14] However, prudent pessimism may be the right approach, taking into consideration the various disincentives for investing in information security explained above.

The information security market is heterogeneous, with various firms developing particular mixes of security activities that broadly fall into four categories. The first is identity management. The second is securing communications and transactions either by using Internet-based virtual private networks[15] (VPNs) or public key infrastructures (PKI). A third sector is security information management – tools and processes that help organizations manage an often diverse and heterogeneous amalgamation of security technologies. Finally, application-specific integrated circuits are increasingly being designed and deployed to perform security specific tasks, as in VPNs or firewalls, as hardware appliances, supplanting discrete security applications.

The security technology sector is not as concentrated as that of computer software or hardware. Nearly all software and many hardware companies provide services around their own or licensed security products, including industry giants such as IBM and Microsoft. Nevertheless, several companies have established themselves as market leaders in information security and are often cited as bellwethers for the sector. Table 5.2 gives an overview of several basic parameters for a number of these companies while omitting firms that generate important revenues outside the information security services niche.[16] The diversity in size is significant, with the largest companies providing comprehensive security solutions, while smaller ones occupy the innovative niches of biometrics or encryption technologies. From a financial perspective, since the dot.com bubble burst in March 2000, investors have generally not resumed the positive expectations for the sector that were common in the late 1990s, in spite of frequently alarming news coverage about the vulnerability of ICT networks, infrastructures and appliances brought on by a diversity of viruses, malicious codes and direct hacking activities.

The larger firms are well-known because they are industry leaders and produce popular anti-virus software and firewall systems. RSA Security is interesting

Table 5.2

Selected vendors of information security technology

Company	Market capitalization on 2 September 2005 (billions of dollars)	Revenue* (millions of dollars)	Number of employees (2003)
Computer Associates	15.74	3,600	15,300
Symantec	25.35	2,730	6,500
Verisgn	5.73	1,530	3,206
McAffee	4.99	94	2,950
Check Point Software	5.48	55	1,344
RSA Security	0.90	31	1,144
Entrust	0.35	98	491
Viisage	0.21	76	211
Identix	0.43	74	480
Watchdata Technologies	n/a	39	258

* Trailing twelve months.
Source: Yahoo Finance, Hoovers.com.

from a historical perspective. It was founded by Ron Rivest, Adi Shamir and Len Adleman, who pioneered the development of an algorithm for asymmetric encryption and signing and commercialized the first technology enabling PKI. A discussion on the RSA algorithm is presented in part D of this chapter. Verisign, a 1995 spin-off of RSA Security, is a diversified company that offers a range of ICT products and PKI services, and operates a large array of network infrastructure, including two of the Internet's 13 root servers and the generic top-level domains for .com and .net. Entrust is a Canadian company that develops PKI technologies and uses them for secure messaging, identity management, and authentication solutions. Viisage and Identix develop biometric authentication technologies. While most of the technology developments and use originates in developed countries, information security services are increasingly present in developing countries. For example, Watchdata Technologies, a Chinese company, has developed a proprietary smart card operating system and is a provider of electronic transaction applications, data security, and encryption and PKI technology. The service and interdisciplinary nature of information security provides opportunities for companies like WIPRO from Mumbai or Odyssey from Chennai, Comtrust from Abu Dhabi or Infocus Consulting Group from Buenos Aires, to establish and develop local business operations and seek growth in their regions and internation-

ally. Box 5.1 provides an overview of information security issues in several developing countries.

Aside from firms, government and academic institutions are often heavily involved in information security and infrastructure development, since the issues of standards, interoperability and regulation validating the use of electronic signatures fall squarely within their research interests or political mandates. Examples of such activity are the EuroPKI project, the Dartmouth College PKI Lab or the Internet2 PKI Labs.[17] Outside the traditional business or mainstream public sector, information security technology is also being developed in free and open-source frameworks such as the Open Source Security Information Management project, the OpenCA Lab, CAcert or the Smartsign Project.[18] National computer emergency response teams (CERTs) have been established in many developed and developing countries, and their cooperation has been encouraged through various international agreements and treaties.

The sector will most likely be subject to a vast array of acquisitions aimed at diversifying existing business portfolios, as well as buying new or breakthrough technologies from more innovative and typically smaller companies.[19] While the current crop of firewall, anti-virus or PKI products will certainly maintain their brand profile, in the near term information

---

Box 5.1

Information security in developing countries: Mainstreaming Latin America? [i]

The need for information security in developing countries is growing constantly. Security has become a big issue today, not only because of school children trying to understand and embrace the cyber world but also because Latin America is suffering from organized crime which has discovered the virtual world as its new medium. Kidnap, ransom and fraud are some of the real world crimes that are assisted by information extractions from our ICT infrastructure with increasing frequency. This extraction of vital information from personal archives is often achieved without the concerned knowing about it. The need for information security is rising, and it will continue growing because of the change in social structures and commercial relations that technology has brought to everyday life.

In managing the challenges of information security, Latin American firms and Governments are investing in security technologies but are unfortunately under-investing in personal training for their employees. Having started with firewalls, many have moved to managed security services, and a fast-growing market is emerging for virtual private networks, intrusion detection, penetration testing and cryptography. In addition, the maturing of many open-source platforms and applications has led many companies to implement security by using software such as GNU/Linux, which can provide a solid, robust, fail-safe platform at very small cost.

If we look at particular countries, we see that there is a variety of experience. In Mexico, awareness building and security training in general is insufficient, and while companies are aware of the possible threats, they are not investing money for their security. Only government and financial institutions are willing to invest in information security. Nevertheless, demand for security consulting and education and training services is expected to rise during the next six to twelve months.

In Argentina, opportunities for ICT business are stabilizing, in part because North American and European companies are migrating their ICT product development there. Argentina today is increasingly playing host to international security firms such as Core Technologies, which has established a development centre in Buenos Aires that works on software applications for comprehensive penetration testing to accurately identify specific information security risks. This is, in turn, assisting the development of local ICT and security skills and transforming Argentina from a consumer market into an ICT producer market.

Brazil is perhaps the country with the highest potential for firms providing security training, security hardware, penetration testing, etc. In the past, the small size of the ICT security market was perhaps due to language barriers or commercial issues. Medium-size and large enterprises, as well as many government institutions, are now concerned about information security and have increasing economic resources to invest in it as their security awareness matures and financial strength improves. A good indicator is the use of the Internet for filing income tax declarations and Brazil has managed an impressively high level of 16.5 million fillings, representing 95 per cent of the total. This was achieved using Giss online technology[ii] developed by Eicon Auditoria e Consultoria LTDA, a 100 per cent Brazilian technology firm specializing in networked intelligence business applications.

---

[i] The overview was provided by Mr. Eduardo Moreno Lopez, Chief Executive Officer, Infocus Consulting Group, an information security consulting firm active in the Latin America region; http://www.infocuscg.com/.

[ii] See http://www.gissonline.com.br.

---

security is likely to be increasingly integrated in contracts for ICT network or infrastructure products and services. However, as security threats and challenges evolve with commercial and public use of IT, new threats and problems may require appropriately innovative solutions, and this could motivate the development of novel technologies and the entry of new competitors. From a developing country perspective, it is important to appreciate the dual growth opportunities resulting from an increase in security needs as local governments and businesses increasingly adopt the Internet as a communications and commercial medium, as well as the potential for innovation in the area of new security applications and technologies.

Developing a strategic and policy approach to information security requires, among other things, a basic understanding of what is on offer from the informa-

tion security industry. Appreciating the current palette of solutions can be facilitated by understanding how they evolved within their own historical context, rather than by categorizing them according to technology or functionality type and diving into technical detail.

D.   Development of security technologies

1.   Early development

Security technology develops and progresses hand-in-hand with information and communication technology. As the written word was, in a sense, the first communication technology, cryptography became its security partner. For centuries it relied on simple cyphers that used monoalphabetic transposition or substitution of letters to convert the original text into an encrypted cyphertext.[20] Monoalphabetic cyphertexts, by their nature, gave away data that could be statistically analysed and were thus easily unlocked without the cypher. But the security was good enough as long as a point-to-point transport (e.g. a private courier) was used instead of a communications infrastructure,[21] such as a postal service.

The first real change and challenge for modern information security came about with wireless communications, as the airwaves presented the first truly global and public communications infrastructure.[22] Wireless technology immediately drew the attention of military establishments, as instant communication meant remote command and feedback. Unfortunately, ease of communication also meant ease of interception (Singh, 2000), as anyone could eavesdrop on radio transmissions without any sign of an intrusion. The "public" nature of the airwaves rendered existing encryption technologies inadequate. What resulted was the development of mechanical computer or encryption "rotor" machines that produced polyalphabetic cyphertext based on keys. "Polyalphabetic" meant several substitution tables were used in the same message. A secret key indicated what number, sequence and combination of substitution tables were to be used. While polyalphabetic encryption was theoretically proposed as early as the fifteenth century, its mechanical "computerization" using rotor machines in the early twentieth century made it usable for everyday communications by operators uninitiated in the underlying mathematical complexities.[23] In practice, any two users that had the same encryption machine would merely have to synchronize the use of a secret key that, when punched in, would reset both machines to identical states that would then provide automatic encryption and decryption.

The most famous of all rotor machines was Enigma. It was developed by Scherbius and was awarded a patent in 1918. Mass production had to wait until after Churchill's *The World Crisis* was published in 1923, explaining the achievements of British cryptography experts and the resulting and detrimental high level of intrusion in German communications during the First World War. This realization prompted large orders of Enigma machines by the German military. Another historically important machine was the Lorenz SZ40/42. Somewhat more complex and less portable than Enigma, it produced text output on a teleprinter. The effort to crack the Enigma and Lorenz codes during the Second World War by allied cryptographers at Bletchley Park[24] using electromechanical "bombes" and the Colossus computer is important for security experts, as it draws attention to several fundamental issues that have not lost their validity more than 60 years later and are presented in box 5.2.[25]

2.   Recent history

As the Colossus computer was top secret and a German prototype called Z3 was destroyed during the Second World War, the ENIAC – designed and constructed at the University of Pennsylvania between 1943 and 1946 – was deemed, for many years, the first fully electronic computer. The invention of the transistor and the resulting improvements in speed and reliability, the move towards binary logic and the development of programming languages in the late 1940s and 1950s accelerated the development of information technologies to the point where, by the late 1960s, many government and commercial entities began to rely on ICTs for data processing tasks and communications.

The development of the Internet and the universality of its protocols (e.g. TCP/IP, http, ftp) enabled the networking of disparate computer resources and further boosted intensity of use and innovation in computer technology. The problem with Internet-based communications is that they use infrastructures and public protocols that are, much like radio waves, easy to access but also open to interception. Furthermore, the Internet was designed to be failsafe and reliable while security was not given a high priority as, in its early stages, all the network nodes were trusted entities. Therefore, security needed to be purposefully designed and deployed in order to maintain the safety of data and information handled, as well as the integrity of the associated computers and networks. The question of the standardization of security technology arose in the early 1970s, when establishing a standard that would allow different institutions to communicate with each other became an important concern, as it could help avoid the complexity of establishing numerous bilateral protocols. Thus, in 1973 the United States National Bureau of Standards formally requested proposals for the establishment of a data encryption standard (DES) algorithm.[26] The algorithm that was eventually accepted in 1976 was proposed by IBM and was based on the work of Fiestel and his development of the so-called "Lucifer" cipher. The strength of the DES was eventually

---

Box 5.2

Lessons learned from the past – Still valid half a century later?

An obvious first lesson is that Enigma's security came from the strength of its keys, not the secrecy of its electro-mechanical design or encrypting process – these were known quantities.[i] This axiom, often referred to as Auguste Kerckhoffs[ii] second law, remains valid, and many present-day experts advise against placing excessive confidence in proprietary security systems that have not undergone public scrutiny, while recommending public-domain or free and open-source technologies (Diffie, 2003; Perens, 1998; Schneier, 2000). A misguided trust in secret systems and protocols is often referred to as "security through obscurity".

A second lesson is that underestimating the technological capacity of your opponent is a source of failure. Cracking the Enigma and Lorenz codes was greatly assisted by brute force computing. Turing, a pivotal expert at Bletchley Park and considered by many to be the father of modern computing, designed a method of electronically interconnecting 12 Enigma machines into a device called a "*bombe*". By the end of 1942 there were 49 *bombes* in operation that were capable of cracking the current key within an hour (Singh, 2000; Khan, 1996). In order to crack the Lorenz cypher, Newman and Flowers set out to design and construct the world's first electronic computer. The Colossus could perform 5,000 calculations per second, thus helping to break the Lorenz code in about two hours (Good, Michie and Timms, 1945/2000).[iii]

A third lesson is that people are the weakest point of a security system. Breaking security often relies on human error and physical espionage; technology is needed but is insufficient. Cracking the Enigma cyphers often relied on "cribs" – an obvious match of non-encrypted text to encrypted text – that could be found at the start or end of a communication in the from of a topic or greeting or from repeated transmissions of slightly altered messages using the same key and cypher. Physically stealing codebooks that contained key and transmission instructions and data was also a significant contributor to the success of Bletchley Park operations.

A fourth lesson is that security systems that do not actively monitor for suspicious traffic or interference, will fail. Hackers will avoid leaving trails or indications of intrusion. Intelligence from Enigma cracks was not always acted upon, and redundant scouting missions would be ordered to cover up the fact of a successful decryption.

---

[i] The user instructions for an early model of Enigma machine were revealed to the French authorities in 1931 by a disgruntled German government employee (Singh, 2000).

[ii] Auguste Kerckhoffs was a 19th century Flemish linguist and cryptographer. Kerckhoffs' law is widely embraced by cryptographers as contrary to "security through obscurity".

[iii] The estimate is based on a quote from Anthony Sale, Director of the Colossus Rebuild Project, and as posted on the National Valve Museum website. See http://www.r-type.org/static/valvecpu.htm and the BBC news story on http://news.bbc.co.uk/1/hi/technology/3754887.stm .

---

improved through an increase in its key size from 56 to 168 bits in 1999, and the resulting standard is commonly known as Triple DES.[27] Today, that standard has been largely superceded by the Swiss-developed International Data Encryption Algorithm (IDEA)[28] and the Advanced Encryption Standard (AES) that was adopted in November 2001 by the United States National Institute of Standards after a five-year stand ardization process.[29] The main weakness of these systems is that they are symmetric: the same cryptographic key is used to encrypt and decrypt the communication, and this key has somehow to be shared between the two parties, thus providing a point of attack. Information security is decreasing with the increase in the use of and reliance on the Internet and telephony networks, and thus using these for a key exchange *and* the ensuing communication is a fundamentally flawed and unwise practice.[30]

To resolve this problem, in 1976 Diffie and Hellman proposed a key exchange system in their seminal study *New Directions in Cryptography,* for which, together with Merkle, they received a patent in 1980.[31] The ideas presented enabled the evolution of

a plethora of asymmetric key technologies and were foundational for the development of commercial and secure Internet use. The task was simple: how can two people establish and share a secret without telling it to each other. The partners in communication, often called Alice and Bob in cryptographic research, would each have a private and public key. The exchange of their public keys could be conducted over a public, non-encrypted, communications network. Once the public keys are exchanged, Alice and Bob would, each on their own, combine the other's public key with their own private key using a one-way mathematical function – a function that is difficult to reverse – to create the final key to be used to encrypt and decrypt their messages. The process is analogous to agreeing to a secret color of paint. Box 5.3 illustrates this example in more detail with an analogy proposed by Singh (2000). Details of the underlying modular mathematics are provided in the annex to this chapter.

Unfortunately, the so-called Diffie-Hellman key exchange was not practical for remote communications. Both Alice and Bob would need to enter into non-encrypted contact, share their public keys and perform calculations in order to establish the common secret key, upon which they could start an encrypted and secure exchange. This system is also bilateral, as each pair of partners would need to establish a separate set of private and public key pairs, thus creating key management problems. The proposed solution to this problem was for Alice to have only two separate and distinct keys: a public key to encrypt and a private key to decrypt the message. The keys would be related, but it would be impossible, or more precisely unfeasible, to derive the private – and secret – key from the public one. If Bob wished to send a secret message to Alice, he would retrieve Alice's pub-

lic encryption key from a public key repository and use it to encrypt. When Alice receives Bob's message she will use her private key to decrypt it. This process also solves the authentication problem: how can Alice know that a message is really from Bob? In this case Bob would do the opposite. He would establish a public-private key pair for authentication. His public key could be used by anyone to decrypt Bob's messages, while Bob would use his private – and secret – key to encrypt his message. Alice would retrieve Bob's public decryption key that, by definition, only works on Bob's messages, and a successful decryption would therefore confirm that the message could only be from Bob.

Box 5.3

A colourful public key exchange system analogy of Diffie-Hellman

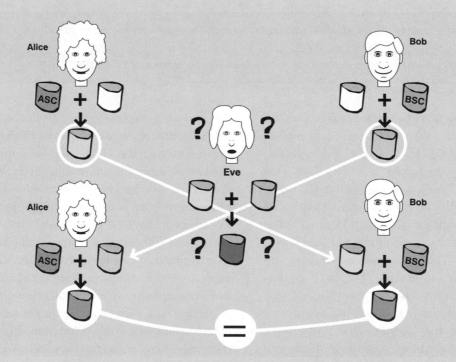

Both Alice and Bob start off with a litre of identical paint to which they each add another litre of paint of a secret color. They then swap the two- litre mix and to each add another liter of their own secret colour. They should now both have the same colour. An eavesdropper, often called Eve, would find it very difficult to discover the new secret color even if she intercepted both exchanges: it is plainly difficult to unmix paint, at least with the same technology used for mixing it. Even if Eve intercepts the pots, she cannot learn their key. She can get hold of what Alice sends (Y + ASC) and what Bob sends (Y + BSC), but she has no way of removing the yellow from either pot, and no way of combining the two to get the secret colour. If she mixes them, she will end up with 2Y +CA+CB, which is altogether too yellow. There is also no way of knowing which precise shade of yellow, blue or green was used to mix up the public colors; indeed an infinite variation of different greens and yellows can be used to produce Alice's public lime green or Bob's aquamarine (Singh, 2000).

The mathematics allowing the derivation of such a public-private key pair were developed by Rivest, Shamir and Adleman (RSA) while working at the Massachusetts Institute of Technology Laboratory for Computer Science and were published in 1977.[32] The RSA system relies on a *public key* that is arrived at by multiplying two prime numbers – a number that can be divided only by 1 and by itself.[33] The *private key* is derived using the original pair of prime numbers. If the prime numbers are sufficiently large, say 100 digits each, and thus produce an enormous public key, it becomes unfeasible to discover them. In 1977, a challenge appeared in *Scientific American* magazine asking its readers to discover the two prime numbers that when multiplied give a number 129 digits long. At the time of the challenge it was thought that the prime pair would never be found. The pair was eventually calculated in 1994, thus enabling the key to hold up for 17 years (Atkins, Graff, Lenstra and Leyland; 1995).[34] RSA Laboratories have continued posting challenges and prizes for factoring ever-larger keys. Currently, the largest cracked key is 174 digits or, in binary form – 574 bits long, and its pair of primes was discovered by Franke and Kleinjung in 2003.[35] It is widely accepted that minimum encryption security needs a public key at least 309 digits or 1,024 bits long.

Asymmetric key systems coupled with ever-increasing key size currently provide reliable security.[36] However, in practice they are often used to encrypt and decrypt a more efficient and smaller symmetric key, such as the aforementioned IDEA or AES, instead of the actual message.[37] This was the approach used by Zimmermann when he set out to design Pretty Good Privacy (PGP) – a widely used e-mail encryption and authentication (i.e. signature) tool. Before PGP, cryptography-based information security was the domain of large corporations and government. PGP allowed individuals using personal computer hardware to take advantage of security technologies. PGP ran into several problems early on. One issue is that PGP provides full privacy to all citizens, including those engaged in legally questionable activities. Thus, if government security authorities wish to monitor communications, they would need to find some way of obtaining the private key beyond reverse engineering the public key. A range of solutions have been debated without convincing outcomes – from the creation of a government key escrow repository to embedding hardwired or software "back-door" technologies in appliances, ICT infrastructures and programmes.

While developments in cryptography algorithms often receive significant attention in professional and, on occasion, popular media, the true workhorse of online security applications is the cryptographic hash function. A hash function takes a data string of any length as an input and produces a fixed length data string as an output – a digital fingerprint. In conjunction with public-key algorithms, hash functions are used for digital signatures and integrity checking. In 1990, Rivest invented the MD4 hash function that was eventually evolved and adopted with modifications by the United States National Security Agency (NSA) as the Secure Hash Algorithm (SHA) in 1993. In 1995, the NSA revised SHA to SHA-1, which remained unbroken until February 2005.[38] SHA-1 is employed in a large variety of popular security applications and protocols, including the Secure Socket Layer (SSL) and its successor the Transport Layer Security (TLS) protocols used to secure the transfer of payment data in e-commerce, the Secure Shell (SSH) programme and protocol for network log-in and access, the S/MIME public key standard for signing email, and IPSec – a standard for securing Internet communications by encrypting and authenticating data packets,[39] thus providing security at the network layer and enabling the design and implementation of VPN infrastructures (Schneier, 1996).

Other notable developments include the ElGamal encryption algorithm of 1984[40] and elliptic curve cryptography. An evolution of the Diffie-Hellman key exchange system, ElGamal was used as the base for the NIST Digital Signature Algorithm (DSA) (Adams and Lloyd, 2003) and in the GNU Privacy Guard – a free and open-source personal cryptography tool and replacement for PGP.[41] Elliptic curve cryptography (ECC) was pioneered by Koblitz and Miller in 1985.[42] The main benefit of ECC is that under certain situations it uses smaller keys than other methods – such as RSA – while providing an equivalent or higher level of security. Use of ECC is still in its early phases, perhaps because its key algorithms are still subject to patent protection (Zwicky, Cooper and Chapman, 2000).[43] Its best-known use is in the Blackberry handheld e-mail device.[44]

In conclusion, cryptographic technologies are being used to achieve many of the goals of information security described in table 5.1. They have served historically as a starting point for reflecting on information security concerns. They have become so successful that security threats have adapted and evolved to take aim at weaknesses beyond actual cryptographic technology. While it is inconceivable for Eve to unmix the paint in the illustration in box 5.3, she may decide to continuously taint the paint exchange, for example by adding her own colors, and frustrate Alice and Bob's dialogue to such an extent that they will give up on their scheme and revert to using unsecured paint exchange. Or she may befriend Bob. Or corrupt Alice. Or get a job in the paint factory.

3. Current issues

Given the steady improvement of cryptographic technologies, one would be forgiven for being puzzled at seemingly everyday news about some criminal or malicious event compromising some well established and regarded commercial or public institution's computers and data. Headlines such as "Instant messaging viruses and worms up 271% in Q1 2005"[45], "Have hackers recruited your PC?"[46] or "Cost of malware soars to $166 billion in 2004"[47] have become commonplace.

The world of Alice, Bob and Eve has changed. Until recently, the use of ICTs and the need for security was limited to the few that had access, usually as tools for their professional activities. Cryptography may have been the main and usually sufficient tool used to provide security. In contrast, today's computers and computer-like appliances, the Internet, and the software that runs them are commonplace. Cryptography seems to be less effective in an environment where multitudes of unsupervised users develop a broad spectrum of interaction with ICTs. Security threats have thus moved away from exploiting weaknesses in technology to exploiting weaknesses in the *use of technology* (Schneier, 2000) – a fertile field of opportunity, in particular when we consider the positive growth of the Internet population in developing countries.

This shift means three things. First, it alerts us to a general need for education and awareness building about information security issues and how we encounter various threats at home, in our private lives, as citizens, as firms and as public entities. Public policy and government action may follow with varying levels of practical application. Secondly, it highlights the need to adjust national legislation and international conventions to accommodate and deter malevolent activities. Chapter 6 of this Report, on cybercrime, as well as chapter 6 in UNCTAD's *E-Commerce and Development Report 2004*, on protecting privacy rights, describe recent developments from a legal perspective. Thirdly, and most importantly, the

approach to information security is changing from a technology focus to a risk management focus. Still, the technologies themselves remain important, and their scope and use will be briefly described within the risk mitigation component of an overall risk management approach to information security in the following section.

E. Information security and risk management

Risk is the uncertainty as to the outcome of an event when there are several possibilities (Outreville, 1997).[48] In other words, risk is the variability of an occurrence of an event around its statistical probability. The larger its uncertainty, or variance, the more risky the event is. In less formal terms, risk is a "... condition in which there is a possibility of an adverse deviation from a desired outcome that is expected and hoped for." (Vaughan, 2002) The objective of risk management is to devise and implement a system that will support the operational and financial stability and effectiveness of an individual, firm or public body in the case of an unfortunate, loss-generating event. In practice, risk management is the process of identifying and assessing risk and developing strategies to manage it – i.e. to decrease variance. A risk management strategy would be a defined process that would guide us through several decisions.

Initially we would need to identify and quantify a risk. After this first phase of risk assessment, we may try to find ways to avoid the risky event – often referred to as a "peril" in risk management literature. We would also attempt to lessen the hazardous conditions under which the peril materializes. Having exhausted avoidance options, we may try to find ways to reduce the frequency of the threats and the severity of the damage we may face, if and when the peril materializes. This often relates to using safety and emergency features and tools. Inevitably, we must accept that some damage will occur at some point, and we may choose to transfer some risk using insurance, thus securing a source of financial compensation for part of the loss. Having done all this, we have probably reduced the potentially negative financial outcome of the risk to such an extent that we can decide to internalize what remains within the cost structure of the core business. Chart 5.1 outlines the basic elements of the risk management process flow.

In order to gain some insight about implementing a risk management approach to owning and using ICTs, it is useful to highlight the basic elements of the process in greater detail. In practice, risk management can demand inputs from diverse fields and competencies and thus should not be limited to exchanges between management and technical staff, such as network administrators or programmers. The same will apply to government policy and governance: a risk management approach to information security policy is multi-stakeholder by nature.

1.   Risk assessment

In order to use a risk management approach, it is fundamental to define risks, to evolve ways to keep risk perceptions current, and to measure or develop methodologies to quantify risks. It is immediately apparent that the task at hand may be more difficult for information security and ICT risks than, for example, for physical property risks. Part of the problem lies with the ever-expanding scope of use of ICTs. It is therefore important to maintain flexibility and alertness to the changing notions and categories of information assets and threats. At the same time, Governments and their statistical offices may choose to institutionalize some aspects of information security risk measurement within their efforts to provide quantitative data for policy makers involved in information society

and economy issues, in the same way that physical traffic data will be complemented by statistics on traffic accidents. Chapter 1 of this report provides an overview of current progress in e-measurement issues.

In order to establish a risk, it is important to define the asset and the perils and threats it is subject to. From an information security perspective, assets can be data, software, hardware and network infrastructure, and the resulting connectivity. General accounting concepts such as those applied to physical assets will have difficulty accommodating information assets, as the cost of the technical components of an information technology system will not be a measure of its value. Resolving the problem of how to evaluate information assets may require a major review of accounting practice to include intellectual capital and to evaluate information in the light of its contribution to management or to core financial indicators, in particular if information products or services are an inseparable part of a firm's main activity or business (Wilson, Stenson and Oppenheim, 2000). A number of approaches have been proposed for short-term evaluation of intangible intellectual assets, such as market capitalization methods, whereby the difference between a firm's market capitalization and its stockholders' equity is the value of its intangible

Chart 5.1

Risk management and information security

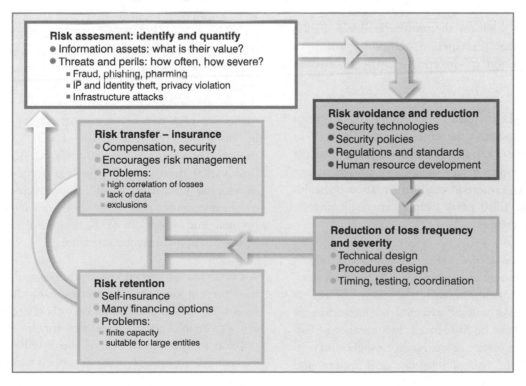

assets, or return on assets methods, whereby the earnings of a company in one period divided by its tangible assets value and then compared with the industry average, with the difference indicating earnings from the intellectual capital (Sveiby, 2004). The problem of isolating the information asset component from the intellectual capital is also unresolved. It is also obvious that these methods are limited in that they would apply only to publicly listed firms. The use of hedonic demand theory has been proposed for valuing information technology investment in public sector organizations (Cilek, 2001).[49]

By comparison, defining perils and threats seems simpler. Threats usually appear as disclosure, modification, loss or destruction, and interruption of one or several information assets. A risk management approach requires research and analysis of possible threats to information security. The research should consider and evaluate sources of threats and perils that relate to an entities interaction with people, operational processes and the deployment and use of technology (Siegel, Sagalow and Serritella, 2002). It requires an estimation of frequency: how often do particular threats occur during, say, one year? Furthermore, the determination of maximum exposure is also necessary: what is the worst-case damage scenario per threat? Answering these two questions is an exercise specific to a firm or institution, and generalizations are therefore difficult to make. Information security threats may present themselves as one or a combination of several risk types.

First party risks manifest themselves as losses arising from the damage, destruction, temporary malfunction or corruption of an entity's own information assets.

Third party risks materialize as losses arising from liability claims against the entity, its management or employees. These can include a broad range of perils such as distributing malicious code or breach of privacy related to, say, credit card information or health records. Thus, third party claims can result directly from security failures.

Business interruption risks are those that prevent a planned or contracted delivery of goods or services. From an information security perspective, business interruption risks will be affected by infrastructure risks, and this may be influenced by a number of factors, such as a diversity of hardware, bespoke and proprietary software, overall reliability and uptime, and

the ultimate dependency of business processes on ICT infrastructure.[50]

Reputation risks occur when a firm suffers damage to its reputation or brand identity. They are sometimes considered separately because they can be difficult to assess as they involve quantifying difficult variables such as expected business revenue or future market capitalization. More practically, they may need to be treated separately, as insurance cover for first party risks is unlikely to cover this class.[51]

Catastrophic risks can generate losses of such severity that, should they occur, they can on their own terminate an entity. As such, if suffered by an entity, they necessarily render its business or activity unsustainable.[52] Accordingly, actively managing catastrophic risk often leads to using risk transfer mechanisms, such as insurance. From an information security perspective, catastrophic risks can affect users, perhaps more so than ICT service providers. A typical case would be identity theft or theft of confidential information. From the perspective of an ICT service provider, data services and even certain information security applications can create *catastrophic points of failure* if they function using centralized databases and thus become identifiable targets for attack. However, beyond an irrecoverable breakdown or clogging up of the Internet, very few risks can be termed truly catastrophic in the traditional sense, as the value of ICT services is only partly reflected in the value of its technical infrastructures.

It is important to note that not all entities in all countries will be subject to the same perils, nor will the same threats appear with similar frequency or severity. In spite of global interconnectivity, differences in the value and nature of underlying information assets and in the thoroughness of the implementation of a risk management strategy will result in vastly different outcomes. Table 5.3 uses an example of three Asian countries to describe just how varied these may be. Such differences among developing countries should be expected, as they would necessarily reflect the diversity of their development and adoption of ICTs in everyday social, business and governance activities.

An overview of several known threats and perils that may present one or a combination of the outlined risks follows. Their scope and numbers are not fixed. Some overlap is possible, and new threats are likely to develop in the future. All of the listed threats can present one or several of the described types of risks.

Table 5.3

Security attacks by type of threat in 2003

	China	Thailand	Malaysia
Number of reported incidents	28.424	386	4.294
Type of attack as a % of reported incidents	25.35	2.730	6.500
Virus or worm	5.73	1.530	3.206
Spam	4.99	94	2.950
Scans of probes	5.48	55	1.344
Denial of service attacks and Intrusion	0.90	31	1.144

Source: APCERT Annual report for 2003, MyCert.org.my.

Fraud

Fraud regularly attracts media coverage, as the consequences are easily described in money terms, rather than in terms of technology. Fraud is the crime of deliberate deception in order to unjustly obtain property or services. Quite a few threats fall into this category. Credit card fraud is the classic example and continues to grow with the development of e-commerce activities. Recent reports indicate that merchants from the United States expect to lose an estimated $2.6 billion to online fraud in 2004, $700 million more than in 2003 and more than the prior fraud loss record of $2.1 billion established in 2002.[53] Recent reports also indicate that almost 85 per cent of fraudulent transactions on the Internet originate from computers in the United States. Canada is in second place with 5 per cent, while Australia, Germany and Japan hover around the 1 per cent mark.[54]

Phishing and pharming

Phishing is a more recent phenomenon. It consists of masquerading as an official-looking and trustworthy telephone service, e-mail or website in order to acquire someone's sensitive personal information such as passwords and credit card details. According to a recent Anti-Phishing Working Group (APWG) report on phishing activity, 37 per cent of phishing web sites were hosted in the United States. China was in second place with 28 per cent and the Republic of Korea was third with 11 per cent. Other top countries were Brazil with 4 per cent, Germany with 3 per cent, Japan with 2.5 per cent and Canada with 2.3 per cent.[55]

Pharming is the exploitation of vulnerability in domain name server software that may enable a hacker to gain control over the domain name of a legitimate web site (e.g. Unctad.org) and to redirect traffic from that web site to another bogus, defamatory or competitive web site. If the phony web site is a copy of a website of a trusted organization, such as a bank, a hospital or a government institution, it can be used to phish users' passwords, personal identity numbers or account numbers and gain access to their personal data or access to the organization's computer resources.

Infrastructure threats

At a basic level, infrastructure depends on the reliability of power supplies, hardware, operating systems and network connectivity. This issue is often of concern to developing countries, as it underlies efforts to establish universal access to ICTs. However, the energy crisis in California during 2000 and 2001, and the accompanying shortages and price volatilities, indicates that even in developed countries, overconfidence can be misguided and risk management should not assume away risks related to the provision of public utilities.[56]

This category also compromises the whole range of viruses and worms – often jointly referred to as malware – and any other type of attack aimed at destroying or seriously reducing the functionality of ICT resources. Often, the objects of attack are particular software applications or websites and portals. Material gain may not be an objective, although reports have recently surfaced of blackmail advanced by criminals threatening to take down websites using denial-of-service attacks if demands are not met.[57] The major vendors of anti-virus programmes maintain current information on the activity and danger level of various types of malware. A number of portals monitor ongoing developments in common applications, such as operating systems, web servers and database applications. Attacks will aim to take advantage of an unintended functionality to cripple or gain control over an ICT system.[58]

Intellectual property theft

This is an important and significant issue in itself. UNCTAD (2003, 2004) has described the intellectual property issues that occur when the Internet interfaces with software development or the music industry, and has considered the issues related to domain name assignments and disputes from a trademark perspective. Here too, the democratization of computing power and the availability of bandwidth change everything. While it is perfectly reasonable that individuals, firms and organizations want to control the distribution of and access to any creative content they may produce, such control is "...contrary to what the digital world is all about" (Schneier, 1996). The Internet is functionally and fundamentally designed to facilitate the copying of files using a robust communications infrastructure: even the simple act of viewing a web page means that a browser will copy a file from a server into its local memory and often hide an extra copy (in its "cache") on its hard disk in order to speed up browsing. Creative content industries and organizations may appreciate these notions and choose to consider them within their risk management strategies.

Identity theft

Identity theft is the deliberate assumption of another person's identity. The underlying problem is that, as technology increases its use of identity recognition, identity theft becomes a more commonplace and tempting criminal activity. For individuals, identity theft can present a catastrophic risk. People whose identities have been stolen can spend enormous time and resources re-establishing their good name, credit and legal record. In the meantime, they may lose job opportunities, be refused finance, education and other benefits, and they may even get arrested for crimes they did not commit. Techniques for obtaining identification information range from rummaging through rubbish to infiltration of organizations that store large amounts of personal information. Identity theft often works together with privacy violations.

Privacy violation

Privacy violations can be divided into targeted attacks and data harvesting. Targeted attacks are difficult to defend against, in particular if the attackers have large resources at their disposal. The digital nature of communications also allows attackers to leave few if any traces of a violation, making post-event detection difficult. Therefore, defenses must be pro-active and based on monitoring. Cryptographic tools may also be useful to the extent that the data and the associated ICT infrastructure are under the control of the owner. Using encryption in e-mail correspondence is one example – provided the recipient is trustworthy and exercises a similar level of prudence. Aside from violating content, traffic analysis of Internet-based communications can reveal significant information. Changing reaction times, message lengths and patterns of communications can indicate activity and organizational or command structures.

Broad surveillance activities coupled with data harvesting are generally increasing and are becoming easier with improving technology and increasing technology use. Wireless LANs can easily be subject to surveillance. A biometric identity system can exclude unauthorized staff from company premises, but it is necessarily powered by a database of personal details that, in itself, can become a point of attack. Commercial entities can, and often do, record and track everything purchased with a credit card. E-commerce firms use such private information to propose a more personalized level of service, but at what cost to privacy? More and more data are being collected as people leave increasingly larger digital footprints during their online activities. Legislation protecting privacy and databases can be an important deterrent and has been discussed in a previous edition of this report (UNCTAD, 2003).

Regulatory threat

Compliance with new and expanding regulations on information security may be seen as a threat in the sense that it may require adjustments in operations and improvements in security, security audits and certification, and corresponding expenses. Regulatory change may also be perceived as a threat if requirements evolve to become significantly different in one country or when required adjustments are above or even contrary to regulatory requirements in other countries. However, regulation can be better appreciated as a policy tool for risk avoidance and hazard reduction and will be discussed as such in the next section.

2. Risk avoidance and hazard reduction

Risk avoidance and hazard reduction policies and activities will be developed on the basis of a successful understanding of the frequency and potential damage of predetermined information security threats. They may span a wide range and would include:

- Using information security technologies;

- Developing institution-level information security policies and procedures;

- Implementing information security regulation and self-regulation; and

- Training and developing human resources to understand information security and use the technology, execute information security polices and comply with regulations.

Information security technologies

The development of modern security technologies was described in part D of this chapter. Most of that discussion covered the development of cryptographic tools and applications, as these were central to most security concerns until recently. Part D.3 noted that the Internet and the ubiquitous use of networked computers introduce greater diversity in the security technology landscape, which necessarily corresponds to the increasing diversity of security threats.

Information security technologies can be categorized by the object they control or monitor. The five basic categories are:

- System access controls;

- Content access and cryptography controls;

- System integrity controls and monitoring;

- System audit and monitoring technologies; and

- System management controls.

An individual, firm, or public or civic organization will need to implement a certain mix of several of the listed technologies. Not all of these technologies will scale perfectly, and their successful use will depend on the ICT readiness of administrators and users. It is important to implement several technologies at the same time, thus creating security density and depth through a layered system. System access controls restrict access to computer resources to authorized users. Content access and cryptography achieves a similar goal but can make fine distinctions in terms of the accessibility of particular information and content, and authorization can be generated by individual users as well as administrators. System integrity and monitoring defends against unwarranted and often illicit modification or corruption of system and data files. System audit and monitoring technologies are used to investigate security breaches and their impact. System management controls are used to effect and verify security settings and implement defensive measures when encountering a threat. Box 5.4 describes the individual technologies in brief. Public key technology and free and open-source software merit some additional attention, as they have been advanced as solutions for improving information security, with public key technology being particularly necessary for developing e-business activities (UNCTAD, 2001, 2003).

The technological development of asymmetric key or public key cryptography was discussed in part D.2 of this chapter. In application, public key cryptography may use an infrastructure to provide for third-party confirmation of user identities and the matching of public keys to users. The purpose of a public key infrastructure is to manage keys and certificates and consists of a public private key pair generator, a registry and a certification authority.[59] Going back to the traditional naming scheme, Alice will register her identity and request a key pair. Alice will then digitally sign messages using her private key. Bob, the recipient, will read the digital signature using Alice's public key, which will be certified as belonging to Alice by the PKI's certification authority. The certificate will unambiguously match up Alice to her key because Alice has already established her identity with the PKI's registrar. Thus, Bob will have established the integrity and authenticity of the message without having exchanged any secret information in advance with Alice. Certain definitions of public key infrastructures will include the legislation on electronic signatures (Ford and Baum, 2000).

There is a diversity of PKI infrastructure types, and firms and Governments are often presented with difficult choices on what could be a good match for their activities and would scale well. Questions as to how many certification authorities there should be, whether there would be a hierarchical relationship between them or would they be peers, how they will relate to certification authorities in other PKIs etc., await managers and administrators.[60] Given the sometimes impenetrable complexities and corre-

Box 5.4

Information security technologies

1. **System access controls** are designed to exclude unknown or unauthenticated and unauthorized users from gaining access to computer system resources and forbidden data and content from entering into the system. In this sense, all five categories of security technologies can be broadly understood to be access controls. Passwords are an authentication tool, as are biometric tools and smart cards and tokens. However it may be exaggerated to call them a security technology, given that they favour convenience at the expense of security.

   Firewalls control communication between different zones of trust. Typically they are placed between zones of no trust, such as the Internet, and zones of high trust, such as a firm's internal local network. Firewalls prevent or allow communication according to a prescribed security policy.

   Content screening applications monitor communications for inappropriate content such as Spam or unauthorized file types and thus deny access to content that may be offensive or constitute a non-productive use of resources.

   Biometric security tools measure and analyse personal physical characteristics, such as fingerprints, eyes, voice or facial patterns, signature, gait and keyboard typing patterns that are processed for entry into a database. Authentication will require a match between the user requesting access and one or several biometric characteristics stored in the database. Biometrics have raised concerns about privacy, as the databases contain personal data. From a risk management perspective, if the databases are centralized, they then present a single point of potential catastrophic failure.

   Smart cards and security tokens are distributed devices that store and process authentication data and have some level of imbedded cryptography technology. They will typically be used in conjunction with a personal identification number or a biometric screen and this may, to some extent, decentralize the access authentication process and thus ease catastrophic failure concerns.

   Rights and privileges policies are designed to give authenticated users access to particular data or resources. This process is often called authorization – a process by which one entity attempts to confirm that another entity is allowed access and thus becomes a trusted party.

2. **Content access and cryptography** controls embrace digital signatures and certificates, encryption applications and the use of virtual private networks. They are different from the access controls described above in that they function within existing system resources and their policies can be highly individualized and controlled by actual users or groups of users.

   Digital signatures are electronic signatures that use some cryptographic technique to assure the integrity or authenticity of a message. Public key cryptography has become the choice technology because it removes the need to establish public-private key pairs between each and every party; in this sense it is a multilateral rather than a bilateral construct.[i]

   Secure virtual private networks (VPN) are private communications infrastructures providing remote users with the functionalities of a local private network. A secure VPN will tunnel a private communications network through a public one, such as the Internet, by encrypting and authenticating all data packets using security protocols such as IPsec, SSL or PPTP. IPsec has become a part of IPv6, the new protocol standard for Internet traffic.

3. **System integrity controls and monitoring** applications consist of anti-virus software and integrity checkers. Anti-virus software attempts to detect foreign and malicious applications that may try to corrupt, destroy or exploit a user's computer or data. Integrity checkers monitor any alterations to files that are considered critical to the system.

4. **System audit and monitoring technologies** include systems for intrusion detection and prevention, event monitoring and forensics. Intrusion detection and prevention will identify inappropriate, incorrect, or anomalous activity on a network or computer system and will take action to prevent them from being successful.

   Monitoring applications will document actions on network devices and analyse the actions to determine if an attack is ongoing or has occurred, which enables an organization to determine if and with what effectiveness information security activities are operating according to prescribed security policy.

   Computer forensics tools are used to identify, preserve, extract, and document computer-based evidence.

   Countermeasure applications or aggressive network self-defense are a set of graduated responses that include strike back capabilities.[ii]

5. **System management controls** include applications that assist administrators to enforce security policies, manage computing resources, provide failsafe continuity of operation, scan for vulnerabilities and provide remedies. System controls consist of a number of distinct tools and applications.

   Policy enforcement applications enable system administrators to engage in centralized monitoring and enforcement of an organization's security policies.

   Network management tools are used to control and monitor networks, including the management of faults, configurations, performance, and security.

   Continuity of operations is supported by a scope of tools that provide for a complete backup infrastructure to maintain the availability of systems or networks in the event of an emergency or during planned maintenance.

   Scanners are tools that analyse computers or networks for security vulnerabilities.

   Patch management tools acquire, test, and apply multiple patches to one or more computer systems.

---

[i] Electronic signatures are a broader category and may include cable and Telex addresses, as well as facsimile transmissions of handwritten signatures.

[ii] For more details on countermeasure application, see Nathan (2004).

sponding difficulty in matching existing PKI solutions to market needs (Gutmann, 2002), it may not come as a surprise that the deployment of PKIs has not met the expectations of the late 1990s.[61]

In recent years, a number of IT firms or firms notable for their intensive use of information technology have been increasingly using free and open-source software (FOSS), in part because of perceived security benefits. The software used is often for infrastructural computing tasks, such as operating systems, web servers or database applications. When assessing competing proprietary and FOSS applications for security, technical experts and decision makers will need to appreciate the various quantitative and qualitative issues that make cross-comparisons between software difficult. A security flaw can attract few or many attacks. Flaws may be more or less critical, depending on the amount of damage they invoke. There is therefore a certain scope for judgment and for weighing the different factors in a final evaluation of comparable solutions. There is also the subjective user experience to contend with, as the most dissatisfied users are the most vocal ones as well, while it is entirely possible that the majority can be untroubled or content with a programme's security performance. Anderson (2002) suggests that there should be no difference from the perspective of achieving technical reliability, all other things being equal. However, in practice things are not equal, and due to information asymmetries, network effects and imperfect markets, actual outcomes may vary. UNCTAD (2003) has analysed these issues and suggests that the FOSS development model may have some hypothetical advantages, while there are no practical guarantees. Wheeler (2003) advances that FOSS has more security potential.[62] Free and open code allows users to inspect and fix bugs, including security vulnerabilities, should they have the resources and competencies. Certain FOSS applications are less likely to be targets of attacks because of either design principles or their still relatively small install base.[63] Malicious hackers would logically choose to exploit systems that have been broadly deployed, as this increases the chances of success. As previously noted in box 5.2 of this chapter, the simple fact that certain technologies are proprietary and that their inner workings and logic are not easily knowable is not a security feature. On the contrary, the secret source code of proprietary software may in itself be a security liability, in particular when public reporting by third parties on exploits and vulnerabilities may be in conflict with anti-circumvention provisions of international treaties and national legislation.[64]

Policies and procedures

An information security policy is a document that defines the rules and requirements that must be followed and met and identifies what behaviour is appropriate when accessing the computing resources of an institution. A policy will document potential threats and define responses to a security attack or failure, often specifying detailed procedures for particular types of incidents or security breaches. Information security policies are a fundamental component of and an input into the risk management process. In order to be successful, information policies need to be integrated into institutions' and companies' overall strategic and operational planning and procedures.

Policies will usually address very specific use issues such as "acceptable use" or "dial-in access", and should outline what tools and procedures are needed to deal with them. It will often be important to have policies define and communicate a state of consensus reached between users and administrators, as the ownership of a policy will be crucial to its success. Information security policies provide a foundation for human resources development, as their design can help identify where training and education may be needed to meet the policy's requirements, as well as broader issues related to the use of computer technology. The process of policy design will also define responses for certain types of behaviour of users and administrators that are incompatible with its prescriptions. Accordingly, a policy will also serve as a reference for establishing factual circumstance in the case of a policy breach.

Information security policies may be constructed in accordance with an international standard of best practices, such as ISO/IEC 17799, in particular where international commerce will depend or indeed focus on information technology. Such standards and related regulations are discussed in the next section. There are also technical standards, such as the ITU X.800 series; these will not be explored in this chapter.[65]

Self-regulation

Self-regulation is established through standards and voluntary quality certifications. Their function is dual: they indicate a certified level of performance, and they present a path for improving managerial and operational activities. Self-regulation can have a number of potential advantages over government regulation. It can be easier to evolve and faster to implement. Commitment may be stronger when the actual stakeholders participate in its conception. It is often in response to a market need, and funding may be more accommodating from those with a vested interest in its success. There are a number of standards that may be used.[66] The discussion will however focus on a selected few that seem to be attracting particular attention from specialized media.

The International Organization for Standardization and the International Electrotechnical Commission (ISO/IEC) 17799 standard issued under the title "Information technology - Code of practice for information security management" is an important information security standard. ISO/IEC 17799 was published in 2000 and a revision is planned for 2005. It provides best practice recommendations for initiating, implementing or maintaining information security management systems. ISO/IEC 17799 specifically addresses a number of issues, some of which have been discussed in this chapter, such as security policies, asset classification or access control. For each issue, objectives are specified and best practice means of achieving them are outlined. Specific actions are not recommended, as an institution seeking certification is expected to perform an information security risk assessment before selecting actions relevant to its information security profile. ISO/IEC 17799 has a number of equivalent national standards.[67]

Another international standard for computer security is the Common Criteria, also registered as ISO/IEC 15408.[68] The Common Criteria originated out of three standards: ITSEC, a European standard developed in the early 1990s by the United Kingdom, France, the Netherlands and Germany, TCSEC – or the "Orange Book" – the Unites States' standard, and CTCPEC, the Canadian standard. By unifying these pre-existing standards, companies selling computer products for defense or intelligence use only need to have them evaluated against a single standard. The Common Criteria allow users to specify their security requirements, allow developers to specify the security attributes of their products, and allow evaluators to determine whether products actually meet their security claims. The Common Criteria Mutual Recognition Agreement was signed in 1998 and recognizes evaluations against the Common Criteria standard done by other parties other than the original signatories.[69]

The Generally Accepted Information Security Principles (GAISP) project is an initiative aimed at self-regulation, in particularly with a view to preparing for the possible impact of a number of regulatory developments discussed later in this subsection. It aims to promote information security principles and practices that are scalable to varying levels of risk tolerance and that would apply equally to government or corporate infrastructure assets or the equipment and environment of a home user. GAISP is managed by the Information Systems Security Association, a not-for-profit industry-based information security resource with members in 89 countries.[70] The GAISP provides three levels of guiding principles addressed to security professionals of all levels of technical and managerial responsibility. The first level, "Pervasive Principles", targets government policymakers and executive-level management and provides guidance to help organizations achieve an effective information security strategy. The second level, "Broad Functional Principles", defines more precisely the elements needed to build effective security architecture. Finally, the third level, "Detailed Principles", serves as a framework for action for information security professionals and provides specific, comprehensive guidance for consideration in day-to-day information risk management activity.

Regulation

Regulation, in comparison to self-regulation, has its strengths as well. Enforcement may be simpler, as there is often legislative backing. Adherence is frequently obligatory and can reduce selection problems – whereby only the willing and successful come forward – in evaluating the overall impact of the prescribed standards or activities.[71] Regulation can be better aware of its societal context, as the regulatory body will itself be accountable to higher government instances, while regulations would need to be compatible with other accepted legal notions and rights, such as civil liberties and privacy. Firms outsourcing to clients under such regulation need to appreciate the current regulatory environment and develop competencies on the emerging standards, and achieving compliance may become a central marketing message (UNCTAD, 2003).[72] As notions of trust habitually decrease with distance and dissimilar business environments, firms from developing countries may have to make relatively greater efforts in supporting importers and clients in developed economies when these need to validate their own regulatory compliance. Such support and cooperation would necessarily involve the application of risk management concepts in information security activities. Four regulatory developments have been singled out in this subsection, three of which are related to the United States, as it is an important outsourcing market.[73] The regulations discussed relate to information security issues and are complementary to cybercrime legislation as discussed in chapter 6.

Basel II is a capital adequacy framework agreement among banking regulators from 55 countries, of which 18 are from developing countries. Chapter 3 of this report deals with the implications of its new financial rating system on enterprises' access to bank-related trade finance and e-finance. Basel II proposes improved methodologies for accurately calculating capital provisions made against credit and commercial, and operational risk and asserts that the framework "…will promote the adoption of stronger risk management practices by the banking industry, and views this as one of its major benefits."[74]

Basel II is not overly explicit about information security measures *per se*. Information security in Basel II needs to be understood within the context of operational risk: the more effective a bank's operational risk management effort is, the less money it needs to set aside in reserve. Basel II defines operational risk as "…the risk of loss resulting from inadequate or failed internal processes, people and systems or from external events. This definition includes legal risk, but excludes strategic and reputation risk."[75] Recent computer security failures, such as hacked databases or virus and worm infections, are meaningful examples of the operational impacts of failed or insufficient information security controls. In this sense Basel II positions information security controls as a useful tool for operational risk management.

Information is critical to the operation of every financial institution. If the confidentiality of sensitive or private information is compromised, lawsuits or regulatory sanctions may result in penalties, and violated trust may result in loss of business. The integrity of critical information can be corrupted. When critical information is not available where and when it is needed, important processes may fail completely, with similar results. Recovery costs that follow such failures can become a major, or even detrimental, issue if damages turn out to be catastrophic. Thus, the degree of risk mitigation from a formal and well-organized information security programme can be significant. In practice, many of the Basel II operational risk principles can be met through use of the information security standards such as the ISO/IEC 17799 or the

Organization for Economic Cooperation and Development (OECD) Guidelines on Information Security that are discussed in part F of this chapter.[76]

The United States Federal Information Security Management Act (FISMA) was enacted in 2002. The objective of the act is to improve computer and network security within the Federal Government and government contractors by mandating yearly security audits. Federal agencies will "develop, document, and implement an agency wide information security program … [in order] to provide information security for the information and information systems that support the operations and assets of the agency, including those provided or managed by another agency, contractor, or other source."[77] This will include periodic assessments of risk policies and procedures, security awareness training, periodic testing and evaluation, remedial action, and implementing measures to mitigate risks associated with security incidents before substantial damage is done, as well as plans and procedures to ensure continuity of operations when information security is under threat.

The United States Public Company Accounting Reform and Investor Protection Act of 2002, more commonly known as the Sarbanes-Oxley Act (SOx), was enacted after a series of corporate financial scandals, including those affecting Enron, Arthur Andersen, and WorldCom. Through its Titles VIII and XI, SOx aims to prevent third parties or corrupt management from destroying or falsifying financial documents. Information security aspects and audit ability are important for its realization, as many firms will use electronic means to store and analyse financial data. The deadline for compliance with SOx was 15 April 2005, but an online poll at a SOx discussion forum shows that almost 60 per cent of companies surveyed have not started any kind of implementation.[78]

More specifically, SOx article VIII criminalizes destroying, altering, concealing or falsifying records, in particular audit records, with intent either to obstruct or influence an investigation, and the failure of an auditor to maintain audit or review work papers for a five year period. Article XI takes issue with tampering with records and impeding official proceedings by, among other, altering, destroying, mutilating, or concealing a record, document, or other object, with the intent to impair the object's integrity or availability for use in an official proceeding. As certain outsourcing activities may involve data management that can include financial and accounting data, service providers from developing countries may consequently be affected.

Another regulation that can impact outsourcing firms is the Statement on Auditing Standards No. 70 (SAS 70) of the American Institute of Certified Public Accountants. Established in 1993, SAS 70 elucidates how external auditors should assess the information security in an outsourcing firm and the nature of the attestation. While the attestation implies that an in-depth audit of controls over information technology and related processes was performed, much like the ISO/IEC 17799 standard, SAS 70 does not provide a predetermined set of objectives or activities that a firm must achieve. The full "Type 2" SAS 70 report would include, besides the auditor's opinion, the firm's description of its security controls, a description of the auditor's tests of operating effectiveness, the results of those tests and any other information provided by the firm.[79]

However, the SAS 70 Type 2 audit may not be sufficient for SOx compliance. The SAS 70 standard was developed long before SOx regulations and does not focus on SOx controls and issues. An important distinction is that the burden of SOx compliance is with the entity receiving an outsourced service. For the outsourcing service provider, a single SAS 70 audit could cover multiple clients. However, recipients may demand additional controls and documentation beyond the requirements of SAS 70 Type 2 in order to achieve a satisfactory level of SOx compliance. SAS 70 requirements may eventually change to achieve compatibility with SOx, and outsourcing firms in developing countries may need to keep track of related developments.[80]

Human resource development and training

Without the knowledge conveyed through training and test exercises, users may inadvertently expose parts of the organization to security threats. For example, users might reveal sensitive information if they contact the wrong person when observing an intrusion. The term "social engineering" is often used to describe the practice of obtaining confidential information by manipulation of legitimate users to perform actions that are against established information security policies (Schneier, 2000). "Social engineers" will exploit the natural tendencies of people to be trustful and helpful, rather than attempt to discover and attack computer security flaws.

The human factor in information security manifests itself as intentional or involuntary employee transgression of established conduct norms and security policies. The proverbial disgruntled employee is the most obvious source of intentional security breaches, and an awareness of the criminal consequences and the forensic traceability of online activity may act as deterrents. To mitigate such risks, human resources policy will need to interface with risk management policy, and employee training may need to include issues related to intentional and criminal information security breaches. Enhancing recruitment processes, gauging levels of acceptance and trust in information security reporting systems and taking into account subjective levels of satisfaction as related to recognition of merit and financial reward will support the development of well-targeted human development and training policies and content at the firm or institutional level.

Moving to the notion of involuntary actions, employees may not be focused on information security threats as they go about performing their duties and doing their work. Security risks can be compounded by ignoring or not respecting poorly applied or designed policies and technologies in order "to get the job done". Involuntary transgressions can also result from a fundamental lack of training and awareness of security issues. While information resources and technologies are growing and improving daily, accessing them securely is becoming an issue of some complexity. It is therefore not surprising that demand is growing for biometric technologies and identity management systems that promise to simplify authentication and authorization.[81]

Firms and organizations need to provide training and education on applying prescribed policies in order to minimize response times and even pre-empt certain threats.[82] Employee buy-in is crucial to validate any investment in information security risk management, hardware and software technologies and the establishment of policies to support them. However, incentives for buying in and the consequences of opting out are management issues, and thus the human factor introduces the problems of information security into the managerial and strategic levels of an organization and warns against leaving its application to insular and detached computer departments. Consistent reporting on security threats can be achieved if employees do not face disincentives; they need to be confident that they can report incidents without fear, ridicule or retribution.

Human resource development will usually start with an awareness-building programme designed to develop an information security mindset. The awareness-building phase can be used to gauge aptitudes and competencies and generate feedback for the design of more practical training. Practical training may follow on from the basics of security and how information and privacy are protected. This is particularly relevant when a business or public institution is responsible for private or sensitive information. There may be a need to educate on the importance and application of privacy laws, both domestically and in the country of the client, in particular if a firm is involved in outsourcing activities.

Building an understanding of security-related policies and their logic can be an important role for government, in particular in guiding public administration and public sector enterprises towards better security.[83] For such entities, market incentives may be non-existent, and security valuation and cost-benefit analysis may be complex and difficult. Accordingly, a clear security strategy and policy commitment may be needed and would necessarily be supported through human capacity and awareness building activities. For many developing countries that have already established e-strategies or information economy development policies, embracing or strengthening information security and the respective human resources development perspectives would increase the spectrum of possibilities for practical implementation.

3. Reduction of frequency and severity of loss events

From an information security perspective, reduction of the frequency and severity of loss events will be related to the design and implementation of policies that govern the use of an information system, as well as with the fundamental technical design of the system. While technical design issues are beyond the scope of this chapter, suffice it to say that any security that users need should be actively implemented within their own environment. Relying only on legislation, regulation or audits of third parties may not be a sufficiently prudent strategy.

Decreasing the response time from a security attack to the implementation of the first active measures, such as bringing redundant systems online, is the basis for loss severity reduction. Accordingly, policies and supporting procedures that are the subject of training, that are well written and clearly documented,

communicated and enforced, can prepare an institution to respond to security threats in a timely and controlled manner. Policies should also foresee practicing security breach procedures in advance of a real attack. When experiencing a security attack or breach, policies will have determined what actions to take, what data to gather and preserve, and how to protect data, systems and networks from further damage. Documenting plans, conducting training and testing procedures in advance will allow users and administrators to coordinate their activities efficiently when responding to an intrusion.

Computer security incident response teams (CSIRTs), sometimes also called computer emergency response teams (CERTs), can be extremely valuable organizations when a security attack is imminent or under way. A CERT performs, coordinates and supports the response to security incidents that involve sites within a defined group of users, sites, networks or organizations.[84] In doing so they will monitor trends in information security breaches, cooperate with security experts to identify solutions to security problems, post alerts, and disseminate information to the public. CERTs may also analyse the security features and performance of various hardware and software products, publish research on information security issues and cooperate with other government or business entities in developing and delivering information security training. Many developing and developed countries have one or several CERT or CSIRT teams hosted by a variety of institutions, ranging from universities to businesses and government. In order for CSIRTs be successful, it is "...paramount that coordination and cooperation occurs among governments, law enforcement, commercial organizations, the research community, and practitioners who have experience in responding to IT security incidents" (Killcrece, 2004).[85] The need for regional and global coordination between CSIRTs is of prime importance as well. This is discussed in part F of this chapter.

4. Risk transfer – insurance

Insurance for information security risks is often called cyber-risk insurance. The objective of insurance is to provide financial stability for individuals, organizations and businesses by providing a risk transfer mechanism in exchange for a premium payment (UNCTAD, 2002). By presenting financial compensation when a loss occurs, insurance helps individuals and organizations continue their activities. Even when no loss occurs, insurance reduces uncertainty and allows people and firms to focus on their objectives. In this sense, insurance and cyber insurance can provide improved security for investors, in particular those with high exposure to information security risks. However, some studies (Böhme, 2005) have questioned the fundamental insurability of information security risks and therefore the development of cyber insurance products. The near monolithic dominance of a few technological platforms could lead to a high correlation of losses from some of the threats previously discussed. To compensate, insurance premiums would surcharge, with a corresponding shrinkage in demand and a potential increase in adverse selection problems.

Using cyber-risk insurance may improve the adoption of risk management concepts and processes, as insurers will necessarily request clients to comply with any one or several regulatory or self-regulatory standards. Requirements for insurance may actually force companies to increase internal network security, and there have been suggestions that the insurance industry will eventually drive security reforms in the information technology industry (ITU, 2002; Schneier, 2000). The insurance industry can also play an important role in improving information security by working with Governments to increase public and corporate awareness of information security risks and promoting best practices.

Cyber-risk insurance cover is available primarily as a stand-alone policy for first- and third-party coverage. Policies can cover both internal and external threats. They may cover attacks aimed specifically at the policyholder or those that affect the Internet in its entirety. Examples of cyber-risk insurance policies are covers for web content liability, professional liability, network security third-party liability, intangible or information property loss, loss of e-revenue or cyber-terrorism. In practice, the total cyber-risk insurance market has probably not reached the $1 billion mark (i.e. less than 0.05 per cent of global premiums). One possible reason may be that the insurance industry lacks sufficient data to quantify security risks. As a result, insurers may set premiums higher in order to compensate for unknown risk. Such high-cost premiums may be beyond reach for small and medium-sized companies, and as a consequence many of them will retain risk and self-insure. Compounding the problem of a lack of data is the fact that the actual nature of security flaws and threats evolves and changes daily, and future risks are difficult to know. Businesses may also be reluctant to report security failure incidents, as they may result in a loss of reputa-

tion and business (Kesan, Majuca and Yurcik, 2004; ICLR 2004).

Another explanation may be that certain exclusions that severely decrease potential clients' perception of the value of cyber insurance covers. These may include, for example, disgruntled employee exclusion, which by any token is a major security risk factor. Territory exclusions may be included, with the result that claims from losses due to wrongful acts in particular parts of the world will not be reimbursed - a fairly awkward proposition given the global nature of the Internet. Abusing available material may also be excluded. These are security attacks that are performed using passwords, authorizations or other employee identification stolen in the physical world.

5. Risk retention

Risk retention is often treated as the final component in a risk management process.[86] After all means and tools have been exhausted to avoid, reduce and transfer information security risks, a certain ultimate risk component inevitably remains and falls on the individual, firm or organization. Organizations will sometimes practice risk retention only because many risks may not be assessable in advance. Beyond this "unplanned" component, formal risk retention is planned and conscious and is sometimes referred to as "self-insurance". While the notion may be simple, in practice risk retention requires setting up a risk financing mechanism. Depending on the size, importance, competencies and regulative environment of the risk taker, the financing mechanism may be managed internally or by a financial service provider. It may range from a pay-as-you-go policy to systematically setting aside funds, creating a captive insurance company, setting up insurance pools with similar institutions or establishing a finite risk insurance scheme. Whatever the solution, it needs to be put in place for two basic reasons.

The first is that some financial losses from information security incidents are inevitable, and their size may affect, at the very least, short-term cash flows. Financial problems may in turn lead to non-performance towards clients or stakeholders that provokes supplementary liability. The second is that without the surety of a risk retention mechanism, the resulting financial uncertainty may inhibit or distract entities to the point where they may forego opportunities that are in their best interest. Thus, a firm striving to maximize its value or an institution aiming to excel at meeting its objectives may under-perform without organized and financed risk retention.

If an entity is confident that future losses will be fairly constant and predictable, and if it makes financial sense in the light of insurance premium prices, the entity may choose to retain more and insure less. However, such choices may be the privilege of large companies and organizations that, during a given financial year, accumulate enough loss events that are statistically representative of the general averages of occurrence and severity for a particular information security risk. This would enable them to forecast with confidence and surety the financial implications of security threats and set aside funds to compensate the impending damage.

F. International and national policy developments and issues

Today, Governments are faced with the certainty of information security threats and various disincentives for using and investing in information security, as well as the notion that information infrastructures are becoming part of national and global critical infrastructures. In response, Governments may engage policies to remedy security problems and seek benefits from enabling a safer, and thus wider, use of information technologies.

Awareness building and education, standard setting, promoting self-regulation, using risk management methodologies, and legislating to deter cybercrime have become important areas of activity for Governments and their institutions. Such efforts find their corresponding expression in international policy forums, where concerns have been voiced and guidelines formulated to tackle the increasingly important issue of information security as we move towards a global information economy and society. This section will review several recent policy processes and events at the international level. It will then highlight several issues of importance for national policy.

1. International policy

A number of international organizations and processes are considering information security issues. Their work goes against any prejudgment of sameness and reflects a wide diversity of concerns and approaches. A certain distillation of these notions has been achieved in UN General Assembly resolutions 55/63 and 56/121, highlighted in part B.3 of this chapter. The General Assembly also took up the cybercrime issue in resolution 56/261, where in paragraph 5 it recommends action at national and international levels against high-technology and computer-related crime.[87] General Assembly resolutions 57/239 and 58/199 expand on these issues and speak of the creation of a global culture of cybersecurity and the need for the protection of critical information systems.[88] The UN Economic and Social Council (ECOSOC) has taken up this issue as well and has reviewed UN-wide activities in this area.[89] ECOSOC has provided guidance on cybercrime issues on several occasions. In its resolution 1999/23, it mandated research on national and international policy for the prevention and control of computer-related crime, and in resolution 2001/18 it took up the issue of the use of computer and telecommunication systems for international and national drug trafficking.[90] The issue of the use of ICT and criminal activities has been dealt with in detail in the report of the International Narcotics Control Board for 2001.[91]

More recently, the World Summit on the Information Society (WSIS), a high level UN initiative on the development of the information society, has specifically addressed information security issues in its Declaration of Principles and Plan of Action. Article 5 of the Declaration notes that building trust is the focus of information security and a prerequisite for the development of the information society. The Declaration affirms the need for building a global culture of cybersecurity, supported by increased international cooperation and taking into account the level of social and economic development of individual countries. The Plan of Action, in part C.5, details these notions and recommends addressing them through international cooperation, public-private sector partnerships, and activities focused on education and awareness building. Particular issues were singled out, such as privacy, spam, cybercrime law, development of best practice guidelines, establishment of response teams and the effects of information security on trade and commerce.[92]

In general, it may be fair to say that policy reactions to information security issues often initially address legal implications and act to adjust legislation to deal with cybercrime. As the issue matures, international policy discussions and cooperation will increasingly engage in technical issues, such as standards or specific technologies, and move on to more holistic notions of risk management and security cultures. Evidence of such processes is already surfacing today.

Council of Europe

The Council of Europe has been actively pursuing the information security theme since 1996. In 2001 its Committee of Ministers adopted the Convention on Cybercrime, an international treaty creating a cross-border "criminal policy aimed at the protection of society against cybercrime, *inter alia* by adopting appropriate legislation and fostering international cooperation."[93]

European Union

The European Union has addressed the issue from a legal perspective (for example through its electronic signatures directive and its data protection legislation). Under its eEurope 2005 action plan, the EU has also undertaken activities in fields such as network and information security and secure communications for e-government. The European Network and Information Security Agency (ENISA) was formally established in 2004 with the objective of supporting the development of a culture of network and information security.[94] ENISA will provide expertise on security-related issues in hardware and software products, security standards, interoperability, and risk assessment.[95]

OECD

The Organization for Economic Co-operation and Development (OECD) produced a primary set of information security recommendations in 1992 and reviewed them in 1997.[97] Given the vast increase in the global use of ICT resources, the OECD responded by re-establishing the guidelines in their present format and substance. The "Guidelines for the Security of Information Systems and Networks: Towards a Culture of Security" were formally adopted as a Recommendation of the OECD Council on 25 July 2002.[97] One obvious difference between the present guidelines and the 1992 version is the inclusion of networks. More importantly, the guidelines propose an overarching theme of promoting a culture of security and focus on nine core principles that can be seen to suggest and support a risk management approach to information security issues. This is most apparent in the principles dealing with risk assessment, risk response, security design and security management. However, the recommendations go beyond risk issues and point to the human principles of ethics

and democracy that can be foundational for understanding information security and its applications in modern society. The principles also address the role of the individual and comment on the need for awareness and skill development and the notion of responsibility. On a final note, the principles explain that information security is a continuous process where the reassessment of risks and the ongoing evolution of security systems is a permanent feature.

In launching the revised principles, the OECD Council made a number of policy recommendations to member countries that urged consultation, coordination and cooperation in dealing with information security issues, at both national and international levels. The Council further recommended the broadest dissemination of the Guidelines throughout public, private, government and civic organizations, and individual users, in member and non-member countries as well. A review schedule of five years has been established in order to address evolving concerns and to provide a forum for international cooperation and exchange of experience. The Guidelines were followed up by an implementation plan suggesting that Governments need to work the information security culture into their international cooperation policies and activities in order to achieve a global effect.[98] Legal cooperation to combat cybercrime was an immediate task. Supporting the establishment, work and cooperation of Computer Emergency Response Teams (CERTs) and developing closer cooperation between government and business was necessary as well. Outreach activities focusing on awareness-raising, education and exchange of experience were also highlighted as beneficiaries of government support. The plan also recognized that Governments are often owners and operators of information systems and networks, and that this presents an opportunity to lead by example and contribute to the development of best practice in information security.

In an effort to gauge implementation, the OECD conducted a survey (2004) on the implementation of the information security Guidelines. Member Governments gave the highest degree of attention to the development of a national policy framework and a legal environment, and to the implementation of the Guideline's principles, in particular those related to awareness building and response capacity. Strengthening cooperation and collaboration and fostering an exchange of practical experiences and best practices among participants, as well as with non-member economies, were declared priorities for future work.

APEC

Asia-Pacific Economic Cooperation (APEC) is a forum for facilitating economic growth, trade and investment in the Asia-Pacific region by cooperating on the basis of non-binding commitments, equality and open dialogue.[99] The APEC Telecommunications and Information Working Group is mandated to develop ICT policies and cooperation strategies on general issues, such as the transformation of the Asia-Pacific region into an information society and reducing the digital divide, as well the specific topics of protecting information and communications infrastructure and cybersecurity. The Fifth APEC Ministerial Meeting on Telecommunications and Information Industry, held in May 2002 in Shanghai, issued a specific statement on information security[100] and a programme of action,[101] which were followed up with the establishment of a cybersecurity strategy. The strategy recommends activities in six specific areas: legal issues and cooperation, information sharing, security and technical guidelines, public awareness, training and education, and wireless security. Promoting cooperation among local, national or regional CERTs was highlighted, and training activities have commenced through a project and a series of seminars on anti cybercrime legislation and capacity building.

G8

The Group of Eight evolves informal agreements on current issues, such as the effects of globalization or information security.[102] The first G8 multilateral meeting devoted to the protection of critical information infrastructures took place in March 2003.[103] This expert meeting was followed up by the G8 member States' Ministers of Justice and Home Affairs, together with the European Commissioner in charge of Justice and Home Affairs, who met in May 2003, in Paris, to engage in a policy discussion on more general security issues, such as terrorism and organized crime. The deliberations made particular reference to the protection of critical information infrastructures and, more specifically, to the use of biometric security technologies.

The G8 meetings stressed the importance and interdependence of critical information infrastructures, as well as the need to increase international cooperation to ensure their protection against potential terrorist attacks. The meetings resulted in a set of 11 internationally agreed principles for protecting critical information infrastructures that would serve as a foundation for further work in this area.[104] The principles noted that effective protection requires "...communication, coordination, and cooperation nationally and internationally among all stakeholders – industry, academia, the private sector, and government entities, including infrastructure protection and law enforcement agencies." They also define information security in terms of a process approximating a risk management approach, rather than an amalgamation of technologies. From the perspective of direct government involvement, the principles point to the need for countries to have early warning and crisis communications networks and bodies, as well as to the role of Governments in supporting awareness building and training. Biometric technologies and their use in travel procedures and documents received special mention and have progressed up the G8 agenda to the highest level in the form of the Secure and Facilitated International Travel Initiative.[105]

Professional initiatives

Practitioners of information security will certainly support international developments while developing less formal mechanisms for international cooperation. The main advantage of such bodies is their unhindered capacity for rapid reaction. Noted disadvantages are a possible lack of transparency of operations and the lack of legal enforcement of their agreements (ITU, 2002). Most will have government or government-funded institutions as their members, so the designation of "non-governmental" may not strictly apply. The Forum of Incident Response and Security Teams (FIRST) was established in 1989. The FIRST membership consists of computer emergency response teams from educational, commercial, vendor, government and military organizations.[106] FIRST describes its purpose as assisting an information technology community in preventing and handling security-related incidents by fostering cooperation and coordination in incident prevention, enabling rapid reaction to incidents and promoting a culture of information sharing among its community. The Computer Emergency Response Team Coordination Center (CERT/CC) was created by the United States Defense Advanced Research Projects Agency in November 1988 after the Morris worm struck. It is a multilateral initiative and coordination centre dealing with Internet security problems. CERT/CC is run by the United States government-funded Software Engineering Institute (SEI) at Carnegie Mellon

University. The Asia-Pacific Computer Emergency Response Team (APCERT) is a coalition of CERTs from 13 economies across the Asia-Pacific region.[107] APCERT has gained the formal support of Governments in the region and has been invited to participate and contribute at the intergovernmental forums of APEC. Latin American countries and CERTs are involved through the Inter-American Committee against Terrorism, which is hosting an initiative for the establishment of a framework for regional coordination among CSIRTs. The framework was adopted in June 2004.[108]

2. National policy

Governments have been intimately involved in defining, engineering and using information security technology from the earliest days. The requirements of diplomatic services and military organizations drove security technology development until the middle of the twentieth century. The change in the role of government from innovator to standard-bearer has only occurred recently and, as explained in part D, has been caused by the broad take-up of computer and Internet technology by firms, organizations and individuals. The decentralized nature of Internet computer networks and the development of intelligent applications that run on its periphery have led to an almost complete loss of direct control over technology users or the network itself.[109]

Governments will need to set policies while appreciating the notion that information security has become a part of the national critical infrastructure. The level of acceptance will vary from developed to developing and least developed countries, but there will rarely be outright rejection. Economic activities are becoming increasingly and strategically dependent on information technology, and therefore the importance of information security has become indisputable. Public sector functions, such as transport and utilities, as well as civil administration, are increasingly using technology to maintain or improve their quality of service and enrich their offerings.

In part B.4, the chapter discussed the problem of incentives. Governments will need to analyse how investment in information security is related to actually achieved security. Should the conclusion be that there is a general under-investment due to problems stemming from a tragedy of the commons or first-mover advantage and network externalities,

incentives may need to be adjusted through a combination of fiscal and regulatory policies.

Government policy and practice are often faced with tough decisions: sound policies may enhance security, while misconceived regulation may be detrimental (Sadowsky et al, 2003). Regulating and legislating is often seen as the natural course of action, and indeed adjustments to incorporate the notion of cybercrime in national legislation have for many Governments been a first practical and determined step in the right direction. This is discussed in chapter 6. However, just because some regulation is good does not mean that more is better, and Governments will need to balance regulating with encouraging innovation. Several regulatory initiatives were discussed in part E.2 of this chapter.

More broadly, in order to develop a national security policy, Governments may conduct a national information risk analysis, not dissimilar to what a firm or an organization would do. Awareness, education and capacity building for information security, within both administrative and other public bodies, schools, universities and training centers, as well as among the general public, can and should be a strategic activity. The promotion of information sharing on critical issues for information security through the establishment and support of national CERTs has become an established activity judging by the broad memberships of organizations such as FIRST or APCERT. The only part of the risk analysis process that may be given less prominence at a government policy level may be any prescription on particular types of applications and technologies, beyond the formulation of minimal standards and requirements. Technological neutrality may eventually be adjusted, with a preference for security technologies that support public standards or that have endured public scrutiny and testing.

While all developed and many developing countries have implemented policies supporting various types of information security activities, it may be doubly important to bring such activities into officialdom by embracing them within a broader national e-strategy framework. This will facilitate the involvement of all stakeholders in information society development. It will also support the notion of evolving information security into a risk management exercise, as the activities of risk assessment and avoidance will generate data and inputs on which to base actual policy actions targeting concrete problems and issues.

G. Concluding remarks

The widespread and growing use of information technology implies shared responsibilities among developed and developing countries, as well as among individuals, firms and Governments, for the threats and weaknesses it presents. The position of developing countries is not conceptually different from that of developed countries. As is indicated in chapter 6 on cybercrime, here too the common wisdom applies to all.

The objective of having in place an appropriate level of information security at all levels is complicated by a number of factors, several of which may be considered as the domain of government policy. Unlike other issues where government involvement is questioned, information security policy and practice are not fundamentally disputed, perhaps because of their strong links and history with national security. Another reason may be the strong realization that information technology, and therefore security, has become part of a nation's critical infrastructure much like physical security, certain utilities or an assured minimum standard of welfare.

Government policy

Trade, financial transactions, government administration and education are examples of activities that are increasingly dependent on technology infrastructures and therefore on information security. Globalization enables – or indeed compels – firms, organizations and individuals to explore opportunities for better business, to compete and to cooperate. Government policy needs to reflect these realities and is increasingly requested to provide leadership and foresight. The productive and intensive use of ICTs requires a high level of trust in the technologies and among its users. In this sense, the application of risk management to information security and the environment of trust it creates and supports is a foundational element for information economy development, and it follows that developing countries would need to support this notion within their e-strategy or digital development policies and practice.

Impact on the ICT service sector

Governments can investigate and assess the intensity and modes of use of security technologies and may regulate minimum general standards or specific guidelines for a particular sector or group, such as financial services or government suppliers. Voluntary self-regulation can also affect demand, as consumers request certification of a standard of quality of services before buying. Meeting increasing regulatory demands may provide additional incentives for the development of information security services in developed and developing countries as well – in particular in those countries that are active in business process outsourcing services. When judging business prospects, ICT and information security services firms may find focusing on trends in ICT purchases important but insufficient. Even though spending on information security is still a subset of the information technology market, security firms will need to monitor international and national regulatory developments and adjust their commercial expectations accordingly. In this sense, the information security industry is both a global and a local business. However, information security services may not be perfectly tradable from an international perspective as local provision may necessarily require locally relevant knowledge and production cost structures. Accordingly, an increasing demand for information security services may present an opportunity for local and national ICT service sector development, in particular in developing countries.

Risk management

Underlying these notions is a shift away from technology-centric treatment of information security and towards a risk management approach. Instead of reaching for a technical fix, risk management requires consideration of the problem and its context. Threats are evaluated, but so are the assets subject to compromise. Incentives and disincentives are analysed, and security policies, human resource development and legal instruments can be used to change their weight and influence on the intensity of applied security measures. The purpose of such an exercise would be to adjust the level of applied information security in order to bring it closer to a perceived or theoretical optimum. However, policy makers in developing countries may benefit from a better historical, social and economic understanding of the progress of information security technologies as, at second glance, many recent issues may not be fundamentally or technically novel. Given comparatively limited resources, developing countries need to make better strategic choices, and they may achieve this by using a risk management framework instead of a technology-centric and reactive approach.

Standards and regulations

The importance of standards and regulations is highlighted by the opportunities presented when firms in developed countries outsource particular business activities. Increasingly stringent regulation aims to, among other things, designate liabilities and fault in case of security compromises. The substantive engagement of the international community in providing security guidelines and addressing particular issues that may need policy consideration and action may offset the difficulties presented by such increased regulatory requirements. Opportunities for global sharing of security information and experience are increasingly accessible, and non-governmental forums are engaging in cooperation with established multilateral institutions.

The way ahead

In closing, it should be noted that developing countries may need to address several issues more specifically. The scope for building awareness may be larger than in developed countries, and government policy may reflect this by extending activities and support to all educational and training institutions. Furthermore, as developing countries have less infrastructure and fewer ICT assets to protect, incentives for applying information security may be significantly different given that the majority of the world's information resources and technologies are owned or managed by entities from developed countries. However, if information security is of global strategic concern, it can only be improved at an equally global level. This suggests that international technical and policy cooperation with developing countries should be encouraged and supported, in particular by the most technologically advanced countries, as there is only mutual benefit to be had. Export and outsourcing opportunities will in the future, if not already, depend on satisfying security regulations in the export destinations. Accordingly, undemanding regulation does not do any ICT exporter a favour – the regulations that apply are those of the importer, and exporting firms may need information and guidance on how to achieve compliance. Establishing an information security policy, preferably within the framework of an overall e-strategy where one exists, based on a risk management approach and regulating an appropriate set of incentives for its use, can provide important support for the development of information security practice.

Annex I

A simplified mathematical illustration of the Diffie-Hellman key exchange

This example owes much to the wisdom of simplification presented in Khan (2000). The actual mathematics use much larger numbers. The purpose of the key exchange process is to allow Alice and Bob to each, on their own and in secrecy, establish the identical secret key without revealing any information about it. Mathematically minded readers are encouraged to explore the process through a referential text such as Schneier (1996).

Step 1	Alice and Bob decide to use the one-way modular function Y^X (Mod P where "mod P" (or modulo P) means calculate the whole number remainder of Y^X divided by P. For example, if $Y^X = 6^2$ = 36, and P = 7, Y^X(mod P) would be the remainder of 36÷7, or 36 minus 35 (which is 7 x 5), which equals 1. However, if someone gave away the result, i.e. 1, and asked to have the equation reversed to find out Y^X and therefore X, even with knowing that P = 7, it would be time consuming to do this. If Y and P are sufficiently large, the exercise becomes unfeasible.
Step 2	In step 2 Alice and Bob will agree on the values for Y and P. Let us assume they have chosen Y = 7 and P = 13. These numbers are not secret.
Step 3	In step 3, Alice and Bob will choose each, in secret, their own values for "X", which are now referred to as A and B Alice chooses A = 5. Bob chooses B = 8.
Step 4	In step 4, Alice and Bob will apply the pre-agreed modular function to their choice of "X". Y^X(mod P) = Y^A(mod P) Y^X(mod P) = Y^B(mod P) 7^5(mod 13) = 16,807(mod 13) = 11 7^8 (mod 13) = 5,764,801(mod 13) = 3 We will call 11 "a". We will call 3 "b".
Step 5	In step 5 Alice and Bob will swap a and b. They can do this over a public communications network without any worry. Eve the eavesdropper may intercept a and b, but will find it very difficult, if not unfeasible, to reverse the calculation to get A and B. Therefore, Alice and Bob can use an unsecured Internet connection or telephone line for swapping a and b.
Step 6	In step 6, Alice and Bob will use each other's b and a instead of the original Y they had agreed upon. b^A (mod P) a^B (mod P) 3^5(mod 13) = 243(mod 13) = **9** 11^8(mod 13) = 214,358,881(mod 13) = **9** The reason being that $(Y^B$(mod P)$)^A = (Y^A$(mod P)$)^B$; Y^{BA}(mod P) = Y^{BA}(mod P) or $b^A = a^B$.
Step 7	In the final step 7, having agreed the secret key is **9**, Alice and Bob will establish an encrypted communication based on this key.

References

Adams C and Lloyd S (2003). *Understanding PKI: Concepts, standards and deployment considerations*, Addison-Wesley Professional, Second edition.

Anderson R (2001). Why information security is hard - An economic perspective, paper presented at the 17th Annual Computer Security Applications Conference, 10-14 December, New Orleans, Louisiana.
http://www.ftp.cl.cam.ac.uk/ftp/users/rja14/econ.pdf

Anderson R (2002). Security in open versus closed systems - The dance of Boltzman, Coase and Moore, paper presented at the Conference on Open Source Software: Economics, Law and Policy, 20-21 June 2002, Institut d'Economie Industrielle, Toulouse, France.
http://www.ftp.cl.cam.ac.uk/ftp/users/rja14/toulouse.pdf

APEC (2002). Shanghai Declaration, Program of Action, Statement on the Security of Information and Communications Infrastructures, Fifth APEC Ministerial Meeting on Telecommunications and Information Industry, TELMIN5/1.
http://203.127.220.112/content/apec/ministerial_statements/sectoral_ministerial/telecommunications/2002.downloadlinks.0001.LinkURL.Download.ver5.1.9

Atkins D, Graff M, Lenstra AK and Leyland PC (1995). The magic words are squeamish ossifrage, *Advances in Cryptology - Asiacrypt '94*, Springer-Verlag, 263-277.
http://www.mit.edu:8001/people/warlord/rsa129.ps

Belrose J S (2001). A radioscientist's reaction to Marconi's first transatlantic wireless experiment, Antennas & Propagation Society International Symposium, Boston, 8-13 July 2001.

Böhme R (2005). Cyber-Insurance Revisited, paper presented at the 2005 Workshop on the Economics of Information Security.
http://infosecon.net/workshop/pdf/15.pdf

Cashell B, Jackson WD, Jickling M and Webel B (2004). The Economic Impact of Cyber-Attacks, Congressional Research Service, Report for the Congress, The Library of Congress, Order Code RL32331.
http://www.cisco.com/warp/public/779/govtaffairs/images/CRS_Cyber_Attacks.pdf

Cilek P, Janko W, Koch K, Mild A and Taudes A (2001). The evaluation of IT-investments in public sector organisations, Proceedings of the 8th European Conference on IT Evaluation, Oxford, UK.
http://wwwai.wu-wien.ac.at/~koch/forschung/bpr/ecite01.pdf

Diffie W (1988). The first ten years of public-key cryptography, Proceedings of the IEEE, Vol. 76, No. 5.
http://cr.yp.to/bib/1988/diffie.pdf

Diffie W (2003). Risky business: Keeping security a secret, ZDNet.
http://news.zdnet.com/2100-9595_22-980938.html

Diffie W and Hellman ME (1976). New directions in cryptography, Institute of Electrical and Electronics Engineers, Transactions on Information Theory.
http://crypto.csail.mit.edu/classes/6.857/papers/diffie-hellman.pdf

ECOSOC (2002). Effective measures to prevent and control computer-related crime: Report of the Secretary-General, E/CN.15/2002/8.
http://www.unodc.org/pdf/crime/commissions/11comm/8e.pdf

Ford W and Baum MS (2000). *Secure electronic commerce*, Prentice Hall PTR, Second edition.

G8 (2003). G8 Principles for Protecting Critical Information Infrastructures.
http://www.usdoj.gov/ag/events/g82004/G8_CIIP_Principles.pdf

Good J, Michie D and Timms G (1945, declassified in 2000). General Report on Tunny, National Archives of the United Kingdom, HW 25/4 and HW 25/5.
http://www.alanturing.net/turing_archive/archive/index/tunnyreportindex.html

Gutmann P (2002). PKI: It's not dead, just resting, IEEE Computer Society, August edition.
http://www.cs.auckland.ac.nz/~pgut001/pubs/notdead.pdf

ICLR (2004). Cyber-incident risk in Canada and the role of insurance, Institute for Catastrophic Loss Reduction, Research paper series - No.38.
http://www.iclr.org/pdf/Cyber-Incident%20Risk%20Final%20Report_April%202004.pdf

ITU (2002). International coordination to increase the security of critical network infrastructures, International Telecommunication Union, CNI/04.
http://www.itu.int/osg/spu/ni/security/docs/cni.04.pdf

Kesan JP, Majuca RP and Yurcik WJ (2004). The economic case for cyberinsurance, University of Illinois College of Law, Law and Economics Working Papers.
http://law.bepress.com/cgi/viewcontent.cgi?article=1001&context=uiuclwps

Khan D (1996). The codebreakers : The comprehensive history of secret communication from ancient times to the Internet, Scribner, Revised edition.

Killcrece G (2004). Steps for Creating National CSIRTs, Software Engineering Institute, Carnegie Mellon University.
http://www.cert.org/archive/pdf/NationalCSIRTs.pdf

Menezes A, van Oorschot P and Vanstone S (1997). Handbook of Applied Cryptography, CRC Press.
http://www.cacr.math.uwaterloo.ca/hac/

Nathan PX and Erwin MW (2004). On the rules of engagement for information warfare, Symbiot, Inc.
http://www.whurley.com/pdfs/iwROE.pdf

OECD (2002). OECD Guidelines for the security of information systems and networks, OECD Publications.
http://www.oecd.org/dataoecd/16/22/15582260.pdf

OECD (2003). Implementation plan for the OECD guidelines for the security of information systems and networks: Towards a culture of security, OECD Publications, DSTI/ICCP/REG(2003)5/REV1.
hhttp://www.oecd.org/dataoecd/23/11/31670189.pdf

Outreville JF (1997). Theory and Practice of Insurance, Springer, first edition.

Perens B (1998). Why security-through-obscurity won't work, Slashdot.
http://slashdot.org/features/980720/0819202.shtml

Rivest R, Shamir A and Adleman LM (1977), (1978). A Method for Obtaining Digital Signatures and Public-Key Cryptosystems, Communications of the ACM 21,2, 1978.
First published in 1977 as MIT Memo MIT/LCS/TM-82.
http://theory.lcs.mit.edu/~rivest/rsapaper.pdf

Sadowsky G, Dempsey JX, Greenberg A, Mack B and Schwartz A (2003). Information Technology Security Handbook, The International Bank for Reconstruction and Development, Washington, DC.
http://www.infodev-security.net/handbook/

Schneier B (1996). Applied cryptography, Wiley Publishing, Inc., Indianapolis, Second edition.

Schneier B (2000). Secrets and lies: Digital security in a networked world, Wiley Publishing, Inc., Indianapolis.

Siegel CA, Sagalow TR and Serritella P (2002). Cyber-risk management: Technical and insurance controls for enterprise-level security, CRC Press.
http://www.aignetadvantage.com/content/netad/CyberRisk_Article_043002.pdf

Singh S (2000). The code book: The science of secrecy from ancient Egypt to quantum cryptography, Anchor Books, New York.

Surendran K (2005). Information security: Nurturing a security conscious workforce, Knowledge Platform White Paper.
http://www.knowledgeplatform.com/presentation/information_security.html

Sveiby KE (2004). Methods for Measuring Intangible Assets, Sveiby Knowledge Associates.
http://www.sveiby.com/articles/IntangibleMethods.htm

UNCTAD (2001). E-Commerce and Development Report 2001, United Nations Publications.
http://r0.unctad.org/ecommerce/docs/edr01_en.htm

UNCTAD (2002). E-Commerce and Development Report 2002, United Nations Publications.
http://r0.unctad.org/ecommerce/ecommerce_en/edr02_en.htm

UNCTAD (2003). E-Commerce and Development Report 2003, United Nations Publications.
http://r0.unctad.org/ecommerce/ecommerce_en/edr03_en.htm

UNCTAD (2004). E-Commerce and Development Report 2004, United Nations Publications.
http://r0.unctad.org/ecommerce/ecommerce_en/edr04_en.htm

United States General Accounting Office (2004). Information security, Technologies to secure federal systems, GAO-04-467.

Varian H R (2000). Managing Online Security Risks. The New York Times. 1 June.
http://www.nytimes.com/library/financial/columns/060100econ-scene.html

Vaughan E, Vaughan TM (2002), Fundamentals of Risk and Insurance, Wiley, New Jersey, 9th edition.

Wheeler DA (2003). Secure Programming for Linux and Unix HOWTO.
http://www.dwheeler.com/secure-programs/Secure-Programs-HOWTO/index.html

Williamson LC (2001). A discussion of the importance of key length in symmetric ad asymmetric cryptography, SANS Institute, GIAC Practical Repository.
http://www.giac.org/certified_professionals/practicals/gsec/0848.php

Wilson RMS, Stenson J and Oppenheim C (2000). Valuation of Information Assets, The Business School of Loughborough University, Research Series Paper 2000:2.
http://www.lboro.ac.uk/departments/bs/research/2000-2.pdf

Zwicky EDtt, Cooper S and Bren Chapman D (2000). Building Internet firewalls, O'Reilly, Second edition.
http://www.oreilly.com/catalog/fire2/
http://www.hn.edu.cn/book/NetWork/NetworkingBookshelf_2ndEd/fire/index.htm

Notes

1.   This definition has been attributed to George McDaniel and his text IBM Dictionary of Computing (1994). See http://www.sei.cmu.edu/str/indexes/glossary/information-security.html.

2.   UNCTAD (2003) presented an initial discussion of information security issues in its first chapter. It noted that, while technology can help reduce information security risks, the key to a secure online environment is not technical, but a combination of market efficiency, industry initiatives, political will and an appropriate legal environment.

3.   See part F.1 for more details on international policy cooperation.

4.   We will often permanently monitor our trust level during the exchange as we continue to judge the sincerity and intent of the other conversant by reading, sometimes unconsciously, body language or speech mannerisms.

5.   The privacy of spoken discussion can range from an interview for public or news media or an exchange of views at a conference, to a business meeting among negotiating teams or an intimate consultation with a medical expert.

6.   See http://www.unhchr.ch/udhr/lang/eng.htm .

7.   See http://www.un.org/Depts/dhl/resguide/r55.htm and http://www.un.org/Depts/dhl/resguide/r56.htm .

8.   See http://www.nta-monitor.com/fact-set.htm .

9.   Zombie computers are computers that have had malicious software installed, without the knowledge of their users. This software allows malicious hackers to use them to launch massive and coordinated attacks against websites or a firm's computer infrastructure.

10.   The tragedy of the commons is a metaphor used to illustrate the conflict between individual and community interests that can often result in the overexploitation of a public good or service.

11.   For an example of the limited liability of a common software license, see http://www.microsoft.com/windowsxp/home/eula.mspx.

12.   Freedonia, Information Security, Study #1761, February 2004; Silicon.com, IDC: Companies must spend more on security, 28 April 2004, http://software.silicon.com/security/0,39024655,39120310,00.htm .

13.   Estimates are from Cashell (2004) citing reports from Computer Economics Inc. and Mi2g. The quoted figures do not include damage caused by spam.

14.   Computerworld, "The new information security market puts the old in the rearview", 6 December 2002, http://www.computerworld.com/ .

15.   A VPN is a private communications network superimposed over a public network (e.g. the Internet). VPNs use cryptographic tools to provide confidentiality and authentication and to prevent message alteration, thus achieving a desired level of privacy over an unsecured network.

16.   The firms were chosen by observing the competitors' listings for each, on the Yahoo Finance and Hoover's company information websites. As such, they are only examples illustrating the breadth, scope and diversity of the security information sector.

17.   See http://www.europki.org/, http://www.dartmouth.edu/~pkilab/ and http://middleware.internet2.edu/pkilabs/.

18.   See http://www.ossim.net/, http://www.openca.org/ , http://cacert.org and http://smartsign.sourceforge.net/ .

19.   See http://news.com.com/2102-7350-3-5624251.html

20.   Monoalpahbetic means that the equivalent "code" letter or symbol does not change throughout the message.

21.   While there are many definitions for infrastructure, here we will be using the term to distinguish it from point-to-point systems set up privately by entities that have an established level of mutual trust. In this sense, drawing a dedicated wire between two localities is not infrastructure.

22. Tesla, Edison and others had explored wireless telegraphy in the 1860s. Marconi started experimenting with radio signals in 1894. By 1896 he could send and receive signals over distances of several kilometers and was awarded a patent that same year. In 1902 Marconi claimed to have radio-telegraphed the letter "S" in Morse code across the Atlantic Ocean from England to Newfoundland, an event that kick-started the race in global wireless communications. Given the relative lack of sophistication of the equipment used, doubts have been expressed over what was actually transmitted and the possibility of misinterpreting noise for a signal (Belrose, 2001).

23. Polyalphabetic cyphers were proposed by the Florentine architect Alberti and developed into a practicable system in the sixteenth century by the French diplomat and cryptologist Vigenère.

24. Bletchley Park (BP) was the site of a secret British military intelligence operation during and just before World War II. The site was named after the mansion in the grounds of which it was established.

25. Many cryptographic rotor machines were used until the 1980s. Besides the Enigma and Lorenz machines, the original Hebern machine from 1918 (United States), the Fialka (Soviet Union), the HX-63 and NEMA (Switzerland), the Hagelin M-209, SIGABA and KL7/Adonis (United States) and the Typex (United Kingdom) are well known.

26. Standards have been commissioned and designed more recently by other organizations and entities, for example the Gosudarstvennyi Standard GOST 28147-89 (Soviet Union – see http://ietfreport.isoc.org/ids-wg-smime.html), NESSIE - New European Schemes for Signatures, Integrity and Encryption (European Commission, see https://www.cosic.esat.kuleuven.ac.be/nessie/) or CRYPTREC - Cryptography Research and Evaluation Committee (Japan, see http://www.ipa.go.jp/security/enc/CRYPTREC/).

27. See http://csrc.nist.gov/cryptval/des.htm .

28. See http://www.mediacrypt.com/ .

29. See http://www.csrc.nist.gov/publications/fips/fips197/fips-197.pdf .

30. Recent studies confirm this notion, and the European Commission's *"Report on the existence of a global system for the interception of private and commercial communications (ECHELON interception system)"* (2001) can be singled out as being particularly comprehensive. See http://www.europarl.eu.int/tempcom/echelon/pdf/rapport_echelon_en.pdf or http://webdomino1.oecd.org/COMNET/STI/IccpSecu.nsf .

31. See http://crypto.csail.mit.edu/classes/6.857/papers/diffie-hellman.pdf . See also http://patft.uspto.gov/netahtml/srchnum.htm and search for patent number 4,200,770. There have been suggestions that a comprehensive public key system was developed by Cocks, Ellis, and Williamson before 1975 while working for the British Government Communications Headquarters. See http://www.nytimes.com/library/cyber/week/122497encrypt.html#1 and http://www.cesg.gov.uk/site/ast/index.cfm?menuSelected=3&displayPage=31 .

32. See Rivest, Shamir and Adleman (1977)

33. The more precise definition of a prime number is a positive integer (1, 2, 3, 4, ...) whose only positive integer divisors are 1 and itself.

34. See http://mathworld.wolfram.com/RSANumber.html .

35. See http://www.rsasecurity.com/rsalabs/node.asp?id=2093 .

36. A discovery of a method for factoring large prime numbers would break certain asymmetric systems, regardless of their key length.

37. For a discussion on why asymmetric keys need to be longer than symmetric keys, see Williams (2000).

38. "Broken" would mean that a method has been found to reverse the hash value back into the message in less time than it would take a theoretical brute-force computational attack. A hash function would also be considered broken if it could be demonstrated that two different messages would produce an identical hash value. The reported attacks on SHA-1 are described as working on a subset of SHA-1 keys and under specific circumstances. Therefore, SHA-1 and derivative technologies are still considered to be secure at the time of writing. See http://www.schneier.com/blog/archives/2005/02/sha1_broken.html and http://www.schneier.com/blog/archives/2005/02/cryptanalysis_o.html .

39. Unlike telephony, where a dedicated connection is established and reserved for those speaking, data travels on the Internet in a multitude of independent data packets. The sender's computer will take a file and divide it into many packets and each will receive an indication of origin, destination and reassembly instructions. These will travel through the Internet and sometimes will use different routes to reach the recipient computer, where they will be reassembled and presented in an application such as a browser. If the packets are encrypted to disallow access to a third party intercepting and lodging copies of the data packets, this creates a virtual private network (VPN) within, or on top of,

the Internet. Unlike telephony, this does not require any change in the Internet communications protocols and standards, nor does it require sequestering bandwidth or infrastructure. VPNs are powered by applications that sit on the computers of those communicating without affecting the underlying Internet.

40. See http://www.nullify.org/docs/elgamal.pdf .

41. For more details, see and http://www.itl.nist.gov/fipspubs/fip186.htm .

42. The original discussions on elliptic curve cryptography were presented in Koblitz (1987) "Elliptic curve cryptosystems" in Mathematics of Computation 48; and Miller (1985) "Use of elliptic curves in cryptography" in CRYPTO 85.

43. For a list of Certicom patents on elliptic curve cryptography, see their letter to the Standards for Efficient Cryptography Group (SECG) at http://www.secg.org/download/aid-398/certicom_patent_letter_SECG.pdf and SECG's commentary on patent issues at http://www.secg.org/?action=secg,about_patents .

44. See Certicom, *Code & Cipher,* Vol.2, No.1, http://www.certicom.com/download/aid-391/codeandcipher2-1.pdf .

45. See http://www.imlogic.com/news/press_107.asp .

46. See http://news.bbc.co.uk/2/hi/technology/4354109.stm .

47. See http://www.vnunet.com/news/1160924 .

48. This definition is often attributed to the American Risk and Insurance Association. Outreville (1997) provides an excellent overview of various definitions of risk.

49. Hedonic demand theory is a method of estimating demand or prices and can be used to assess information technology investments in non-profit or public organizations. An obvious effect of new information technology would be a change in the pattern of use of human resources from lower value to higher value functions, with a corresponding change in the overall wage-per-function structure of the organization. By classifying employee types and functions and assuming wages weightings for each employee type-function combination, "before" and "after" new technologies scenarios can be compared and the difference understood as the creation of an intangible technology asset.

50. For more details see http://www.willis.com/Services/Risk%20Management%20Operational/Operational.aspx .

51. See "Managing Reputation - an Holistic Approach" in AON Dimensions: Corporate Governance Special at http://www.aon.com/about/publications/pdf/dimensions/dimensions_1002.pdf .

52. A more conventional definition is that catastrophic risks are infrequent events that cause severe loss, injury or property damage and affect a large population of exposures.

53. For more details consult CyberSource, 6th Annual Online Fraud Report, at http://www.cybersource.com/fraudreport.

54. See http://www.verisign.com/static/030910.pdf .

55. See the full report of the APWG at http://antiphishing.org/APWG_Phishing_Activity_Report_Feb05.pdf .

56. For more detail and various analyses of the power crisis in California, see http://business.baylor.edu/Tom_Kelly/California%20Power.htm as well as the CNN brief at http://www.cnn.com/SPECIALS/2001/power.crisis/backgrounder.html .

57. For reports and examples see: http://www.itweek.co.uk/news/1162306 , http://www.itweek.co.uk/news/1160555 and http://www.winneronline.com/articles/april2004/distributed-denial-of-service-attacks-no-joke.htm .

58. For examples of vulnerability tracking and reports, see http://secunia.com/ , http://www.frsirt.com/ , http://www.us-cert.gov/ or http://www.niscc.gov.uk/niscc/index-en.html . It is sometimes ironically noted that software vulnerabilities, exploits and bugs are in fact "undocumented features".

59. If we define PKI from the perspective of what it does, we can say that it is an infrastructure that creates public key certificates, provides a certificate repository, provides for certificate revocation, maintains a key back-up and recovery facility, provides support for non-repudiation of digital signatures, automatically updates key pairs and certificates, provides management of key histories, provides support for cross-certification with other PKIs, and ensures that client software properly supports the public key functionalities in a secure, consistent and trustworthy manner. UNCTAD (2001) provides an overview of the functioning of PKI in its chapter 6, on managing payment and credit risks online. For a more detailed description, see http://www.entrust.com/resources/docs/pki.htm .

60. An approachable overview of various PKI architectures and their suitability for use by the New Zealand Government can be found at: http://e.govt.nz/docs/see-pki-paper-4/chapter3.html .

61. For a critical commentary on PKI technologies and implementations, see http://www.schneier.com/paper-pki-ft.txt or http://infosecuritymag.techtarget.com/articles/october01/columns_logoff.shtml .

62. For an interesting discussion on the argument for and against FOSS and proprietary software from a security perspective, see http://www.dwheeler.com/secure-programs/Secure-Programs-HOWTO/open-source-security.html .

63. For an example of opposing views on the issue, one can consult the papers "Is Linux more secure than Windows?" at http://www.microsoft.com/windowsserversystem/facts/analyses/vulnerable.mspx and "Windows v Linux security: The real facts" at http://www.theregister.co.uk/2004/10/22/linux_v_windows_security/ .

64. Some examples are the 1996 WIPO Copyright Treaty (Article 11), the European Copyright Directive (Article 6(1)) or the Unites States Digital Millennium Copyright Act (Section 1201). In general, legislation is formulated to deter the circumvention of so-called digital rights technologies that content owners use with the aim of reducing the scope of use. Examples of this would be that a legally downloaded music file will only play on specified computers or will be copied a limited number of times.

65. The ITU website has a comprehensive explanation of its standards at http://www.itu.int/rec/recommendation.asp?type=products&lang=e&parent=T-REC-X .

66. Examples of other types of self-regulation, often called "control frameworks", would be COBIT (http://www.isaca.org/template.cfm?Section=COBIT6 , FFIEC (http://www.ffiec.gov/ and NIST SP 800 (http://csrc.nist.gov/publications/nistpubs/ . Their application may enable firms and organizations to achieve regulatory compliance.

67. For more information see http://csrc.nist.gov/publications/secpubs/otherpubs/reviso-faq.pdf .

68. For more information, see http://www.commoncriteriaportal.org/public/files/ccintroduction.pdf .

69. The original signatories were the United States, Canada, France and Germany.

70. To form GAISP, the ISSA merged its predecessor, the Generally Accepted System Security Principles, with a related initiative, the Commonly Accepted Security Practices and Recommendations. For more details, see the GAISP Project Overview at http://www.issa.org/gaisp/_pdfs/overview.pdf .

71. For example, the United States Federal Information Security Management Act affects all federal Government resources, and thus the range of improvements in everyday practice is surveyed across all federal agencies, rather than just those that have volunteered or have had success, and in this way provides a healthy level of transparency of governance. See http://reform.house.gov/GovReform/News/DocumentSingle.aspx?DocumentID=22247 .

72. UNCTAD (2003) includes an extensive discussion of the outsourcing phenomenon in its chapter 5: Business process outsourcing service for economic development.

73. There are other relevant regulations in the United States that should be reviewed by ICT service providers and exporters of outsourcing services. These would include the Gramm-Leach-Bliley Act, whose main purpose was to repealed the Glass-Steagall Act in order to open up competition among banks, securities companies and insurance companies and which has impacted financial institutions though added responsibilities for the protection of customers' non-public personal information, and the Health Insurance Portability and Accountability Act, which aims to increase the transfer of health care information from one insurer or provider to the next and which required the development of privacy regulations to protect the confidentiality of individually identifiable health care information. For more details, see http://www.ftc.gov/privacy/glbact/glbsub1.htm and http://www.legalarchiver.org/hipaa.htm .

74. Paragraph 4 of the full text of the framework available at http://www.bis.org/publ/bcbs107.pdf .

75. See paragraph 644 of the full text of the framework available at http://www.bis.org/publ/bcbs107.pdf .

76. For a detailed discussion of information security implications of Basel II see Bruce Moulton, "Basel II: Operational Risk and Information Security" at http://ses.symantec.com/Industry/Regulations/article.cfm?articleid=3270 &EID=0

77. See United States Bill H.R.2458 on the management and promotion of electronic government services, SEC. 301. Information Security, § 3544. Federal agency responsibilities, at http://csrc.nist.gov/policies/FISMA-final.pdf .

78. See http://www.sarbanes-oxley-forum.com/modules.php?name=Surveys&op=results&pollID=1 . If anything, the survey should have a positive bias, as only business with intent to implement SOx would visit the forum and vote at the poll.

79. For more details, see http://www.sas70.com/about.htm .

80. For more details, see http://searchcio.techtarget.com/originalContent/0,289142,sid19_gci963032,00.html

81. For more details, see http://www.csoonline.com/analyst/report3172.html or http://magazine.digitalidworld.com/Sep04/Page46.pdf .

82. Regular patching and virus database updates are among the simplest of such measures.

83. See Surendran K (2005).

84. See the Internet Engineering Task Force best practice paper on CRIST at htp://www.ietf.org/rfc/rfc2350.txt .

85. Killcrece (2004) provides a useful description of the necessary steps in creating a national CSIRT.

86. From a process point of view, risk retention may precede the risk-transfer/insurance phase. Many firms may first explore what they can retain and then seek insurance cover for risks they cannot keep.

87. See General Assembly resolution 56/261 (A/RES/56/261) http://daccessdds.un.org/doc/UNDOC/GEN/N01/497/54/PDF/N0149754.pdf .

88. See http://www.un.org/Depts/dhl/resguide/r57.htm and http://www.un.orgDepts/dhl/resguide/r58.htm .

89. See ECOSOC (2002).

90. See ECOSOC resolution 1999/23 (E/1999/INF/2/Add.2) at http://www.un.org/documents/ecosoc/docs/1999/e1999-inf2-add2.pdf , and resolution 2001/18 on the implementation of the computer and telecommunication system for international and national drug control (40th plenary meeting, 24 July 2001) at http://www.un.org/docs/ecosoc/documents.asp?id=144 .

91. See chapter 1 of the INCB annual report for 2001, "Globalization and new technologies: challenges to drug law enforcement in the twenty first century", at http://www.incb.org/incb/annual_report_2001.html.

92. See http://www.itu.int/wsis/docs/geneva/official/dop.html and http://www.itu.int/wsis/docs/geneva/official/poa.html for the text of the WSIS Declaration of principles and Plan of action.

93. From the Preamble of the Convention on Cybercrime at http://conventions.coe.int/Treaty/en/Treaties/Html/185.htm. As of 28 June 2005, 11 countries had ratified the Convention, and an updated list is available at: http://conventions.coe.int/Treaty/Commun/ChercheSig.asp?NT=185&CM=1&DF=&CL=ENG .

94. For more details, see the dedicated ENISA website http://www.enisa.eu.int and the Regulation (EC) No 460/2004 of establishment at http://europa.eu.int/eur-lex/pri/en/oj/dat/2004/l_077/l_07720040313en00010011.pdf .

95. More information on the European Commission's work on security issues can be found at their dedicated website http://europa.eu.int/information_society/eeurope/2005/all_about/security/index_en.htm and in the document "Proposal for a regulation of the European Parliament and of the Council establishing the European Network and Information Security Agency " (2003) (COM(2003) 63 final).

96. For the original 1992 text of the OECD Guidelines for the Security of Information, see http://www.oecd.org/document/19/0,2340,fr_2649_201185_1815059_1_1_1_1,00.html .

97. The full text of the OECD Guidelines on information security is available at: http://www.oecd.org/dataoecd/16/22/15582260.pdf .

98. The full text of the OECD implementation plan for the OECD guidelines for the security of information systems and networks: Towards a culture of security (2003) is available at: http://www.oecd.org/dataoecd/23/11/31670189.pdf .

99. See http://www.apec.org/apec/about_apec.html .

100. See http://webapps.apec.org/content/apec/ministerial_statements/sectoral_ministerial/telecommunications/2002.downloadlinks.0001.LinkURL.Download.ver5.1.9 .

101. See http://www.apectelwg.org/admin/document/documents/telmin5sub021.htm .

102.   See http://www.g8.gov.uk/servlet/Front?pagename=OpenMarket/Xcelerate/ShowPage&c=Page&cid= 1078995913300 .

103.   See http://www.g8.utoronto.ca/summit/2003evian/press_statement_march24_2003.html .

104.   The conclusions are available at http://www.usdoj.gov/ag/events/g82004/G8_CIIP_Principles.pdf .

105.   See http://www.fco.gov.uk/Files/kfile/Art%2013%20SAFTI,0.pdf . During the expert consultations in 2003, establishing standards for biometric technologies was considered of particular importance in order to achieve interoperability and ensure their technical reliability and fast progress in implementation.

106.   A list of members is available at http://www.first.org/about/organization/teams/index.html .

107.   A list of members is available at http://www.apcert.org/member.html .

108.   See "Adoption of a comprehensive inter-American strategy to combat threats to cybersecurity: A multidimensional and multidisciplinary approach to creating a culture of cybersecurity", at http://www.cicte.oas.org/Docs/ CyberSecurityConference/Cyber%20Strategy-English.doc for the

109.   Telephone and radio technologies have not have the same effect as the Internet because in both cases the infrastructures have a high level of centralized control and centralized intelligence. From a security perspective, this allows direct control and solutions and facilitates implementing information security processes and technologies – something the Internet does not do.

Chapter 6

PROTECTING THE INFORMATION SOCIETY: ADDRESSING THE PHENOMENON OF CYBERCRIME

A. Introduction

As developing countries embrace, exploit and integrate computer and communications systems at an economic and social level, concerns arise about the vulnerability of such systems to deliberate attack. An attack may target the data being processed by systems, or the integrity, confidentiality and availability of the systems themselves. Most users, for example, will have experienced and suffered from viruses infecting and corrupting their data and the operation of their systems. However, where such attacks are targeted at, or inadvertently impact on, a country's critical national infrastructure, such as power systems or transportation networks, the consequences may be significant and cause substantial damage.

Protecting systems from attacks via the Internet obviously relies primarily on the implementation of appropriate technical, physical and operational security measures. It must therefore be the concern of policymakers that users, whether public sector or private sector, implement such security measures to protect their data and systems. However, a parallel requirement for appropriate security is the establishment of a legal framework that deters such attacks by criminalizing the different forms of activities being carried out against systems and enabling law enforcement agencies to adequately investigate and prosecute such activities.

This chapter examines why countries, and in particular developing countries, need to address the threat of cybercrime and what measures need to be taken to ensure that an adequate legal framework is put in place. In the first section, the phenomenon of cybercrime will be examined in its many manifestations, together with its prevalence and economic cost, particularly for developing nations. In the second section, consideration will be given to the appropriate criminalization of particular types of acts.

Cybercrime can generally be classified into three broad categories: computer-related, content-related and computer integrity offences. Each category raises unique issues, and addressing all forms of cybercrime will generally require amendment of the current criminal code, as well as the adoption of *sui generis* offences.

However, reforming the criminal code is only one step towards the effective legal treatment of cybercrime. Law enforcement agencies also require the necessary powers, expertise and resources to be able to tackle instances of cybercrime. The third section of this chapter will examine what procedural law reforms are needed to adequately equip law enforcement agencies to investigate cybercrime.

Cybercrime is often international in nature, occurring across boundaries and impacting on users in different countries. Developing countries will obviously be both victims and the source of cybercrime. As noted at the Eleventh United Nations Congress on Crime Prevention and Criminal Justice, in April 2005, developing countries "have become staging grounds for attacks by cyber criminals" on developed countries, due to the greater prevalence of unprotected systems.[1] To address this interrelated vulnerability, greater harmonization evolves between jurisdictions in order to be able to effectively prevent criminal activities, as well as pursue perpetrators. In recent years, there have been a number of initiatives at the intergovernmental level, including the United Nations, the Council of Europe, the G8 and the Commonwealth. These will be used as a benchmark to consider the needs of developing countries.

While examining the threat of cybercrime and suggesting means of combating it, the chapter will keep its focus on issues addressed in the recommendations of United Nations General Assembly Resolution 55/63 (see excerpts from the resolution in box 6.1).

Box 6.1

United Nations General Assembly Resolution 55/63, Combating the criminal misuse of information technologies

(January 2001)

"...notes the value of, inter alia, the following measures to combat such misuse:

(a) States should ensure that their laws and practice eliminate safe havens for those who criminally misuse information technologies;

(b) Law enforcement cooperation in the investigation and prosecution of international cases of criminal misuse of information technologies should be coordinated among all concerned States;

(c) Information should be exchanged between States regarding the problems that they face in combating the criminal misuse of information technologies;

(d) Law enforcement personnel should be trained and equipped to address the criminal misuse of information technologies;

(e) Legal systems should protect the confidentiality, integrity and availability of data and computer systems from unauthorized impairment and ensure that criminal abuse is penalized;

(f) Legal systems should permit the preservation of and quick access to electronic data pertaining to particular criminal investigations;

(g) Mutual assistance regimes should ensure the timely investigation of the criminal misuse of information technologies and the timely gathering and exchange of evidence in such cases;

(h) The general public should be made aware of the need to prevent and combat the criminal misuse of information technologies;

(i) To the extent practicable, information technologies should be designed to help to prevent and detect criminal misuse, trace criminals and collect evidence;

(j) The fight against the criminal misuse of information technologies requires the development of solutions taking into account both the protection of individual freedoms and privacy and the preservation of the capacity of Governments to fight such criminal misuse;"

B.   Addressing the phenomenon

As Gibson's notional "Internet"[2] has materialized as the "network of networks" that constitutes the Internet and the communication and content services made available over it, so there has been an inevitable growth in the criminality associated with this environment. The Internet spawns cybercrime: "Since crime tends to follow opportunity and the Internet provides many new opportunities, then new crimes will certainly emerge".[3]

There is no agreed definition of what constitutes computer crime or cybercrime. The computer may constitute the instrument of the crime, as in murder or fraud; the object of the crime, as in the theft of processor chips; or the subject of the crime, as in hacking and distributing viruses. The latter could be defined narrowly to refer to those activities that are unique to the Internet, such as "hacking" and distributing viruses. However, the impact of computers on

criminal law has been much more substantial than this narrow field of activities, both challenging traditional criminal concepts, and facilitating particular types of crime, such as child pornography. In addition, criminal law is not just about whether a particular act should be considered criminal or not. It is also about law enforcement, investigating those that commit criminal acts and prosecuting them, a process often considerably more difficult in a computer environment. This chapter therefore adopts a broad approach to the topic, focusing on crimes involving interconnected computers, which use in whole or part the Internet as a communications platform.

For the purpose of this report, the boundaries of what is considered cybercrime and the categorization used to distinguish between different types of cybercrime are those adopted in the primary international legal instrument in this area, the Council of Europe's Convention on Cybercrime (2001).[4] In the Convention, substantive offences are classified into three categories. The first category is traditional types of criminal offence that may be committed using computers as the instrument of the crime, referred to as computer-related crime, such as fraud. The second category concerns content-related crimes, primarily involving, for example, the violation of copyright or trademark. These first two categories could perhaps be more accurately described as "information crimes", since the object of the crime is the information processed by computers, whether accounting data or a music file, rather than the computer itself.[5] The third category is offences that have been established to specifically address activities that attack the integrity of computer and communications systems, such as distributing computer viruses. However, it could be argued that the public policy rationale underpinning this category is also the protection of the information being processed rather than of computers and systems for their own sake.

While this tripartite categorization will inform our discussion, it should also be recognized that the adoption and dispersion of Internet technologies are not uniform, particularly between developed and developing nations. Wireless communication technologies, for example, have rapidly eclipsed wireline systems in many developing countries, where the legacy fixed infrastructure was greatly underdeveloped. Thus, it should be recognized that differential technological use may mean different patterns of threats and vulnerabilities in terms of cybercrime.[6]

1. The incidence and cost of cybercrime

While this report is concerned with how legal systems need to evolve to address the phenomenon of computer crime, a preliminary question is why they need to evolve. What is the scale of the problem? Public policy agendas generally respond to a need articulated through one or more channels, such as the media or business. Such needs generally emerge from the experience of victims of cybercrime, often coupled with a real or perceived sense of inadequate protection by the law and the agencies responsible for its enforcement. Therefore, how great is the threat of cybercrime?

Reliable statistics about the scale of crime are notoriously difficult to measure,[7] and cybercrime presents particular challenges. A lack of consensus about what constitutes cybercrime is clearly one obstacle to the collection of data. Such a paucity of empirical data

concerning computer crime is generally seen as being due to a range of factors:

- *Under-reporting*

  There is a lack of reporting by victims, since commercial organizations avoid adverse publicity in order to protect their reputation and share price.[8] One approach to addressing this problem has been to impose a legal obligation to report incidents. Since 2003, for example, the State of California has obliged public businesses and government agencies to report if a hacker has gained access to personal information and financial data.[9]

- *Law enforcement experience and resources*

  A lack of experience and resources among law enforcement and prosecuting authorities has often meant that investigations and prosecutions are not considered a priority area, particularly when competing for attention with other public concerns, such as violent crime. This will often be exacerbated by inadequate training of personnel. This second factor obviously contributes to the first, under-reporting, since where victims perceive that they will receive a poor response from law enforcement agencies, they will be less likely to make the effort to report.

- *International nature*

  A third factor is the transnational nature of computer crime and the associated jurisdictional problems that contribute to the complexity of investigating and prosecuting offenders. All law enforcement agencies are under to pressure to perform, either expressly or implicitly, and are short of resources. Tackling international crime is resource-intensive, but there are low clear-up rates, namely successful prosecutions.

- *Statistical recording*

  Law enforcement agencies often fail to specifically collate data in relation to computer crime. This may be due to a lack of resources, but is more likely due to the complexities of recording such events.

- *Forensic and evidential challenges*

  Computers, particularly when networked, create significant forensic challenges to law enforcement agencies when obtaining evidence and subsequently presenting it to the courts.

Where figures are published, they are often from commercial entities operating in the data security sector, which clearly have an incentive to overstate the problem, and extrapolate the economic costs of computer crime on the basis of scant real data.[10]

The absence of reliable empirical data to support the frequent public claims made about the growth and impact of computer crime creates problems for policymakers. On the one hand, adopting legislative measures against a phenomenon that is little known may easily result in an inappropriate set of rules, either failing to adequately address the mischief or overextending criminal law to activities that should not be criminalized. On the other hand, the basis for taking any measures at all is weak, and therefore potentially flawed; this undermines the rationale for public policymakers to act and again leads to the overextension of criminal law.

Although the true figures concerning cybercrime may be suspect, certain common characteristics do emerge from the data available, and these provide important insights to help guide policymakers. First, a significant proportion, if not the majority, of cybercrime, is committed by, or with the assistance of, persons within the victim organization, such as employees. A survey from India, for example, reported that two thirds of data theft incidents were attributable to employees (current or former), while the majority of acts of unauthorized access originated within the affected company.[11] Such insider-instigated crime may mean that policymakers see primary responsibility as resting with the victim organizations themselves, rather than Governments. In addition, civil proceedings under employment law may be seen as providing for alternative legal redress against the perpetrators. Second, while cybercrime is most popularly associated with acts of hacking and viruses, its most prevalent form would seem to be computer-related crimes, where computers are simply a tool for the commission of economic and financial crimes[12]

When measuring the incidence of computer crime, the concern is with not only the volume of such activities but also their value, in terms of the damage and loss they cause to the victims themselves as well as the collateral damage incurred by others, including wider society and the nation State.

Clearly, the scale of the loss or damage caused will vary greatly according to which form of cybercrime is involved. In terms of computer-related offences, the nature of the loss and damage will obviously be dictated by the underlying criminal activity for which the computer, as a tool, was being used. Most modern large-scale economic and financial crime, for example, will utilize computers at some point, whether in terms of the inputting, processing or outputting of fraudulent data. In 1994, for example, Citibank suffered a significant breach of security in a case management system for financial institutions. Having hacked, the perpetrator was able to transfer funds out of the accounts of certain Indonesian banks.

For perpetrators of computer integrity crimes, the Internet offers individuals and criminal networks possibilities unparalleled in other environments, in terms of anonymity, mobility, geographical reach and the scope of the damage that can be inflicted. The range and scale of potential loss that may flow from attacks against computers and data are substantial and well reported[13] from individual inconvenience when a virus infects and corrupts a system, to substantial loss of revenue resulting from interruption of business. Where such attacks are targeted at, or inadvertently impact on, a nation's critical national infrastructure, such as power systems or transportation networks, their consequences are obviously of great significance and concern. In 2003, for example, the Port of Houston in the United States was brought to a standstill after a denial-of-service attack crippled the computer system on which the port's operations were dependent.

Box 6.2 sets out the key findings of a survey on the impact of computer-related crimes on major businesses in the United Kingdom.

The scant empirical data from developing countries are obviously fraught with difficulties and are potentially meaningless. The economic activity of developing countries may be viewed as being less dependent on computers and communications networks. Computers are also less integrated into every aspect of people's daily lives. The cost and resources required in order to secure systems against attack and exploitation, whether in terms of organizational, physical or logical measures, may often be beyond the means of those using those systems, the result being that there is greater vulnerability in developing countries than in developed ones.

Box 6.2

The impact on UK business

The following are the findings of a 2004 survey by the United Kingdom's National Hi-Tech Crime Unit:

1. Of 201 respondents, 167 had experienced hi-tech crime in 2003.

2. For those 167 companies, the total estimated cost was over £195 million, with financial fraud taking the lion's share at £121 million.

3. Seventy-seven per cent of all respondents faced virus attacks. Viruses affected all types and sizes of company.

4. Of the 44 financial services organizations which responded, three companies had experienced financial fraud totalling over £60 million.

5. Acts of sabotage and data theft most often originated internally. In addition, over a third of recent incidents of financial fraud were either wholly or partially, perpetrated by employees.

6. Almost three quarters of respondents agreed that the single most important impact of a computer-enabled crime was whether the company could continue to operate, function and do business with its customers.

As with other forms of loss and damage, there may be a range of options available to mitigate the loss suffered by certain categories of victim. The adequate provision of insurance cover, for example, is a standard developed-nation response to the risks of doing business. However, the complex nature and the scale of cybercrime-related losses have created problems in the market for the supply of such products in developed countries, which will only be greater in developing nations.

In terms of legal recourse, while cybercrime is primarily addressed through the criminal or penal code, Governments may adopt supplementary compensatory provisions, offering the possibility of the granting of compensation orders in addition to any punitive fine or jail term. In Singapore, for example, the Computer Misuse Act 1993 expressly grants a court the power to make an order against a person convicted of an offence to pay compensation to any party that has suffered damage from the offending activity. Similarly, in the United States, the Computer Fraud and Abuse Act provides that "any person who suffers damage or loss…may maintain a civil action…to obtain compensatory damage and injunctive relief or other equitable relief."[14]

2. Policy objectives

Law and regulation are about facilitating certain types of behaviour and restraining others. The imposition of criminal sanctions on an activity, particularly where the sanction involves the deprivation of liberty through imprisonment, clearly falls at one end of the spectrum in terms of the enforcement of public law. As such, criminal sanctions are not generally imposed without clear policy objectives being identified and articulated by the legislature through statute. Governments have a traditional role as guardian, but the adoption of protective measures, particularly criminal, can also be viewed as demand-side mechanisms supporting the development of e-commerce.

In terms of the development of a nation's information economy and society, it is widely recognized that engendering trust among users, both as citizens and consumers, is a critical element in facilitating the take-up of such techniques and technologies. Indeed, the need for a "global culture of cyber-security" was recognized as a key principle by the delegates at the World Summit on the Information Society (WSIS)[15] in Geneva in 2003 and, together with cybercrime, is a topic being examined by the UN Working Group on Internet Governance (WGIG).[16]

The policy objectives underpinning the criminalization of computer-related activities are generally unaltered by the use of computer technology. The objectives driving the criminalization of activities specifically targeted at computer systems and networks, particularly hacking and the distribution of viruses, range from concerns about the cost to users, both business and consumers, to a broad recognition of increasing societal dependence on such systems, especially with reference to "critical national infrastructure", such as power networks and air traffic control systems.

Prevention being better than cure, criminalizing specific activities is not a complete or sufficient response to the threat of hackers, virus writers and cyber-terrorists. The targets or potential victims of attacks are usually best placed to implement the appropriate physical and organizational security measures that will prevent, deter or limit the consequences of such attacks. While the virtuous link between data security and cybercrime should clearly be in the interests of users, there is much evidence that data security measures are not given adequate attention or are not properly understood within many organizations.[17] However, since an interconnected and interdependent environment means significant negative externalities and collateral vulnerabilities resulting from a failure to take measures, policymakers must recognize the need to facilitate data security through a variety of mechanisms, including the imposition of legal obligations to implement "appropriate security measures"[18] and encouraging compliance with internationally recognised security standards such as ISO 17799 and ITU Recommendation X805.[19]

As concern about cybercrime as cyber-terrorism has increased, Governments have expressly addressed the vulnerabilities created by the Internet for so-called critical infrastructures, those "facilities, networks, services and assets which, if disrupted or destroyed, would have a serious impact on the health, safety, security or economic well-being of citizens or the effective functioning of governments."[20] While the specific scope of what constitutes "critical infrastructure" may vary between countries, computer and communications networks, including the Internet, are always explicitly identified. In South Africa, for example, requirements exist for the identification and management of "critical data", defined as data that the Minister of Communications considers "of importance to the protection of the national security of the Republic or the economic and social well-being of its citizens".[21] Obligations are placed on "critical database administrators" to implement measures to protect databases, and a failure to comply may itself be the commission of an offence. At the G8 level, member States have adopted a set of principles specifically aimed at the protection of "critical information infrastructures".[22]

While Governments are keen to promote the security of, and trust, in the Internet, as a mechanism for facilitating its development security technologies themselves are a source of vulnerability. Cryptographic products in particular, as the dominant technological solution to the need for authentication, integrity and confidentiality on the Internet, are categorized as "dual-use", having military as well as civil applications, and have been, in the past, subject to export controls. While there has been a relative deregulation of export controls, some regulation is still present at the national level and through international treaties. In the United States, the Department of Commerce's Bureau of Industry and Security controls exports of cryptographic products. Some export restrictions still exist for bespoke or military-grade systems. However, the general prescription is that exports are unrestricted, provided that the software is generally available to the public by being sold in retail outlets, that the cryptographic functionality cannot be easily changed by the user, that the software is designed for installation by the user without further substantial support from the developer, and that the developer agrees to provide the software for inspection in order to ascertain compliance with all requirements.[23] Internationally, the trade in cryptography software is the subject of the Wassenaar Arrangement on Export Controls for Conventional Arms and Dual-Use Goods and Technologies.[24] The Wassenaar Arrangement was established after the end of the Cold War and is seen as a successor to the Coordinating Committee for Multilateral Export Controls (CoCom). Its provisions are compatible with the prescription of the US Department of Commerce – namely, that software is not necessarily a restricted technology if it is generally available to the public or in the public domain. This is in recognition of the fact that many important cryptographic technologies are either in the public domain, their patents having expired several years ago, or are available as free and open source software that freely circulates on the Internet.[25]

Therefore, a duality in the nature of the vulnerability created by the Internet can be seen: as a source of vulnerability, the conduit for those that wish to attack State infrastructure; and a vulnerable entity in its own right, as an essential infrastructure.

3.   Enforcing the law

Despite continuing public ignorance, it is now widely recognized by experts that the Internet does not suffer from a lack of law, but an excess of law coupled with an enforcement problem.[26] As noted above, one central issue in tackling cybercrime is the availability of law enforcement resources. Law enforcement can be seen as a two-stage process: the investigation of illegal activities and the prosecution of offenders. Both stages are traditionally perceived as tasks to be carried out by the police, with the intelligence services operating where issues of national security are involved. However, the reality is that the "policing" of cybercrime will involve a diverse range of public and private sector entities.

In most developed-nation jurisdictions, a wide range of regulatory authorities are granted powers to investigate and prosecute persons for offences within their regulatory jurisdiction. These authorities have functions to investigate specific types of conduct, such as financial services authorities (e.g. in an Internet securities fraud) or trading standards bodies (e.g. preventing the sale of unauthorized signal decoders).

In some legal systems, a private person as well as a public authority may be able to pursue a prosecution for certain offences. In the area of criminal copyright infringement, for example, rights holders such as the Business Software Alliance and the International Federation of Phonographic Industries may lead the investigation and prosecution of perpetrators. Most notably, in France, the League Against Racism and Anti-Semitism and the French Union of Jewish Students brought a successful action against Yahoo! for the sale of Nazi memorabilia available via its auction service in breach of French penal code.

In terms of criminal investigations, the private sector is clearly needed to assist public law enforcement and may, through self-regulatory initiatives, establish entities with a specific remit to receive complaints, and investigate and report on illegal activities. The following are some examples:

- In 1999, the International Chamber of Commerce (ICC) established a Cybercrime Unit to provide a mechanism for reporting criminal activity in the area and alerting members.[27]

- Many countries have established Computer Emergency Response Teams (CERTs), with public and private sector funding, which are tasked with warning users of emerging cybercrime activities, as well as developing a core of skilled professionals able to help tackle incidents.[28]

- In December 2004, a group called "Digital PhishNet" was established to tackle online identity theft, comprising financial services companies, ISPs and law enforcement.[29]

The need for a partnership between State authorities and the private sector to enhance enforcement is an inevitable feature of the Internet. However, private sector law enforcement activities also raise concerns in terms of vigilantism, infringement of rights and a blurring of traditional concepts of accountability.

4. International harmonization

Computer crime has an obvious international dimension and policymakers recognize the need to ensure that legal protection is harmonized among nations, so as to prevent the emergence of cybercrime havens. The "I love you" virus, which first emerged in 2000, is the classic example of such a threat. The virus spread rapidly around the world affecting some 45 million Internet users and causing great financial losses.[30] The source was eventually traced to a virus writer named Onel de Guzman based in the Philippines.[31] However, under Philippines law at the time, there was no suitable offence to charge Guzman with, and after the local courts threw out an attempt to proceed against him for theft and credit card fraud, no proceedings were brought.

Attempts have been made within various international organizations and forums, such as the G8 member States' "Principles and Action Plan to Combat High tec Crime"[32] and the United Nations,[33] to achieve a harmonized approach to legislating against computer crime and thereby try to prevent the appearance of "computer crime havens". The first major attempt was under the auspices of the Organisation for Economic Co-operation and Development (OECD). It published a report in 1986, which listed five categories of offence that it believed should constitute a common approach to computer crime.[34] However, the most significant intergovernmental institution in the field has been the Council of Europe.

The Council of Europe first examined the issue of computer crime in 1985, with the establishment of a committee of experts. The committee produced guidelines for national legislatures on a "Minimum List of Offences Necessary for a Uniform Criminal Policy", which outlined eight offences seen as critical areas of computer misuse requiring criminalization, including damage to computer data and programs. In addition, the report presented an "optional list" of four offences, which failed to achieve consensus among member States, but were thought worthy of consideration, including unauthorized use of a computer. The report was endorsed in a Recommendation by the Council of Ministers urging Governments to review and legislate accordingly (Recommendation No. R(89) 9). A similar instrument, addressing procedural issues (Recommendation No. R(95)13), was adopted in 1995.

Council of Europe Recommendations are not binding legal instruments and, inevitably, had limited effect. However, as the Internet emerged as a new environment for the commission of crime, the attention of policymakers was refocused on the need for a harmonized response. In April 1997, the Council of Europe embarked on the adoption of a Convention, which member States would have a legal obligation to implement. In November 2001, the Council of Ministers adopted the Convention on Cybercrime (Cybercrime Convention), which was opened for signature in Budapest on 23 November 2001, and has since been signed by 34 of the 46 members of the Council of Europe. However, of particular significance to the status of the Convention, four non-members were also involved in the drafting process, the United States, Japan, South Africa and Canada, and became signatories. The Convention also contains a mechanism whereby other non-members can sign and ratify the Convention. The Convention entered into force as of 18 March 2004, when Lithuania became the fifth ratifying State.

Since the adoption of the Convention in 2001, an additional protocol to the Convention was agreed by member States, "concerning the criminalisation of acts of a racist and xenophobic nature committed through computer systems", in January 2003. The protocol requires the establishment of a range of substantive offences concerning "racist or xenophobic material", including the dissemination of such material, threats and insults, and denial of genocide and crimes against humanity. However, owing to the complexities of legislating against such material, member States have considerable autonomy not to adopt such measures, where, for example, issues of freedom of expression conflict.[35]

The comprehensive nature of the Cybercrime Convention, as well as the geographical spread of its signatories, means that it is likely to remain the most significant international legal instrument in the field for the foreseeable future. The success of the Convention as a spur to harmonization can be measured on the basis not only of the number of signatories, including non-European countries, but also of the fact that it is the source of other harmonization initiatives, such as the Commonwealth Model Computer and Computer-related Crimes Bill (October 2002),[36] which addresses the needs of some 53 developed and developing nations. In 2005, the international police organization, Interpol, adopted a resolution describing the Convention as "providing a minimal international legal and procedural standard" and recommending that its 182 member countries consider joining it.[37] However, concerns have been expressed about the Convention by both human rights groups and providers of communication services, and there have been calls for a treaty to be drafted under the auspices of the United Nations.[38]

C.   Reforming the criminal code

To address the threat of cybercrime and to enhance the security of the Internet, Governments have been keen to establish an appropriate legal framework that deters attacks. Such a framework is a question of substantive law, which must appropriately criminalize the different forms of cybercrime.

In general, law reform in respect of computer-related and content-related crime will involve considerations of adaptation designed to ensure that the criminal code is capable of being applied against acts involving the use of computers, rather than wholesale revision of the existing criminal code. The criminal code will generally have been drafted at the time of a modern State's establishment, on the basis of national historical precedents as well as borrowing from colonial and regional sources. As such, the code will often have been drafted using concepts and terminology that reflect the physical world rather than the virtual world.

It is beyond the scope of this Report to consider each and every type of computer-related and content-related crime; however, the following highlights some of the areas where jurisdictions have faced issues when applying the traditional criminal code in a cybercrime environment:

- *Information acquisition*: As information has become a more valuable commercial asset, such as intellectual property and personal data, the illegal appropriation of such information may need to be made subject to criminal sanction (e.g. identity theft) or to enhanced penalties (e.g. counterfeiting).

- *Dealing with machines*: Some criminal acts may be cast in terms of doing something to someone, such as deception (fraud). In a cybercrime environment, acts will often involve no human interface, being completely automated. The criminal code must ensure that machine-to-machine criminal acts are fully subject to the law.

- *Intangible damage*: The nature of computer and communication technologies means that damage may be done to a system which is not tangible or directly perceivable by persons, such as altering the magnetic state of a disk to erase data. Such intangible damage should be recognized by the criminal code.

- *Digital manipulation*: Digital information is capable of manipulation to an unprecedented extent. Consequently, statutory provisions based on fixed conceptions of capturing and presenting information (e.g. an indecent photograph) may need to be amended to reflect such flexibility.

- *Digital time*: It is recognized that events can happen on the Internet on a time scale that is different from that of traditional conceptions. The criminal code may need to reconsider the use of terminology such as "recorded" or "stored", which may imply a requirement for something more permanent than the transitory nature of events on the Internet.

- *Determining location*: As in the case of time, traditional criminal-law concepts of location may be challenged on the Internet. The criminal code needs to reflect the potential transnational scope of cybercrime activities.

Policymakers and legislators will therefore need to review the existing criminal code in order to address such issues and to reflect the nature of criminal activities in a Internet environment.

1. Computer integrity offences

In contrast to the other two categories (computer-related and content-related offences), computer integrity offences generally present countries with the need to establish *sui generis* offences, rather than reform the existing code. The computer integrity activities addressed in the international instruments can be broadly classified into four categories:

- Offences concerning access to data and systems;
- Offences relating to interference with data and systems;
- Offences concerning the interception of data in the course of their transmission;
- Offences concerning the use of tools or "devices" to carry out any of the above acts.

The two key elements of all these offences are intention – the traditional criminal-law requirement for the necessary mental element, or *mens rea* – and that the person must be acting "without right", "authorisation" or "lawful excuse".

Interference is generally considered to be of greater seriousness than the "mere" access offence, since the main mischief being addressed is threats against the integrity of data being processed and the operation of systems. Obviously, access may be gained in order to commit any number of further offences, whether fraud or terrorism. In the United Kingdom, for example, a terrorist act is defined as including actions "designed seriously to interfere with or seriously disrupt an electronic system".[39] In such cases, the access offence may be viewed as primarily "facilitative" in terms of the investigation and prosecution of cybercrime activities, since it will rarely be the main charge laid against the accused.[40] However, by criminalizing all forms of computer "trespass", such as access sought simply as an intellectual challenge or out of curiosity, an anomaly can be created with the legal treatment of analogous situations in the physical world.

In terms of interference, whether with data or systems, the concept is elaborated to cover all forms of modification, including deletion and suppression, as well as rendering such data or systems inaccessible or inoperable. The latter would be applicable to activities known as 'denial-of-service' attacks, where a person or persons bombard a system with data requests, thereby overloading the system and leading to its eventual shutdown. In the draft EU Framework Decision, interference which has "affected essential interests", a term presumably designed to encompass "critical infrastructure", is considered an "aggravating circumstance" which should be subject to more substantial penalties.

The interception of data in transmission is carried out in order to compromise the confidentiality of communications. Such espionage or surveillance will generally be for reasons of political or economic gain. Indeed, the political overtones attaching to interception activities have meant that communications privacy is given statutory or even constitutional protection in most jurisdictions. Historically, legal controls in respect of interception have been directed more towards the manifestations of the State, particularly law enforcement agencies, than towards individuals or networks of cybercriminals or cyber-terrorists.

The provisions in respect of "devices" are intended to address those that supply or possess the tools that are used to access or interfere with data or systems, or intercept communications, such as password "cracking" software and other "hacker tools".[41] These provisions have been controversial, since such tools will often encompass both legitimate and illegitimate purposes. In relation to supply, such offences could also be categorized as "facilitative", to the extent that they address the availability of the tools needed to commit cybercrimes. The possession offence can be categorized as a "preparatory" offence, criminalizing the steps taken prior to the commission of an integrity offence.

Harmonization of substantive offences is a prerequisite intergovernmental response to network-based crime. Identifying and criminalizing specified activities place a common legal framework on decentralized, informal and mobile transnational criminal and terrorist networks. However, concerns about over-criminalization may also be raised in respect of the *sui generis* computer integrity offences, particularly concerning access and devices.

2. Locating cybercrime

Computer crime often inevitably has a transnational aspect to it that can give rise to complex jurisdictional issues, involving persons present and acts carried out in a number of different countries. Even where the perpetrator and the accused are located in the same jurisdiction, relevant evidence may reside on a server located in another jurisdiction, such as a "Hotmail" account.

In terms of general law, as with most aspects of network-based activities, traditional concepts and principles are sometimes challenged by the nature of the technology. The general principle of international criminal law is that a crime committed within a State's territory may be tried there, although the territoriality

of criminal law does not coincide with territorial sovereignty.[42]

However, where criminal activity is information-based a jurisdictional distinction between the initiation and termination of an act often results, such as in the case of the release of a virus and its execution within a recipient's system. One consequence of this jurisdictional dissonance, especially in an Internet environment, is that criminal law has had to be amended to extend the territorial reach of certain offences. In addition, the general concern about the growth and societal impact of computer crime has led Governments to apply extraterritorial principles to computer crime.

In terms of ensuring legal certainty, general principles of international criminal law are made concrete through express jurisdictional provisions in the substantive legislation. Such rules generally claim jurisdiction if one of the elements of the offence occurs within the State's territory. Under the United Kingdom's Computer Misuse Act 1990, for example, jurisdiction is asserted through the concept of a "significant link" being present in the domestic jurisdiction, for example if either the computer or the perpetrator is in the United Kingdom. In the United States, the USA Patriot Act of 2001 amended the Computer Fraud and Abuse Act to extend the concept of a "protected computer" to include "a computer located outside the United States that is used in a manner that affects interstate or foreign commerce or communication of the United States".[43] This effectively extends the territorial scope of the domestic offence, when the attacked computer is in another jurisdiction.

While the jurisdictional norm of criminal law is the territorial principle, there are four broadly recognized principles under which extraterritorial jurisdiction is claimed or exercised in cases of international criminal activity:

- The "active personality principle", which is based on the nationality of the perpetrator;

- The "passive personality principle", which is based on the nationality of the victim;

- The "universality principle", for crimes broadly recognized as being crimes against humanity, such as genocide;

- The "protective principle", to safeguard a jurisdiction's national interest, such as the planning of an act of cyber-terrorism.

Both the Convention on Cybercrime and the Commonwealth Model Law address the question of establishing jurisdiction. The Convention states that jurisdiction should exist when the offence is committed:

(a) In the Party's territory; or

(b) On board a ship flying the flag of that Party; or

(c) On board an aircraft registered under the laws of that Party; or

(d) By one of its nationals, if the offence is punishable under criminal law where it was committed or if the offence is committed outside the territorial jurisdiction of any State. (Article 22).

The fourth scenario, based on the nationality of the offender, is an example of the "active personality" principle referred to above.

However, the adoption of extraterritorial provisions does not necessarily provide an easy solution to trans border cybercrime. First, there are practical difficulties arising from the need to gather evidence overseas and the possibility of bringing witnesses from abroad. Second, there may be potential conflicts with local laws, which may prevent evidence from being gathered or the accused being extradited. Third, doubts may be raised as to whether the public interest is served in the prosecution of cases where there is no impact on the jurisdiction in question.

D. Addressing the data problem

Cybercrime investigations and the gathering of appropriate evidence for a prosecution, the science of forensics, can be an extremely difficult and complex issue.[44] Steps will obviously be taken by perpetrators to hide or disguise their activities, such as "communications laundering" routing transmissions through a series of jurisdictions to frustrate attempts to trace the source or the extensive use of cryptographic techniques to render data unintelligible. However, the environment itself also raises significant challenges owing, in part, to the intangible and often transient nature of data involved. The nature of the technologies bestows upon data the duality of being notoriously vulnerable to loss and modification, as well as being surprisingly "sticky" – subject to a thorough inspection, a hard disk will reveal much data that may have been assumed as deleted – at one and the same time. The "stickiness" of data is attributable, in part,

to the multiple copies generated by the communications process, as well as to the manner in which data are stored on electronic media. Such technology renders the process of investigation and recording of evidence extremely vulnerable to defence claims of errors, technical malfunction, prejudicial interference or fabrication, which may lead to such evidence being ruled inadmissible.[45]

A lack of adequate training of law enforcement officers, prosecutors and, indeed, the judiciary will often exacerbate the difficulties of computer forensics. In developed countries, substantial efforts have been made over recent years to address this training need and specialized courses and facilities have established. In addition, computer forensics has become a recognised academic discipline and numerous organizations now offer such services on both a commercial and a non-commercial basis. Law enforcement agencies have also formalized their treatment of computer derived evidence, through the issuance of guidance.

Box 6.3 provides an example of principles designed to ensure good practice when collecting computer-based electronic evidence.

Relevant evidential data may be found in the systems of the victim, the suspect and/or some third party, such as a communications service provider. Alternatively, evidence may be obtained from data in the process of being transmitted across a network, generally referred to as intercepted data. Specific rules of criminal procedure address law enforcement access to both sources of evidence data at rest or data in transmission although the Internet raises a range of issues in relation to the operation of such rules.

Any criminal investigation interferes with the rights of others, whether the person is the subject of an investigation or a related third party. In a democratic society any such interference must be justifiable and proportionate to the needs of society to be protected. However, the growth of cybercrime has raised difficult issues in respect of the appropriate balance between the needs of those investigating and prosecuting such crime, and the rights of data users to privacy. This section considers some of the problems raised by data for law enforcement agencies investigating cybercrime and examines proposals for procedural law reform.

Box 6.3

ACPO *Good Practice Guide for Computer Based Evidence*[1]

The following principles should guide the practice of all law enforcement agency investigations:

Principle 1: No action taken by law enforcement or their agents should change data held on an electronic device or media which may subsequently be relied upon in Court.

Principle 2: In exceptional circumstances where a person finds it necessary to access original data held on an electronic device or media that person must be competent to do so and be able to give evidence explaining the relevance and the implications of their actions.

Principle 3: An audit trail or other record of all processes applied to electronic evidence should be created and preserved. An independent third party should be able to examine those processes and achieve the same result.

Principle 4: The person in charge of the investigation (case officer) is responsible for ensuring that the law and these principles are adhered to.

---

[1] Association of Chief Police Officers (ACPO), Good Practice Guide for Computer Based Evidence (3rd edition, 2004), available at www.nhtu.org.uk

1.   Data at rest

Communications involve at least two parties   the caller and the called. In data communications either party, or both, may be machines or more accurately software or files residing on machines, rather than people. Law enforcement agencies will generally access forensic data once they have been recorded or stored, whether in the systems controlled by the calling or called parties, or during the process of transmission. However, access to stored data has raised a number of issues in relation to criminal procedure, in respect of the seizure of such data, particularly when held remotely, protected data, communications data and the preservation or retention of data.

Seizing data

Data stored in the computer system of the suspect are generally obtained through the execution of a court order for search and seizure. A search and seizure warrant can give rise to problems where the relevant material is held on a computer system being used at the time of the search, since any attempt to seize the material for further examination may result in either the loss or the alteration of the evidence.[46] Another problem for law enforcement is the volume of data that are generally subject to seizure, especially since

the cost of data storage has fallen and capacity increased dramatically in recent years. The time and expense involved in shifting and scrutinizing seized data are a serious impediment to the process of investigation.

One aspect of the use of search and seizure warrants in a Internet environment concerns the geographical scope of a warrant, issued by a court and authorizing such acts. The Cybercrime Convention, for example, states that the right to search and access should extend to any other computer system on its territory which "is lawfully accessible from or available to the initial system" (Article 19(2)). Thus, an authorized search at a single site can potentially be extended to interconnected systems located anywhere within the jurisdiction.

However, where the remote computer is based in another jurisdiction, important issues of sovereignty and territoriality may arise. In 2000, for example, as part of an investigation into the activities of two Russian hackers, Vasiliy Gorschkov and Alexey Ivanov, the FBI accessed computers in the Russian Federation via the Internet, using surreptitiously obtained passwords to download data from computers operated by the accused, who were already under arrest in the United States. In retaliation for this breach of sovereignty, the Russian authorities charged the FBI agent responsible for the intrusion.[47]

To address these potential conflicts, member States parties to the Cybercrime Convention accepted that access to data stored in another jurisdiction might be obtained without the authorization of the State in which the data reside in two situations:

a. access publicly available (open source) stored computer data, regardless of where the data is located geographically; or

b. access or receive, through a computer system in its territory, stored computer data located in another Party, if the Party obtains the lawful and voluntary consent of the person who has the lawful authority to disclose the data to the Party through that computer system. (Article 32)

Article 32 details two circumstances which all parties to the Convention could accept, but does not preclude other situations being authorized under national law. An example of a more aggressive stance to accessing remote data is Australia, where a specific warrant-based procedural mechanism was adopted to enable the Australian Security Intelligence Organisation to access remotely held data. These provisions not only authorize the seizure of data, but also permit the modification of any obstructive access control and/or encryption systems to obtain access to the data. Such proactive policing, utilizing the techniques and tools of the cybercriminal in the course of an investigation, even potentially to launch an attack against a foreign perpetrator, raises serious issues of legitimacy, due process and the potential for sovereignty disputes.[48]

Protected data

As discussed above, evidentially relevant data may be obtained through intercepting a communication session or from a party who has stored the data. However, the data once obtained may be in a form that is designed to protect it from being disclosed to third parties; for example, data could be encrypted in order to ensure its confidentiality. In the United States, for example, when the notorious hacker Kevin Mitnick was finally arrested, many of the files found on his computers were encrypted and investigators were never able to access them.[49]

The nature of data security technologies means that investigating authorities have essentially three options in respect of gaining access to protected data:

- Require the person from whom the data have been obtained to convert them into an intelligible plain-text format;

- Require the person to disclose the necessary information and/or tools to enable the authorities to convert the data into a legible format themselves;

- Utilize technologies and techniques which enable the data to be converted without the active involvement of the person from whom the data were obtained.

The first option represents standard criminal procedure in most countries. Under the second option, proposals have been made in some jurisdictions for specific requirements to deliver up "keys" to render data intelligible. Such an obligation differs from the approach taken in traditional investigations. Criminal procedures do not, generally, contain express requirements to provide, for example, the combination to open a metal safe. However, modern data security techniques have been seen by some policymakers as requiring a specific legislative response.

The viability of the third option, converting the data into an intelligible form by utilizing available techniques, would seem to depend on a number of factors, including the strength of the technology used by the party applying the security technique, the functional design of future technology[50] and the period within which the data realistically need to be converted. However, technological developments may create security mechanisms which are incapable of being overcome, such as quantum cryptography.[51] Some Governments have already established "in-house" technical capabilities to support law enforcement agencies,[52] and although such resource allocation is likely to be beyond the capacity of most developing countries, cross-border forensic services could be made available by such institutions.

Communications data

Establishing the identity of a person suspected of criminal activity is obviously crucial to the commencement of any legal proceedings. However, network users are often not readily identifiable from the naming and addressing information processed in the course of a communications session. There will often be a need, therefore, for the investigator to map a user's electronic identity to his real world identity. A third party, the user's ISP, generally holds such information, and accessing it interferes with the interests both of that third party and of the person being investigated.

One of the classic aphorisms of the Internet age is Peter Steiner's famous cartoon captioned "On the Internet, nobody knows you are a dog".[53] However, in the course of an investigation, the investigator will need to identify the person carrying out the illegal activity, whether canine or not! The process of establishing a real world person's identity from their Internet-related identity creates a significant forensic and legal hurdle.

When utilizing an Internet-based service such as e-mail, the originator of a message requires an IP address, for example 38.111.64.2. That IP address is then logically linked to the originator's pseudonym and domain name, e.g. john.smith@first.com. However, whilst the IP address is unique, the person to whom it is linked will usually vary. ISPs and corporate networks will generally, for reasons of efficiency, dynamically assign an IP address to a user each time he or she logs onto a service or at the commencement of each communication session.

Identification is often a two-stage process. First, it is necessary to identify the person to whom an IP address has been assigned. This can be relatively straightforward, for example using "whois" software to interrogate one of the regional registry databases, which detail IP address allocation. Where the person has a fixed IP address, the registry will effectively identify the owner of the machine unless the address has been "spoofed"[54]. However, where a block of IP addresses belong to a service provider or organization, the second stage will be to approach the holder in order to match the IP address to a specific user. This will clearly not be possible where the holder either provides anonymous public services, such as cybercafe, or does not maintain a historical log of IP address allocation.

From the investigator's perspective, the first legal issue concerns the second-stage process: what legal obligations does the holder of the IP address have, whether a public communications provider or a corporate entity, to disclose information to an investigator identifying an individual user? Reliance on voluntary mechanisms is likely to result in inconsistent practice, perhaps constrained by conflicting legal obligations such as privacy laws or contractual constraints. It may therefore be necessary for investigating authorities to have specific powers to require the delivery of information upon receipt of a properly authorized request.

Preserved or retained data

The patterns created by the communications attributes of criminal and terrorist networks on the Internet are increasingly valuable to law enforcement agencies for discerning the operational nature of such networks forming, dissolving and reforming according to the logic of the opportunities being pursued. Such evidential data will be generated by the networks that comprise the Internet, as traffic passes into, across and out of each network, and will often be as transient as the communication session itself. To address such transience, Governments have looked to the imposition of express preservation and retention obligations upon the providers of communication services.

The Cybercrime Convention addresses the right of law enforcement agencies to request that stored or transmission data be preserved upon notice for certain periods of time, the so-called fast freeze-quick thaw model. Such an order will normally be made against an ISP. However, in the normal course of business traffic data are generally retained for relatively short periods of time, owing to the cost to the ISP as well as compliance with data protection rules, designed to protect the privacy interests of subscribers and users.

Concerns about security threats from the Internet led to calls for the imposition of a general data retention obligation on ISPs to enable law enforcement to access historical as well as real-time traffic data. Prior to the events of 11 September 2001, most Governments rejected such calls, recognizing that such wholesale retention obligations were a threat to privacy as well as an unnecessary cost burden for ISPs. Only expedited data preservation rules made it into the Cybercrime Convention, not general retention obligations, primarily owing to trenchant opposition from the United States.

In the United Kingdom, for example, provisions were incorporated in the Anti-Terrorism Crime and Security Act 2001, establishing a voluntary regime for the retention of communications data, with the possibility of imposing mandatory directions. In April 2004, the Governments of the United Kingdom, Ireland, France and Sweden proposed a EU Council Framework decision to harmonize traffic data retention among EU member States.

However, large-scale data retention must itself be seen as vulnerable to abuse a new security risk and considerable concern has been voiced that provisions for retention breach data protection and human rights laws as a disproportionate response to an unmeasured threat.

2. Intercepted data

Evidence may also be obtained during the transmission of data between computers across communication networks. Such evidence may comprise the content of a communication, such as a list of passwords, or the attributes of a communication session, such as the duration of a call or the location of the caller, referred to as "traffic data" in the Cybercrime Convention and Commonwealth Model Law.

The interception of the content of a communication is usually subject to relatively strict procedural controls, designed more to protect against privacy infringements by law enforcement agencies than to deter cybercrime. Interception in the course of a criminal investigation will generally require authorization from a third party, usually in the form of a judicial or executive warrant. The Cybercrime Convention provides that authorization should be available only for "serious offences", which would obviously include cyber-terrorist activities, but not necessarily all forms of computer integrity offences, such as mere unauthorized access.

Historically, national legal systems have distinguished between the interception of the content of a communication and the traffic data related to the communication session itself, such as number called. Access to the latter has generally been subject to less stringent procedural hurdles, such as the need for a warrant. Such a distinction would seem to be based on a widely held perception that access to the content of a communication represents a greater threat to personal privacy than access to the related traffic data. However, developments in communications would seem to have led to a qualitative and quantitative shift in the nature of traffic data, from the generation of location data in mobile telephony to the ever-expand-

ing range of daily activities carried out online. As a consequence, the volume of traffic data potentially available to law enforcement agencies and its value as an investigative tool have increased considerably. It would therefore seem arguable that the threats to individual privacy from accessing traffic data, compared with communications content, are of a similar nature in terms of revealing a person's private life and activities and should therefore be subject to comparable access regimes.

One procedural issue raised by differential legal treatment is that in a Internet environment the distinction between traffic data and content is becoming increasingly blurred. A web-based Uniform Resource Locator (URL), for example, may contain not only details of the IP address of the website being accessed, akin to a traditional telephone number, but also further information in relation to the content of the requested communication, such as a particular item held on the site or a search string containing the embedded parameters of the search, for example:

http://www.google.com/
search?hl=en&q=aliens&btnG=Google+Search

In the URL example above, how should the "traffic data" be separated from the associated content? Reliance on law enforcement agencies to distinguish such data would seem unacceptable, and this therefore requires us to consider the role of the communication service provider, over whose network the data are being sent during the interception process. The relevant service provider would need to be able to identify the relevant data and then automatically separate traffic data for forwarding to the appropriate requesting authority.

The consequences of the blurring between traffic data and content in a Internet context and their differential legal treatment are potentially significant in terms of eroding an individual's traditional privacy rights. In addition, communication service providers face legal, procedural and operational uncertainties with regard to the obligations to obtain and provide data that have been requested by an investigating agency.

3. Communication service providers

In a traditional voice telephony environment, the general principle was that an interception would be carried out as physically close to the suspect as possible, which usually meant at a local loop or exchange level. In a Internet environment, the principle is no longer necessarily applicable as the proliferation of intermediary service providers within the network hierarchy structure presents a range of alternative points of interception (e.g. a web-based e-mail service and cached web pages).

Historically, in order to enable law enforcement agencies to intercept communications, the incumbent operator, often State-owned, has maintained the technical capability to intercept communications. However, in an environment of multiple networks, of vastly varying size and nature, Governments have had to establish formal obligations and procedures concerning "intercept capability". These generally differentiate between the different types of communication service providers (CSPs) and networks.

CSPs have a number of concerns arising from an obligation to ensure an "intercept capability". First, considerable reservations have been expressed about the feasibility of achieving a stable "intercept capability" solution in a rapidly evolving communications environment. "Intermediary service providers" in particular are concerned that their freedom to design, build and operate innovative data communications networks and services, in accordance with the dictates of newly available technologies and commercial imperatives, would be significantly restrained by the need to meet an ongoing obligation to ensure an "intercept capability". It is generally accepted that a single technological solution to the requirement for "intercept capability" is not going to be available; this will have associated cost implications for CSPs and, potentially, procedural implications for law enforcement agencies.

Second, the costs arising from compliance with an obligation to provide "intercept capability" are an important factor. Such costs can be categorized as fixed costs, in relation to building the "capability" into the network (e.g. switches with intercept functionality), and variable costs, arising from the operational aspects of carrying out an interception (e.g. personnel). It is beyond the remit of this report to suggest the most appropriate division of costs between Governments, as holders of public funds, and the providers of communication networks and services. In many jurisdictions, fixed costs are borne by the CSP, whilst variable costs are covered by the relevant public authority.[55] It is generally accepted that shifting some of the financial cost arising from

an investigation to the investigating agency acts as an effective restraint on the use of such techniques.

Significant concerns have been expressed, however, particularly by representatives of newly emerged "intermediary service providers", that the costs involved in implementing "intercept capability" in modern communication networks are likely to be substantial. Such concerns have been reflected in some jurisdictions through express statutory reference to the parties required to bear the costs.

4.   Cooperating against cybercrime

Another aspect of the governmental response to Internet crime is improvement of cooperation between national law enforcement agencies. At one level, cooperation will involve mutual assistance in the obtaining and exchange of information, whether as intelligence or evidence. In this regard, agencies have established "network" structures in an attempt to mimic the responsiveness and flexibility of other networks. However, such an approach would not seem appropriate where the cooperation involves the movement of suspected perpetrators, further up the enforcement chain.

Moving evidence

The investigation and prosecution of transnational cybercrime will usually require substantial co-operation between national law enforcement agencies, prosecuting authorities and private sector entities such as ISPs. Obtaining such cooperation, generally referred to mutual legal assistance (MLA), in a timely and efficient manner will often be critical to the success of a cybercrime investigation. Historically, however, MLA procedures have been notoriously slow and bureaucratic.

A request for evidence from another jurisdiction is known as a "letter rogatory", and will generally be issued only where it appears that an offence has been committed and that proceedings have been instituted or an investigation is under way. The request may be sent to a court in the relevant jurisdiction, to a designated authority or, in an urgent case, through the International Criminal Police Organization (Interpol). The evidence, once received by the requesting State, should then be used only for the purpose specified in the request; this principle is known as the "specialty principle", a principle also present in extradition treaties, requiring the requesting State to prosecute the accused only for the crimes detailed in the extradition request.

Despite the existence of MLA procedures, there is always a time lag created by the need to channel a request through the appropriate authorities. As a consequence, law enforcement agencies have adopted alternative informal approaches to the need for a rapid and flexible exchange of information. In the United States, for example, the extension of the concept of a "protected computer" to include non-US based computers, as noted above, means that when a foreign law enforcement agency contacts the US authorities, they can provide assistance informally on the basis that the perpetrator's activities also constitute an offence under US law, rather than comply with MLA procedures. Such an approach may be seen as an alternative version of the "double criminality" principle, discussed below, where the act is in actuality an offence in both jurisdictions, rather than theoretically. While the US authorities may have no intention of pursuing a domestic prosecution, the possibility provides an informal alternative to the mutual legal assistance route.

Many of the international harmonization initiatives have been designed to address the institutional and procedural obstacles to the investigation of a crime, as much as the substantive offences themselves. One key mechanism is the establishment of a network of designated law enforcement contacts, available 24 hours a day, 7 days a week. In 2003, Interpol established a global police communications system, referred to as "I-24/7", to facilitate a rapid response and information exchange among its 182 member countries. In addition, Interpol has established regional working parties (i.e. European, American, African and Asia-South Pacific) to develop good practice through sharing expertise.[56]

As well as reacting to requests, such networks offer a channel for the proactive exchange of intelligence. The Cybercrime Convention, for example, envisages the provision of "spontaneous information", namely intelligence, where by agencies in one State disclose information uncovered during their investigations to another State for the purpose of initiating or assisting an investigation (Article 26). However, such disclosures should be subject to the domestic law of the disclosing State, such as data protection rules, which may impose restrictions on the transfer of personal data.

Moving people

Clearly, when a system is attacked, the perpetrator may be located anywhere in the world. Therefore, if a prosecution is to be mounted, the accused has to be brought to the prosecuting State. The formal procedure under which persons are transferred between States for prosecution is known as extradition. Either bilateral or multilateral treaties or agreements between states generally govern extradition. In the absence of such a treaty, the State where the perpetrator resides is not required under any rule of public international law to surrender the person. In such situations, informal mechanisms may be used to bring the perpetrator to justice. In the *Levin* case referred to above, for example, the accused was enticed to leave the Russian Federation, with which the United States did not have an extradition treaty, and was arrested as soon as he landed in a country with which the United States did have an extradition arrangement, namely the United Kingdom.[57]

In an action for extradition, the applicant State is generally required to show that the actions of the accused constitute a criminal offence exceeding a minimum level of seriousness in both jurisdictions, the country from which the accused is to be extradited and the country to which the extradition will be made. This is referred to as the "double criminality" principle and is generally a threshold of a minimum of 12 months' imprisonment in both States (Cybercrime Convention, Article 24). Meeting the 'double criminality' standard is clearly an objective of harmonization initiatives in respect of substantive offences. In *Levin*, for example, the defendant was accused of committing wire and bank fraud in the United States. No exact equivalent exists in English law, and therefore Levin was charged with 66 related offences, including unauthorized access and unauthorized modification.

Most countries will not extradite juveniles, although a significant proportion of cybercrime perpetrators fall into this category. In addition, some jurisdictions, such as France, make a distinction between nationals and foreign persons, extradition being only available in respect of non-nationals. To address this potential lacuna, the Cybercrime Convention provides that member States shall establish jurisdiction over and prosecute offenders that they refuse to extradite.[58]

E. Concluding remarks and policy recommendations

The Internet can be viewed as the ultimate transnational communications network, offering an unrivalled capability for accessing data and computer systems on a global level. As economies and society become dependent on the Internet, it becomes a critical information infrastructure over which nearly all Governments have only limited control.

Combating cybercrime is one of the greatest challenges facing society today. Evidence of the scale of the threat from cybercrime and cyber-terrorism remains scant, although Governments and, indeed, the wider general public are convinced of the need for action. The Internet can be used to undermine State control and circumvent State laws; however, law reform can address aspects of cybercrime and enhance security on the Internet: as a spur to action for system controllers, as a deterrent for perpetrators and as a tool for law enforcement agencies

Technologically neutral statutes

It is generally accepted that online conduct should be treated no differently from offline conduct. Laws should be technologically neutral and based on the act rather than the technology used to commit the act. As FBI Director Louis Freeh noted in testimony before the United States Senate, "Statutes need to be rendered technology neutral so that they can be applied regardless of whether a crime is committed with pen and paper, e-mail, telephone, or geosynchronous orbit personal communication devices".[59]

Balance between law enforcement and human rights

Criminalization of computer wrongdoing is a prerequisite for combating cybercrime. Thus, in response to threats to the integrity of computer systems and the data that they process, Governments have pursued the harmonization of legal rules and greater law enforcement cooperation. While public perception of cybercrime revolves around specific types of behaviour, such as "hacking",[60] policymakers have primarily been concerned with reforming the procedural aspects of investigating and pursuing cybercriminals. Since the events of 11 September 2001, law enforcement agencies have been granted substantially enhanced powers of investigation. However, there is a fear that the desire to secure the Internet may result in a concomitant erosion of individual privacy and other fundamental liberties. Thus, it is necessary to ensure a proper balance between the interests of law enforcement and respect for fundamental human rights as enshrined in international human rights treaties, such as the 1966 United Nations International Covenant on Civil and Political Rights.

International cooperation

As cybercrime has become a threat, harmonization and cooperation have gathered pace and re-engaged the attention of legislators. It is acknowledged today that an effective fight against cybercrime requires increased, rapid and well-functioning international cooperation in criminal matters.[61] Initiatives in this connection can be seen as extensions of State authority in the face of the erosion of State control. Despite the early territorial assertions for the Internet, cybercrime activities take place and have effects in and between territories. Consequently, Governments may be prepared to trade a loss of some degree of *de jure* State control, in terms of criminal procedure, reflecting their loss of *de facto* control, in return for extended jurisdictional reach, enhancing State authority.

Capacity development

It is recognized that in many developing countries there is a lack of sound, basic knowledge and experience in investigating cybercrime. Thus, it is recommended that adequate awareness programmes be established for decision makers, cybercrime units, justice departments, the private sector and academic institutions .Moreover, it is important that adequate resources in terms of finance, staff and equipment be devoted to addressing cybercrime.[62]

Recommendations

The following highlights some policy considerations and recommendations that policymakers in developing countries may need to address when considering a comprehensive response to the phenomenon of cybercrime:

- Review the existing legal framework and enact a comprehensive set of laws relating to cybersecurity and cybercrime that are consistent with the provisions of international legal instruments, including UN General Assembly Resolution 55/63 (see box 6.1) and the Council of Europe Convention on Cybercrime.

- Cooperate in the exchange of experience and information about legislation and judicial and law-enforcement procedures applicable to computer crime.

- Promote public awareness of the need to implement appropriate data security measures, at a physical and organizational level, encouraging compliance with international standards and the development of sectoral codes of practice.

- Facilitate training among law enforcement officers, State prosecutors and the judiciary in cybercrime technologies and techniques.

- Identify critical national infrastructure that may be vulnerable and susceptible to deliberate attack or accidental damage, and put in place a risk management strategy designed to deal with such risks.

- Consider the imposition of obligations to report to an appropriate government department any breach of data security experienced by certain categories of commercial entity, such as banks.

- Consider the establishment of specialized law enforcement units, combining personnel who have traditional policing skills with computer professionals.

- Establish mechanisms to facilitate greater liaison and cooperation between public sector law enforcement agencies and the private sector, especially providers of telecommunications services.

- Establish mechanisms to develop computer crime prevention and victim assistance programmes.

Notes

1. See Macan-Markar M, Developing Countries Not Immune From Cyber Crime Ø U.N., Inter Press Service, posted 25 April 2005, available at http://www.ipsnews.net/africa/interna.asp?idnews=28430.

2. Gibson W, *Neuromancer*, Harper Collins, 1984.

3. Wall DS, *Internet Crime,* Dartmouth, Aldershot, 2003, at p. xv.

4. See section 1.5 below.

5. The G8 categorizes computer-related and content-related together as "computer-assisted threats", as distinct from "threats to computer infrastructures".

6. Measures to Combat Computer-related Crime, Workshop 6: Background Paper (A/CONF.203/14), at para. 14 *et seq.* Presented at the Eleventh United Nations Congress on Crime Prevention and Criminal Justice, Bangkok, April 2005.

7. See generally The state of crime and criminal justice worldwide (A/CONF.203/3), Report of the Secretary-General, presented at the Eleventh United Nations Congress on Crime Prevention and Criminal Justice, Bangkok, April 2005.

8. See Computer Security Institute and Federal Bureau of Investigations, *Computer Crime and Security Survey,* 2004 (CSI-FBI 2004), available at http://www.gocsi.com/.

9. California Senate Bill 1386, available at http://info.sen.ca.gov/pub/01-02/bill/sen/sb_1351-1400/sb_1386_bill_20020926_chaptered.pdf.

10. See Kabay M, Studies and Surveys of Computer Crime, 2001, available from www.securitystats.com/reports/Studies_and_Surveys_of_Computer_Crime.pdf.

11. ASCL Computer Crime & Abuse Report (India) 2001-02, quoted in UNCTAD, *E-Commerce and Development Report,* 2003, p. 54.

12. See Discussion Guide presented at the Eleventh United Nations Congress on Crime Prevention and Criminal Justice, Bangkok, April 2005, at para. 103.

13. E.g. CSI-FBI 2004.

14. 18 U.S.C. § 1030(g).

15. WSIS Declaration of Principles (WSIS-03/GENEVA/DOC/4-E), 12 December 2003.

16. See Draft WGIG Issue Paper on Cybersecurity and Cybercrime, available at http://www.wgig.org/docs/WP-cyber-sec.pdf.

17. See, for example, Schneier B, *Secrets and Lies,* Wiley, 2000.

18. E.g. European data protection laws. Directive 95/46/EC states in Article 17(1): "Member States shall provide that the controller must implement appropriate technical and organizational measures to protect personal data against accidental or unlawful destruction or accidental loss, alteration, unauthorized disclosure or access, in particular where the processing involves the transmission of data over a network, and against all other unlawful forms of processing".

19. WGIG at p. 2. For more details on security issues see chapter 5 of this Report

20. Commission Communication to the Council and the European Parliament on Critical Infrastructure Protection in the Fight against Terrorism, COM(2004) 702 final, Brussels, 20 October 2004.

21. Electronic Communications and Transactions Act 2002, Article 52(1)(a).

22. G8 Principles for Protecting Critical Information Infrastructure, adopted May 2003, available at www.usdoj.gov/ag/events/g82004/g8_CIIP_Principles.pdf.

23. See http://www.access.gpo.gov/bis/ear/txt/ccl5-pt2.txt for the text of the US Department of Commerce's Bureau of Industry and Security regulation on US DoC BIS Category 5 Ø Telecommunications and "information security".

24. The Wassenaar Arrangement signatories are Argentina, Australia, Austria, Belgium, Bulgaria, Canada, the Czech Republic, Denmark, Finland, France, Germany, Greece, Hungary, Ireland, Italy, Japan, Luxembourg, the Netherlands, New Zealand, Norway, Poland, the Republic of Korea, Portugal, Romania, the Russian Federation, Slovakia, Spain, Sweden, Switzerland, Turkey, Ukraine, the United Kingdom and the United States. For more details see http://www.wassenaar.org/.

25. See chapter 5, part C, for details of the development of particular cryptographic technologies.

26. Reed C, *Internet Law: Text and Material*, Cambridge University Press, 2004.

27. www.iccwbo.org/ccs/menu_cybercrime_unit.asp.

28. See www.cert,org.

29. See http://www.digitalphishnet.org/.

30. Brenner S, and Goodman M, Cybercrime: The Need to Harmonize National Penal and Procedural Laws, 2002, International Society for the Reform of Criminal Law, 16th Annual Conference Technology and Its Effects on Criminal Responsibility, Security and Criminal Justice.

31. Grossman L, 15 May 2000, Attack of the Love Bug, Time Europe, at http://www.time.com/time/europe/magazine/2000/0515/cover.html.

32. See also the G8 Recommendation on Transnational Crime. The Recommendation was endorsed at the G8 Justice and Interior Ministers' Meeting in Canada, 13–14 May 2002 (http://www.g8j-i.ca). See in particular, Part IV, Section D, "Hi-Tech and Computer-Related Crimes"

33. General Assembly Resolution 55/63, Combating the criminal misuse of information technologies, 22 January 2001. See also the *United Nations Manual on the Prevention and Control of Computer-related Crime*, United Nations publication, Sales No. E.95.IV.5.

34. Computer-Related Criminality: Analysis of Legal Policy in the OECD Area, Report DSTI-ICCP 84.22 of 18 April 1986.

35. Article 3(3).

36. http://www.thecommonwealth.org/shared_asp_files/uploadedfiles/{DA109CD2-5204-4FAB-AA77-86970A639B05}_Computer%20Crime.pdf.

37. www.interpol.com/Public/TechnologyCrime/Conferences/6thIntConf/Resolution.asp.

38. See Discussion Guide, supra n. 14, at para. 190.

39. Terrorism Act 2000, s. 1(2)(e).

40. Smith R, Grabosky P and Urbas G, *Cyber Criminals on Trial*, Cambridge University Press, 2004.

41. Council of Europe Convention on Cybercrime, Explanatory Report, para. 71 *et seq.*

42. Cassese A, *International Criminal Law*, Oxford University Press, 2003, p. 277.

43. § 1030(e)(2)(B).

44. See generally Casey E, *Digital Evidence and Computer Crime*, Academic Press, 2004.

45. Sommer P, Evidence from Internet: Downloads, Logs and Captures, pp. 33–42, *Computer and Telecommunications Law Review*, vol. 8, no. 2, 2002.

46. See, for example, the US Department of Justice Report *Searching and Seizing Computers and Obtaining Electronic Evidence in Criminal Investigations*, July 2002: available at http://www.usdoj.gov/criminal/cybercrime).

47. Brenner S and Koops B-J, "Approaches to Cybercrime Jurisdiction", 4 *Journal of High Technology Law*, 1, 2004.

48. Reidenberg J, States and Internet Enforcement, 1 U. Ottawa L. & Tech. J. 1, 18 (2004), http://papers.ssrn.com/sol3/papers.cfm?abstract_id=487965.

49. See generally www.freekevin.com.

50. US-based hardware and software manufacturers, such as Intel, have been in discussions with law enforcement agencies about the possibilities of "building-in" certain functionalities into their products to assist criminal investigations.

51. See Stix G, Best-kept secrets, *Scientific American*, January 2005.

52   E.g. in the United Kingdom, the Government has established a National Technical Assistance Centre.

53.   *New Yorker cartoon*, 5 July 1993.

54.   This means that a false IP address is inserted in the packet headers.

55.   In Belgium and Finland, the costs involved in a criminal investigation may ultimately be recovered from the perpetrator, if found guilty.

56.   See http://www.interpol.int/Public/TechnologyCrime/default.asp.

57.   R v *Governor of Brixton Prison and another, ex parte Levin* (1996) 4 All ER 350.

58.   Article 22(3).

59.   *Foreign Economic and Industrial Espionage Remains a Threat in 1999*, National Center for Counterintelligence, p. 2, http://www.nacic.gov/fv99.htm.

60.   Many computer scientists and programmers will refer to the criminal misuse of computer code as "cracking" while reserving the term "hacking" for the more mundane tasks of writing non-infringing computer code. For an example, see http://tlc.discovery.com/convergence/hackers/hackers.html.

61.   See Preamble to the Convention on Cybercrime.

62.   See 5th Meeting of the Interpol Working Party on IT Crime Africa, Pretoria, 17-19 May 2005, http://www.Interpol.int/Public/TechnologyCrime/WorkingParties/Africa/5thMeeting/.

Questionnaire

Information Economy Report, 2005

In order to improve the quality and relevance of the Information Economy Report, the UNCTAD secretariat would greatly appreciate your views on this publication. Please complete the following questionnaire and return it to:

Electronic Commerce Branch, SITE **UNCTAD, Palais des Nations, Room E.7075** **CH-1211 Geneva 10, Switzerland**	**Fax: +41 22 917 0052** **E-mail: ecommerce@unctad.org**

The questionnaire can also be completed on-line at: http://r0.unctad.org/ecommerce/ecommerce_en/edr05_en.htm
Thank you very much for your kind cooperation.

1. How do you judge the quality of the 2005 Information Economy Report?

	Excellent	*Good*	*Adequate*	*Poor*
Overall assessment	[ ]	[ ]	[ ]	[ ]
Policy conclusions and recommendations	[ ]	[ ]	[ ]	[ ]
Quality of analysis	[ ]	[ ]	[ ]	[ ]
Originality	[ ]	[ ]	[ ]	[ ]
Timeliness of chosen themes	[ ]	[ ]	[ ]	[ ]

2. How useful was the Report for your work?

Very useful	*Useful*	*Of some use*	*Irrelevant*
[ ]	[ ]	[ ]	[ ]

3. What is your main use of the Report? (click one or more)

   [ ] Academic work or research
   [ ] Government policy work
   [ ] Legal or regulatory activities
   [ ] Journalism or media work
   [ ] NGO support activities
   [ ] Education and training
   [ ] Business / commerce
   [ ] Other

4. Please list any topics that you would like to see covered in future editions of the report. If you have any suggestions for improvement, both on the Report's substance and its form, please make these here:

5. Will you be interested in next year's report?

   Yes   Perhaps   Unlikely

   [ ]   [ ]   [ ]

Answering "yes" or "perhaps" and fully completing this survey will reserve a copy of the 2006 edition for you.

In this case, Please provide us with your mailing details.

Tile (Mr., Mrs.):	
Names and Surname	
Function or profession:	
Company or institution:	
Street address or PO Box:	
City:	
Postal code or Zip code:	
Country:	

Printed at United Nations, Geneva
GE.05-51966–October 2005–5,985

UNCTAD/SDTE/ECB/2005/1

United Nations publication
Sales No. E.05.II.D.19

ISBN 92-1-112679-7